The Interview

ASA Monographs

ISSN 0066-9679

The Relevance of Models for Social Anthropology, ed M. Banton
Political Systems and the Distribution of Power, ed M. Banton
Anthropological Approaches to the Study of Religion, ed M. Banton
The Social Anthropology of Complex Societies, ed M. Banton
The Structural Study of Myth and Totemism, ed E R. Leach
Themes in Economic Anthropology, ed R. Firth
History and Social Anthropology, ed I M. Lewis
Socialization: The Approach from Social Anthropology, ed P. Mayer
Witchcraft Confessions and Accusations, ed M. Douglas
Social Anthropology and Language, ed E. Ardener
Rethinking Kinship and Marriage, ed R. Needham
Urban Ethnicity, ed A. Cohen
Social Anthropology and Medicine, ed J B. Loudon
Social Anthropology and Law, ed I. Hamnett
The Anthropology of the Body, ed J. Blacking
Regional Cults, ed R P. Werbner
Sex and Age as Principles of Social Differentiation, ed J. La Fontaine
Social and Ecological Systems, ed P C. Burnham and R F. Ellen
Social Anthropology of Work, ed S. Wallman
The Structure of Folk Models, ed L. Holy and L. Stuchlik
Religious Organization and Religious Experience, ed J. Davis
Semantic Anthropology, ed D. Parkin
Social Anthropology and Development Policy, ed R. Grillo and A. Rew
Reason and Morality, ed J. Overing
Anthropology at Home, ed A. Jackson
Migrants, Workers, and the Social Order, ed J S. Eades
History and Ethnicity, ed E. Tonkin, M. McDonald and M. Chapman
Anthropology and the Riddle of the Sphinx: Paradox and Change in the Life Course, ed P. Spencer
Anthropology and Autobiography, ed J. Okely and H. Callaway
Contemporary Futures: Perspectives from Social Anthropology, ed S. Wallman
Socialism: Ideals, Ideologies and Local Practice, ed C M. Hann
Environmentalism: The View from Anthropology, ed K. Milton
Questions of Consciousness, eds A P. Cohen and N. Rapport
After Writing Culture: Epistemology and Praxis in Contemporary Anthropology, eds A. James, A. Dawson and J. Hockey
Ritual, Performance, Media, ed F. Hughes-Freeland
The Anthropology of Power, ed A. Cheater
An Anthropology of Indirect Communication, ed J. Hendry and C W. Watson
Elite Cultures, ed C. Shore and S. Nugent
Participating in Development, ed P. Sillitoe, A. Bicker and J. Pottier
Human Rights in Global Perspective, ed R A. Wilson and J P. Mitchell
The Qualities of Time, ed W. James and D. Mills
Locating the Field: Space, Place and Context in Anthropology, ed S. Coleman and P. Collins
Anthropology and Science: Epistemologies in Practice, ed J. Edwards, P. Harvey and P. Wade
Creativity and Cultural Improvisation, ed E. Hallam and T. Ingold
Anthropology and the New Cosmopolitanism: Rooted, Feminist and Vernacular Perspectives, ed P. Werbner
Thinking Through Tourism, ed J. Scott and T. Selwyn
Ownership and Appropriation, ed V. Strang and M. Busse
Archaeology and Anthropology, ed D. Shankland

The Interview
An Ethnographic Approach

Edited by
Jonathan Skinner

B L O O M S B U R Y
LONDON • NEW DELHI • NEW YORK • SYDNEY

Bloomsbury Academic
An imprint of Bloomsbury Publishing Plc

50 Bedford Square
London
WC1B 3DP
UK

1385 Broadway
New York
NY 10018
USA

www.bloomsbury.com

Bloomsbury is a registered trade mark of Bloomsbury Publishing Plc

English edition first published in 2012 by Berg
Reprinted by Bloomsbury Academic 2013
Reprinted 2014

British Library Cataloguing-in-Publication Data
A catalogue record for this book is available from the British Library.

ISBN: HB: 978-1-8478-8940-9
PB: 978-1-8478-8939-3

Library of Congress Cataloging-in-Publication Data
A catalog record for this book is available from the Library of Congress.

Typeset by Apex CoVantage, LLC, Madison, WI, USA.
Printed and bound in Great Britain

This volume is dedicated to
my mother
who always asked a question or two

Contents

III. INTERVIEW CASES

Acknowledgements

I should like to thank a number of people and institutions involved in 'the happening' of this volume. For inspiring this topic, I should like to thank Peter Collins and Anselma Gallinat who, though they don't know it, challenged me to develop some ideas and work I had with them about 'Sarah'. That was the seed for further examination of the interview topic. I have, then, to also thank 'Sarah' for her considerate and considerable involvement in my dance research in Sacramento, California. Precursors to them are John McLeod and colleagues at the University of Abertay Dundee for supervising and sponsoring my training in person-centred counselling.

In terms of developing this volume, I should like to thank contributors for their part in this project, for making it such enjoyable, pleasant and edifying work. Those who did not make it to the volume are thanked for their support in this project too. The volume represents the best papers from the ASA annual conference held at Queen's University Belfast, Easter 2010. It is therefore appropriate to thank the ASA committee for its intellectual and financial support for this topic and conference; Stranmillis College for hosting the affair and providing us with such a lovely venue, accommodation, garden grounds and student bar; and the School of History and Anthropology, and Faculty of Humanities at Queen's University Belfast for contributing to the support of this endeavour. We should like to thank the volunteer student helpers for their courteous and professional assistance during the conference: especially 'MK' Rallings for leading the team, and Dave Kanter and Ioannis Tsioulakis for leading the musical breaks. Jenny Elliott, from the Arts Care charity and Belfast Health and Social Care Trust, very kindly dovetailed a student/Orbit Dance and Kompany Maine dance performance during our conference. Rohan Jackson and Megan Caine coordinated and administrated the conference from start to finish—indeed, from venue reconnoitering and salsa-tasting trips in 2009, to packing up displays and wrapping up finances. They will, I am sure, also appreciate a thanks to Eyjafjallajökull for making the end of the conference so memorable. Everyone is indebted to your calm-under-crisis and consummate rebooking skills.

A special thanks is owed to Dominic Bryan for co-convening the conference with me. Thank you for joining in and taking part. Thank you for your tireless engagement with the topic, the people, the dancing… for your good humour throughout, and for developing such an engaging and controversial Forum on Ethics and Reconciliation. I look forward to the next one!

Final thanks go to those who assisted in the final stages of the project: John Skinner, Barnaly Pande, Fiona Murphy for reading parts of the manuscript and offering corrections, and especially Kirk Simpson who added suggestions to the corrections. Anne Montgomery for being such a friendly face and intelligent voice over coffee breaks. Yazmin and Leonardo for introducing me to tango and so getting me 'outside' over the Belfast Summer. Essential Secretary for its online transcription services. Anna Wright at Berg and the Berg team for such support, encouragement, and diplomatic distance when deadlines were looming. Massa for sitting patiently through all the work.

Jonathan Skinner
Bangor, Northern Ireland

About the Editor and Contributors

Editor

Jonathan Skinner is senior lecturer in social anthropology at Queen's University Belfast. He has done fieldwork in the Caribbean and the United States and the United Kingdom. He has interests in tourism, dance and embodied research methods. He is author of *Before the Volcano* (Arawak, 2004), editor of *Writing the Dark Side of Travel* (Berghahn, 2012) and co-editor of *Great Expectations: Imagination and Anticipation in Tourism* (Berghahn, 2011).

Contributors

Anne Cazemajou holds a PhD in the anthropology of dance from Blaise Pascal University (Clermont-Ferrand, France) and is currently undertaking postdoctoral research at the Lyon Conservatoire National Supérieur Musique et Danse and the Centre National de la Danse Lyon, where she is also developing a phenomenological pedagogy. She studies bodily experience in the transmission of dance combining ethnography and the explicitation interview, a technique in which she continues to be trained as a member of GREX (Groupe de Recherche sur l'Explicitation).

Vincent Crapanzano is distinguished professor of comparative literature and anthropology at the Graduate Center of the City of New York. His most recent book is *The Hakis: The Wound That Never Heals* (University of Chicago Press, 2011).

Markieta Domecka has been working with biographical method for several years, applying it in various research projects on borderland identities, career patterns in postsocialist business fields (PhD thesis), the peace process in Northern Ireland and two FP7 projects: EUROIDENTITIES (http://www.euroidentities.org) and LOCAW (http://www.locaw-fp7.com). Currently she is working at the University of Surrey in the research group of environmental psychology.

Sandra Fahy holds a PhD in Social Anthropology from the School of Oriental and African Studies. She is currently a Sejong Society Post-Doctoral Fellow in the Korean Studies Institute at the University of Southern California. Her work is situated in the East Asian post–Cold War context, focussed on North Korea, involving fieldwork with refugees in South Korea and Japan. She has written on famine and food shortage; government irresponsibility and hindrance towards humanitarian or international intervention; refugees, migrants and internally displaced persons.

Madalina Florescu holds a PhD in Social Anthropology from the School of Oriental and African Studies. She is currently a research fellow at the Centre of African Studies at the University of Porto, Portugal.

Martin Forsey is lecturer in anthropology and sociology at the University of Western Australia, where he teaches Australian studies and the anthropology of business. His publications include *Challenging the System? A Dramatic Tale of Neoliberal Reform in an Australian High School* (2007). His research interests include schools and community formation; neoliberalism and education; school choice amongst students, parents and teachers; and, more recently, qualitative research methods.

Georgiana Gore is professor of anthropology of dance and bodily practices at Blaise Pascal University (Clermont-Ferrand, France) and a member of the research group Corporeal Experience and Practices of ACTé. She co-convenes several masters programmes including the Erasmus Mundus International Masters in Dance Knowledge, Practice and Heritage—Choreomundus. Her research focusses mainly on dance transmission, the politics of embodiment and epistemological issues in dance anthropology (*Anthropologie de la danse: Genèse et construction d'une discipline* with Andrée Grau, 2006).

Alexandra Greene is a senior research fellow in medical anthropology in child health and the behavioural and social sciences teaching lead in the Dundee Medical School at the University of Dundee.

Jenny Hockey trained as an anthropologist and is Emeritus Professor of Sociology at Sheffield University. Her research interests include death and dying, ageing and the life course, memory and material culture, gender, heterosexuality and masculinity. Recent publications include *The Matter of Death: Space, Place and Materiality* (Palgrave, 2010, co-edited with C. Komaromy and K. Woodthorpe) and *Masculinities in Transition* (Palgrave, 2011, coauthored with V. Robinson).

Lisette Josephides is professor of anthropology at Queen's University Belfast. Her two most important publications on her lengthy Papua New Guinea fieldwork are *The Production of Inequality* (Tavistock, 1985) and *Melanesian Odysseys* (Berghahn, 2008). Her current interests focus on cosmopolitanism, philosophical anthropology and issues of knowledge and the person.

Nick McCaffery is an independent researcher based in Belfast, Northern Ireland. Since completing his doctoral research in social anthropology with the Hopi Indians of Northern Arizona, Nick has focussed on topics closer to home, such as perceptions of historical conflict amongst young people in Northern Ireland and on the impact of learning circus skills amongst adults living with learning disabilities.

Anne Montgomery is a doctoral researcher at the Centre for Primary Care and Public Health at Queen Mary University of London. Her research centres on the interface between public and private discourses of prostate cancer and the struggle by actors around a prostate cancer health social movement to invest aspects of this illness with their preferred meaning to men with prostate cancer and other attentive audiences. She has gained expertise in video interviewing and has worked at Queen's University Belfast on research projects investigating walker–driver risks in the city and learner–teacher interactions in interprofessional settings.

Nigel Rapport is professor of anthropological and philosophical studies at the University of St Andrews, where he directs the Centre for Cosmopolitan Studies. Recent books include *Human Nature as Capacity: Transcending Discourse and Classification* (editor, Berghahn, 2010); and *Anyone, the Cosmopolitan Subject of Anthropology* (Berghahn, 2012).

Géraldine Rix-Lièvre holds a PhD in sports and human movement studies. She is senior lecturer at Blaise Pascal University (Clermont-Ferrand, France) and a member of the research group Corporeal Experience and Practices of ACTé. She studies the embodied dimensions of practices, especially those of refereeing situations and of polar expeditions, and has developed new methods to make these dimensions of human experience explicit.

Marilyn Strathern is Emeritus Professor of Social Anthropology, Cambridge University. Over the last twenty years she has written on reproductive technologies, intellectual and cultural property, and 'critique of good practice', an umbrella rubric for reflections on audit and accountability.

Maruška Svašek is reader in the School of History and Anthropology, Queen's University Belfast. Her main research interests include emotional dynamics, migration, art and artefacts. Her recent publications include *Anthropology, Art and Cultural Production* (2007), the edited volumes *Emotions and Human Mobility: Ethnographies of Movement* (2012), *Postsocialism: Politics and Emotions in Central and Eastern Europe* (2006) and the co-edited volume *Mixed Emotions: Anthropological Studies of Feeling* (2005). She has used biographical methods in various research projects, examining identity formation, mobility and ageing.

Olivier Wathelet holds a PhD in anthropology from Sophia Antipolis University Nice and specializes in the ethnographic study of sensory skills. After studying the familial transmission of mundane olfactory know-how, he now focusses on culinary abilities in professional and domestic settings. He is 'innovation project leader—anthropologist' in the innovation department of the Kitchen Electrics Business Unit of the Group Seb, a French industry providing small domestic appliances.

Helena Wulff is professor of social anthropology at Stockholm University. Her research is in the anthropology of communication and aesthetics based on a wide range of studies on the social worlds of literary production, dance and visual arts in a transnational perspective; current focus is on contemporary Irish writers. Amongst her recent publications are the monographs *Ballet across Borders: Career and Culture in the World of Dancers* (Berg, 2001) and *Dancing at the Crossroads: Memory and Mobility in Ireland* (Berghahn, 2007), as well as the volumes *The Emotions: A Cultural Reader* (editor, Berg, 2007) and *Ethnographic Practice in the Present* (editor with Marit Melhuus and Jon P. Mitchell, Berghahn, 2010).

Figure 1 Interview relations

A Four-part Introduction to the Interview: Introducing the Interview; Society, Sociology and the Interview; Anthropology and the Interview; Anthropology and the Interview—Edited

Jonathan Skinner

Introducing the Interview: Two Openings

First, fieldwork for me was a rucksack, some lab books for notetaking, a pen gifted to me by a fellow anthropologist, a tape recorder, some spy novels for escapism and Robert Burgess's *In the Field: An Introduction to Field Research* (1993). I took all these materials and myself to the field, a small British Dependent Territory in the eastern Caribbean, Montserrat, where I intended to live for at least a year examining colonial and postcolonial relations and expressions of identity. For ten months I lived, limed and hung out—deep hanging out—with various groups on the island: the calypsonians, the development workers, the Writers' Maroon writing collective, the tourists. At that point in time, and despite having filled most of my notebooks with stream-of-consciousness fieldnotes—collected all the local newspapers; worked with the calypsonians sorting and thereby learning their materials, concerns and 'social commentary'; hiked with tourists and biked with development workers all over the island; produced and analysed poems and pamphlets, and studied West Indian history with my fellow writers—I developed a growing sense of panic that all my activities and conversations and insights into local knowledge, local issues and reactions, indeed, a local social world which was increasingly becoming my own, would all be to no avail; that I was not going to return to my university with 'data'.

I panicked and went into interview mode. I spent a fortnight cycling around the island visiting all the people I had been working with, reholding the conversations we had had over the months. It was as if those friendly meetings had been rehearsals for this interview show. We replayed the conversations about their lives, their work and their social worlds. A lot of the questions were expressly for the tape, and so too the answers. Interviewees paused in midsentence when the tapes ran out and they needed changing over. Respondents queried my questions, knowing that I knew the answers to the questions and that we were just talking for the tape, that we were interviewing for the record. Friends-turned-informants recreated our previous exchanges. It was an awkward culmination of months of relationship building. I knew the questions to put to them just as I knew the answers they would put back at me.

When I returned from the field, the interviews more than 'complemented' the participant observation as Burgess (1993: 106) suggests of them. The interviews overshadowed my fieldnotes and became the core of the writings, leaving the fieldnotes to become timelines and context points. The interviews had been semi-structured in that the question topics had been prepared. Whilst the fieldwork leading up to the meetings allowed me to judge the questions and to critique the answers, such that the questions and follow-ons were probing and the answers consistent with previous conversations, these 'interviews as conversations', again as Burgess (1993: 101, 101–22) phrases them, a method of field research particularly favoured by sociologists, were strained conversations if that. They changed the relationships I had with the people I was living and working with. Fortunately, they indulged me with their responses.

* * *

More than a decade later and I am coming to the end of a long-term comparison of social dancing between Belfast, Northern Ireland, and Sacramento, California. This has been a particularly immersive and embodied project working as a dancer (see Skinner 2007), first learning and then training with fellow enthusiasts, some of whom have gone on to become teachers, competitors and professional dancers in their own rights, though most have stayed as part-time pleasure dancers—cosmopolitans with salsa second skins using their physical skills for mobility (Skinner 2009b, 2010a). Besides dancing, training, watching, travelling, performing and competing with my respondents, I have again resorted to interviews in my research. This interviewing and recording is digital now rather than on tape and takes place at all stages of the research from brief chance encounters with promoters and visiting teachers to interviews whilst dancing on the dance floor—letting the physicality of the close dance personal space very quickly move the interview into the interviewee's intimate headspace (Skinner 2010a)—to giving video cameras to informants and letting them film and narrate the evenings unfolding before them, to long-term periodic interviews over nearly a decade with key respondents, to interviewing myself after some of my interviews. In all, there are nearly 200 interviews with other people ranging from ten-minute snapshots to four-hour reflections.

Following is an extract from June 2011 from an interview with Elizabeth, a married dance friend in her fifties, a Protestant from East Belfast who is aware of my research and work in the university, and whom I have danced with socially on and off for the last two to three years. After lunch we talk about her dancing, her relations with her husband and dance partner, how she got into the dancing and what it means for her to be out dancing three nights a week. A key theme to emerge in the semi-structured interview is 'appropriacy', a term which comes up and I probe for from several different angles (religious, sexual, moral). The religious angle elicits the following explanation:

Interviewer (I): You mentioned religion a couple of times, church. Are you a religious person?

Respondent (R): No, we're not religious any more.

I: So you don't have any issues with the dancing?

R: No, no. We would have gone to church regularly but it was many, many years ago we stopped going and part of the reason was because my eldest child, we had put them into crèche in the church when we were at the service and we came back and the girl who was looking after the crèche had him in her arms and apparently my eldest son had been running around and running around, but instead of coming in and getting us, obviously the people who had children at the crèche would have been at the back, she just let him and I think eventually he bit her because she was trying to restrain him. So she literally... I just said, 'That's fine. You should have got me,' and I took him on my hip, because he would have only been about eighteen months, two years, and she tried to take him off me again. And I said, 'No, give me my child,' and that was it because I said, 'No person is going to take my child from me.' So apart from going to some services, that was the last time we stepped in... you can still be a religious person, but I don't have an issue... I don't think you have to have to go to...

I: And the appropriacy doesn't come from that?

R: No, I think it was probably more the way I was brought up, that it was a very strict household I was brought up in and you certainly weren't allowed to wear makeup or anything like that. You had to be in at a certain time. Northern Ireland would have been very much you couldn't do this on a Sunday because it was just not appropriate. You couldn't cut your nails on a Sunday. You couldn't play cards because it was just not appropriate because it's Sunday. It's only in latter years even that the shops have opened on Sundays. It was very much a religious island.

Elizabeth went on to discuss how she is aware of her Protestant background and upbringing, her relationships and how they play into but do not overdetermine her dancing or dressing for dancing. In 'Leading Questions and Body Memories' (Skinner 2010a), I introduced Sarah, an anaestheticist who taught salsa in the operating theatre, making the point that she was particularly responsive in her interview with me because we had shared the dance together such that her cognitive memories flowed easily following our co-constructed physical memories. Ours was 'a symbiotic' relationship (Sparkes 1997) of words and movements. Returning to the field the year following our interview, and following the drafting of an article about how one shared knowledge facilitates the sharing of another, Sarah revealed how she had been trained in interview skills and, whilst I—with some person-centred counselling training—had been checking my questions with her and using imagery in the interview, she had been checking her answers with me, that they answered my questions according to my responses, as if I were a patient questioning her about my treatment. In effect, during our interview we had continued the dance, around each other rather than with each other in this instance.

Elizabeth also has medical training and is used to interviewing and assessing her patients before starting triage. Indeed, she had expectations about the interview ever since she heard that I was conducting them in the dance scene in Belfast. She expected to be interviewed, was flattered to accept and intrigued by the possible questions I might ask her. At the end of the interview, we talked about the interview, its lead-in, and the interview process in general. Elizabeth regularly reviewed patients before their treatment, probing them with health-related questions. Moreover, one of Elizabeth's colleagues had conducted a semi-structured interview with her for his master's dissertation, so Elizabeth was expecting something similar. The following is an extract from our impromptu interview debriefing:

R: It was just more than expectations that I was answering, not necessarily questions appropriately, but I would answer the questions appropriately, but I was giving you enough information that you required—because I realized from the semi-structured interview that you were guided to a point of what I was saying. For then, for you to prompt me to ask me, for me to go down a different angle or [sure] rein me back in to go back to what we were talking about.

I: How did you, did you feel that I did that or what?

R: No. Well, we're used to talking to each other anyway but…

I: Have you been interviewed before?

R: I have been interviewed before so I have an idea that I know the techniques of trying to, to get people round the subject again. I would also review patients regularly [yes] so they could go off on a tangent, and we all can do that. So, it's appropriate to try and rein things back again. So, I realized you were doing it and I suppose responded to that once I finished what I wanted to say. I would go back again to where…but that's because I would know, I know as well that you're doing it [yeah]. So, although I was aware of it, I suppose, because I use that technique regularly myself, I probably noticed it.

I: So, you were checking with me to see whether it was appropriate from my perspective?

R: Yes, in respect that I want to make sure the material that I had covered for you [yes] was what... I don't mean what you needed, was required rather than what was appropriate [yeah], what was required. Because it's all very well us discussing things, but it's just in case it wasn't what you need it for, your case research.

I: And do you think it was comprehensive?

R: I think it was very thorough. Yeah, I think it was very thorough. I would think that it should probably—the thing with semi-structured interviews is really that, it gives the person who's being interviewed, the interviewee as such, an opportunity to give you more information than ultimately if they were doing a questionnaire or yes/no. We're allowed to go off [yeah] and talk rather than yes/no answers as such. In a way, you're guiding by what [yeah] I've answered.

In a way, I was partly guided by her answers, just as Elizabeth was partly guided by my questions. The interview lasted nearly eighty minutes and Elizabeth expressed shock that it had gone longer than the thirty minutes it had felt like for her. Whilst answering my questions and checking for my reactions, as well as showing an awareness for the main avenues and tangent side-streets in the interview, Elizabeth also felt immersed in the exchange between us, to being on the receiving end of the interview society.

Approximately one month later, and after reading some of my articles and dancing together—but both of us perhaps deliberately holding off from mentioning the interview—Elizabeth sent me an email adding to the interview. Therein, she mentioned how she had found the interview thought-provoking and edifying, and that she had some additional comments that she wanted to make. The first was to note that even in the short time of an interview, an interviewee might 'try to be protective of oneself', particularly in a private conversation in the public space of a quiet cafeteria. She wrote, then, exposing herself further, about her abusive childhood, of beatings and attacks, and of finding 'solace' from an early age in music: 'It made me feel as if I was somewhere else.' Now, though, there is still an element of escapism in the music and dancing but it is one of choice and enjoyment rather than necessity and survival: the music moves Elizabeth to enjoy and 'express oneself with it' rather than use it to take herself away from her 'new' home and family life. Elizabeth compensates in her dancing nights with her husband, structured physical evenings, safe and limited, from her father's physical abuses, his assaults on her ears and her body.

The interview is an uncertain art or skill, sometimes productive (one of a set of methods triangulating about Elizabeth and her social world, eliciting the meaning in her life story and turning up new materials and insights) and sometimes counter productive (damaging personal relationships on Montserrat and resulting in over-reliance on the interview in my writing). The interview—a conversational meeting with at least one other self—is the subject of this volume. Our consideration of the interview in anthropology is by no means uncritical. The chapters in this volume represent the best papers from the 2010 annual meeting of the Association of Social Anthropologists of the United Kingdom and the Commonwealth that was held at Queen's University Belfast on the theme of 'The Interview—Theory, Practice, Society'. They cover the gamut of topics pertaining to the interview: they range from the nature and structure of the interview, its relationship as a method with participant observation, to ethics and knowledge construction in interviews, and to experiments in working with interviews (from transcription to biographical narrative and interview stimuli), and a selection of case studies in interviewing—the difficulties, the problems, the silences, the successes of using the interview in anthropological research. Loosely, then, the volume puts the interview itself in the proverbial 'hot seat' by exploring the positioning of the interview, interview techniques, and interview cases. Each chapter interrogates the interview as understood and used by anthropologists: illustrative, reflexive, methodological and ethnographic. The remainder of this introduction presents an overview of the interview and its use in other disciplines, most notably sociology—once referred to as 'the science of the interview' (Benney and Hughes 1956, cited in Burgess 1993: 101)—before turning to its place and use in anthropology. These sections are then followed by an introduction to the chapters in this volume.

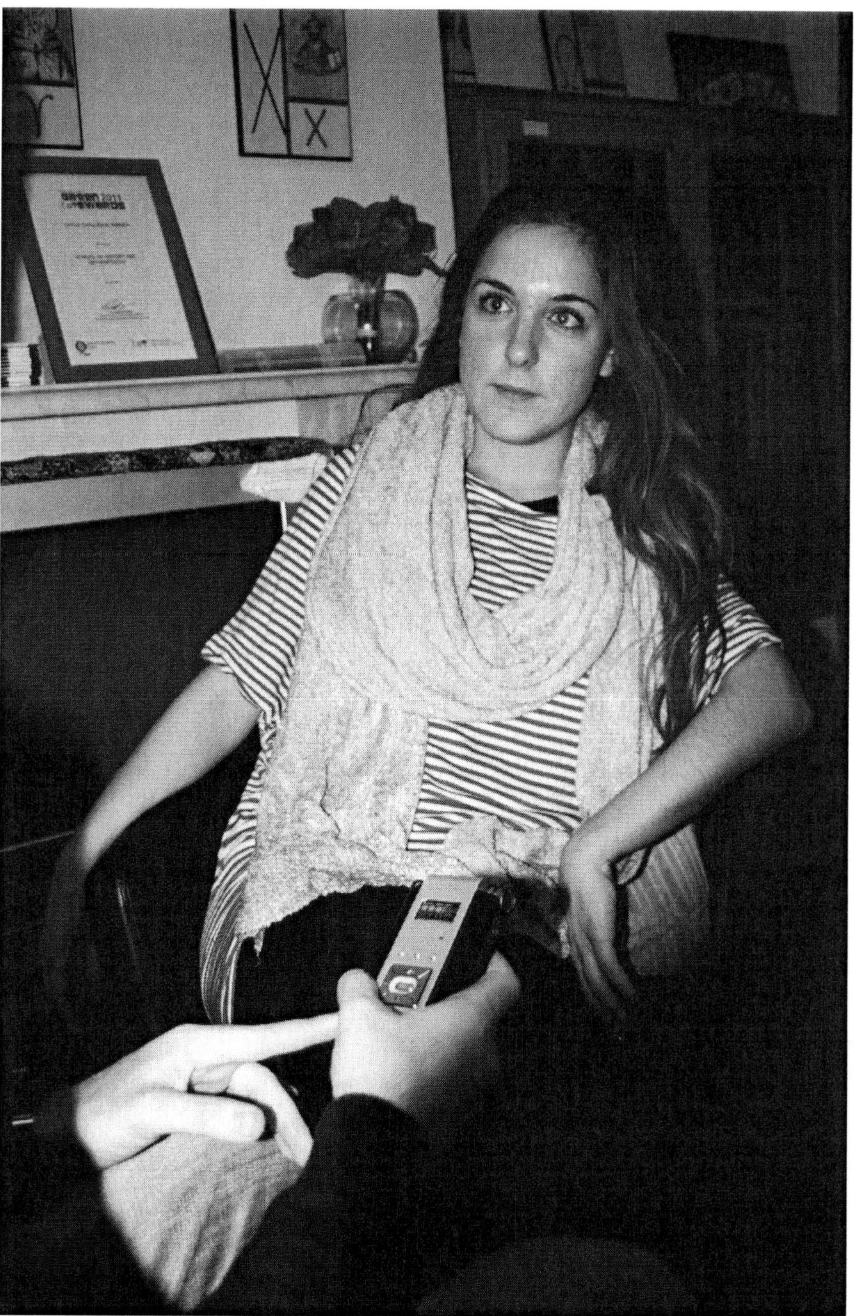

Figure 2 Interviewer perspective

Society, Sociology and the Interview

'I don't do interviews in my fieldwork,' was one of the responses to holding an anthropologists' conference on anthropology and the interview. Before exploring this tenuous, problematic—and perhaps unacknowledged—relationship, I propose to set up 'the interview' from other disciplines, to review how they define, deploy and debate the interview. This entails drawing, especially, from sociology where there has been a significant use of interview techniques in research and considerable methodological examination of the interview. I will also touch upon other disciplines where the interview is expressly in use such as journalism, healthcare, psychology, criminology, counselling, education and oral history. I am also devoting a specific initial section to the work of educational psychologist Steinar Kvale whose book *InterViews: An Introduction to Qualitative Research Interviewing* (1996) remains a key influential text on the interview and its place in social science research.

Kvale and Qualitative Interviewing

Whilst referring to the 'interview as conversation' in his field research manual, Burgess narrows his gaze to focus upon the unstructured interview in social research. He distinguishes between the structured interview—often associated with survey research and generally involving a fixed set of questions with little to no control on the part of the respondent (Burgess 1993: 101)—and the unstructured (informal or semi-structured) interview which has more open-ended questions on themes, can involve probing or follow-on/supplementary questions relating to the answers, is conducted more as a conversation and is supposed to be more natural and egalitarian in the relationship between the interviewer and interviewee. The association of the 'interview as conversation' suggests that there is a give-and-take to the semi-structured interview. Certainly, for Kvale, the give-and-take is at the heart of the interview, a conversation that coproduces, cocreates knowledge. 'Interviews are conversations where the outcome is a coproduction of the interviewer and the subject', Kvale (1996: xvii) asserts in the preface to his book. It is 'a construction site of knowledge' (2), a conversational journey, 'a professional conversation' (5)—with a 'professional stranger' in the anthropologist (Agar 1996). More explicitly, the research interview entertained by Kvale is defined as '*an interview whose purpose is to obtain descriptions of the life world of the interviewee with respect to interpreting the meaning of the described phenomena*' (1996: 5–6, author's emphasis). It has 'structure' and 'purpose' as well as definition: the interview has a beginning and an ending, and in-between there is typically questioning, answering and listening.

One of the strengths of Kvale's work is to situate the interview within the philosophy of research methods. He credits it as a craft technique to unfold the subject's life world—the native's point of view for the traditional anthropologist. This interview is quite literally an *inter view*, 'an inter-change of views' (Kvale 1996: 14) to varying degrees, a privileged conversation with the Other. Done well and the InterView, as Kvale also characterizes it, can give access, insight and information. The qualitative research interview has a number of aspects to it, and is connected with several philosophies. This type of interview is themed and seeks to understand the actor's understandings of his or her life world, his or her interpretations, meanings and narrations.[1] It is qualitative and descriptive, seeking the nuances and particularities of the human condition in a humanist tradition. It is expansive rather than reductive, preferring the complexity, ambiguity and irony of a memory or explanation such as Elizabeth's loss of religion to the generalizing population sample. Kvale adumbrates further themes that can link the interview to the philosophy phenomenology and to the discipline anthropology (more of the latter in the following section), both of which are inclined towards the detail of human experience.

There is a presuppositionless naïveté about the interviewer who, ideally, shows an openness, curiosity and sensitivity to the interviewee in order to stimulate, engage and elicit in the interview rather than to judge, criticize or deride. It should be a safe space for the interviewee, physically as well as mentally, so that the person can speak unencumbered. In this, Kvale makes the point that a relationship is acted out by the interviewer and the interviewee during the interview. The interview is a ritualized performance space where '[t]he interviewer and the subject act in relation to each other and reciprocally influence each other' (Kvale 1996: 35; see also Bauman 1977). Moreover, Kvale makes the point that just as in participant observation, in this interpersonal dynamics, the interviewer comes to embody the research method, hence, perhaps, the blurring and confusion for my respondents on Montserrat as our relationships and conversations became mediated and repeated for the record—for the tape as opposed to the scratchnotes jotted down during our meetings and the fieldnotes dutifully written up the following morning.

Considering the conversation, Kvale notes that the interview roles in the conversations are not reciprocal 'interchanges' but responses by respondents to directed questions. There is thus methodological technique to the interview. From the philosopher Richard Rorty, Kvale proposes that the conversation, such as that taking place in an interview, though probably a more contrived than 'natural' encounter, is 'a *basic mode of knowing*' (Kvale 1996: 37, author's emphasis). It is in the conversation that knowledge is constituted; we learn and develop through conversation, with conversation as the context for understanding knowledge, to paraphrase Rorty (1979: 389, cited in Kvale 1996: 37). Further to this, we constitute ourselves through conversation as linguistic beings. Human language makes for human reality. As such, Kvale proposes three understandings of the conversation: methodological, epistemological and ontological. And in this overview on the conversation, Kvale suggests hermeneutical, postmodern and phenomenological understandings and interpretations of the interview from interview dialectics to interview transcripts.[2] The interview has the potential to give us access to the life world of the respondent, to articulate lived meanings, 'to make the invisible visible' (Kvale 1996: 53), not just in exploring the subject's consciousness, but in gaining insight into his or her deliberations, perspectives, viewpoints, understandings, points of view, reactions, plans, imaginings, jealousies, strategies, hostilities, madnesses, reasonings, hurts, ambitions, loves, losses—verily, his or her life stories past, present and future.

But is it science? Certainly the interview is a qualitative rather than quantitative research method in that the information and knowledge gained is 'narrative' as opposed to 'digital'. The narrative is language-based and so open to the difficulties of translation, interpretation and gender bias.[3] The interview with its branching and chain question structures, its channelling and probing, mutation and internal coherence can be produced with replicability with the same or similar questions posed in successive interviews. They are comparable, as one narrative can be juxtaposed or examined against another or many others. They are open to falsification and are testable for coherence and verifiability within the narrative, between narratives and with other methods as triangulation. As such, it is possible to classify the interview as either or both subjective and objective, science and art, depending upon the definitions used. Objectivity could, for example, refer to the reliability of the narrative, the nature of the 'object' researched (Kvale 1996: 65), the removal of leading questions from the interviewer's schema to avoid bias, the use of a computer program me or coding in the analysis of the data. Kvale's (1996: 66) point is that at the heart of the interview is 'intersubjective interaction'. Rubin and Rubin (2005) refer to this qualitative interviewing as 'The Art of Hearing Data' in the subtitle of their interview guidebook and manual. They advocate a 'responsive' conversational partnership between interviewer and interviewee (Rubin and Rubin 2005: 14). Qualitative interviewing, for them, is similarly *between.* It is also dynamic, iterative, flexible and falls within a naturalist-interpretive research paradigm (Rubin and Rubin 2005: 22) taking place in the interviewee's setting and also perhaps alongside extensive participant observation. It can be the exciting final flourish in qualitative research or, as they put it: 'Qualitative interviews have operated for us like night-vision goggles, permitting us to see that which is not ordinarily on view and examine that which is often looked at but seldom seen' (Rubin and Rubin 2005: vii). Such qualitative interpretive research is 'ideopathic', according to King and Horrocks (2010: 11), in that it describes aspects of the social world rather than seeks to establish general patterns of behaviour. It elicits detailed instances about meaning and experience from the actors' perspectives rather than attempts to establish more positivistic causal relationships—participants' *perceptions* of causality notwithstanding (King and Horrocks 2010: 26).

Sociology and the Interview

The interview is not just a popular qualitative research method and means for knowledge coproduction. In this section I shall review and consider the rise of the interview and the suggestion that we now inhabit an interview society. The interview has become both research trajectory and contemporary trend, particularly as expressed through the discipline of sociology. Through the latter half of the twentieth century and into this twenty-first century, the interview has percolated into not just research practice but also public consciousness. Not in small part due to the dominance of the press and other media where the interview is standard working practice (see following subsections), there is certainly interview familiarity and interview expectation with implications for interview practice: we now live in an 'interview society' (Atkinson and Silverman 1997; Gubrium and Holstein 2001). '[I]nterviews have become a ubiquitous aspect of contemporary life,' mark King and Horrocks (2010: 1). Further to this, and perhaps more critically, King and Horrocks (2010: 1) add that interviewees also 'usually have a pretty good idea about the kind of encounter they are agreeing to'. They, like Elizabeth above but unlike many of the Montserratians, are well versed in the interview: they encounter interviews daily in the newspapers, television, and perhaps also in their clinical practice. The interview has become more than just a popular mode of inquiry; it is now 'a significant constituent of the kind of society we live in' (King and Horrocks 2010: 5).

King and Horrocks are referring to the interview society thesis proposed by British sociologists Paul Atkinson and David Silverman (1997) in their now-classic article in *Qualitative Inquiry*, 'Kundera's *Immortality*: The Interview Society and the Invention of the Self', a thesis subsequently taken up and developed especially by American sociologists Jaber Gubrium and James Holstein in their interviewing collections and methods books, *Postmodern Interviewing* (2003) and the comprehensive *Handbook of Interview Research* (2001)—both of which feature their chapter, 'From the Individual Interview to the Interview Society'.

Atkinson and Silverman warn of a potential naïve and uncritical reliance upon the interview in the social sciences. They do this through an assessment of writer Milan Kundera's novel *Immortality*, a complex metafiction in parts about the construction of character, author and ultimately the self.[4] They use Kundera to stress the culturally situated and produced nature of the self, commonly expressed through the revelations of the interview. 'Immortality' comes through the media images, the sound bites and now even the research methods and writings. There is a convergence, for them, of mass media techniques with social research in the interview. They warn against an uncritical and undertheorized adoption of the interview and the interview text as a stable, authentic and secure representation of the self (Atkinson and Silverman 1997: 310). If the *zeitgeist* of this age is towards confessional self-revelations, then the interview process and product substantiates and encourages such practice. An attraction of this is to promote and affirm the interiority of the self—a therapeutic act in itself for the speakers as well as the listeners; a research soft porn, if you will, entrapping an emotional life and a private experience in public. Notwithstanding the ethical, moral, ontological and feminist problematics[5] associated with this cheap mode of inquiry—'the interview [as] a personal confessional' (Atkinson and Silverman 1997: 305)—there are contentious assumptions being made that the interview is an accurate and approximate revelation of the interviewed self, that there is coherence in the narrative, stability of self and an authenticity and accuracy about the reconstructions of experience from memory (see for example Scott 1999).

According to Atkinson and Silverman, the interview society affirms the speaking subject. The interview narratives taken from the interview are inevitably rehearsed, repeated stories from multiple tellings of the self (Atkinson and Silverman 1997: 314). We might say, then, that in the interview society, the interview narratives sound good, feel good and look good for the interviewer and the interviewee. But this is a rehearsed self up for analysis. This is research by repetition rather than insight. Furthermore, in their responses to researching within the interview society, Atkinson and Silverman draw from the work of medical anthropologist Arthur Kleinman on illness narratives, critiquing the suggestion that his subjects' stories—empathic experiential accounts from social actors—are gained as mini-ethnography. Ethnography is not necessarily just romantic and heroic, a casting of protagonists as fighters and survivors. Atkinson and Silverman are not against such conclusions, but only so long as they are the results of theoretical and critical analysis. Self-revealing subjects should be scrutinized, techniques questioned, narratives challenged. Nor, too, should there be, ironically, an uncritical substitution of the author's monologue replaced by the monologue of the privileged subject (Atkinson and Silverman 1997: 322). Their conclusion is to hold a healthy scepticism towards the rise of the interview in our research: 'There is clearly the danger that in concentrating on speaking voices, and narrating selves, current sociological and anthropological research may ground itself in technologies of the interview society rather than systematically questioning its root assumptions and methods' (Atkinson and Silverman 1997: 322).

Sociologists Gubrium and Holstein are advocates of 'the active interview'. They consider all interviews to be 'reality-constructing, meaning-making occasions' (Holstein and Gubrium 1995: 4). The interview is thus an active encounter, and researchers should consider the *hows* of social process in the interview setting as well as the *whats* of the lived experience in the interview content in their interview work (Holstein and Gubrium 1995: 5; see also Douglas (1985) on 'creative interviewing' and mutual disclosure in the interview relationship). They give us a careful examination of the shift from the individual interview research approach to the interview society social condition (Gubrium and Holstein 2003). They associate the rise of the interview with 'the democratization of opinion' (Gubrium and Holstein 2003: 22; see also Lee 2004 on the history of interview recording technologies) found post–World War II, with the use of new techniques of social inquiry such as the standardized survey. Robert Merton, for example, spent his US wartime effort interviewing Army trainees to get responses to their training films, formative work for his 1956 'focused interview' manual (Merton (1956) 1990: xvii–xviii). In the same year, Benney and Hughes published their special issue on the importance of the interview—'a relatively new kind of encounter in the history of human relations' (1956: 138), 'a bridge between social strata' (140)—suggesting, carefully, that it is a role-playing interaction, a 'balance of revelation and concealment of personal thoughts and intentions' (137). The dominance of newspaper media since the nineteenth century, and an emergent interest in Freudian psychoanalysis in the early twentieth century, also accounted for this new research interest in the interview, according to Reisman and Benney (1956). Such factors informed this new form of research communication which encourages rather than suppresses the words of the people (Reisman and Benney 1956: 13). It is part of the 'modern temper' (Reisman and Benney 1956: 7), an expression picked up by Gubrium and Holstein (2003: 22–3).

Whilst it might be declared that we inhabit Atkinson and Silverman's interview society—one with an increasingly individualizing discourse and subjectivity (Gubrium and Holstein 2003: 24, 29)—Benney's work in particular shows us that there has always been a careful and sceptical consideration of the interview. So too we might suggest that not every society has an interviewing mass technology about it. The romantic, confessional impulse might also be a luxury afforded to only some in open and wealthy societies. It might not be for all, but it might not be a possibility for many. Continuing their historical review of the interview and interview literature, Gubrium and Holstein (2003: 30–3) review interview relations from 'mining' and 'prospecting' interview participants to passive and active interviewer and respondent subjects. Gubrium and Holstein (2003: 32) favour active interviews with 'animated participants', empowered practitioners co-implicated in the production of knowledge. The interview material should subsequently give voice and ownership to the interviewed. This is more complicated than the interviewees 'telling their story' with the interviewer subsequently 're-telling their story'. The language, the extracts, the mode of representation of this communication all shift and reorient, largely at the behest of the author of the research text rather than the author of the interview text, and also subject to the demands and expectations of the cultural production and reception of research writing. Life story and oral history narratives, so Gubrium and Holstein (2003: 45) point out, 'extend the biographical particulars of the subject and subject matter in time'. This is *contra* the snapshot picture from the *vox pop* interview or cross-sectional survey. This can be further developed in the interview or written account that blurs the lines between interviewer and interviewee in the aim for symmetry and which can include layers of interviewer reactions and feedback in the text. This is the globalization of the interview, now 'a worldwide form of cultural production' (Gubrium and Holstein 2003: 47), but one ever changing and dynamic, an art form as well as a scientific practice. This is the interview society we inhabit, more blurred and collaborative than before (see Ellis and Berger 2003; Narayan and George 2003), one that 'provides both a sense of who we are and a method by which we represent ourselves and our experiences' (Gubrium and Holstein 2003: 47).

Oral History and the Interview

The interview method and product has been used and examined in other disciplines, one of which is oral history or historiography which relies upon the interview at its core and is a subject also with an affinity with anthropology given that its aim is 'pursuing the past through the spoken word' (Henige 1988: 3). It is a popular method for historians as well as anthropologists, and Henige advocates formal interviewing or even, controversially, informal 'eavesdropping on the past' to supplement traditional archival research (1988: 55). For him, interviewing is an art form not without its own challenges such as lying and deception in informants (see Salamone (1977) on the Tiv), as well as researchers, apparently; interference from the venue; informant choice; and letting the interviewee reminisce and ramble (Henige 1988: 109). For Henige, this democratization of the past can lead to introspective life histories, personal memories and stories. These, for him, lead to 'a cellular rendition of the past' (Henige 1988: 110), oral histories that are not comparable with each other. The danger is that the democratization of the past can lead to the trivialization of the past, a criticism applicable to the interview society thesis in general. In these interview instances, the interviewer learns about the interviewee, but not his or her larger context world. For Henige, the oral life history—essentially 'a spoken autobiography' (Henige 1988: 106)—is an inefficient way of learning about the past.

Whilst others take a softer stance towards the oral and/or life history or are less critical of this conceptual shift acknowledging 'interviewer's reactions [and] intrusions' into the research (Yow 2006: 212), Henige does draw attention to difficulties in using the interview, an ethnographic interview (Henige 1988: 76). He also makes the valid point that these sessions are oral performances, speech acts and events,[6] performing arts in their own rights; a storytelling occasion. In these research settings, not only is the interview a theoretical performance event, but it could be treated as a performance by the speaker who is used to holding forth through the medium of orality. In other words, orality as a label can be unpacked itself and is not just a medium but a series of mediums with different meanings and manners. There are rhetorics, aesthetics, paralinguistics and patterns to all forms of communication and verbal texts such as the interview, as anthropologist Ruth Finnegan (1992: 13, 19) suggests in her methods guide *Oral Traditions and the Verbal Arts* (1992: 13, 19). Further, there is no necessary 'equivalence' between the spoken and written 'texts' of the interview (Finnegan 1992: 195). Neither should be treated as 'a social' (Finnegan 1992: 45).

Context and intertextuality and indeterminacy and ambiguity from performance to reception (the word 'Yes' for example can be interpreted variously as: 'I heard you'; 'I understand you'; 'I see this as important for you'; 'I agree with you' as well as a soft form of 'No' (Fontes 2008: 299); kinesics and proxemics; accent, intonation and emphasis; acoustic and visual elements; transcription and interpretation: all are at play in this 'ethnography of speaking' (Finnegan 1992: 42; see also Hymes 1974; Tedlock 1983) that we struggle to represent. 'Looking to words on their own is too narrow' (Finnegan 1992: 233), especially when spoken 'across' and subsequently written or typed 'up'.

Where Finnegan opens conventional thought on the interview text in *Narrating Our Pasts: The Social Construction of Oral History*, fellow anthropologist and oral historian Elizabeth Tonkin adds memory to the interview nexus with her attention to our 'representations of pastness' (1995: 16). For Tonkin, our present is lived in an amalgam of memories from our past, social memories tied to relationships with others. 'We live in other people's pasts' (Tonkin 1995: 9), and so our research seeks to explicate that foreign country, ever wary towards the open spaces in the texts, the danger of treating them too literally and the ability of memory to play tricks with us in all its condensations and displacements (Tonkin 1995: 91, 114 with an allusion to Freud). Memory is different to recall. Memory is subject to revision, fragmentation and deflection and is inevitably refracted upon layers of experience. Memory is anecdotal and potentially prone or even stimulated to exaggeration in the presence of an interviewer (Summerfield 2004: 66). In orating our selves, whether in one-to-one interviews involving reminiscence or in public storytelling oral tradition, we can maintain or develop our selves, create personas of our selves manipulate the distance between our commentary and our selves or use the speaking to come out of our selves (Tonkin 1995: 48–9). It is emancipatory and empowering. Michael Jackson attaches 'narrative warrant' to our storytelling (2002: 35). Anthropologist Barbara Myerhoff gives a good example of this reminiscence work interviewing an elderly Jewish community in Venice Beach, California ((1979) 1994). In *Number Our Days*, Myerhoff gained insight into the lifeworlds of retirees through a living history class, interviewing and community participation. In this ethnography, one which stays very close to the interview transcripts, the telling and retelling of Holocaust survivors' stories has particular poignancy and serves as 'witnessing', whether or not the telling and retelling of their stories made life bearable in the present (Myerhoff (1979) 1994: 271; see also Zelizer 2005; Felman and Laub 1992; Skinner 2012). We are multiple, and the interview—existential in the sense that it reconstructs an existence from the debris of a collapsed past all around us (McGuire 1987: 61)—enables but one facet or face of our selves. The self, the subject, the text, the interview are all single words, but they are far from simple or unitary. They are, to return to Tonkin (1995: 132), open and diverse, indeterminate and complex, whether used individually or collectively.

It would seem that our interview society is both a method as well as an identity-forming practice—with the interview also often serving as an entrée to or exit from the field.[7] It has developed and it has percolated through the disciplines, mediating our world—now pitched to as 'secondhand' by Denzin (2003: 141) referring to the performative/cinemative-interview society (Denzin 2001). Perhaps we now live in a secondhand society. The interview as well as the interview society can be unpacked and shown to be a complexity of subjects, acts, events and 'ephiphanies' (Denzin 1989), and texts by oral historians. Other disciplines such as journalism, healthcare, psychology, criminology and politics and market research all also make use of the interview. An extensive range of literature covers these disciplines, too much for this introduction to cover in full, but several titles are worthy of mention as possible reading avenues. I concentrate on journalism, counselling and healthcare, touching upon the applied 'active' interview: news, clinical, person-centred, forensic.

Interview Uses in Other Disciplines

The word *interview* has origins associated with the French *entre voir*, meaning 'to be in the sight of' and referring to a meeting of people face to face. It also has Latin origins with the prefix 'inter' meaning among and between and 'view' referring to seeing, looking or inspection. The term thus connotes a level of introspection for Fontes, who defines the interview as 'the intermingling of distinct ways of seeing' (2008: 3). It has become the staple practice in journalism whether working in print or broadcast media. Clayman and Heritage describe it as an 'interactional encounter' (2002: 1–2), spoken, spontaneous and emergent, inexpensive and attractive in the sense that it is easily consumed by readers, listeners and viewers. There is a format to interviews and, to return to the interview society thesis, the interview allows the journalist to perform a democratic function. Robin Day, Jeremy Paxman, Larry King, David Frost, David Letterman and Piers Morgan have built successful careers as professional interviewers—sometimes investigative, sometimes adversarial, sometimes hagiographic, all using the interview to reach a mass audience. Despite the changing medium of the interview, it remains interpersonal, spoken and largely contributory on a turn-by-turn basis. It is, then, a 'speech exchange system' (Clayman and Heritage 2002: 21), symbiotic, loosely contractual, with an opening and a closing, with questions and probing in between. For some it is a game of strategy and spin, the interview—the production of talk—as 'dark art'. Stuart Hall (1973) characterizes the news interview as a mix of consensus, toleration or conflict. There is, inbuilt into the interview, a querying presumption by nature of the questions asked, as well as some inevitable cultural encoding in the questions put such as attitude, point of view or hazarded answer. The skilled interviewer might, for all this, attempt to mask the adversarial setup of the interview to appear impartial or neutral by for example speaking on behalf of a third party ('Minister, critics have used the expression "not fit for purpose" to describe your Department, how do you respond?'). Frost positioned himself as a tribune of the people in his legendary exchange with President Nixon, both legitimizing and neutralizing his controversial call for the president to admit to his crimes with the words '"people need to hear"' (Clayman and Heritage 2002: 176).

Contra the position of the interviewer, figuratively or sometimes quite literally the 'attorneys for the public' (Adams and Hicks 2001: 54), many interviewees now have received media training and have practised maintaining their agenda at interview, evading questions, steamrolling their points, how to waffle, 'loop' or use a 'word-bridge' from the question to take control of an interview in their answers. Note the key tense shift in President Clinton's now-notorious answer to Jim Lehrer's public interrogation about allegations of an affair with White House intern Monica Lewinsky (Clayman and Heritage 2002: 295):

Lehrer: You had no sexual relationship with this [young woman].

Clinton: There is not a sexual relationship. That is accurate.

This is more verbal fencing than news interview as conversation. It is an example of rhetoric used to achieve socially acceptable answers. It also shows us that we should treat carefully the recent association between the interview and the democratization of society. This is more of a case of the 'pseudo-democratisation' of political discourse as seen in the interview (see Fairclough 1992, cited in Clayman and Heritage 2002: 339).[8]

For all the different mediums, agendas and interpretations, the interview remains a dialogue of talking and listening. It is responsive cajoling as the interviewer tries to build a rapport with his or her subject, practises his or her interview art and elicits 'his or her' answers. These characteristics are present to a varying degree in synchronous face-to-face verbal exchanges in the here and now and over the telephone as synchronous 'callers' (a category to which we can now include Skype calls or written instant messaging), as well as in the asynchronous questioning by post, email, Internet relay chat or texting. Displaced time-space interviewing—'online interviewing' (James and Busher 2009) which can generate discontinuous 'narratives on the net' (Skinner 2002)—is fast becoming a necessary core or adjunct technique in the social scientist or journalist's repertoire: ethnography gone 'virtual' (Hine 2000) or 'cyber' (Skinner 2009a; Christensen 2002), 'netnography' (Kozinets 2010) even for the sociologist or anthropologist.[9] These new research techniques and fields challenge ethnography's romantic legacy that treats speech as more authentic than writing. In these last cases, the field and narrative results are more 'temporal collage' (Hine 2000: 95) than linear engagements; the 'screentalk' (Denzin 1999: 114) is textual ethnography engaged through ever more complex time quotients. Moreover, the anonymity of net-interviewing can encourage less willing interviewees into taking part, and frequently the spontaneous nature of the written medium such as instant messaging can foster a particularly immersive and unguarded encounter (see also Voida et al. 2004), as though, ironically, the interviewer and interviewee were reading each other's minds, unmediated. Murray (1997: 252) has described this World Wide Web as a 'global autobiography project'. However, it seems wise to make cautious use of it given the potential for deception in whatever the medium the dyadic encounter—and yet anthropologists Salamone (1977) and Metcalf (2002) argue that there is great significance and merit from discerning respondents' motives to lie (see also Harrison et al. 1978).

In the medical setting, the clinical interview has a different dynamic. It might be that the interview is not voluntary as the interviewee is a patient under assessment. McConaughy advocates the use of clinical interviews in the assessment of intervention needs ranging from initial understanding of problems to psychiatric diagnoses, designing mental health treatments, evaluating the effectiveness of current treatments and screening clients for at-risk status (2005: 2). For her, the interview is part of a multimethod approach, with naturalistic observation providing more behavioural assessment information. She notes, after Sattler (1998), that, though they are bidirectional interactions, such interviews differ from conversations in that they are formally arranged, specific in purpose, the topic is decided by the interviewer and the relationship is predefined in terms of adopting the questioner and answerer roles. Furthermore, the interview differs from a conversation in that the interviewer is using questioning techniques to sustain the interaction and gather information in a particular format, that the interviewer often explicitly states for the sake of the interview what would often generally be left unstated in ordinary conversation and, finally, that the interviewer is abiding by guidelines on ethical behaviour and confidentiality. These interviews have *gravitas* to them and can have far-reaching and possibly life-changing implications for the interviewee who might be abused, suicidal, addicted to drugs, dyslexic. In these cases, the interviewee is seen to be in need of assistance and the interviewer is acting as his or her gatekeeper to services. These are controlled conversations; the interview serves as an efficient trawl net for information (cf. Wolcott 2005: 98–9).

In this clinical context, where the interview is a precursor to intervention, Morison points out that lying constitutes breach of the therapeutic contract between patient and healer (2008: 202–3). It is, though, still important to gain insight into the deception, be it fear, shame, worry or other emotions, for social or financial gain or a pathological condition from a highly experienced interviewee. In the clinical interview, the motive is to assess with a view towards treating the interviewee/patient. The interview prompts change. I would suggest that it is more than 'helping people talk about themselves' (Morison 2008: 1). It is a pre-action evaluation. And so the interviewer might be particularly attuned to the mood, the inner state of the interviewee; to the rate and intensity of the speech; to the flow of thought and associations being made from 'derailment' (loose associations common in psychosis such as example A) to 'clang' associations rhyming words (example B), echolalia repetition of words (example C) to incoherence:

IR: When did you enter the hospital?

IE (A): I came in on Monday. Monday is wash day. That's what I'm gonna do—wash that man right outta my hair. He's the tortoise and I'm the hare.

IR: Who brought you to the hospital?

IE (B): My wife, she's the wife of my life, no strife.

IR: How long were you in the hospital that time?

IE (C): How long were you in the hospital? I was in the hospital a long, long time, that's how long I was in the hospital. (Morison 2008: 126–7)

The clinical interview gathers a patient's history with a view towards diagnosis and treatment. It can also be a mental status assessment, an established cognitive and behavioural assessment of the patient (see also Sullivan 1954; Rutter and Cox 1981). Writing for healthcare practitioners, Rollnick et al. refer to this motivational interviewing as a 'productive conversation' (2008: 4), one which encourages behaviour change in the interviewee. It is gentle counselling by asking, listening and informing the patient; by 'chunk-checking' (Rollnick et al. 2008: 94) them as the session develops (providing the subject with chunks of information and checking on its understanding). For them, the success is in eliciting 'changetalk' (Rollnick et al. 2008: 35) so that they are motivated and empowered to make subsequent lifestyle changes. This approximates some of the psychotherapeutic talking therapies such as cognitive behavioural therapy found in counselling settings.

In the counselling setting, the talking relationship is one of 'working alliance' (Rennie 1998: 102). It is a broad modern discipline perhaps developing as a response to the empty self (see Cushman 1995). The analysis of counselling techniques and research into interviews and/or counselling sessions is sophisticated and detailed and is where many of the advances in interviewing come from (see McLeod 1994: 79–89). Post-Freudian psychodynamic counselling, for example, pays heed to the problem of transference and counter–transference as either respectively the client or counsellor project feelings or characteristics into his or her working partner based upon his or her previous experiences with other people (McLeod 1998: 47). As with deception, Heiman (1950) uses counter transference as an important tool in the analysis of the interviewee. The 'conversational model' is a development within the psychodynamic where the counsellor deliberately develops a language of feelings with the client (McLeod 1998: 54).

The person-centred approach is the one I was trained in, practised for two years and find useful in my interview practice as an anthropologist. In these interviews, I recognize that the interviewer watches himself or herself as well as our narrators, that they watch us and themselves, sometimes 'catching themselves', and that both interviewer and interviewee can be involved and affected by the interview (see also Yow 2006). Associated with American psychologist Carl Rogers, this 'Rogerian' approach is client-centred and nondirective. Humanistic in orientation, it aims to work in the here-and-now of the client's experiences, nonjudgemental, walking with the client metaphorically. The person-centred counsellor seeks empathy, congruence and acceptance with the client. Congruence is when feelings and awareness are synchronized with each other. These conditions are thought to best 'self-actualize' the client, to make him or her feel safe to speak and disclose. Elizabeth and I were not very congruent in our interview debrief. Several times she corrected me, illustrating an ease in the encounter—also evinced by the subject of the conversation—but also indicating that I had been incongruent in my comments and suggestions. This is evinced through the Barrett-Lennard (1981) empathy cycle model. I was checking for when congruence was maintained between us, confirmed or not in her replies. In my interview with Sarah (see Skinner 2010a: 116), the responses were positive ('*Yeah*', '*Exactly*'). With both interviewees I was listening, reading, gauging, measuring and probing their responses; I was using rich visual and evocative language to visualize aspects of the interview and so assist with the checking and comprehension. Checking mechanisms are in play to ensure that the conversation is flowing between each other rather than past or over one another.

Person-centred interviews require a high degree of reflexivity and reflection in the counsellor. Person-centred advocate David Rennie (1998: 103) notes that this form of counselling necessitates the active listening presence of the counsellor, but an absence of his or her personality. The counsellor is a foil and a reflecter of the client. His or her counselling self encourages an awareness of his or her consciousness and the various streams of thought we move in and out of. Without the reflexivity there is no conversation. With reflexivity there is conversation and, if it is mutual, there is communication and metacommunication as both counsellor and client communicate the meanings behind their communications. Here is an example of a counsellor's metacommunicative invitation to the client to share his sense of the counsellor's impact on him (from Rennie 1998: 93):

Client (Cl): For some reason, the sense that you're on my side isn't as strong today. [Pause] I don't know why.

Counsellor (Co): Is it because of something that I have done today? Perhaps I've somehow taken you away from where you were the last time we met. Is that possible?

Cl: No, I don't think so. It doesn't seem to be that.

Co: Mmmm. [Pause] Since we've met today, there's been something going on in me that I haven't told you about. I'm feeling upset about something that happened to me at the university today. I'm still carrying that with me. Maybe you picked that up. Have you been feeling that I'm a bit more distant from you today?

Cl: No, I haven't been feeling that.

Such 'two-way metacommunication' (Rennie 1998: 91) is neither necessary nor practical in all interview or conversation scenarios, but it does demonstrate the levels of acuity and detail possible. Such awareness and reflection can percolate into research behaviour and relations (see Josselson 1997), the research interview questions and postinterview interpretations.[10] These considerations are less at the forefront of the forensic or investigative interview conducted by the police where vulnerability (age, disability, illness), capacity for consent and competence (do they understand the question?) and reliability and security of testimony are the priorities (Smith and Tilney 2007). The UK police for example interview according to UK Ministry of Justice/Home Office frameworks endorsed by the Association of Chief Police Officers (Ministry of Justice 2011). These are easily remembered and deployed by the mnemonics PEACE and ABE (Achieving Best Evidence):

ABE	**PEACE**
Planning and Preparation	Planning and Preparation
Establishing Rapport	Engage and Explain
Initiating and Supporting a free narrative account	Account, Clarification and Challenge
Closing the Interview	Closure
Evaluation	Evaluation

Conversation management is central to their forensic interview. So, too, is the management of the interview data. From a legal perspective, the security of interview recordings is essential with master copies sealed and put in storage and records kept of the movements and access of the copies.

In 'Active Interview Tactics', Hathaway and Atkinson (2003) advocate a very different conversational relationship. They suggest a good cop–bad cop persona interviewing technique when faced with 'public deviants'. They are sympathetic to conflict methodologists, noting that '[s]ocial scientists tend to adopt a more artificial, conciliatory style of questioning in the spirit of protecting, respecting, and maintaining rapport with informants' (Hathaway and Atkinson 2003: 172). This 'safe questioning' (Hathaway and Atkinson 2003: 172) results in safe data. On some occasions, with a good working knowledge of the context and strong relationship with the informant, it can be productive to pose him or her sceptical questions, to 'play dumb' or to even challenge him or her outright, no matter the discipline. The interviewee might set up a tactical interview, particularly when faced with resourceful and experienced interviewees who might have their own agenda and use the interview as a conduit for their ends (see also Collins and Gallinat 2010: 16), for the deceptive interviewee or interviewee courting publicity or exposure as in the case of jazz musicians understudied by Daniels (1987) trying to ingratiate themselves, to curry favour, to demonstrate 'respect', to please authority and authority figures. (It is worth bearing in mind that many interviews are 'downward' in terms of hierarchy and that the researcher is often seen as a powerful and lucrative gatekeeper by the interviewee.)[11] Sociologists Pierre Bourdieu et al. saw fit to challenge the accounts of two young Frenchmen so as to actualize an 'extraordinary discourse' in their responses, to cut through their presentations of self (1999: 614). Anthropologist Judith Okely notes that such an approach would not work with gypsies:

> The Gypsies' experience of direct questions is partly formed by outsiders who would harass, prosecute or convert. The Gypsies assess the needs of the questioner and give the appropriate answer, thus disposing of the intruder, his ignorance intact. Alternatively, the Gypsies may be deliberately inconsistent.
>
> Interviewers should be conscious of the subtleties of the interview context (1998: 45).

Paraphrasing psychologist Lisa Fontes, the interviewer should be aware that he or she has great power and potential in his or her questions to direct the interview and tell the interviewee what he or she should be talking about, to set and keep to the agenda of the interview (2008: 239, 73–7). Sensitive interviewers can show an awareness of this; pragmatic, Machiavellian interviewers have been known to use it to their advantage. To elaborate, the words chosen have a particular valence to them and can influence the interviewee as well as the reader of the final text or report. They 'embody' intentions and contain certain assumptions and are but one of a number of influences. Their impulse is to make the interviewee passive. This can be used to interviewer advantage but, generally, this should be acted against. The interviewer should also be conscious that the interviewee is reacting to him or her:

> Even when we think we are 'just listening', we are talking through our bodies, and interviewees watch us as we listen, trying to gauge our response. They are trying to find out how much attention we are paying, whether we like them, whether we believe them, if we are horrified or amused by what they are telling us, if we find them interesting and appealing, and so on. (Fontes 2008: 81)

Open-ended questions are more invitational and devolved to the interviewee: they can elicit a more free narrative and are one means of devolving agency to the interviewee. This devolution is but partial as the interviewer builds upon his or her initial questions (unless using the BNIM technique; see chapter 4, this volume).

Holstein and Gubrium contend that 'all interviews are interpretively active [...] reality-constructing, meaning-making occasions, whether recognised or not' (1995: 4). This applies to the applied interview between the journalist, the counsellor, the policeman and their clients, just as much to the qualitative research interview discussed by Kvale and evinced in the opening of this introduction. On the interview continuum, the latter represent a 'vessel-of-answers' (Holstein and Gubrium 1995: 8) view of the interviewee, where interviewer and interviewee are passive subjects in a scripted process. Such interviews have their merits as surveys, especially as large-scale fact-finding exercises, for behavioural, economic or demographic information for instance. Holstein and Gubrium, however, tend towards the creative side of interviewing; of improvization, mutual disclosure and reciprocity in the encounter (1995: 12).[12] There are no neutral or culture-free frames in the interview, no matter how standardized it is. Further, without the attention to the narrative linkages in the interview—the meaning trails, the 'horizons of meaning' in Holstein and Gubrium's (1995: 58) terminology—the interview becomes a disparate and meaningless set of words or scores. In Holstein and Gubrium's 'active interview' the focus is upon the interrelatedness of the information elicited. For Keats, the interview 'provides an opportunity to explore the reasons behind the person's answers and to verify the reliability of those answers with further questioning' (2000: 5). The working metaphor for these approaches to interviewing is to concentrate 'as much on the assembly process as on what is assembled' (Holstein and Gubrium 1995: 79), if not more so. In this fashion, shying away from the precoded response format in favour of immediacy and the context just as much as the content of the interview, Holstein and Gubrium refer to their active interviewer as an 'ethnographer of the interview' (1995: 78). This links their narrative approach to the interview to the new critical ethnography of the *Writing Culture* school (Clifford 1988; Clifford and Marcus 1986; Marcus and Fischer 1986) in anthropology as the interviewee/informant is re-positioned, and is actively involved in interpreting and representing himself or herself.

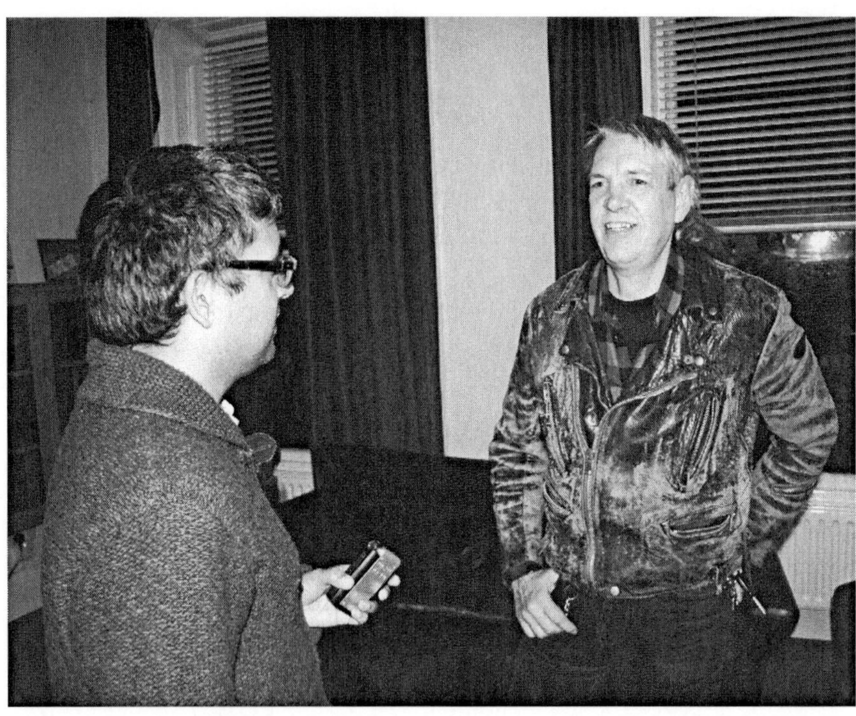

Figure 3 Standing interview

Anthropology and the Interview

> The best plan seems to be to devote as much time as possible to the photographic camera or to making careful drawings, for by these means the traveller is dealing with facts about which there can be no question, and the record thus obtained may be elucidated by subsequent inquirers on the same spot, while the timid answers of natives to questions propounded through the medium of a native interpreter can but rarely be relied upon, and are more apt to produce confusion than to be of benefit to comparative anthropology. It is almost impossible to make a savage in the lower stages of culture understand *why* the questions are asked, and from the limited range of his vocabulary or ideas it is often nearly as difficult to put the question before him in such a way that he can comprehend it. The result often is that from timidity, or desire to please, or from weariness of the questioning, he will give an answer that he thinks will satisfy the inquirer. If time serve, these difficulties can easily be overcome by friendly intercourse, and a careful checking of answers through different individuals. The information obtained will probably be more accurate if the examination takes place on the spot to which the questions relate; and the practice of making sketches of obsolete objects or customs, for correction by the natives, is also useful. They will also be found to answer more freely when the interrogator places himself on the same level as themselves, *i.e.*, if they sit upon the ground he should do the same. (Read (1874) 1892: 87–8, author's emphases)

Thus begins the second part of the Anthropological Institute's classic *Notes and Queries on Anthropology*, a volume first published in 1874 by the British Association for the Advancement of Science and edited by John Garson and Charles Read ((1874) 1892). This book is a comprehensive survey manual of topics and questions for the 'general traveller' to gather ethnographic data in the name of science. It remains in print after more than six reprints, though it is now more of an historical document than the latest revised handbook on methods that it was until the 1950s (Fürer-Haimondorf 1952). This extract evinces simultaneously self-consciousness in the reflexive position of the interviewer and contempt for the uncivilized interviewee. It shows us that questioning, conversing, interviewing has been integral to the anthropological project, though there have been paradigm shifts in its practice and regard for the investigating subject and the questioned object. Urry (1972) notes the shift from this observational survey-like recording to Malinowski's participant observation revolution of the 1920s.[13] In his pre–World War II lectures, Marcel Mauss was advocating 'the sociological method' of questioning people—especially 'the old people, whose memory is usually perfectly precise' (Mauss 2007: 16)—about their tribal histories, or asking natives to detail their biographies which would then be available for 'cross-questioning' (Mauss 2007: 17). These are the mixed methods of the 'extensive' ethnographer (Mauss 2007: 17) seeking social facts. Writing in 1939, anthropologist Fred Nadel propounds the use of the interview to also gather 'the "objective facts" of culture and society' (1939: 317). For him, the anthropological interview is different from the psychological or psychiatric in that we access 'informants' for information about their society and customs, whereas interviews in other disciplines seek to access the personality of their client.

Nadel adds the participatory element of the interview to the previous more distanced practice of observation. He writes: 'In anthropology the interview should if possible always be combined with direct observation. Observation can be used to check information obtained in interviews, and interviews to obtain information about facts which have been or are being observed' (1939: 318). The fieldworking anthropologist might, thus, consider the interview the participation in the new avant-garde participant observation formula. Nadel favours training and paying his key informants so they can cope with the systematic nature of questionnaire use or questioning—'the native manner of thinking... apparently [being too] circuitous' (Nadel 1939: 324). He finds it productive setting informants against one another in order to make their information explicit.[14] And he is also not adverse to using 'bullying' techniques of quizzing (Nadel 1939: 323) to obtain his informant's 'social and cultural facts' (Nadel 1939: 317–18).

As fieldwork became more participatory—the gentleman traveller giving way to the professional 'cross-cultural private eye' (Lewis (1976) 1988: 26)—the interview became an adjunct to the *habitus* of the fieldworker. Interviewing, whether using scripted or unscripted questions, allowed the anthropologist to learn the native point of view, namely, 'how the members of the culture see their own institutions and traditions' (Beattie (1964) 1982: 88), but at a remove from the routines of the field. It is stepping out from '[l]iving in the village with no other business but to follow native life' (see Malinowski (1922) 1984: 18). The interview is a step forward to, and a step back from, the field: it is an interjection into the activity under observation; it is an interruption of the interrogative with the respondent. In the latter, the interviewer and interviewee critically reflect on their activities: the anthropologist's interview as person-centred metafieldwork, after Rennie. The interviewing just before my departure from Montserrat is an extreme example of this talking about rather than just doing.

Of course, the ethnographic interviews do not always go easily, as Evans-Pritchard demonstrated in the now-notorious opening to his classic monograph *The Nuer.* Here, he cites the suspicions and evasions of one of the visitors to his tent:

Interviewer (I): Who are you?

Cuol (C): A man.

I: What is your name?

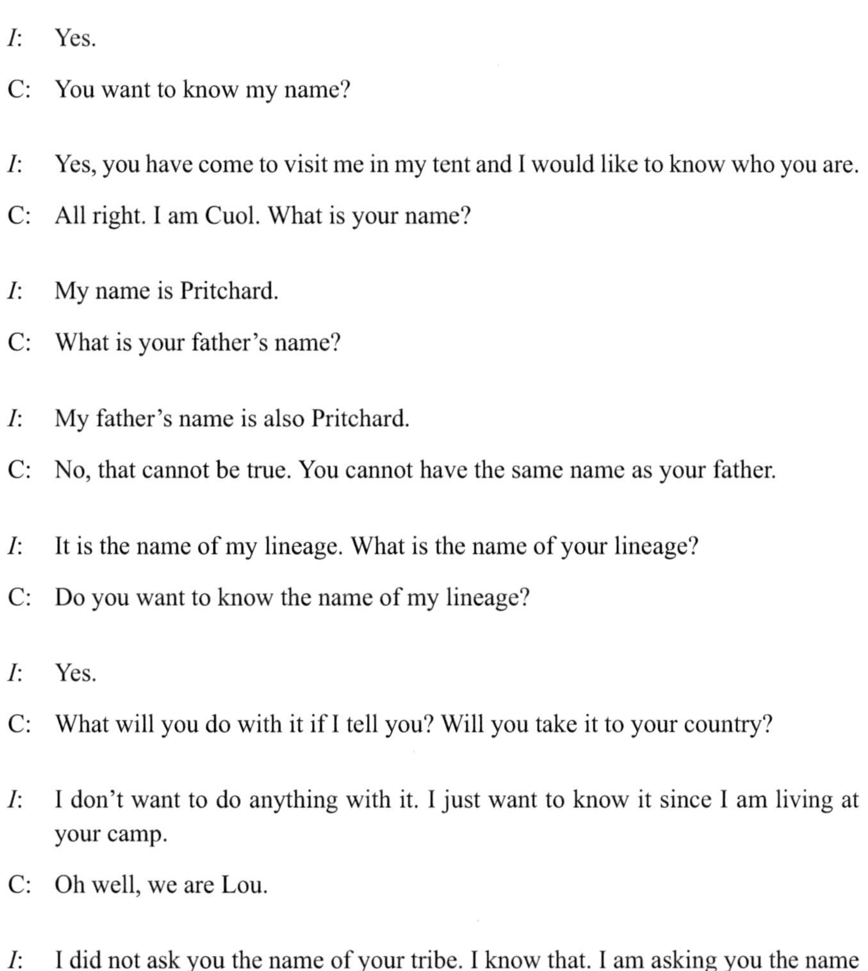

C: Do you want to know my name?

I: Yes.

C: You want to know my name?

I: Yes, you have come to visit me in my tent and I would like to know who you are.

C: All right. I am Cuol. What is your name?

I: My name is Pritchard.

C: What is your father's name?

I: My father's name is also Pritchard.

C: No, that cannot be true. You cannot have the same name as your father.

I: It is the name of my lineage. What is the name of your lineage?

C: Do you want to know the name of my lineage?

I: Yes.

C: What will you do with it if I tell you? Will you take it to your country?

I: I don't want to do anything with it. I just want to know it since I am living at your camp.

C: Oh well, we are Lou.

I: I did not ask you the name of your tribe. I know that. I am asking you the name of your lineage.

C: Why do you want to know the name of my lineage?

I: I don't want to know it.

C: Then why do you ask me for it? Give me some tobacco (1940: 12–13).

This example comes at the start of *The Nuer* where Evans-Pritchard gives a *drôle* introduction to his fieldstudy. The native sabotaging of his questioning he jokingly refers to as leading to fieldworker 'Nuerosis' (Evans-Pritchard 1940: 13).

Evans-Pritchard has been taken to task for glossing over the socio political context of this encounter, criticizing Cuol's oppositional complexity but not sparing mention of the recent government raids and hence local suspicions towards strangers (Rosaldo 1986: 91; see also Geertz 1988: 49–72). One can add to this by noting that despite the candour of his ethnographic methods, Evans-Pritchard does not give other instances of his conversations or interviews, and that this episode was recounted more to make an humorous point about the difficulties he had to endure in the field than as a serious comment contextualizing the basis of the knowledge production in his book.

Nisa: The Life and Words of a !Kung Woman by Marjorie Shostak ((1981) 1990) is perhaps a turning-point text in ethnographic conversations and interviews and their representation. It took approximately ten years to gestate into an ethnography of words, an interweaving of voices between Shostak and Nisa, a fifty-year-old !Kung woman who seemed 'to get' more than others what the interviewing questions were about and how to respond to them. Despite the fact that talking and telling stories is a popular 'aesthetic pleasure' (Shostak (1981) 1990: 22) amongst the !Kung, Shostak found that other !Kung women, such as Bey, did not interview well or work to Shostak's paid interview format (taped conversations of stories or information about the range of life for a !Kung woman, an hour per day) ((1981) 1990: 20). They were unable to present their stories, to summarize their lives chronologically, to delve into the required detail, to repeat in different ways when misunderstood. In short, Nisa became Shostak's key informant; 'her voice persisted' (Shostak (1981) 1990: 29) because she understood the requirements of the interview—Shostak's requirements. The result is an amalgam of the life of the !Kung native Nisa as translated and told through the anthropologist Shostak. The account is the interpreted highlights as selected by the anthropologist as author. Kenny (1987: 72) suggests that this makes the anthropologist the client and the informant our patron as we seek out people we can work with; as we are sponsored or develop brokers giving us our entrée into their chain of patronage (Kenny 1987: 77). This is a similar stance to that taken by Sidney Mintz who warns that, 'until the interview relationship is firmly established, the ethnographer may be figuratively at the mercy of the informant, quite the opposite is likely to be the case thereafter' (1979: 23). That working talking relationship is best sustained over time rather than by any 'one-night stand' approach to interviewing (Kenny 1987: 73)—interview collecting, to pastiche Leach.

The time accrued in the field is time spent building relationships, coming to terms with the field and gaining insight with which to fathom the intricacies of 'the ethnographic interview' (see Mintz 1979: 19) that can range from dialect to background and common knowledge. For Kenny, there is a qualitative difference between the chance, serendipitous interview in the field and the repeated interviewing of an intimate key informant who you have worked with over time (1987: 75). These interviews benefit from 'the vantage-point of ethnography' (Mintz 1979: 19) and are opportunities to see the informant interacting in his or her group—narrative and behavioural evidence of a single informant silhouetted against the backdrop of the group, to paraphrase Mintz (1979: 25). They also complement and give insight to the sustained interactions of the field. Yet, even with the trained informant or the most cosmopolitan patron, 'there is [still] nothing neat and evolutionary and articulate about it', Kenny reminds us, especially concerning the oral life history interview (1987: 78).

Anthropologists are 'privacy-snatchers' (Di Leonardo 1987: 17) in their ethnography of the intimate and private lives of their informants. They collect 'the droppings of talk' (Moerman 1988: 8). Nigel Rapport, for example, joins in the sets of 'talking relationships' in the English farming village of Wanet, but stays quiet in the pub, concentrating upon memorizing key words and phrases to jot down in the toilets and write up later back in his caravan on the farm (1993: 77, 63). These covert conversations with 'Nige', the rum bugger with the weak bladder, were an attempt at naturalistic conversational research, to record—undisrupted—Sid, Doris and the local regulars' habits of interaction. In further covert research in Newfoundland, Nigel, now 'Basil' or 'Bas', went on to look at the talking of violence, at the situational use of language by which we constitute and contradict ourselves—and society—in diverse and egocentric fashion (Rapport 1987: 13, 150). These captured ethnographic encounters and conversations differ from the more explicit ethnographic interview with Nisa where insight is by consent; or examples such as the alleged reported conversations Carlos Castañeda ((1969) 1998) had with Don Juan, the Yaqui shaman from Mexico that he reconstructed from memory. Or the 'incipient communication' Dumont (1978: 52) had with the headman and other tribesmen of the Panare of Venezuela Guiana in his exploration of the relationship between the fieldworker 'I' and the informants 'they', to his examination of 'the [very] texture of anthropologizing' (Dumont 1978: 6) itself. Or Kevin Dwyer's (1982: xix) interrupted dialogues with Faqir Muhammad, a Moroccan cultivator, an ethnographic confrontation or existential intrusion of 'structured inequality and interdependence of Self and Other, [...] the individual's action and his or her own society's interests'. Or Vincent Crapanzano's (1980) life of a tile maker, *Tuhami: Portrait of a Moroccan*, a reconstruction through his words, a 're-creation' (Crapanzano 1980: 151) with reflexivity and questions only coming from Crapanzano, the answering words seductive and entrapping, turning the interviewer into 'an articulatory pivot' (Crapanzano 1980: 140) about which Tuhami spins his own recreations and fulfills his own fantasies. The result is a puzzle, a realist modernist text of extracts inviting the reader in to interpret the text (see Marcus and Fischer 1986: 71). This is a shift indeed from active interviewer to active reader (Roulston 2010; see also Crapanzano, chapter 10, this volume).

These ethnographies represent a dialogic anthropology. This is the reconstruction of auto/biography and voice of the Other: Tuhami is by extract; Faqir Muhammad by extended quoting; Sid and Doris by textualizing headnotes and fieldnotes. This conversation work is not without its critics in anthropology from fieldwork practice to textual (literary) production—the latter as creative, engaging, antiessentialist, challenging, experimental and effective ethno-poetics according to advocates Marcus and Fischer (1986: 74). These ethnographies, however, represent postmodern narcissistic twaddle for others (see Fardon 1990). Dwyer declares Crapanzano's interviews with Tuhami 'insulated' in their psychoanalytic manner (1982: 279ff). They are, by virtue of their structure and their content, cut off from the wider context and almost therapeutic as a client–patient relationship. In this case, the focus is upon the Other and the Self remains largely unexamined (see also Paul 1989).[15] Perhaps there is more commentary on the Self than Dwyer credits Crapanzano with—Seidman suggests that the interview experience can transform Self and Other as Crapanzano's interviews with Tuhami shift an 'I–thou' interview relationship into a 'we' relationship (1991: 73)—but Dwyer's wider point is that our fieldwork experiences should be open to journeys together and new meanings and mutual understandings, and that our texts should reflect the like, that to engage with the fieldworker's experiences and to be able to confront, challenge or criticize them, the conversations represented should be dialogic so that both the Self and the Other are visible to the reader. Both should be experience-near. Moreover, the timing of the dialogues should be maintained so that we can 'listen' to them (Dwyer 1982: 279), so that the texts—built from utterances in the field—speak to us and them (see Feld 1987), just as the experiences and conversations spoke to the fieldworker.

This context is more than a background setting for ethnographers John and Jean Comaroff. They resist the 'dialogic' impulse in favour of a 'dialectics' one (Comaroff and Comaroff 1992: 11). Linking the conversation to ethnography, the Comaroffs suggest that ethnography 'does not speak *for* others, but *about* them' (1992: 9, authors' emphasis). For them, it does not set out to achieve the realist representation that postmodern new ethnographic critics deny. It is an historically situated practice, 'an inescapably Western discourse' (Comaroff and Comaroff 1992: 10), and should be recognized as such. But, in that inescapable ethnocentrism, we should beware 'the bourgeois subject' (Comaroff and Comaroff 1992: 10) and its many manifestations such as in the legacies of American cultural anthropology. This is reductive; a rendering down of the human subject to the product of Western humanism. It is chilly scholarship.[16] The Comaroffs deny such asocial agency in their writings:

> Under these conditions, culture becomes the stuff of intersubjective fiction: a web to be woven, a text to be transcribed. And ethnography becomes 'dialogical', not in Bakhtin's thoroughly socialized sense, but in the narrower sense of a dyadic, decontextualized exchange between anthropologist and informant. We would resist the reduction of anthropological research to an exercise in 'intersubjectivity', the communing of phenomenologically conceived actors through talk alone [. . .] To treat ethnography as an encounter between *an* observer and *an* other—*Conversations with Ogotemmeli* (Griaule 1965) or *The Headman and I* (Dumont 1978)—is to make anthropology into a global, ethnocentric interview. Yet it is precisely this perspective that warrants the

> call for ethnography to be 'dialogical'—so that we may do justice to the role of 'the native informant', the singular subject, in the making of our texts (1992: 10, authors' emphasis).

Though, as Michael Jackson points out, it is precisely from 'the dynamics of intersubjectivity' that stories, biographies, answers and confessions arise (1998: 23), the Comaroffs propose an historical anthropology, one in which ethnographic texts are as grounded in the grounds of the informants they try to represent. For them, it is not about the 'inter-locution' (Jackson 1998: 3). It is the task and responsibility of the anthropologist to include and account for the 'processes of production', 'the orbits of connection and influence' (Comaroff and Comaroff 1992: 34) that give life to their fields of study. This is as opposed to the 'inter-existence', the 'inter-action', the 'intercorporeity' of being-in-the-world existential-phenomenologicalism stressed by Jackson (1998: 3).

Charles Briggs (1997) successfully does this in his study of the interview based upon his communicative blunders amongst *Mexicanos* of northern New Mexico. He uses his ethnographic experiences to draw attention to the communicative norms and speech forms of the community of people he has studied over the years. To go into a community and ask questions is to ignore native metacommunicational skills and repertoires. It is imposing the researcher's conversational forms upon the interviewee. The result can be incompatibility as evinced by Evans-Pritchard. Briggs is not ruling out the interview in social science research. He is making the point that the interviewer needs to be more sophisticated in that nebulus of the interview as 'a communicative event' (Briggs 1997: 2). This extends from the interview process through to the engagement with the interview text—'dialogical texts that are largely structured by the interviewer' (Briggs 1997: 13). Is the interview using casual everyday speech that the interviewee would use? How does the structure of the interview—a series of speech events from rapport-building entrée to diplomatic closure—impact the interview? Briggs notes that interview success relies upon native communication routines working their way into the interview situation (1997: 28). This means that the interview is best accomplished late into the fieldwork encounter so that interviewees are not impeded by an alien discourse as well as the constraints of circumstance. The referential frame of the questions needs to be understood regardless of whether it relates to the lineage system (Cuol) or the nature of an interview (Elizabeth). Their answers demonstrate an awareness or a lack of comprehension (or a mask or play of incomprehension, or word and tense subversion such as in Clinton's case) for the referents in the question.

As an unmarried nineteen-year-old male researcher, Briggs could only work with certain social groups with particular roles in the Córdova community he was studying. He was only able to acquire 'metacommunicative competence' as he aged with the community, as he came to imitate local language terms and structures, and he became aware of the danger of imposing 'communicative hegemony' over his respondents; '[t]his refers to researchers' efforts to impose their own communicative strategies on their subjects or consultants regardless of the possibility that these techniques may be incompatible with those persons' own communicative repertoire' (Briggs 1997: 90). Briggs challenges ethnographers or oral historians who pick their respondents as the 'best' or 'key' people to easily work with, or who train up their respondents. Instead, you might say that he was the one trained up over the many years of fieldwork and longitudinal interviewing he conducted. From Read to Shostak to Skinner, we are guilty of communicative hegemony to varying degrees. Interviewing Elizabeth, however, I was at least very aware of the dance background she had—I had been a significant part of it. I knew about the politics of dance she was referring to in our interview. I had been a victim of it. I knew what she danced, with whom and how. I had danced with her. And yet, I was selecting her from other potential interviewees: selecting her by excluding others; and asking her pointed questions, some of which I knew the answer to or were reprising events for the recording, some of which were designed to keep her 'on track' with the interview, all of which were grounded in our dance experiences. I wanted a rapport with her and for her to be at ease to enrich our communication, and I wanted considered answers, not just reply answers. Atkinson suggests that this level of detail in a dialogue distinguishes an interview from a more relaxed and general conversation (1988: 32). After the interview, I spoke my own notes and reactions to the interview into the recorder, self-interviewing so that the transcript of the interview would have notes that maintained the context of the utterances, so that it didn't turn into decontextualized knowledge. In short, I am suggesting that one should never rely on interviews alone. The material should be interpreted and analysed according to its referentiality (local semantic meaning, 'semantic density' (Hastrup 1990: 51–3) in the field; local ethnographic context; metaphorization (see Alvesson 2011; Gallinat 2006)). And that entails a degree of reflexivity.

With a sociolinguist's ear for detail, Briggs warns us against formulaic interviews and interview analyses. '[I]nterview data lulls us into being content with business-as-usual interpretive techniques', he writes (1997: 118). Fieldwork, ethnography, participant observation allows us to appreciate the interviewees, their words, their social worlds. It is 'a means of learning to provide a rapprochement between native meanings and the requirements of anthropological discourse' (Briggs 1997: 119–20). This can lead to an 'ethnographic interview' (Spradley 1979: 19), an opportunity to make explicit tacit knowledge practised and lived by people, an 'apprehensive' and 'uncertain' (Spradley 1979: 79, 80) task, ultimately, of translation competence from one cultural form, forum and format to another; or interviewing with an 'ethnographic imaginary' for Forsey (2010), the ethnographer as 'participant listener' (Forsey 2010: 561) treating the interview as an ethnographic encounter. Would Jarvie (1969) approve of the 'ethical integrity' of this more involved orientation?

Briggs would dispute this synchronicity with his suggestion that interviewing is Janus-faced: it is both in-the-field and at-the-desk (2007: 565). It has presumed distance and it has assumed proximity. The result for Briggs is a simultaneity apparent in anthropological writing.

Clearly, interviewing favours working with the aural soundscapes (see Rice 2005) more than the physical bodyscapes (see Ness 1995). In her ethnography of contemporary dance training, Caroline Potter (2008) notes that we privilege certain senses over each other such as sound over touch, when some informants—and anthropologists[17]—might be more experienced and comfortable moving than talking. The dancer's way of knowing (Crosby 1997)—an informant's kinaesthetic knowledge—is difficult to translate into the logocentric. Yet both are careful expressive articulations of being-in-the-world nevertheless. Hockey suggests that in anthropology there is even more of a methodological hierarchy with 'stand-alone interviews [...] as the poor relation or handmaiden of a participant observation study' (2002: 210). But it is fieldwork all the same, a punctuation point in relations, a research topic in itself just as the writing of ethnography became a research topic for the *Writing Culture* school. Such fieldwork in our interview society—in what Fernandez refers to as the 'sound bite cannibalism [...] of the modern world' (1993: 183)—needs to be attuned to the conversational production of ethnography and not just its textual representation. This means being aware of how ethnographic data is gleaned—the active listener's ear added to the *Writing Culture* writer's voice (cf. Clifford 1986: 12).

Michael Moerman (1988) works a micro-ethnography, preferring interviews leading to detailed conversational analysis, word for word, sentence by sentence. This is the micro politics or multi politics of elicitation. John Wengle (1988) assesses conversation recordings in terms of character vulnerability and identity maintenance, interviewing fieldworkers in this case as they persevere whilst feeling displaced in the world. This is the psychology of fieldwork research. Vieda Skultans 'borrowed the pain' (1998: 14; see also 1999) of her Latvian interviewees when they gave her their autobiographies of illness, all shaped by turning points in Soviet history. Judith Okely became 'the silent therapist who triggered off fantasies and monologues' (1992: 15). Hastings Donnan and Kirk Simpson (2007) helped border 'subjects' find a voice in troubled South Armagh. Michael Angrosino (2004) endured 'concealment' and 'monkish reticence' amongst Benedictine monks. Allan Young 'replays' group psychotherapy sessions amongst trauma-torn war veterans (1995: 227). Allan Feldman repeats the mimesis of the past in the present of the body, a coincidence of pain and memory for the Republican prisoner tortured under interrogation (1991: 128–36). Anselma Gallinat explores *zeitzeugen* in former East Germany, the reworking of the past by the state and former political prisoners, both institution and individual giving testimony—talking cures as 'time's witnesses' (2006: 344). The interview in anthropology is ubiquitous. It is here to stay. When used well, it accesses the native point of view. When well represented, it iterates the native viewpoint.

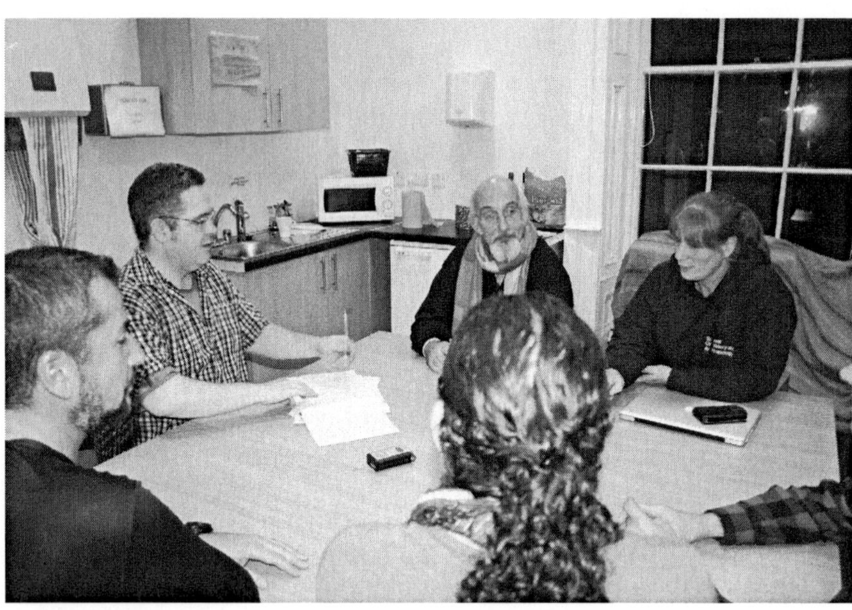

Figure 4 Focus group interview

Anthropology and the Interview—Edited

This volume answers Briggs's recent criticism of anthropology when he wrote the following: 'Anthropologists [...] seldom focus sustained, critical attention on how their interviewing practices produce subjects and objects, texts, and authority or what they might learn by making interviews and their place in society an object in anthropological inquiry' (2007: 531).

We heed his call to arms. The contributors to this volume use ethnographic cases to develop their arguments—taking the reader from the form and ethics of the interview through to interview dynamics, interview transcription and integrating the interview into one's writing. This develops from the typical 'how to interview' manual approach to interviewing and situates this volume in its own niche *between* the generic methods text and the typical edited collection focussing on an academic topic. The interview—whether professional, conversational, phenomenological, active, forensic, ethnographic—is a glimpse into the particular world of another. It is more than just a data-gathering or knowledge-producing exercise, a second choice method often taken as implicit and unscrutinized in the researchers' professional toolkit. But what is a successful and representative interview? How are they best transcribed and integrated into our writing? Is interview knowledge production safe, ethical and representative? And how are interviews used by anthropologists in their ethnographic practice and production of ethnography? The contributors to this volume reject the position of the interview occupying the methodological low ground. To be sure, in her epilogue, Marilyn Strathern gives us postinterview annotations, tying chapters together and relating them to the nature of qualitative research.

This introduction recommends the interview as *a part of* participant observation and not *apart from* participant observation. It is first amongst equals, just as '[e]thnography without questions would be impossible' (Agar 1996: 95). They are 'the "dynamic duo" of field research' (Sperschneider 2007: 275). Ideally, that interview is a mutual 'inter-view' (Finch 1984), edifying, and not 'a one-way pseudoconversation' (Fontana and Frey 2003: 82) in which the researcher elicits research information by acting out a relationship but without really relating to the speaker (Benney and Hughes 1956). As we've already seen, the context and media of the interview are important. So are the techniques of elicitation used whilst sitting, standing, walking or even dancing through the interview (Irving 2005; Skinner 2010a; see also Lee 2004). There are clearly identifiable pros and cons of various interviewing techniques (Biographical Narrative Interpretive Method; Rogerian nondirective; Responsive (Rubin and Rubin 2005); Barrett-Lennard congruence (1981); open/closed questioning, etc.) and devices (scratch notes, sound recording, telephone, video (see figures 1 through 4 in this introduction)).[18] For Sarah Pink the video camera in a video interview can act as a nonhuman agent in the interview process of knowledge production (2004: 64). It can enhance the interview and involve the interviewer and interviewee in different ways, interweaving visual and verbal representations and eliciting additional commentary: Pink encourages her informants to video their sensory home and to give the (inter)viewer a tour which they narrate. This is part of a growing 'sensory methodology' that has developed from conventional 'talk-based' research (Pink 2006: 57) and in part out of the ethnographic *After/Writing Culture* debates (James et al. 1997). It can be seen in chapter 5 where a team of French anthropologists experiments with headsets to film decision-making events elicited further whilst the interviewee watches and comments upon the recordings.

Besides being active, the video interview is 'relational' (Tietel 2000) and transformational; in its narration, there is an inevitable change to the interviewee's memories: healing, reinforcement, reappraisal, remembering and re-authoring in the telling of stories. To paraphrase Hertz (1997), an interview results in the interviewee retelling his or her past experiences whilst the interviewer lives and negotiates his or her present. Interpretation, subject construction and expression also take place in the coding, transcribing and eventual writing about the interview—a translation from speech to text, a writing and re-righting of reality in ethnography (see Rapport 1994). This movement is equally deserving of attention as the interview precedings and proceedings. Anne Montgomery examines the importance of transcription technique in research interpretation in chapter 6.

This volume is more than just an introduction to techniques of elicitation for ethnographers. Here are twelve chapters from senior and junior anthropologist scholars engaging with the nature of the interview, taking the reader from initial scrutiny of the interview (its form, its place, and as an ethical tool for knowledge production) to interview techniques (from the biographical to the experimental embodied and visual, and the importance of the interview transcription itself) through to an illustrative range of interview explorations making particular key conceptual points (about silence, displacement and rhetoric in the interview encounter; as well as inspiration, disciplinary authority and avoidance). Each of these cases, techniques and positions draws from specific ethnographic experience with interview use, giving the volume an international ethnographic dimension from England, the Harkis of Algeria, Scotland, Papua New Guinea, France, North Korea, Northern Ireland, Angola, Ireland and the Hopi of Arizona. Similarly, the anthropologists contributing to this volume are international themselves, institutionally based in the following countries: Northern Ireland, Australia, Scotland, the United States, Sweden, England and France.

The twelve chapters in this book are divided into three sections: Positioning the Interview, Interview Techniques and Interview Cases. These three sections are bookended by this general introduction to the interview and its place in anthropology and Strathern's epilogue, which considers each chapter in the volume, drawing them together, teasing out connections and pushing forward some of the theorization on the interview.

In the first section, 'Positioning the Interview', Rapport examines the form of the interview; Hockey and Forsey, the interview as participatory research; Josephides, the interview and knowledge production. These chapters raise the questions of what and when is the interview. Rapport develops his talking-partners thesis discussed in the previous section. For Rapport, the conversation is dialectic—not in the Comaroffs' sense of the word, but as a zigzag, the give-and-take of an encounter. The research interview differs from this in that it is nonroutine, it is purposive and it is bounded. Added to this, Hockey and Forsey advance their respective suggestions that the research interview is ethnographic and that the ethnography is participant listening. Rather than complement participant observation with the interview, they propose reconceptualizing interview-based studies as ethnographic in themselves. This is an especially fruitful strategy for preserving disciplinary identity for anthropologists doing 'anthropology at home'. In Papua New Guinea, Josephides refers to the interview as a technique for knowledge production. It has prerequisites to it in that an interview relies upon shared understandings and the adequate emplacement of the interviewer. Issues of confidentiality and individuality come to the fore in a group-living village community, raising questions as to the suitability and appropriacy of the interview and drawing attention to the interview as a modern phenomenon and export.

In section two, 'Interview Techniques', Svašek and Domecka, Gore et al. and Montgomery showcase work integrating interviewing into the heart of their anthropological practice. Svašek and Domecka evaluate the biographic-narrative-interpretive method (BNIM) that has growing popularity particularly in sociology. It is an example of attentive interviewing with the interviewer asking questions only at the end of the initial interview narrative. Gore et al. use experimental techniques to elicit tacit knowledge in the interview. They attend, especially, to the physical, to eliciting verbal reflection on the embodiment of activity, be it refereeing, cooking or dance teaching. Finally, Montgomery demonstrates the importance of transcription in conversational analysis. She treats the interview as a discursive event, using an awkward example of respondent vulnerability and interviewee complicity to make her point. What does it mean to be a good interviewer? This is the question at the heart of her chapter.

The third section, 'Interview Cases', features a variety of examples of interview use highlighting issues ranging from creativity to rapport, silence to subversion and apology. Wulff considers the interview an instance of inspiration, a rebounding or zigzagging of creativity (see also chapter 1, this volume). These moments are natural but also induced with the dancers and writers she interviews. They show varying degrees of engagement and experience with the body and the verbal and with the interview society in traditional and modern Ireland. Florescu scrutinizes the lead-in to the problematic interview of an Angolan priest on the topic of children accused of sorcery. There is a context to the interview and a complexity of relations at play between and within interviewer and interviewee: it has material traces, Florescu observes. These factors frame and intrude upon the interview be they levels of imagination, disparate agendas or subtle cultural registers. Just as the interview has interruptions, the interview itself is an interruption of relations.

Migrants and exiles, the dispossessed Harkis from Algeria now living in France are the subject of Crapanzano's chapter. They are invisible people. Their story has been silenced. There is no *zeitzeugen* for the Harkis. Their personal narratives remain entrapped within themselves, more so for the older generations for whom the story of their collective past weighs particularly heavily over their individual stories. We turn from the trials of an ethnic population to a clinical trial with Greene's discussion of medical reluctance to include the interview in their assessment processes. How is the interview constrained? Who should set the interview script? In addressing these questions and Greene's difficulties of interviewing alongside a national screening programme in the United Kingdom, we get an exemplification of how to integrate the interview as qualitative research. Fahy unpacks the oral accounts of North Korean famine survivors in her chapter. She looks at the difficulty of articulating atrocity, quite literally the silence or the unspeakable in her narratives. Is the silence in the testimony an example of self-censorship or state silencing? Like the atrocity itself, silence resists our ability to represent it, but neither are beyond it. If anything, silence frames and draws attention to the awful. In the final chapter, the silence is more teasing as though the silence of a trickster. In his field research, McCaffery struggled with the authenticity of the interview—when he was not being manipulated or 'fobbed off' by his interviewees, Hopi Native Americans in northeastern Arizona. They are experienced interviewees, 'media savvy' research subjects skilled in evasion and resistant to triangulation techniques, no matter the researcher who has them in his or her sights. In this modern-day cowboy and Indian c(h)ase, the Hopi were helping the anthropologist by trying to avoid the essentialization—the stereotyping—of their words. Thus, from Evans-Pritchard's tent amongst the Nuer where the suspicious Cuol avoids giving out lineage details to McCaffery's mobile home amongst the Hopi where they offer him spoof clan names to draw attention to offensive New Age projections of identity, their 'Hopification', we have the interview embedded in anthropological practice but ever increasingly acknowledged by researcher and researched alike.

Notes

1. See Mattingly (1998; also Mattingly, Lutkehaus and Throop 2008) on emplotment, Bruner on narrative knowing (1990, 2008), and Ricoeur (1992) on lived and told narrative configurations of the shattered 'cogito' and the narrative conception of personal identity in general. Narrative also features in the approaches and analyses of interviews (King and Horrocks 2010: 213–32): Free Association Narrative Interviewing (FANI) where there are narrative incentives in the questioning or requests for stories (Holloway and Jefferson 2000); Biographic-Narrative-Interpretative Method (BNIM) where there are no interruptions in the initial interview but deliberately 'narrative-pointed questions' in subsequent

interviews (King and Horrocks 2010: 223; see also Wengraf 2001 and chapter 4, this volume); and the Life Story Interview approach that calls for 'nuclear episodes' in the person's life (McAdams 1993).

2. Smith and Osborn's (2008) Interpretative Phenomenological Analysis (IPA) recognizes a double hermeneutic in interview interpretation with the interviewee articulating his or her interpretation of his or her lived experience and the interviewer interpreting that interpretation for the reader (see also Schuman (2008: 63–91) for the application of Geertzian interpretativism in survey research and Crapanzano (1986) and Dundes (1994) for anthropological critiques of Clifford Geertz's 'constructed understanding of the constructed native's constructed point of view' (Crapanzano 1986: 74)).
3. See collections by Parkin (1982) and Dilley (1999) on semantics and context and Lee (1997) and Devault (1990) on language, stereotyping and feminist interviewing.
4. See also Silverman (1993) for a more comprehensive assessment of Kundera's work.
5. See also McDonald (2000) on Orientalism in the interview process and interview knowledge production.
6. For more detail, see Austin (1962) *How to Do Things with Words* where speech acts are distinguished between locutionary acts (the utterance and its ostensible meaning), illocutionary acts (the force and real meaning of the utterance, the 'doing' of the utterance, such as 'I now pronounce you man and wife'), and perlocutionary acts (the effects of the utterance whether intended or not). Philosopher John Searle (1969) developed this thesis according to the rules of language in *Speech Acts*, and subsequently in an investigation of 'the background' presuppositions and dispositions surrounding the utterance (*Intentionality*, 1983). Anthropologist Michael Agar used interviewing extensively in a study of American independent truckers, building his ethnography out of multiple 'strips' (bonded phenomena loosely approximating the speech event or 'film strip') (1987: 210, 218).
7. Once he had established his position hanging out on the street corner, William Whyte ((1943) 1993: 302–3) learned how to converse in 'baseball and sex' and when to add questions to the conversations or when to 'keep stum'. His place as well as his posture and his interviewing established him. Anthropologist Ulf Hannerz (1969: 202–3) found the same in Winston Street as his conversations and questioning came to define and place him where previously he had been invisible. It is also possible to work secondhand with other people's questions, interviews, 'rounds' and conversations as Atkinson (1995) did in his study of haematologists in a practicing hospital; or secondhand in a team of interviewers in the field and analysts in the university (Donnan and Simpson 2007).
8. Other links with democracy and the interview lie with the democratic principles of governance in and ownership of the interview. This also relates to issues of

blind, informed and continuous consent; anonymity, quoting—including libel (spoken defamation of character) and slander (defamation in broadcast medium)—and the protection of sources; ethics and on and off the record material; and difficult interviewees where status issues, role conflicts, under- and over-communicative interviewees and the muting of interviewers come into play.

9. For virtual methods see also Jones (1997, 1999); and for good examples of internet ethnography see Miller and Slater (2000) and Baym (2000).
10. See also Hook (1994) on anthropology, psychoanalysis and interpretation and Heald et al. (1994) on anthropological engagements, psychoanalysis and cross-cultural critiques of notions of the self.
11. See Grice (1975) on 'conversational implicature' as respondents are constrained to shape and flow their speech to develop the conversation. See also Arksey and Knight on interviewing elites and the need for background knowledge and skill in negotiating access to the interviewee (1999: 122–5).
12. Holstein and Gubrium position themselves closer to Jack Douglas's (1985) *Creative Interviewing* than Jean Converse and Howard Schuman's (1974) *Conversations at Random* survey approach (1995: 9–13).
13. Malinowski ((1922) 1984: 22) expressly targeted 'the natives' views and opinions and utterances'. Their words recorded became 'documents of native mentality' (Malinowski (1922) 1984: 23). Their words came from hunting out local events and listening in to the natives' reactions; as he writes, 'it must be emphasized whenever anything dramatic or important occurs it is essential to investigate it at the very moment of happening, because the natives cannot but talk about it, are too excited to be reticent, and too interested to be mentally lazy in supplying details' ((1922) 1984: 8).
14. Nadel writes, 'In the case of interviews which bear on secret and forbidden topics, I have found it most profitable to stimulate the emotionality of a few chief informants to the extent of arousing almost violent disputes and controversies' (1939: 323).
15. See also Frankenberg on 'sharing subjects' (2008: 175).
16. Psychologist Ruthellen Josselson sums up the shift from responsive interview to unaccountable public representation of interviewee in her reflections upon the various research stages to publication:

    > My guilt, I think, comes from my knowing that I have taken myself out of the relationship with my participants (with whom, during the interview, I was in intimate relationship) to be in a relationship with my readers. I have, in a sense, been talking about them behind their backs and doing so publicly. Where in the interview I had been responsive to them, now I am using their lives in service of something else, for my own purposes, to show something to others (1996: 70).

17. See Stanton (2000) on Stoller and sensuous ethnography.

18. Sturges and Hanrahan (2004) suggest that there is no difference between data gathered in telephone and face-to-face interviewing. Clearly, though, there is a difference in medium as the one 'calls' for particular productions of sound and interpretation and the other relies more upon visual cues (Genovese 2004: 216).

References

Adams, S. and W. Hicks (2001), *Interviewing for Journalists*, London: Routledge.

Agar, M. (1987), 'Transcript Handling: An Ethnographic Strategy', *Oral History Review*, 15(1): 209–19.

Agar, M. (1996), *The Professional Stranger: An Informal Introduction to Ethnography*, New York: Academic Press.

Alvesson, A. (2011), *Interpreting Interviews*, London: Sage Publications.

Angrosino, M. (2004), 'Disclosure and Interaction in a Monastery', in L. Hume and J. Mulcock (eds), *Anthropologists in the Field: Cases in Participant Observation*, New York: Columbia University Press, 18–31.

Arksey, H. and P. Knight (1999), *Interviewing for Social Scientists*, London: Sage Publications.

Atkinson, P. (1995), *Medical Talk and Medical Work: The Liturgy of the Clinic*, London: Sage Publications.

Atkinson, P. and D. Silverman (1997), 'Kundera's *Immortality*: The Interview Society and the Invention of the Self', *Qualitative Inquiry*, 3(3): 304–25.

Atkinson, R. (1988), *The Life-Story Interview*, London: Sage Publications.

Austin, J. (1962), *How to Do Things with Words*, Cambridge: Harvard University Press.

Barrett-Lennard, G. (1981), 'The Empathy Cycle: Refinement of a Nuclear Concept', *Journal of Counselling Psychology*, 28: 91–100.

Bauman, R. (1977), *Verbal Art as Performance*, Prospect Heights: Waveland Press.

Baym, N. (2000), *Tune In, Log On: Soaps, Fandom, and Online Community*, London: Sage Publications.

Beattie, J. ((1964) 1982), *Other Cultures: Aims, Methods and Achievements in Social Anthropology*, London: Routledge & Kegan Paul.

Benney, M. and E. Hughes (1956), 'Of Sociology and the Interview', *American Journal of Sociology*, 62(2): 137–42.

Bourdieu, P., A. Accardo, G. Balazs, S. Beaud, F. Bonvin and E. Bourdieu (1999), *The Weight of the World: Social Suffering in Contemporary Society*, Stanford: Stanford University Press.

Briggs, C. (1997), *Learning How to Ask: A Sociolinguistic Appraisal of the Role of the Interview in Social Science Research*, Cambridge: Cambridge University Press.

Briggs, C. (2007), 'Anthropology, Interviewing, and Communicability in Contemporary Society', *Current Anthropology*, 48(4): 551–80.

Bruner, J. (1990), *Acts of Meaning*, Cambridge: Harvard University Press.

Bruner, J. (2008), 'Culture and Mind: Their Fruitful Incommensurability', *Ethos* (Special Issue: Troubling the Boundary between Psychology and Anthropology: Jerome Bruner and His Inspiration, edited by C. Mattingly, N. Lutkehaus and C. Throop), 36(1): 29–45.

Burgess, R. ((1984) 1993), *In the Field: An Introduction to Field Research*, London: Routledge.

Castañeda, C. ((1969) 1998), *The Teachings of Don Juan: A Yaqui Way of Knowledge*, Berkeley: University of California Press.

Christensen, N. (2002), *Inuit in Cyberspace: Embedding Offline Identities Online*, Copenhagen: Museum Tusculanum Press.

Clayman, S. and J. Heritage (2002), *The New Interview: Journalists and Public Figures on the Air*, Cambridge: Cambridge University Press.

Clifford, J. (1986), 'Introduction: Partial Truths', in J. Clifford and G. Marcus (eds), *Writing Culture: The Poetics and Politics of Ethnography*, Berkeley: University of California Press, 1–26.

Clifford, J. (1988), *The Predicament of Culture: Twentieth-Century Ethnography, Literature, and Art*, Boston: Harvard University Press.

Clifford, J. and G. Marcus (eds) (1986), *Writing Culture: The Poetics and Politics of Ethnography*, Berkeley: University of California Press.

Collins, P. and A. Gallinat (2010), 'The Ethnographic Self as Resource: An Introduction', in P. Collins and A. Gallinat (eds), *Keeping an Open 'I': Memory and Experience as Resources in Ethnography*, Oxford: Berghahn Books, 1–24.

Comaroff, J. and J. Comaroff (1992), *Ethnography and the Historical Imagination*, Boulder: Westview Press.

Converse, J. and H. Schuman (1974), *Conversations at Random: Survey Research as Interviewers See It*, New York: John Wiley.

Crapanzano, V. (1980), *Tuhami: Portrait of a Moroccan*, Chicago: University of Chicago Press.

Crapanzano, V. (1986), 'Hermes' Dilemma: The Masking of Subversion in Ethnographic Description', in J. Clifford and G. Marcus (eds), *Writing Culture: The Poetics and Politics of Ethnography*, Berkeley: University of California Press, 51–76.

Crosby, J. (1997), 'The Dancer's Way of Knowing: Merging Practice and Theory in the Doing and Writing of Ethnography', *Etnofoor*, X(1/2): 65–81.

Cushman, P. (1995), *Constructing the Self, Constructing America: A Cultural History of Psychotherapy*, New York: Addison-Wesley.

Daniels, D. (1987), 'Oral History, Masks, and Protocol in the Jazz Community', *Oral History Review*, 15(1): 143–64.

Denzin, N. (1989), *Interpretive Biography*, London: Sage Publications.

Denzin, N. (1999), 'Cybertalk and the Method of Instances', in S. Jones (ed.), *Doing Internet Research: Critical Issues and Methods for Examining the Net*, London: Sage Publications, 107–26.

Denzin, N. (2001), 'The Reflexive Interview and a Performative Social Science', *Qualitative Research*, 1(1): 23–46.

Denzin, N. (2003), 'The Cinematic Society and the Reflexive Interview', in J. Gubrium and J. Holstein (eds), *Postmodern Interviewing*, London: Sage Publications, 141–56.

Devault, M. (1990), 'Talking and Listening from Women's Standpoint: Feminist Strategies for Interviewing and Analysis', *Social Problems*, 37(1): 96–116.

Di Leonardo, M. (1987), 'Oral History as Ethnographic Encounter', *Oral History Review*, 15(1): 1–20.

Dilley, R. (ed.) (1999), *The Problem of Context*, Oxford: Berghahn Books.

Donnan, H. and K. Simpson (2007), 'Silence and Violence among Northern Ireland Border Protestants', *Ethnos*, 72(1): 5–28.

Douglas, J. (1985), *Creative Interviewing*, Beverly Hills: Sage Publications.

Dumont, J. P. (1978), *The Headman and I: Ambiguity and Ambivalence in the Fieldworking Experience*, Prospect Heights: Waveland Press.

Dundes, A. (1994), 'Gallus as Phallus: A Psychoanalytical Cross-Cultural Consideration of the Cock-Fight as Fowl Play', in A. Dundes (ed.), *The Cockfight: A Casebook*, Madison: University of Wisconsin Press, 241–84.

Dwyer, K. (1982), *Moroccan Dialogues: Anthropology in Question*, Prospect Heights: Waveland Press.

Ellis, C. and L. Berger (2003), 'Their Story/My Story/Our Story: Including the Researcher's Experience in Interview Research', in J. Gubrium and J. Holstein (eds), *Postmodern Interviewing*, London: Sage Publications, 157–83.

Evans-Pritchard, E. (1940), *The Nuer: A Description of the Modes of Livelihood and Political Institutions of a Nilotic People*, Oxford: Clarendon Press, http://ia700300.us.archive.org/17/items/nuerdescriptiono00evan/nuerdescriptiono00evan.pdf, accessed 26 April 2011.

Fairclough, N. (1992), *Discourse and Social Change*, Cambridge: Polity Press.

Fardon, R. (ed.) (1990), *Localizing Strategies: Regional Traditions of Ethnographic Writing*, Edinburgh: Scottish Academic Press.

Feld, S. (1987), 'Dialogic Editing: Interpreting How Kaluli Read Sound and Sentiment', *Cultural Anthropology*, 2(2): 190–210.

Feldman, A. (1991), *Formations of Violence: The Narrative of the Body and Political Terror in Northern Ireland*, Chicago: University of Chicago Press.

Felman, S. and D. Laub (1992), *Testimony: Crises of Witnessing in Literature, Psychoanalysis and History*, London: Routledge.

Fernandez, J. (1993), 'Review Article: A Guide to the Perplexed Ethnographer in an Age of Sound Bites', *American Ethnologist*, 20(1): 179–84.

Finch, J. (1984), '"It's Great to Have Someone to Talk To": Ethics and Politics of Interviewing Women', in C. Bell and H. Roberts (eds), *Social Researching: Politics, Problems, Practice*, London: Routledge, 70–87.

Finnegan, R. (1992), *Oral Traditions and the Verbal Arts: A Guide to Research Practices*, London: Routledge.

Fontana, A. and J. Frey (2003), 'From Structured Questions to Negotiated Text', in N. Denzin and Y. Lincoln (eds), *Handbook of Qualitative Research*, Thousand Oaks: Sage Publications, 61–106.

Fontes, L. (2008), *Interviewing Clients across Cultures: A Practitioners Guide*, New York: Guildford Press.

Forsey, M. (2010), 'Ethnography as Participant Listening', *Ethnography*, 11(4): 558–72.

Frankenberg, R. (2008), 'Role of Ethnographic Argument in the Prediction and/or Creation of Social Futures', *21st Century Society*, 3(2): 175–85.

Fürer-Haimondorf, C. von (1952), 'Review of Notes and Queries on Anthropology, 6th Edition', *Man*, 6(7): 10.

Gallinat, A. (2006), 'Difficult Stories: Public Discourse and Narrative Identity in Eastern Germany', *Ethnos*, 71(3): 343–66.

Geertz, C. (1988), *Works and Lives: The Anthropologist as Author*, Cambridge: Polity Press.

Genovese, B. (2004), 'Thinking inside the Box: The Art of Telephone Interviewing', *Field Methods*, 16(2): 215–26.

Grice, H. (1975), 'Logic and Conversation', in P. Cole and L. Morgan (eds), *Syntax and Semantics 3: Speech Acts*, New York: Academic Press, 41–58.

Gubrium, J. and J. Holstein (2001), 'From the Individual Interview to the Interview Society', in J. Gubrium and J. Holstein (eds), *Handbook of Interview Research: Context and Method*, London: Sage Publications, 3–32.

Gubrium, J. and J. Holstein (eds) (2001), *Handbook of Interview Research: Context and Method*, London: Sage Publications.

Gubrium, J. and J. Holstein (2003), 'From the Individual Interview to the Interview Society', in J. Gubrium and J. Holstein (eds), *Postmodern Interviewing*, London: Sage Publications, 3–18.

Hall, S. (1973), 'A World at One with Itself', in S. Cohen and J. Young (eds), *The Manufacture of the News: Deviance, Social Problems and the Mass Media*, London: Constable, 226–43.

Hannerz, U. (1969), *Soulside: Inquiries into Ghetto Culture and Community*, New York: Columbia University Press.

Harrison, A., M. Hwalek, D. Raney and J. Fritz (1978), 'Cues to Deception in an Interview Situation', *Social Psychology*, 41(2): 156–61.

Hastrup, K. (1990), 'The Ethnographic Present', *Cultural Anthropology*, 5(1): 45–61.

Hathaway, A. and M. Atkinson (2003), 'Active Interview Tactics in Research on Public Deviants: Exploring the Two-Cop Personas', *Field Methods*, 15(2): 161–85.

Heald, S., A. Deluz and P.-Y. Jacopin (eds) (1994), 'Introduction', in S. Heald and A. Deluz (eds), *Anthropology and Psychoanalysis: An Encounter through Culture*, London: Routledge, 1–26.

Heiman, P. (1950), 'On Counter-Transference', *International Journal of Psycho-Analysis*, 31: 81–4.

Henige, D. (1988), *Oral Historiography*, London: Longman.

Hertz, R. (1997), 'Introduction: Reflexivity and Voice', in R. Hertz (ed.), *Reflexivity and Voice*, Thousand Oaks: Sage Publications, vi–xviii.

Hine, C. (2000), *Virtual Ethnography*, London: Sage Publications.

Hockey, J. (2002), 'Interviews as Ethnography? Disembodied Social Interaction in Britain', in N. Rapport (ed.), *British Subjects: An Anthropology of Britain*, Oxford: Berg, 209–22.

Holloway, W. and T. Jefferson (2000), *Doing Qualitative Research Differently: Free Association, Narrative and the Interview Method*, London: Sage Publications.

Holstein, J. and J. Gubrium (1995), *The Active Interview*, London: Sage Publications.

Hook, R. (1994), 'Psychoanalysis, Unconscious Phantasy and Interpretation', in S. Heald and A. Deluz (eds), *Anthropology and Psychoanalysis: An Encounter through Culture*, London: Routledge, 114–27.

Hymes, D. (1974), *Foundations in Sociolinguistics: An Ethnographic Approach*, Philadelphia: University of Pennsylvania Press.

Irving, A. (2005), 'Life Made Strange: An Essay on the Re-inhabitation of Bodies and Landscapes', in W. James and D. Mills (eds), *The Qualities of Time: Anthropological Approaches*, Oxford: Berg, 317–30.

Jackson, M. (1998), *Minima Ethnographica: Intersubjectivity and the Anthropological Subject*, Chicago: University of Chicago Press.

Jackson, M. (2002), *The Politics of Storytelling: Violence, Transgression and Intersubjectivity*, Copenhagen: Museum Tusculanum Press.

James, A., J. Hockey and A. Dawson (eds) (1997), *After Writing Culture: Epistemology and Praxis in Contemporary Anthropology*, London: Routledge.

James, N. and H. Busher (2009), *Online Interviewing*, London: Sage Publications.

Jarvie, I. (1969), 'The Problem of Ethical Integrity in Participant Observation', *Current Anthropology*, 10(5): 505–8.

Jones, S. (ed.) (1997), *Virtual Culture: Identity and Communication in Cybersociety*, London: Sage Publications.

Jones, S. (ed.) (1999), *Doing Internet Research: Critical Issues and Methods for Examining the Net*, London: Sage Publications.

Josselson, R. (1996), 'On Writing Other People's Lives: Self-Analytic Reflections of a Narrative Researcher', in R. Josselson (ed.), *The Narrative Study of Lives: Volume 4—Ethics and Process in the Narrative Study of Lives*, Thousand Oaks: Sage Publications, 60–71.

Josselson, R. (1997), 'The Ethical Attitude in Narrative Research', in D. Clandinin (ed.), *Handbook of Narrative Inquiry*, Thousand Oaks: Sage Publications, 538–66.

Keats, D. (2000), *Interviewing: A Practical Guide for Students and Professionals*, Buckingham: Open University Press.

Kenny, M. (1987), 'The Patron-Client Relationship in Interviewing: An Anthropological View', *Oral History Review*, 15(1): 71–9.

King, N. and C. Horrocks (2010), *Interviews in Qualitative Research*, London: Sage Publications.

Kozinets, R. (2010), *Netnography: Doing Ethnographic Research Online*, London: Sage Publications.

Kvale, S. (1996), *InterViews: An Introduction to Qualitative Research Interviewing*, London: Sage Publications.

Lee, D. (1997), 'Interviewing Men: Vulnerabilities and Dilemmas', *Women's Studies International Forum*, 20(4): 553–64.

Lee, R. (2004), 'Recording Technologies and the Interview in Sociology, 1920–2000', *Sociology*, 28: 869–89.

Lewis, I. ((1976) 1988), *Social Anthropology in Perspective: The Relevance of Social Anthropology*, Cambridge: Cambridge University Press.

Malinowski, B. ((1922) 1984), *Argonauts of the Western Pacific: An Account of Native Enterprise and Adventure in the Archipelagoes of Melanesian New Guinea*, Prospect Heights: Waveland Press.

Marcus, G. and M. Fischer (1986), *Anthropology as Cultural Critique: An Experimental Moment in the Human Sciences*, Chicago: University of Chicago Press.

Mattingly, C. (1998), *Healing Dramas and Clinical Plots: The Narrative Structure of Experience*, Cambridge: Cambridge University Press.

Mattingly, C., N. Lutkehaus and C. Throop (2008), 'Bruner's Search for Meaning: A Conversation between Psychology and Anthropology', *Ethos* (Special Issue: Troubling the Boundary between Psychology and Anthropology: Jerome Bruner and His Inspiration, edited by C. Mattingly, N. Lutkehaus and C. Throop), 36(1): 1–28.

Mauss, M. (2007), *Manual of Ethnography*, Oxford: Durkheim Press/Berghahn Books.

McAdams, D. (1993), *The Stories We Live By: Personal Myths and the Making of the Self*, New York: Guildford Press.

McConaughy, S. (2005), *Clinical Interviews for Children and Adolescents: Assessment to Intervention*, New York: Guildford Press.

McDonald, K. (2000), 'Authorisation of Knowledge in the Interview Process', *On-Line Issues*, 6(1), http://www.ccfi.educ.ubc.ca/publication/insights/online/v06n01/mcdonald.html, accessed 23 February 2011.

McGuire, S. (1987), 'Expanding Information Sets by Means of "Existential" Interviewing', *Oral History Review*, 15(1): 55–69.

McLeod, J. (1994), *Doing Counselling Research*, London: Sage Publications.

McLeod, J. (1998), *An Introduction to Counselling*, Buckingham: Open University Press.

Merton, R. ((1956) 1990), 'Introduction to the Second Edition', in R. Merton, M. Fiske and P. Kendall, *The Focused Interview: A Manual of Problems and Procedures*, London: Collier Macmillan, xiii–xxxiii.

Metcalf, P. (2002), *They Lie, We Lie: Getting on with Anthropology*, London: Routledge.

Miller, D. and D. Slater (2000), *The Internet: An Ethnographic Approach*, Oxford: Berg.

Ministry of Justice (2011), *Achieving Best Evidence in Criminal Proceedings: Guidance on Interviewing Victims and Witnesses, and Guidance on Using Special Measures*, London: Ministry of Justice, http://www.justice.gov.uk/guidance/docs/achieving-best-evidence-criminal-proceedings.pdf, accessed 1 April 2011.

Mintz, S. (1979), 'The Anthropological Interview and the Life History', *Oral History Review*, 7: 18–26.

Moerman, M. (1988), *Talking Culture: Ethnography and Conversation Analysis*, Philadelphia: University of Pennsylvania Press.

Morrison, J. (2008), *The First Interview*, London: Guilford Press.

Murray, J. (1997), *Hamlet on the Holodeck: The Future of Narrative in Cyberspace*, Cambridge: MIT Press.

Myerhoff, B. ((1979) 1994), *Number Our Days: Culture and Community among Elderly Jews in an American Ghetto*, New York: Meridian Penguin.

Nadel, S. (1939), 'The Interview Technique in Social Anthropology', in F. Bartlett (ed.), *The Study of Society: Methods and Problems*, London: Taylor & Francis, 317–28.

Narayan, K. and K. George (2003), 'Personal and Folk Narrative as Cultural Representation', in J. Gubrium and J. Holstein (eds), *Postmodern Interviewing*, London: Sage Publications, 123–40.

Ness, S. (1995), 'Dancing in the Field: Notes from Memory', in S. Foster (ed.), *Corporealities: Dancing Knowledge, Culture and Power*, London: Routledge, 129–54.

Okely, J. (1992), 'Anthropology and Autobiography: Participatory Experience and Embodied Knowledge', in J. Okely and H. Callaway (eds), *Anthropology and Autobiography*, London: Routledge, 1–28.

Okely, J. (1998), *The Traveller-Gypsies*, Cambridge: Cambridge University Press.

Parkin, D. (ed.) (1982), *Semantic Anthropology*, London: Academic Press.

Paul, R. (1989), 'Psychoanalytic Anthropology', *Annual Review of Anthropology*, 18: 177–202.

Pink, S. (2004), 'Performance, Self-Representation and Narrative Interviewing with Video', in C. Pole (ed.), *Seeing Is Believing? Approaches to Visual Research*, Oxford: Elsevier B.V., 61–78.

Pink, S. (2006), *The Future of Visual Anthropology: Engaging the Senses*, Abingdon: Routledge.

Potter, C. (2008), 'Sense of Motion, Senses of Self: Becoming a Dancer', *Ethnos*, 73(4): 444–65.

Rapport, N. (1987), *Talking Violence: An Anthropological Interpretation of Conversation in the City*, St John's: Memorial University of Newfoundland.

Rapport, N. (1993), *Diverse World-Views in an English Village*, Edinburgh: Edinburgh University Press.

Rapport, N. (1994), *The Prose and the Passion: Anthropology, Literature and the Writing of E. M. Forster*, Manchester: Manchester University Press.

Read, C. ((1874) 1892), 'Part II—Ethnography: Prefatory Note', in J. Garson and C. Read (eds), *Notes and Queries on Anthropology Edited for the Council of the Anthropological Institute*, 2nd edn, London: Anthropological Institute, 87–8, http://ia600304.us.archive.org/8/items/notesandqueries00readgoog/notesandqueries00readgoog.pdf, accessed 2 May 2011.

Reisman, D. and M. Benney (1956), 'The Sociology of the Interview', *Midwest Sociologist*, 18(1): 3–15.

Rennie, D. (1998), *Person-Centred Counselling: An Experiential Approach,* London: Sage Publications.

Rice, T. (2005), 'Review Essay: Getting a Sense of Listening', *Critique of Anthropology*, 25(2): 199–206.

Ricoeur, P. (1992), *Oneself as Another,* Chicago: University of Chicago Press.

Rollnick, S., W. Miller and C. Butler (2008), *Motivational Interviewing in Health Care: Helping Patients Change Behaviour*, New York: Guildford Press.

Rorty, R. (1979), *Philosophy and the Mirror of Nature*, Princeton: Princeton University Press.

Rosaldo, R. (1986), 'From the Door of His Tent: The Fieldworker and the Inquisitor', in J. Clifford and G. Marcus (eds), *Writing Culture: The Poetics and Politics of Ethnography*, Berkeley: University of California Press, 77–97.

Roulston, K. (2010), *Reflective Interviewing: A Guide to Theory and Practice*, London: Sage Publications.

Rubin, H. and I. Rubin (2005), *Qualitative Interviewing: The Art of Hearing Data*, London: Sage Publications.

Rutter, M. and A. Cox (1981), 'Psychiatric Interviewing Techniques: I. Methods and Measures', *British Journal of Psychiatry*, 138: 273–82.

Salamone, F. (1977), 'The Methodological Significance of the Lying Informant', *Anthropological Quarterly*, 50(3): 117–24.

Sattler, J. (1998), *Clinical and Forensic Interviewing of Children and Families*, San Diego: Author.

Schuman, H. (2008), *Method and Meaning in Polls and Surveys*, Cambridge: Harvard University Press.

Scott, S. (1999), 'Fragmented Selves in Late Modernity: Making Sociological Sense of Multiple Personalities', *Sociological Review*, 47(3): 431–60.

Searle, J. (1969), *Speech Acts*, Cambridge: Cambridge University Press.

Searle, J. (1983), *Intentionality*, Cambridge: Cambridge University Press.

Seidman, I. (1991), *Interviewing as Qualitative Research*, New York: Teachers College Press.

Shostak, M. ((1981) 1990), *Nisa: The Life and Words of a !Kung Woman*, London: Earthscan Publications.

Silverman, D. (1993), 'Kundera's *Immortality* and Field Research: Uncovering the Romantic Impulse', Unpublished Manuscript, Goldsmith's College, University of London.

Skinner, J. (2002), 'Narrative on the Net: Bill and His Hyper- Lives, Loves and Texts', *Auto/Biography*, X(1/2): 21–9.

Skinner, J. (2007), 'The Salsa Class: A Complexity of Globalization, Cosmopolitans and Emotions', *Identities* (Special Edition on Emotions and Globalization), 14(4): 485–506.

Skinner, J. (2009a), 'Cyber Ethnography and the Disembedded Electronic Evergreen of Montserrat', in M. Srinivasan and R. Mathur (eds), *Ethnography and the Internet: An Exploration*, Hyderabad: ICFAI University Press, 125–48.

Skinner, J. (2009b), '"Live in Fragments No Longer": Imagination and the Connection in Human Nature', in N. Rapport (ed.), *Human Nature as Capacity: An Ethnographic Approach*, Oxford: Berghahn Books, 207–30.

Skinner, J. (2010a), 'Leading Questions and Body Memories: A Case of Phenomenology and Physical Ethnography in the Dance Interview', in P. Collins and A. Gallinat (eds), *The Ethnographic Self as Resource: Writing Memory and Experience into Ethnography*, Oxford: Berghahn Books, 111–28.

Skinner, J. (2010b), 'Work/Leisure Balances and the Creation of a Carnival Cosmopolitanism amongst Salsa Dancers', *Intergraph: Journal for Dialogic Anthropology* (Special Issue: Work Life: Flexibility, Globalization, Life-Project and Identity, edited by A. Dawson and C. Dahl-Jorgensen), 2(2), http://intergraph-journal.com/enhanced/vol2issue2/12.html, accessed 17 July 2011.

Skinner, J. (2012), 'Introduction: Writings on the Dark Side of Travel', in J. Skinner (ed.), *Writing the Dark Side of Travel*, Oxford: Berghahn Books, 1–28.

Skultans, V. (1998), *The Testimony of Lives: Narrative and Memory in Post-Soviet Latvia*, London: Routledge.

Skultans, V. (1999), 'Narratives of the Body and History: Illness in Judgement on the Soviet Past', *Sociology of Health and Illness*, 21(3): 310–28.

Smith, J. and M. Osborn (2008), 'Interpretative Phenomenological Analysis', in J. Smith (ed.), *Qualitative Psychology: A Practical Guide to Research Methods*, London: Sage Publications, 53–80.

Smith, K. and S. Tilney (2007), *Vulnerable Adult and Child Witnesses*, Oxford: Oxford University Press.

Sparkes, A. (1997), 'An Elite Body, Illness, and the Fragmentation of Self: A Collaborative Exploration', *Auto/Biography*, 1(2/3): 27–37.

Sperschneider, W. (2007), 'Video Ethnography under Industrial Constraints: Observational Techniques and Video Analysis', in S. Pink (ed.), *Visual Interventions: Applied Visual Anthropology*, Oxford: Berghahn Books, 273–94.

Spradley, J. (1979), *The Ethnographic Interview*, London: Holt, Rinehart and Winston.

Stanton, G. (2000), 'The Way of the Body: Paul Stoller's Search for Sensuous Ethnography', *European Journal of Cultural Studies*, 3(2): 259–77.

Sturges, J. and K. Hanrahan (2004), 'Comparing Telephone and Face-to-Face Qualitative Interviewing: A Research Note', *Qualitative Research*, 4: 107–18.

Sullivan, H. (1954), *The Psychiatric Interview*, New York: Norton.

Summerfield, P. (2004), 'Culture and Composure: Creating Narratives of the Gendered Self in Oral History Interviews', *Cultural and Social History*, 1(1): 65–93.

Tedlock, D. (1983), *The Spoken Word and the Work of Interpretation*, Philadelphia: University of Pennsylvania Press.

Tietel, E. (2000), 'The Interview as a Relational Space', *Forum: Qualitative Social Research*, 1(3), http://www.qualitative-research.net/fqs-texte/2–00/2–00tietel-e.htm, accessed 14 December 2011.

Tonkin, E. (1992), *Narrating Our Pasts: The Social Construction of Oral History*, Cambridge: Cambridge University Press.

Urry, J. (1972), '"Notes and Queries on Anthropology" and the Development of Field Methods in British Anthropology, 1870–1920', in *Proceedings of the Royal Anthropological Institute of Great Britain and Ireland*, 1972 edn, 45–57.

Voida, A., E. Myatt, T. Erickson and W. Kellogg (2004), 'Interviewing over Instant Messaging', in *Extended Abstracts of CHI 2004 Conference on Human Factors in Computing Systems*, Vienna, New York: ACM, 1344–7, http://citeseerx.ist.psu.edu/viewdoc/summary?doi=10.1.1.64.2808, accessed 12 May 2011.

Wengle, J. (1988), *Ethnographers in the Field: The Psychology of Research*, Tuscaloosa: University of Alabama Press.

Wengraf, T. (2001), *Qualitative Research Interviewing: Biographic Narrative and Semi-Structured Method*, London: Sage Publications.

Whyte, W. ((1943) 1993), *Street Corner Society: The Social Structure of an Italian Slum*, Chicago: University of Chicago Press.

Wolcott, H. (2005), *The Art of Fieldwork*, Oxford: Altamira Press.

Young, A. (1995), *The Harmony of Illusions: Inventing Post-Traumatic Stress Disorder*, Princeton: Princeton University Press.

Yow, V. (2006), '"Do I Like Them Too Much?": Effects of the Oral History Interview on the Interviewer and Vice-Versa', in P. Atkinson and S. Delamont (eds), *Narrative Methods, Volume I: Narrative Perspectives*, London: Sage Publications, 211–34.

Zelizer, B. (2005), 'Finding Aids to the Past: Bearing Personal Witness', in E. Rothenbuhler and M. Coman (eds), *Media Anthropology*, London: Sage Publications, 199–209.

Part I
Positioning the Interview

–1–

The Interview as a Form of Talking-partnership: Dialectical, Focussed, Ambiguous, Special

Nigel Rapport

Ideal Types of Interaction

There is a fundamental form to the interview, indeed to any conversation or dialogue, comprising a to-ing and fro-ing of utterances or responses. Even should one party dominate, a verbal exchange such as an interview comprises a dialectic, an incremental zigzagging, between participants who act as one another's 'talking-partners' (Rapport 1987: 170–90). What are the possible consequences of this dialectic? My starting point is that these can be identified as ideal-types. When, in its simplest form, *A* utters 'a' and then *B* utters 'b' and then *A* utters 'c' and then *B* utters 'd', and so on, a-b-c-d can come to assume an identifiable range of kinds of interaction. Let me elaborate.

Alvin Gouldner observed, in a seminal article, that reciprocity is distinct from complementarity. Complementarity, Gouldner outlined, is when two or more parties to a relationship are linked by difference: one's rights imply another's duties (1977: 33–5). Reciprocity, on the other hand, is when the parties are linked by sameness or equivalence: each is in possession of rights *and* duties vis-à-vis the others. If I borrow this distinction and apply it to the utterances of partners to an interview or a conversation, then I might say that *reciprocity* is a kind of exchange which proceeds by way of an exact and accurate equivalency between talking-partners. *A* says 'I love Scotland' and then *B* says 'I also love Scotland': the utterances of both talking-partners are symmetrical. Such reciprocity does not proceed far. One might say that as an interactional style or effect it is not productive of much new meaning. It might be phatic, and highly pleasing as such: it can be good to be informed that you and a partner share a mutual love and simply to converse confirms this. But there is a closure to this mutuality. What next, now that that mutual exchange of information has been accomplished?

Complementarity is when the utterances of the talking-partners proceed by way of an equivalency less similar in form. *A* says 'I love Scotland' and then *B* says 'Well then I hate Scotland'. One statement follows the other, as in the reciprocal version, but now there is further issue, so to speak. There is a contiguous and meaningful and logical relationship between the two utterances, but they are not the same. And rather than the exchange necessarily ending there, there is room for some development which is different to the kind of stasis that accompanies a possibly endless to-ing and fro-ing of 'I love Scotlands'. Complementarity is more than simple phatic communication (although it may be this too).

But this is only the beginning of considering the possible consequences of verbal exchange. The utterances of talking-partners in a conversation, such as an interview, may be reciprocal and complementary to one another but they might also abut against one another in more complex ways.

A says 'I love Scotland' and then *B* says 'Well in that case why don't we go and live there together?' I would call this the utterances of talking-partners coming together to create an *addition* or a *collaboration.* It is different to complementarity insofar as the second utterance is more than merely an equal but opposite version of the first. *B*'s utterance builds on that of *A*. But then consider this: *A* says 'I love Scotland' and then *B* says 'Well, that's typical: I always knew you were looking for a way out of this relationship'. What has happened here is a kind of *multiplication* or *emergence.* The difference between addition and multiplication (or collaboration and emergence) is that between metonymy and metaphor. When *B* says 'Well in that case why don't we go and live there together?' in response to *A*'s 'I love Scotland', the response keeps the exchange in the same semantic or classificatory domain. But when *B* understands *A*'s 'I love Scotland' to infer that their relationship is at an end, there is a metaphorical reading of the first utterance such that it is transferred into a different emotional and cognitive context. So we have now reciprocity and complementarity, collaboration and emergence.

There is one further consequence I would define. *A* says 'I love Scotland' and *B* says '5 foot 7' or 'Light-brown', or else *B* rushes out to purchase a pineapple. I would call this *distortion.* There is an association and a contiguity between *A*'s and *B*'s utterances or actions but the logic linking them is hard to fathom. It is neither metonymic nor metaphoric. It is not obviously schismogenetic, a deliberate attempt to assert a distinct perspective; nor is it apparently complementary or reciprocal: at least on the level of meaning. Something has occurred, there is a connection, but not one of formal semantics. Perhaps *B*'s response makes emotional sense to *A*. Perhaps *B*'s response makes no sense at all, whether emotional or semantic. *B* has interpreted *A*'s utterance in such a way that only *B* can reveal the logic of her response.

The nature of utterances as being emotional as well as intellectual or cognitive, as having meaning that resides in the words as signs but also as signals, complicates matters significantly. But I feel confident that an elucidation of the consequences of interaction as being reciprocal, complementary, collaborative, emergent or distorted has worth and conveys some truth concerning the nature of verbal exchange.

Conversation and Interview

I have so far used the terms *conversation* and *interview* interchangeably. They are, I have said, both kinds of verbal exchange founded upon a dialectic or incremental zig-zag. But one might also distinguish between them. Jonathan Skinner has assembled some pertinent texts for this purpose in the introduction to this volume. According to Bruce Jackson, 'an interview is not a normal conversation; the rules are different and so are the expectations' (1987: 89). Colin Robson elaborates: interviews are 'conversation with a purpose' (1993: 28). Interviews are limited both in terms of time and of function, they are more focussed than conversations which can last a lifetime and meander and eddy and sprawl and dissipate. The distinction is not hard and fast. One can imagine the conversation of a marriage becoming distilled into an interview of interrogation, accusation, evidence and proof-making; one can imagine the formal interview developing into the love affair that comprises a lifetime. But, again in terms of ideal-types, I shall say the following: *An interview is a nonroutine conversation, with a purpose or design which at least one of the talking-partners has previously determined, and which need not be repeated (the talking-partnership can extend to this one exchange alone).* There are three significant elements here, then: the nonroutine, a purposiveness and a boundedness. The interview is, as an ideal-type, a thing-of-itself, a mini-relationship, a micro-institution.

The phrase 'micro-institution' is one of Anton Zijderveld's in his work on cliché. Zijderveld describes modern society as a 'clichegenic condition' inasmuch as clichés come to form the major component of individual consciousness (1979: 4–18). According to Zijderveld, catchwords and clichés are verbal signals of modernity, of industrialization, urbanization and bureaucratization, which come to serve as 'Durkheimian micro-institutions': they act to crystallize social values and mould individual perceptions into one typical, objective, cohesive structure of summary meanings and, hence, to trigger normative behaviour. At its bleakest, a clichegenic modernity bespeaks for Zijderveld a kind of sociocultural totalization, if not tyranny: in the omnipresence of formulaic expression, daily interaction loses meaningful substance, there being no room for creative reflection and empathy, only hackneyed thoughts and emotions, action and volition.

I have in the past taken exception with Zijderveld's conclusions (Rapport 1994). While contemporary society may be characterized by so-called clichegenic conditions, and much of social interaction may today take place by way of formulaic tokens of exchange, one need not read this as a sign of impoverished significance, of a dearth of individual creativity, an institutionalization and homogenization of meaning and a superseding of the possibilities of exchange by mere social functionality and structuration. Because rather than micro-institutions, catchwords and clichés may serve as shorthands: incomplete pronouncements which stand for but disguise more expansive expressions and verbal associations being deployed at the same time. In other words, individuals talk clichés but think and feel illimitable things. (In Percy

Shelley's famous lyrical formulation, 'a single word even may be a spark of inextinguishable thought' (1954: 281).) At the same time as talking-partners might meet upon the common and appropriate linguistic surface of certain simple phrases—exchange catchwords and clichés—they might at the same time diverge in terms of what those simple phrases imply: the expanded verbal associations to which each would have their shared phrases relate. The cliché comes to be housed, cognitively and emotionally, in contexts of words, memories, intentions and behaviours which need not become publicly apparent but which are responsible for privately and personally animating and sourcing those clichegenic conditions with meaning (Rapport 1993).

I have allowed myself this digression concerning the cliché because I believe it throws interesting light upon the interview. The interview, I have suggested, is a thing-in-itself, a mini-relationship, a micro-institution: nonroutine, purposive and bounded in ways that everyday or 'naturally occurring' conversation might not be. But 'interview', like 'cliché', also encompasses the possibility of a subjective interpretation: whether an interview is taking place at all, never mind the meaning of its dialectical exchange, can reside in the eye of a beholder. I think I am having an everyday conversation with my spouse: from her perspective, this is an interview regarding a possible interruption in the ongoing routine of our cohabitation. What I take to be routine, she takes to be a nonroutine interrogation of the very possibility of there being a routineness to our ongoing talking-partnership. Her purposiveness can bypass my awareness, perhaps forever. If the interview is a specific kind of interaction, with a distinctive modality from other conversation, then it shares with all conversation—all interaction—the ambiguities and variabilities concerning the interpretation of its symbolic forms. Not only, 'What is this clichéd expression to be taken to mean here, what is its purpose?', but also 'Is this expression part of an interview: is there a nonroutine and specific purposiveness to this exchange?'

Do the terms *structured interview*, *semi-structured interview*, *unstructured interview* help here? A little, insofar as they describe kinds of agreed upon social contexts. The researcher has it in mind that he or she will endeavour to glean responses to fixed queries in certain predetermined forms in a prearranged period of time. Alternatively, the researcher has it in mind to cover a vague area of information with a respondent but leaves it to the moment to see what exactly will be revealed, in what form and over how long a period. And so on. But these three types—'structured', 'semi-structured', 'unstructured'—constitute a continuum rather than discrete points. What begins by intending one kind of exchange develops into another... What one talking-partner understands the terms of the prearranged exchange to entail is not what is understood by the other... The researcher or talking-partner who enters into the situation of exchange with particular, nonroutine purposes in mind does not inform his or her interlocutor that he or she is now actually a respondent in a dialectic intended to take a structured, semi-structured or unstructured form... I begin with the intention of having a casual conversation with my daughter about our love of Scotland and end by wishing to interrogate her concerning her love life.

Code and Creativity

What I have so far said tends in two main directions. First, to suggest that there is an ambiguity to the situation of an interview that makes it difficult to define, even to identify. Is this an interview? Is it structured or unstructured? It depends on a subjective act of interpretation. The interview situation is a construction: it may be vague and a matter of point of view. It is far from being a known, unproblematic, shared or deterministic social frame or cultural convention.

I had thought at one point that importing Basil Bernstein's distinction between 'restricted' and 'elaborated' code would be an important source of insight into the ambiguity of the interview. A code, according to Bernstein (1973), is a sociocultural norm which controls 'both the creation and organization of specific meanings and the conditions for their transmission and reception'. Bernstein, as part of a wider exploration of how speech may be regarded as 'the major means through which the social structure becomes part of individual experience' (1964: 258), identified two different ideal-types of codification in everyday use in contemporary Britain. One was a highly coded form of language, impersonal and ritualistic, and suited to an explicitly authoritarian and reactionary social structure; the other was a more open and fluid 'now-coding' language suited to the ongoing realization of personal identities. The former Bernstein (1964) called 'public language' or 'restricted code', and the latter 'formal language' or 'elaborated code'. In elaborated code, language is specifically and newly formed to fit a particular referent (situation and speaker), to serve as an individuating factor in experience and to describe individual experience. A poem in free verse, for instance. Language is here used explicitly to clarify meanings, acting as a mediation of complex personal sensation and cognition: it encompasses analytical thought processes and fine gradations of measured cogitation and subjective sensitivity. In restricted code, a referent is designated using ready-made terms and phrases from a common repertoire, put together quickly and automatically in a well-organized sequence. A military instruction manual, for instance. Syntax is rigid, grammar simple and sentences predictable; likewise the type of content, if not the specifics of what the sentences contain. Meaning is commonplace, largely impersonal and ritualistic—even tautological. The effect is the symbolizing, establishing and reinforcing of the normative arrangements and relations of a social group: restricted code expresses concrete thought processes and a high degree of affect concerning a restricted range of significant subjects and assumptions held in common by the group; social not individual symbols are expressed and exchanged.

While emphasizing that these were ideal-types and that individuals might move between such codes according to social context, nevertheless, Bernstein further argued that particular social contexts could be seen to be dominated by one or other of these codes. Their usage was a function of culture and of particular forms of social relationship (rather than individual psychology). Hence, restricted code pertained characteristically to 'position-oriented' social milieux and relations—armies, prisons, age-grades, long-established friendships and marriages—while elaborated code pertained to 'person-oriented' ones. (In particular, the two codificatory usages could be applied to the British class system: while the 'genes' of working-class sociality and solidarity were transmitted by restricted code, the genes of middle-class sociality and individuality were transmitted by elaborated code.)

I had thought at one point to say that the interview introduced a kind of restricted code into a situation of social interaction. A formality superseded a more naturally occurring exchange due to the precise purposes and timings involved. The talking-partners were constrained by conventions concerning what could appropriately be said and how. But then the very point of an interview—where it is not merely going through the motions, rubber-stamping a prior decision—is that it might elaborate upon things that are not conventionally expressed and have not 'naturally' been as of yet learnt. In other words, the interview is a kind of hybrid form—at least in terms of Bernstein's celebrated differentiation.

In fact, the interview would seem to possess a hybridity or idiosyncrasy vis-à-vis *all* possible social classifications or cultural conventions of expression and exchange. The fact that it is a thing-of-itself, in the eyes of its single or joint beholders, also means that it cannot be preconceived in terms of known, unproblematic or shared sociocultural framings. The interview is not overdetermined socially or culturally.

* * *

The second main direction in which this chapter has tended is to suggest that there *is* a kind of limit to how the zigzagging utterances of an interview may possibly relate to one another. The dialectic can take the form of reciprocity, complementarity, collaboration, emergence or distortion. And this is irrespective of attributes of context. Whether formally structured or unstructured, whether purportedly in situations of codificatory elaboration or restriction, there will necessarily be the potential for reciprocity, complementarity, collaboration, emergence or distortion in the interview—as in any other kind of verbal interaction.

What makes the interview special, I suggest, is the coming together of these two elements. The interview is *sui generis*, and distinct from the routines around it, from the social classifications and the cultural conventions. For one or both or all talking-partners, the awareness that 'here is an interview' leads to a heightened self-consciousness and a predisposition to reflect on the consequences of the exchange. Being nonroutine, bounded and purposive sets up an investigative situation: not only is a researcher taken beyond the everyday but so are all the talking-partners who are aware that this is an interview not merely a naturally occurring exchange. And what will be the outcome? Reciprocity, complementarity, collaboration, emergence, distortion: the range is limited but within this range there is an imponderability. The interview combines idiosyncrasy, self-consciousness and a logically formal set of outcomes and indeterminacy. It is a prime research tool not only for outsiders to a social milieu but insiders too, affording a perspective on the possibilities of interaction and the actuality of particular talking-relationships.

Case Study

I have undertaken four pieces of participant observation fieldwork: among farmers and tourists in a rural English village, 1980–1; among the transient population of a city and suburb in the Canadian province of Newfoundland, 1984–5; among new immigrants in an Israeli development in the Negev desert, 1988–9; and among healthcare professionals and patients in a Scottish hospital, 2000–1. Only at the end of the final fieldwork did I formally interview anyone. Before that it had barely been appropriate that I should ask a question 'as a researcher'. My participant observation had always been conducted more or less incognito: as a farm labourer and builder's mate in the village of Wanet; as a volunteer assistant in a halfway house for parolees and as a student of criminology in the city of St John's; as a new immigrant in Mitzpe Ramon. I had, of course, asked questions of others 'in role' but I had not before overtly played the role of researcher with my informants. At the end of my year of working as a porter at Constance Hospital in the port city of Easterneuk, however (see Rapport 2008b), and in a setting in which at least initially and formally hospital employees knew I was also a university anthropologist—and hence legitimately a 'researcher'—I approached members of the hospital's doctoring and managing staff and asked for interviewees (to supplement the information I had gleaned from working with the ancillary and clerical and other nonprofessional staff).

My main research topic was national identity. With Scotland having its first Edinburgh-based parliament in almost 300 years and with political devolution possibly leading to national independence, how did staff members at Constance Hospital feel affected? Did they practice 'Scottish' medicine? Was Constance a 'Scottish' institution? Should healthcare resist the imputation that sickness could be identified in nationalistic or communitarian terms? A number of doctors and administrators responded to my letter and agreed to meet.

I was anxious at first, very uncomfortable. Having grown into the role of a porter over the previous months, I felt that I would be wasting their time: that the doctors and administrators would see through the guise of my suit and tie to the unskilled impostor asking them unintelligent questions. I hated the fact that the conversation was 'unnatural': brought about solely through my own imported interests and initiative, and, initially at least, dependent on my guidance. But in the best interviews I was wholly mistaken: I came out feeling honoured that I had met such moral respondents and that they had found it appropriate and taken the time to open themselves up to me, the stranger who was so differently positioned regarding their medical expertise Here was the interview as *sui generis*.

Let me offer a transcript of part of an interview I conducted in mid-August 2001 with a consultant surgeon, 'Mr J. L. Taylor' (as I shall call him), in his office on his ward. You will see that he soon put me at my ease and also did most of the talking (setting the terms of our exchange):

Taylor (T): I am not in the least a confrontational person; so would you like it if I sat beside you in a chair and not across the desk?

Rapport (R): That would be good!

T: This is what I do with my consultations. So: I'll sit in this chair and you sit in that. I'm sorry if we are interrupted; I have set aside this time but I know I may get bleeped; sorry.

R: That's fine. Thanks.

T: I was a bit worried when I got your letter because I do not feel that Constance Hospital has *any* Scottish component as such. It is simply an NHS hospital... Nationalism is just not an issue in my work.

R: That's fine: that's interesting in itself. That's the kind of thing I want to learn.

T: But I *do* have to deal with the Scottish Parliament, and it gives me absolutely no confidence at all: I certainly preferred dealing with Westminster. The NHS is part of the Barnet Formula of government funding, within which Scotland was favoured. That means, for instance, that there are three consultants per hospital 'firm' here at Constance not two as in England; and this has meant that private medicine could be kept rare in Scotland—as against in England and Wales.

R: I see.

T: I am the clinical leader on this floor, of four firms and twelve consultants... But the Scottish Ministry of Health is hopeless: they never never never reply to letters. They may as well be on the moon! Fortunately, I have friends there who are secretaries and so I can bypass people to get replies. But you can wait weeks. [*A*] and [*B*] are disasters; [*C*] is the biggest disaster of all: fancy appointing someone who is so thick to running the Scottish NHS!... {I grin at his look of incredulity and distaste} [*D*] was the only exception. A straight man, who stood out. He was not building his career merely, and he was talented. So people were pleased to see him in a position of authority. But [*E*] gives you no confidence whatsoever. [*F*] used to be great—my old climbing partner, in fact. But he has been ill and it was clear he could not continue.

R: So you're a climber!

T: I'm from Lancashire. Not that I don't love living here. Been here twenty-five years. I used to climb but no longer; now I walk everywhere. I am a *crazy* walker, a nutcase! I walk the two miles to work and back each day; but I also walk to the centre of Easterneuk. I make people crazy. {We laugh} I am like this because I am fifty-eight now and I find it hard to do things to a different degree to how I always have. Doing surgery takes absolute confidence in yourself—which I have. I have absolutely no wish to retire—as many at my age do.

R: So you came up here to Scotland in your thirties?

T: Yes. For nineteen and a half years I worked at the university here too; so I see from both sides. I know, for instance, that the academic department of surgery here is wonderful.

R: But you left it?

T: Yes, I left the university because the dean wanted me to give up some surgery to become a medical school administrator. I refused and so I was shunted sideways into the NHS full-time—losing three and a half years' pension in the process! Because originally when I came I was a university lecturer in surgery—qualifying at twenty-two, which would have assured me of 40/80ths for my pension at sixty-two. But I did not start working for the NHS till I was more than twenty-five; so even when I reach sixty-five I will not have made up a full pension... *But* I am not at all driven by money in what I do.

R: Do you regret what happened?

T: No. Because I am from Lancashire, as I say: I have made provision for my future. I am not at all bitter.

R: Where from exactly?

T: Kirkby Lonsdale.

R: Oh! I lived near Sedbergh for a while. Involved in some farming.

T: I know it well. And now there are no sheep around there at all: Wensleydale is empty! But that's an issue that I won't get into.

R: No.

T: But the NHS used to work well here, you know. Now Constance Hospital is being smashed to pieces at every level by management. The so-called debt that Constance has incurred! Something cooked up and now to be taken away from patient care! It was caused by government 'interest' on *rental* charges which the Hospital Trust incurred! And also by combining Trusts that were already in debt. The result is that I have lost thirty beds and one operation per week! Which means that beds for cancer patients are blocked and that they wait twice as long as they should on waiting lists. Yet this is *the* acute hospital in the area. And all this to recoup twenty-one million pounds!... All it's succeeding in doing is making the Scottish NHS worse than the English one; because here there is no tradition of private work to take the place of NHS shortfalls... Also there are Hours of Work Directorates now from the EU. This is something compulsory for housemen: fifty-six hours a week maximum is their limit. There are fifteen housemen on my surgery floor. This means that a partial-shift acute rota is *just* feasible. But no other hospital in this area of Scotland can manage: none has sufficient staff to do this: none can any longer be an acute surgical hospital under these current regulations. Though what I have just said is political dynamite... All this means that restricting senior house officers and registrars and consultants to fifty-six hours per week will never be possible. There is a political nettle here that needs grasping, entailing major change for the continuity of patient care. Or there will be none at all. But of this there is absolutely no comprehension from the Scottish Office. The Scottish NHS *did* have lots to be proud of. Now the Scottish Parliament has succeeded in smashing those achievements through ignorance, making us all less outward looking.

R: What do you mean?

T: Well, national trials, for instance. Easterneuk and Scotland were in the forefront of national trials at one time, including all of England and Wales. Forty per cent of UK trials were supplied by Scotland (10 per cent of the UK population). Such as for colon and heart diseases. Now all that becomes more and more of a struggle, and Constance will supply less... But I am not bitter. I rush around. There is an awkwardness in me which means that I never give up on something. I work all the time.

R: Why do you think that is?

T: Because I was born and raised on a pig farm, where I had no day off. Ever. Now I want to die working.

R: Work fulfils you?

T: I get my main pleasures from work. And from having great colleagues. If I did not have good colleagues on this floor that would make me upset. My colleagues trust me not to lose more beds. And so on... I have no fear of any person on earth. Managers here now avoid discussions with me, because I'm a mine of information as against their arrogance and ignorance. And I've never been depressed in my life... I have no religious side to me. I'm not anti-anybody though (you can believe in religion if you want to). I am not anti-Scottish. I am not anti-Iran either—or these countries that are meant to be our enemies. I am not anti-Jewish—half my graduating class was Jewish—though my dad brought me up to be anti-Semitic and I hated him for it. No: if anybody is ill and they need treatment, I will treat them. All the texts, the Bibles, say 'Love Your Neighbour'. What I do object to is the way belief systems can be changed by national regimes for their own ends: one sort of people I do have little time for is religious leaders—those who alter religious texts to suit themselves…

R: What would you like your own legacy to be?

T: I would like my legacy to be: 'A good teacher'. Teachers have been split from researchers here now but I continue to insist on being both. My teaching is very popular, also. I still go round the wards with people and I take tutorials: neither of these things now figures on the official curriculum. But it is part of my awkward streak.

R: You are an individual in the institution!

T: Yes, I go an individual way. But eventually, I am convinced, the pendulum will swing back to my way of thinking. The 'theorists' will have had their day and it will be again the turn of those engaged in clinical assessment to also do the teaching…Because medicine is a practical skill, working with patients; it is not a matter of simply learning out of books. Admittedly some medicine—pathology, radiology, transfusion etc.—requires no patient contact, so theorists have their place too. But my way of teaching, amidst the patients, is the right way usually. 'Doctor' after all means teacher. In fact, I'm busier and busier, and even at retirement I could keep on doing some of these things…But am I boring you? I'm probably boring you silly. Probably this is not what you need from me? Is it?

R: No: this is perfect! Go on, please.

T: I have a merit award Level B. It's a financial award. Professor Sir [X] has a Level A+—and I don't resent that or begrudge it in the slightest. No one does. For what he does. Compared to [X], I am a far far lesser brain. But management is now trying to *reduce* my B Level award. Because I have made myself monumentally difficult. I have been on national TV and in the newspapers: I will *not* kowtow to their monetary decisions and planning. They want me to cut £900,000 from the floor budget—as part of the savings towards the 'deficit'. No. Instead I have been using money earmarked for initiatives to reduce waiting lists towards keeping open six acute beds—employing cancer nurses, and so on. And I would go public if the management tried to take that money away from me. They say: 'Be a good boy, and your merit award will continue'. They say to me: 'Would you not like a holiday?' No! Because if I were to go away they would take my beds away. They say: 'Would you not be happier at home?' Why would I be?! I say to them: What do you think I work for? What do you think I get out of life?…I will retire at sixty-five—not sixty or sixty-two—*if* my health runs out…

R: Well, I think I'd better get away.

T: So I *was* boring you after all. I thought so.

R: No, no. Not at all. Thank you very much. Really.

T: Look at this {He picks up from the table a pamphlet, seemingly newly received}. The future of the NHS! {He waves it in the air} What do you think I'll learn from *this*!? How much did *this* cost to produce!?

R: 'Nothing', and 'Too much' are the answers to those questions, I think. Well: many thanks again. Bye.

Discussion

I left Mr J. L. Taylor's office feeling not at all bored. Exhilarated, yes, and with a sense of privilege: I found him to be a man of integrity and I was grateful for the time he had taken to explain himself to me so openly, even revealingly. I was also relieved that 'the interview-situation' was over and that the information I had received had been so stimulating. There was a heightened quality to the exchange that I think both of us sensed, owing to its nonroutine character: we were both talking to people we had not met before and may not meet again, and we were talking across worlds, not only social but also disciplinary and intellectual. This heightened quality brought with it its own intensity: I was anxious in the interview, more than usually self-conscious, and it was draining to maintain that level of attention to self and other for a long period. I was relieved for another reason, too. I found Mr Taylor far from boring but he was unusual: his utterance had a quality to it that did make me wonder at times what kind of response I would find it necessary to make. I mean I found his self-intensity a little mad. A line from novelist Olive Schreiner that I find particularly apposite runs: 'When your life is most real, to me you are mad' (1998: 69). The madness of Mr Taylor was his revealing to me, a researcher in the hospital and a stranger, parts of himself that were very authentic, I adjudge. The interview occasioned the evidencing of a kind of individuality normally disguised behind the role-player. This was neither 'restricted' nor 'elaborated' code but both at once: I felt somewhat uncomfortable because it seemed Mr Taylor was choosing not simply to pass as a hospital functionary or a standard member of the NHS or a conventional medical specialist recounting information to a nonspecialist.

Of course, having said all of this, I have no evidence beyond an annotation and an interpretation of one interaction of less than an hour. I have no certain knowledge that Mr Taylor was not a consummate actor putting on a show, no knowledge that Mr Taylor behaved outside his office in the way he suggested, no knowledge of what his motivation might have been in taking the time to see me and express himself in this way before me. I only have his words and my feeling for them. ('Body memories', as Skinner (2010) phrases it, have a central role to play in verbal interpretation.)

This gives me two ways to proceed with my transcription. I can give myself the benefit of the doubt: Mr Taylor was not *that* good an actor such that I was hoodwinked into leaving his office and concluding as I have above regarding the honesty of our meeting. Alternatively, I can privilege the form of our exchange and pass over the ambiguous potential of its meaning.

If our meeting *was* honest, then Mr Taylor was a very self-intense talking-partner. 'Self-intensity' is a phrase with a Nietzschean provenance, and this is also appropriate, I think. Nietzsche wrote of the individual human being who is able (and duty-bound, Nietzsche felt) to make of his life an artwork, a project of overcoming, revaluation and transcendence; the individual existed apart from the society in which he happened to be placed and from the cultural symbology in whose terms his interpretations of self and world took form. One of Nietzsche's more recent biographers, Leslie Chamberlain (1997), uses a phrase in her description of Nietzsche which also fits Mr Taylor: *Machtgefuhl*, possessing a sense of what one could do, and therefore ought to do, with one's talents and powers. I do not intend a biography of Mr Taylor; but I am interested to record an impression that in the interview situation I was meeting a respondent 'out of social time and space', in a way, and that our meeting revealed an individuality I found both gratuitous (or 'mad') and self-intense: empowered by its own sense of what it would do with its life—*that* it would make something—and how it would go about it. Mr Taylor burst out of the context. Even when he sought to explain himself by tying his motivation to a sociological or classificatory profile—Lancastrian, son of a pig farmer—and, I suspect, even when he linked his outbursts to a current political and institutional situation—the Scottish Parliament, the hospital's debt—it was Mr Taylor as his own man that came across most strongly and naturally and happily: he has absolute self-confidence and no fear, he has an awkwardness, he rushes around and will not slow down, he is not driven by money but he has made future provision, he is crazy and he makes others crazy. Finally, it was on personal terms, too, that he interacted with and judged others: Scottish politicians, hospital administrators, colleagues and students alike. How can one be a minister for health and fail in intellection? How can hospital management think they could bully him out of doing his medical duty? The interview as an occasion in which I experienced a kind of supraconventional self-intensity in my talking-partner's utterances would accord with what I have defined as the nature of interview as a thing-in-itself, *sui generis*.

Alternatively: what more can be noted of the interview as *form* of exchange? While a nonroutine occurrence, the interview took place in Mr Taylor's office at work, enabling him to classify it as akin to a (routine) consultation. This brought him first to consider questions of space: how to arrange our chairs (and bodies) such that our exchange would not appear confrontational or too formal. I had not realized that should a desk separate us this could be construed as confrontational, but I appreciated his concern for this all the same and felt put at ease. To use the terms I defined earlier, there was *complementarity* here—his concern with nonconfrontation, my thanks and sense of ease—which initiated a friendly exchange and led me to warm to Mr Taylor as a talking-partner. Indeed, I agreed to his terms throughout the exchange, even though they were different to what he suspected I sought—we would discuss the Scottish Parliament rather than Scottishness or nationalism—because the differentiation afforded me something more than reciprocity: his engagement and motivation to speak on. *Reciprocity* did occur in the exchange, but it came from me, serving as a kind of affirmation or conjunctive utterance which showed I had listened and understood. I summarized Mr Taylor's 'awkward streak' by describing him as an individual amid the hospital institutionalism and he accepted my phrasing, 'Yes, I go an individual way', before proceeding to elaborate upon his hypothesis concerning the institution's future. The interview did not call for much reciprocity, it seems, because of Mr Taylor's motivation to proceed and his forcefulness to get certain things said.

There were occasions when I played more than a merely phatic role in the talking-partnership, however. *Collaboration* occurred, then, when I sought the source of Mr Taylor's individuality—why he set himself against the institution, worked at a rush, felt fulfilled and not bitter—and he concluded that this was a matter of his being 'born and raised on a pig farm'. Here was a development in the exchange, an addition, which led to an introduction of Mr Taylor's father, religiosity, anti-Semitism and a work ethic as topics of debate. By contrast, I would say that a situation of *emergence* best describes the transition in semantic domain which occurred when the interview first shifted from a discussion of the Scottish Parliament and Scottish politicians to revelations concerning Mr Taylor's history of employment and his pensionable salary. This was effected by my responding to his hint that one politician was an old climbing partner and my calculation that he had arrived in Scotland in his thirties. What then emerged was an exchange in which the personal and the professional were merged: conditions at Constance became, for Mr Taylor, part of a narrative that included Lancashire, retirement and ageing, teaching and learning, and personal application and drive.

* * *

Having identified these moments of reciprocity, complementarity, collaboration and emergence in our exchange, however, I have to say that for the most part they do not seem to represent what is most significant in the talking-partnership: I would not be happy if my analytical apparatus could offer no more insight than this. But there is a term yet to be considered: *distortion.* And here I feel more significance lies. It would be my sense that *distortion* describes the entire interaction between Mr Taylor and me. I mean that his utterances are mediated by his own purposiveness to such a degree that my utterances are by and large irrelevant. The interview occasioned the opportunity for Mr Taylor to express himself to me and through me but not really with me. His self-intensity acted as a kind of personal sensorium which insulated him from me, my purposes in being there and my interventions, just as it seemed to insulate him and inoculate him from the pressure exerted on him by the hospital authorities. I do not know how or why Mr Taylor had come to develop this manner of sensorium—other than having the hints he let drop concerning his background and character—but I do feel I am watching it in operation. In short, the interview was a distorted exchange insofar as Mr Taylor was largely talking to himself, talking aloud a version of a personal interiority (Rapport 2008a). Phrasing this somewhat differently, Mr Taylor's main talking-partner was himself. He might not have seemed to wish me to leave, and he did express concern that he may be boring me, but I was the audience to an interview he conducted with himself.

If this is allowed, then the nature of the relations between utterances—whether they concern reciprocity, complementarity, collaboration, emergence or distortion—should also be seen as a matter *internal* to Mr Taylor's own expression: perhaps mostly so. Here is the *reciprocity*, then, of Mr Taylor saying to himself 'now I walk everywhere' and following it by 'I am a *crazy* walker'. Here is the *complementarity* of his utterance 'I *do* have to deal with the Scottish Parliament' being followed by 'I certainly preferred dealing with Westminster'. Here is the *collaboration* of him saying 'I am the clinical leader on this floor, of four firms and twelve consultants' and then realizing that 'the Scottish Ministry of Health is hopeless: they never never never reply to letters'. And here is the *emergence* of the utterance 'I'm from Lancashire' being followed by 'Not that I don't love living here. Been here twenty-five years'. To repeat: Mr Taylor's main talking-partner was himself.

Finally, *distortion* figures here too when Mr Taylor interrupts his own narrative flow by remembering my presence as his audience: 'But am I boring you? I'm probably boring you silly'; '"Doctor" after all means teacher'. These represent moments of semantic dislocation from the main thrust of his personal discourse: moments when his internal conversation is broken and he is brought back to the particular other seated before him. He is motivated not to appear impolite to this person—neither confrontational nor boring—but the interaction he finds of consuming and abiding interest would seem to be an internal one to which he routinely returns.

* * *

The special significance of the interview as a research tool may be the light it shines—a kind of snapshot—on the workings of everyday exchange. And the complexities of these symbolic forms-in-use and their ambiguities may be the most significant insight. One glimpses the tensions, the distance, between forms and meanings; also the variable nature of the relations between one symbolic form and those contiguous with it in the flow of interaction. One glimpses the distortions that can characterize relations between talking-partners; also the distortions internal to conversations with the self that might be responsible for returning the individual to the social other and enabling the formal niceties of exchange to continue. I turn to my talking-partner to take momentary relief from distortions intrinsic to my own interiority.

References

Bernstein, B. (1964), 'Aspects of Language and Learning in the Genesis of the Social Process', in D. Hymes (ed.), *Language in Culture and Society*, New York: Harper and Row, 251–63.

Bernstein, B. (1973), *Class, Codes and Control*, St. Albans: Paladin.

Chamberlain, L. (1997), *Nietzsche in Turin*, London: Quartet.

Gouldner, A. (1977), 'The Norm of Reciprocity: A Preliminary Statement', in S. Schmidt, J. Scott, C. Lande and L. Guasti (eds), *Friends, Followers and Factions*, Berkeley: University of California Press, 28–43.

Jackson, B. (1987), *Fieldwork*, Urbana: University of Illinois Press.

Rapport, N. (1987), *Talking Violence: An Anthropological Interpretation of Conversation in the City*, St John's, NFLD: Institute of Social and Economic Research Press, Memorial University of Newfoundland.

Rapport, N. (1993), *Diverse World-Views in an English Village*, Edinburgh: Edinburgh University Press.

Rapport, N. (1994), '"Busted for Hash": Common Catchwords and Individual Identities in a Canadian City', in V. Amit-Talai and H. Lustiger-Thaler (eds), *Urban Lives: Fragmentation and Resistance*, Toronto: McClelland and Stewart, 129–57.

Rapport, N. (2008a), 'Gratuitousness: Notes towards an Anthropology of Interiority', *Australian Journal of Anthropology*, 19(3): 331–49.

Rapport, N. (2008b), *Of Orderlies and Men: Hospital Porters Achieving Wellness at Work*, Durham: Carolina Academic Press.

Robson, C. (1993), *Real World Research*, Oxford: Blackwell.

Schreiner, O. (1998), *The Story of an African Farm*, Oxford: Oxford University Press.

Shelley, P. (1954), *Shelley's Prose*, ed. D. Clark, Albuquerque: University of New Mexico Press.

Skinner, J. (2010), 'Leading Questions and Body Memories: A Case of Phenomenology and Physical Ethnography in the Dance Interview', in P. Collins and A. Gallinat (eds), *The Ethnographic Self as Resource: Writing Memory and Experience into Ethnography*, Oxford: Berghahn Books, 111–28.

Zijderveld, A. (1979), *On Clichés*, London: Routledge & Kegan Paul.

–2–

Ethnography Is Not Participant Observation: Reflections on the Interview as Participatory Qualitative Research

Jenny Hockey and Martin Forsey

Nearly thirty years ago, Holy and Stuchlik confidently pronounced that the doing of anthropology has always been presented as the act of going out into the field in order to study what people are actually doing (1983: 35). Things have not changed very much in the intervening years; the topics may have gone or been changed, as Marcus (Rabinow and Marcus 2008: 46) has recently pointed out, but the 'norms and forms' of classic anthropology, driven by the 'deeply internalized, self-selected desires of anthropologists committed to a distinguishing research practice', still exercise decisive control over anthropological thought and practice. In a world in which newer forms of anthropology are too often perceived as not fully anthropological (Rees, in Rabinow and Marcus 2008: 45), the major concern of this chapter lies in calling fellow anthropologists to examine the significance for anthropological epistemology and pedagogy of the reality of the gaps between what we say we do and what we actually do in and as *practice.*

Ingold (2008) has recently reminded us that 'anthropology is not ethnography', a point we will return to presently and which we also wish to add to in pointing out that *ethnography is not participant observation.* In arguing against the conflation of these three fundamental disciplinary terms—anthropology, ethnography, participant observation—that has occurred in the relatively recent past (see Gans 1999), we are continuing a stance against anthropological commonsense that we have taken with greater and lesser degrees of directness for a little while now (see Hockey 2002; Forsey 2010a,b). In a similar vein Faubion and Marcus (2009) have recently pointed out that *fieldwork is not what it used to be* and asserted the need for anthropologists to rethink the ways we imagine and teach classical research practices (Marcus 2009: 4). In a conversational text tied very closely to Faubion and Marcus's edited volume, Rees asserts the need for a thorough revision of the concepts, problems, questions and topics that have been constitutive of the discipline (Rabinow and Marcus 2008: 13). Marcus identifies these as 'fieldwork', 'ethnography' and 'culture', key concepts that he argues are in need of refashioning, if not replacing, through a radical refunctioning of fieldwork from its 'traditional formation as method in anthropology' (Rabinow and Marcus 2008: 48).

Gans (1999) has provided a cogent argument for returning to the distinction that used to exist between participant observation and ethnography. In affirming his desire to continue referring to himself as 'a sociologist whose primary research method has been participant observation' (544), he alerts us not only to the possibility of decoupling ethnography and participant observation, but also to the potential usefulness of doing so. Whilst we certainly want to argue the need for greater precision in the use of the three fundamental, constitutive terms identified as key concerns—anthropology, ethnography and participant observation—we do not want to waste *too* much time in a Canute-like endeavour of turning the semantic current.

We proceed by taking it as a given that interviews are a primary research tool in anthropological research (Forsey 2010a), and concern ourselves first with thinking about the anthropological status of interviews and what they offer as a medium for understanding. We want to show that even if we accept commonsense thinking about ethnography that is often invoked by those involved in participatory qualitative research, there are good reasons for describing the research interview as ethnographic.

The Status of the Interview in Anthropological Research

Hockey's (2002) argument that interview-based studies are ethnographic, or more specifically are a culturally appropriate form of participatory research, remains remarkably unchallenged in the anthropological literature. This is not to say that the interview has suddenly scaled the methodological heights of the discipline and sits now on a par with participant observation; in most representations of anthropological and/or ethnographic practice it remains a secondary activity (Forsey 2010b). Disputes over the role of interviews in qualitative research practice are clearly not new, as a notable exchange between Brecker and Geer and Trow in 1957 captures. While this is not the place to relive this particular debate in any depth, we agree with Trow that different kinds of questions require different types of investigation (Trow 1957: 13). We join with him in challenging Becker and Geer's (1957: 28) bold assertion that participant observation presents us with a yardstick by which to measure the value of other methods of data gathering, by pointing to the problems triggered by an exclusive preoccupation with a particular research method or tradition.

Debating the superiority of methods or pitting participant observation *against* interviewing is not our concern here, or at least it should not be. However, as social scientists trained as anthropologists, it is difficult to escape the aesthetics and regulative ideals of the Malinowskian myth that so often reduces the anthropological project to that of extended participatory fieldwork and consigns the interview to a lesser, supplementary role (Marcus 2009: 2; Forsey 2010a: 67). Much of the impetus for this chapter comes from knowing all too well the problems this sort of positioning can cause, especially for neophyte researchers seeking to establish their disciplinary credentials through projects that do not easily fit the rubrics of the imagined anthropological craft (Hockey 2002; Forsey 2010a).

The reality of fieldwork is that we interview in order to find out what we do not and cannot know otherwise; to locate the knowledge people carry in their heads, their 'notions', the beliefs and values driving their actions (Holy and Stuchlik 1983). Cohen and Rapport argue (1995) that the uncovering of human consciousness has been an unacknowledged goal of anthropology through much of its history and we cannot achieve this without *listening* as individuals reveal what they are conscious of (Cohen and Rapport 1995: 11–12). As Holy and Stuchlik show, observation alone will not do: 'If we do not want simply to observe and report physical movements of people in temporal and spatial sequences, but to study and explain their actions, we can do it only by relating them, implicitly or explicitly, to some notions about such movements, to knowledge, beliefs, ideas or ideals' (1983: 36).

In order to make sense of what people do we have to interview them, either formally or informally. And as Trow demonstrates in discussing research problems encountered as part of a major study into the trade union movement in the United States, sometimes you have to remove people from their 'natural' surroundings in order to comprehend what is really going on in certain social scenes:

> The workings of the party system inhibited direct expressions of hostility to the system. In the ordinary give and take of conversation in the shop, party meeting, club meeting, informal gatherings after hours, such expressions were not likely to be expressed; they violated strongly held norms, and called down various kinds of punishments. It was only when we interviewed leaders individually and intensively that we could get some sense of the reservations that they held about the party system, how widely and strongly those reservations were held, and thus could make some assessment of those sentiments as a potentially disruptive force in the party system. (1957: 34)

The research interview provides an opportunity for creating and capturing insights of a depth and level of focus rarely achieved through surveys, observational studies or the majority of casual conversations we hold with our fellow human beings (Forsey 2011).

If interviews are so vital to anthropological knowledge, and if this reality is reflected in anthropological practice to the point where we seem to be reporting more of what we hear than what we see (Forsey 2010a), why do anthropologists persist in referring to our main practice as participant observation? If we were more honest, or clear about what we actually do, and called it engaged listening, there would be much less concern expressed about interview studies not quite being the 'real thing'. Of course observation is usually meant as a cover-all term for much of what is sensed in the field—we realize this, but the visual so dominates Western thought that it relegates the other senses to a lower value, filtering their representation through a visualist framework (Bull and Back 2003; Forsey 2010b: 562).

We are not suggesting interviews are more significant than other forms of anthropological research. Instead, we advocate 'a democracy of the senses' (Forsey 2010b: 562). Sometimes, perhaps even often depending upon the questions one is asking, we can observe human knowledge, ideas, beliefs and values in action. But sometimes this is neither possible nor desirable; sometimes observations do not yield much data of significance. Drawing on our own experiences as interviewers we further develop Hockey's (2002) portrayal of the research interview as a culturally appropriate form of participatory research. More specifically, we use a single case portrait from each of our own extensive interview 'galleries' to highlight the ways in which the engaged encounters with fellow social beings that occur in qualitative research interviews can fulfil the already highlighted criteria for the particular and special insights that all too often are attributed to participant observer research. But before doing this, it is important to explore further the troublesome slippage between anthropology, ethnography and participant observation that has occurred in the relatively recent past.

Anthropology ≠ Ethnography ≠ Participant Observation

In critiquing the ways in which anthropology has become virtually synonymous with ethnography, Ingold (2008) shows the equation to be a development of the past fifty years or so. He cites a grumbling Edmund Leach (1961) to make the point that at some point in anthropology's history, in the United Kingdom at least, it moved from being a comparative, nomothetic discipline to one focussed on producing 'impeccably detailed historical ethnographies of particular peoples' (Ingold 2008: 76). Leach regretted this development because he believed anthropology to have general as well as particular implications (Leach 1961: 1). This reminder of the constructed nature of anthropological practice—for which anthropologists of all people might of course feel they need no prompting—should allow reconsideration of some of the ideas about the anthropological endeavour. Anthropology, ethnography and participant observation slip and slop around contemporary anthropological discourse as interchangeable terms. They do similar things in the social sciences more generally but for the most part we limit our attention to anthropology, even while acknowledging that the boundaries with cognate disciplines such as sociology are often difficult to sustain. We join with Leach in suggesting a need to return to the beginning in order to think through basic issues and name ethnography, anthropology and participant observation, agreeing with Leach that basic ideas are just that: they are 'deeply entrenched and firmly held' (1961: 1). Indeed, they have become part of the commonsense of a discipline in the Gramscian sense of the term, a somewhat rigid form of 'popular knowledge' (Gramsci 1985: 421). Echoing this idea in many ways, Marcus has recently argued that the instillation of fieldwork as 'a valued object of professional culture' significantly restricts the range of discourses anthropologists are allowed around a research process that is much prized for its distinctiveness (2009: 4). He argues that this encourages a 'flexible covering over of the variety of activities, of what is done as research "out there" in fieldwork's name, whether or not they resemble the classic mise-en-scène of fieldwork'.

Previously, Ingold pronounced anthropology to be 'philosophy with the people in' (1992: 696). In his more recent essay asserting the distinction between anthropology and ethnography, he takes this idea further, insisting that anthropologists philosophize better than most, mainly because the discipline is embedded in both observational engagements with the world and in collaborations and correspondences with its inhabitants (2008: 90). Ingold's argument is characteristically subtle and complex, eschewing simplistic oppositions between description and theory, and hence between ethnography and anthropology. But oppositions are not distinctions and he makes the case for anthropology to be considered 'a study *with* people' in which anthropologists learn to 'see things (or hear them, or touch them) in the ways their teachers and companions do' (82). Anthropology, according to Ingold, 'educates our *perception* of the world, and opens our eyes and minds to other possibilities of being' (82, author's emphasis). It is a comparative discipline, considering human difference in order that we might be aware of 'alternative ways of being' (84). Ethnographers on the other hand are involved more often than not in writing about how historically and geographically located people perceive the world and their actions in it.

According to *The Dictionary of Anthropology*, ethnography is 'the systematic description of a single contemporary culture, often through ethnographic fieldwork' (Wood 1997: 157). By contrast O'Reilly, a sociologist specializing in migration research, describes ethnography in her recently published book of key concepts as a method (2009: 3). It is iterative-inductive, draws on a family of methods involving direct, sustained contact with human agents and results in richly written accounts that 'respect the irreducibility of human experience, acknowledges the role of theory...and views humans as part object/part subject'. The differences are important and reflect not only disciplinary variation but also some of the shifts in meaning in the term that have occurred over the past two centuries or so, a point noted by Wood (1997: 157). That said, despite the fact that many an anthropologist also thinks of ethnography as both methodology and a descriptive/analytical piece of writing or film-making, Wood does not directly address this particular and significant change in meaning among his anthropological colleagues.

If we were to limit our conceptualization of ethnography to its descriptive/analytical component, it would allow us to think more clearly about the ways that we gather the data making up such a piece of work. Defining ethnography, therefore, as a written or filmic depiction of a people reminds us that participant observation is but one way among a number of approaches that enable the social researcher to produce an ethnography. Participant observation may well be the most effective way to arrive at the final destination in some, and perhaps even most, cases, but it is not essential to the effective production of a descriptive-analytical account of a social grouping.

Picking up on the point already made by Hockey (2002) about interview-based studies offering a culturally appropriate means of conducting socially engaged forms of research, particularly in so-called Western settings, interviews can sometimes offer the most effective way of producing an ethnography. It is conceivable, in fact, that a statistical survey could produce an effective ethnographic account of a people (see Efferson et al. 2007). This does not appeal to all tastes, perhaps, but this is always the case no matter how we conceptualize the production of ethnographic knowledge. The point is that ethnography should not be conceptualized as a method, rather it should be defined by its purpose or as an outcome.

It is important to rethink the Malinowskian archetype often invoked as the ideal for fieldwork (Stocking 1983; Gupta and Ferguson 1997; Hockey 2002). For one thing, the social spaces captured in many a classic ethnography reflected a cultural and physical climate conducive to extended conversations in outdoor settings, 'open-air anthropology' as Malinowski called it (Stocking 1983: 111). This emphasizes the differences in the socio-spatial arrangements between the settings of so many classic participant studies and Western models of differentiated private and public space (Hockey 2002: 215). For example, spending extended periods of time with families in the industrial West is simply not practicable or even desirable in many instances (Silverstone et al. 1991; Forsey 2010b). Part of the impetus for identifying the difficulties associated with participant observer studies in 'the West' arises from the realities of social interactions that are often 'spatially dislocated, time-bounded and characterized by intimacy at a distance' (Hockey 2002: 211; cf. Passaro 1997).

As Hockey points out, whilst anthropologists can now be less apologetic about researching locally produced 'exotica', participant observation still occupies the methodological high ground. That it does this despite the fact that, as Forsey has recently shown (2010a), much of what passes as anthropology/ethnography is based upon what we hear rather than what we see is fascinating to contemplate. In his analysis of recently published papers in key British, American and Australian anthropological journals, a little less than half of them were based on a roughly equal mix of what is seen and heard in the research process, 45 per cent on interviews and informal conversations, and only 7 per cent on what the ethnographer observed. These results offer clear support to Cohen and Rapport's (1995) claim that what anthropologists do, above all else, is listen. They bolster the case for considering ethnography as flowing more from engaged listening than anything else (Forsey 2010a) or for defining it as participant listening *plus*, to upset a recent pronouncement from Crang and Cook (2007: 1) about ethnography being participant-observation *plus*.

As a means of moving beyond the traps of current terminology and the commonsense it helps produce, we suggest a shift in terminology away from the troublesome notion of participation towards the idea of engagement. The vast majority of papers and monographs that are called 'ethnographies' these days flow from some form of engagement with the people portrayed—engaged listening, engaged observation; both are forms of participant engagement and both reflect the important sense of 'being there' and 'being with' research participants, notions fundamental to a field-based study.

The Interview as Participant Engagement

Giddens makes a telling point about social actors commonly knowing more about what they are up to and its consequences than social scientists often give them credit for (1990: 309). We argue that the often unintentional arrogance of the social researcher that Giddens alerts us to is very apparent in claims made about the ability participant observation/ethnography bestows upon the researcher to see beyond what people say they do to what they actually do, and/or to highlight the contradictions of lived reality (Eyles 1988). It is also evident in claims about the depth of insight one can reach as a participant observer/ethnographer, insights apparently not accessible using other research techniques.

The single interviews we report and reflect upon here were part of a series of conversations we held with persons for whom the phenomena we were interested in—natural burial in the case of Hockey, school choice for Forsey—were either complete or still in process. The natural burial study, to which Hockey's interview contributed, involved participant observation at four such burial grounds. How a new mortuary landscape, where vegetation is allowed relatively unfettered growth, might impact the *emotional* landscapes of individuals who had buried a relative or friend there, could not be understood through participant observation alone. Retrospective accounts were needed, opportunities for people to reflect on the entire period between the burial and the present day. School choice is also a process that does not lend itself to observation, not easily at least. Along with many of his fellow Australians, Forsey knows that parents and children are abandoning government schools, particularly high schools, in favour of fee-paying, so-called private schools, which are nonetheless granted significant funds out of the public purse (see Forsey 2008). What he wanted to know more about was how people perceived and experienced these different types of schools and how this affected their responses to the neoliberal imperative to choose the 'right' sort of education for their children.

We want to reflect on the interview as a moment of engagement, a site of participation in the life of the person we meet and talk with. Furthermore, we want to show that the interview allows us to tap into the knowledge that the particular social actors we engage with as social researchers have about what they are up to and its consequences, to echo the previously cited insight from Giddens (1990: 309). The interviews are drawn from significant projects conducted by us in our respective home nations. Forsey reports on an interview conducted with Kelly (all names of research participants are pseudonyms) about various aspects of her educational choices in and around Perth, the capital of Western Australia. All interviews were conducted with persons who involved in some way with decisions to change school systems from private to public or vice versa. Parents, students and teachers were interviewed and while Kelly was interviewed as a teacher who had changed systems it was her reflections on school choice as a parent that were most intriguing for the project at hand. Hockey's interview took place in the context of a project that explored the cultural, social and emotional implications of 'natural burial', the practice of disposing of the dead in ways that minimize its environmental impact by restricting the use of gravestones, instead helping retain or recover woodland or pasture land, for example.

As should be apparent from the research reports offered here, the interviewees are more than able to show an awareness of the gaps between what they say and what they do; they highlight the contradictions of their social world in interesting ways. In other words, they are quite capable of offering to the interviewer the sorts of insights often said to flow most readily from ethnographic/participant observer studies. But the interview can also allow us to go much further than this and, as Hockey shows in the discussion of a recent encounter she had with Mary, the interview can allow the researcher to immerse herself quite intimately in the life of a fellow human being, one with whom we share the status of offspring, parent, lover; the gifts of creativity and artistry; the struggles of life in general and ultimately for all of us, the tussles and strains, the joys and blessings of mortality, both our own and those we care for and perhaps even love. Rapport (1991) for example describes sharing his Wanet participants' commitment to gossip; he also refers to Berger and the 'struggle to give meaning to experience: to scrutinize a given moment and connect it to a continuing script' (1991: 12) that Berger pursued alongside the French peasants among whom he worked. Jenny's voice takes over now as she introduces the interview with Mary and the issues arising from it that she wishes to highlight here.

Playing Cat and Mouse

Back (2007) notes the belief that hearing is the last human faculty to die—that listening connects people at a profound level. The interviewee I am going to discuss, Mary Stanton, had buried her father 'naturally' at one of the sites where we conducted participant observation. She said that when her father was within a few days of his death, 'I actually made a sort of promise to myself that…just really be there for him and actually I found that things he was saying to me made more sense than he'd ever made before in a sort of weird poetic kind of way.' Previously, she had talked about older people supposedly 'losing their marbles'. Her personal theory was that they were in a kind of dream state where things left unresolved in their lives would surface, but the only way that they could talk about them—that they and other people could cope with—was 'to seem abstracted or seem to talk like King Lear'. Statements such as these exercised a special hold over me and this is what I want to consider in detail.

A colleague and I had been interviewing people in Powys, Wales who had buried someone—or booked their own plot—in a natural burial ground in a remote farmer's field. I was the only driver and we were unprepared for the distances between interviewees and the deeply rural nature of Powys. I drove to meet Mary, worried that I'd get lost, worried about liaising with my colleague whom I'd left with another interviewee many miles away. Mary was an artist who exhibited in London. Separated from the father of her children, she lived with her teenaged son. Despite the rich greenery of the countryside, she and her son lived on a bleak social housing estate with untidy looking properties, makeshift gates hung with hand-scrawled dog warnings, threatening young men sitting out on the curb, a neighbour's frontage covered in washing. Inside, Mary's house itself was untidy, furnished with scuffed up rugs and old settees with crochet throws. Her sitting room was her studio, covered in art materials, books and work, with just two worn-out settees facing each other at one end. Apart from her kitchen and bedrooms, this was her living space.

On reflection, I am aware that I felt protective, not wanting to cause her embarrassment about her chaotic house. In fieldnotes, I wrote: 'She seemed slightly shy/troubled, looked like life had been tough [on her]'. And yet I found what she said hugely compelling. I wanted her to know how much I found myself agreeing with her, sharing everything she said. I wanted her to take me further and further into her view of the world, her experience, her life in that 'here and now'. As anthropologists we are told to be reflexive, to notice the partiality of our listening and remember that we hear through the filters of our preexisting frameworks—and later bring reflection to bear on the co-production of knowledge we participated in. As Clifford notes, '"culture" is always relational, an inscription of communicative processes that exist, historically, *between* subjects in relations of power' (1986: 15). These warnings tend to concern our resistances: to people we find unappealing, to beliefs and practices we dislike or disapprove of. But do we also consider the seduction of someone else's story, the experience of being drawn into an unfamiliar world where we feel more at home than in the world we return to? How can we make sense of the strangeness of the 'familiar' landscape we re-enter postinterview, an experience akin to stumbling out of the magical darkness of the cinema and into unexpected and unwelcome daylight? Okely (1996) describes similar experiences when working 'close to home' yet among Traveller Gypsies. Is it like falling in love? A kind of bewitching? And important, is it a problem or a gift, an inadequacy or a skill? We know the risks of anthropologists 'going native', but what about when this happens during a single interview? How many of us experience this? Do we talk about it? What are its implications for our writing? Questions of this kind have been raised in Coffey's (1999) account of the ethnographic self and here we argue that they need to be asked, not just in the long-running field diaries of those conducting participant observation, but also in the aftermath of a single interview—and indeed, in working with the data it generates.

When I look at Mary's words in the transcript, they do not convey the allure of what she said, of how she looked and dressed or of the freedom she gave the mess of her painting to overwhelm the entire room. I asked her about her work as an artist as part of the project's interview schedule, for we wanted to know what kind of people were burying naturally—was there something distinctive about them, given that this is a new minority practice? Mary said that through her work:

> I think I just want to bring a sort of sense—peace of mind and joy of life and what's possible to people really and to try and show that in a soundless sort of nonverbal way because I've always found with things like religion or anything else, that sometimes words are too specific or they, discrepancies arise but generally with music or with, with painting I think people understand one another more easily and, and so I, yes I would say it's landscaped-based painting generally. Or print making, so the idea is I suppose it's a bit like…the figure in the landscape is a metaphor for our sort of general spiritual journey if you like, if that doesn't sound too airy fairy.

Discussing interview data from women who had experienced the presence of a dead partner in some way, Bennett and Bennett (2000) describe an oscillation between what they call supernaturalist and materialist worldviews. Their interviewees provided graphic descriptions of seeing, hearing, smelling their partners—and then qualified this 'supernaturalist' data with materialist statements, noting that they had been thinking about their partner a lot, had been feeling down, were only half awake. Bennett and Bennett (2000) felt that a materialist position was assumed for their benefit as staff of a university and therefore representatives of a scientific worldview. They suspected that in other situations the supernaturalist worldview was the one women felt more at home with. Something of the kind was taking place in my engagement with Mary. She half apologizes for what she's said, nodding to my supposed location within a rationalist belief system—she refers to 'our general spiritual journey' and then implicitly asks for my permission or assent to it—'if you like, if that doesn't sound too airy fairy'. Just as Bennett and Bennett's (2000) interviewees repeatedly 'touched base' in what they implicitly understood to be a dominant, rationalist worldview, so Mary offers her notion of a collective spiritual journey with the caveat that I may choose to disregard it.

In terms of relations of power, however, I was completely eating out of her hand by now. I had already had a snapshot of a life where someone's passion had swept all before it; any nod towards a conventional sitting room and the containing of her painting within a category called 'work'—or space called 'studio'—was absent. Along with the allure of her artistic and spiritual beliefs, I found the free rein she had given to the messiness of her work intensely attractive—on some level speaking to my desire to escape the domestic orderliness without which I imagined control of my professional life would finally and dramatically escape me.

Yet I maintained my 'materialist' position in the sense of displaying what probably looked like an expression of professional empathy. 'Right' was all I said while she spoke. 'No' was my response to her concern that I might find all this 'airy fairy'.

I then asked Mary if she was a practising spiritualist, something I'd heard from my colleague who had arranged the interview. Again, Mary described her 'supernaturalist' beliefs. And yet she qualified these in various ways:

> Yes, yes, I am... I mean I don't, I don't tend to sort of, I don't tend to tell people because I always think any religion that you have to sell it to people not, probably not a good thing and I think, as I was just saying about the, any kind of descriptions of things which I don't think in essence can really be described in words, then it's always going to end up falling short.

I say 'Oh' at the end of this statement (which went on to describe her father's supernatural experiences). And then she explained what she found when a friend took her to a meeting of the spiritualist church:

> all they were saying really was basically that we come from a sort of heaven or spirit and we return to it and we have this essence within us which is spiritual energy really and as long as everything was channelled in the name of love or God or whatever, light or whatever you'd call, choose to call it, that was the main thing and one spends an evening in the company of really lovely people who all just want the world to be a better place, very supportive, pray a lot for healing other people and the planet in general and lots of singing.

She presented this in a very open way: 'in the name of love or God or whatever, light or whatever you'd call, choose to call it', somehow implying that she was not committed to calling 'it' anything in particular—and indeed giving me a kind of choice: 'whatever you'd call, choose to call it'. She then moved from the supernatural or sacred to the mundane when she said: 'at the end there's this sort of demonstration of mediumship which can vary from the sublime to the ridiculous really and as I don't have a telly sometimes I think it's my form of, of soap opera in some ways, which sounds a bit disrespectful'. What I'm suggesting is that both Mary and I are playing the same kind of cat and mouse game—and the context of the game has two elements. First is the agenda inevitably set by someone from a university carrying out an interview. More broadly, though, we both inhabit a society which, as Marina Warner says, denies the persistence of European magical beliefs long after the Enlightenment emphasis on reason and rationality: 'Uses of magic and fantasy have often been ascribed to the Other, to the Stranger, who is consequently characterised as barbaric, even inhuman' (1996: 13).

My reading of all this is that both Mary and I were concerned to play by rules we ascribed to the university—and neither of us wanted to take on the status of the Other, the Stranger. At a conference on death and dying, Jennifer Iles (2009) described ethnographic work within a spiritualist church and her personal epistemological crisis when she discovered herself channelling messages from 'the other side'; something that escaped the limits of her academic project. What was happening in my interview with Mary is more subtle. Rather than an upturning of epistemologies, the event of the interview teeters unevenly on some kind of boundary between an enchanted and a rationalist worldview—and reveals much about contemporary Western perspectives on human mortality. In Mary's case through a series of explicit references to beliefs that pay heed to, yet also transcend a secular dismissal of 'life after death', and in mine through a self-silenced enthusiasm for her nonmaterialist orientation, we both exemplify a culture where, alongside secularization, residual religiosity persists—both in a diversity of orthodox religious beliefs and practices, as well as a more individualized 'search for meaning that rejects the collectivist and prescriptive structures of established religions' (Howarth 2007: 100).

Three years of research into natural burial has now been completed. How Mary understands natural burial—and particularly her image of a burial field slowly 'healing over' after the insertion of a body—derives from frameworks of belief apparent in what she expressed, however guardedly, during the interview. Her conceptualization—or maybe imagining—of what natural burial is about feels like one of the most valuable things I've learned:

> I think returning to the earth at nature's pace is the best solution really. I mean it gives everybody around long enough to come to terms with it…I think long enough for a burial site to start to heal over and plants to start to regrow and things. It sort of and to return one's sort of vehicle to the earth, just on a physical level…just seems to be the right thing to do really. And I think to actually, to actually be around an object like that and actually see it returning to the earth, I think it's very, well it's sort of obvious but I think sometimes a body in grief needs obvious things to kind of make it plain.

Mary is thus speaking retrospectively, looking back over gradual yet dynamic processes that have been going on in both the natural burial landscape and within the geography of her own emotional world. Only through engaged listening has it been possible to access these temporal trajectories. Martin's voice now takes over as he describes the interview he conducted with Kelly late one morning in 2006.

Choosing Schools in Western Australia: Kelly's Story

Kelly and I met in my office because that is what she requested. Commenting in our initial phone conversation that set up the interview that she did her initial degree at the university, she decided to meet me there as she had not seen it for a while. Kelly also made it clear that she needed to go there soon anyway as she wanted to pick up some forms from the postgraduate office.

Normally, I preferred to meet people for this project in their homes, as I figured that is where most of the thinking behind the decisions I was interested in took place. Somehow it felt more 'ethnographic', more participatory, to be going to their place rather than them coming to mine. But of course I was not going to argue with her on this point: she was the one offering her precious time so I could capture her thoughts and feelings in order to enhance my research project; besides she was doing me a favour as she lived more than thirty minutes' drive from the university, in the southern industrial area of the city.

I met with Kelly because she responded to an article she read in her local paper asking for people to volunteer to be interviewed for a project investigating school choice that was conducted by myself and a research assistant. We recruited parents, students and teachers who had changed systems either by moving from a private school to a public one or vice versa. Kelly was a teacher, but she was also a parent, and as became clear, each of these two aspects of her 'identity' spoke to the other in some very interesting ways.

From my office, where we met for the first and only time, we moved to the tea room in the social sciences building. It is a place where people sometimes come to eat their lunch or grab a cup of coffee or tea as a break from their work. On this occasion, one of my colleagues sat at another table eating her lunch for a little less than half of the seventy or so minutes that I spoke with Kelly. It did not seem to disturb the flow of our semi-structured conversation at all. In keeping with my commitment to avoiding the fragmenting, decontextualizing tendencies of much interview-based research (Nespor and Barylske 1991: 810), I prefer to transform all transcripts into individual 'portraits' of the research participants. The portraits aim at revealing cultural contexts behind the lived experiences of research participants, summarizing the beliefs, the values, the material conditions and structural forces underpinning the socially patterned behaviour of the person that emerged in the interview. Key quotes are incorporated into the portraits to provide added texture. It is analogous in some ways to a gallery curator who in not being able to display all of the available pictures has to select particular pieces and summarize what is not as visible to the audience (see Forsey 2008, 2010a). Miller (2008: 5) draws upon similar imagery to explain his use of interviews, which offers a particularly compelling example of a 'gallery exhibition' of interviews drawn from a much larger body of work. As he says of the approach taken in his book *The Comfort of Things*, the thirty portraits selected for the book 'pay respect to whoever these people happen to be and…paint a bigger portrait that starts to emerge as an image of the modern world'.

What makes the reporting of interviews different to a gallery hanging is the way in which the curator can alter the work to better suit the 'space' and audience. What follows is a highly edited version of the image of the contemporary world provided by Kelly when we met. Among some of the many missing aspects of her story is a discussion of her teaching experiences in two very different sorts of schools, as well as reflections on the contrast between growing up in a leafy suburb of Perth and life as a wife and mother in the industrial area of the same city. I choose to emphasize here Kelly's 'knowingness', her insights into the contentious and sometimes contradictory nature of her notions, beliefs and the actions she has pursued and may well pursue into the future.

Kelly is in her mid twenties. She is a mother and a music teacher. Her first teaching appointment to a Catholic school in the eastern suburbs of Perth lasted a little over a year. As is so often the case with first-year teachers, it was a 'sink or swim' experience and it did not work out as she had hoped. Her next job was a short-term contract at a government school near where she lives with her husband in the Southern Industrial Zone of Perth. Her experience at the government school was quite different. Kelly found both the staff and parents more supportive there.

Kelly has a daughter who was two years old at the time of the interview. Interesting, while Kelly would be happy to continue working at the government school in which she recently had a contract, she is not at all keen for her daughter to eventually attend there. 'I wouldn't want her in the classes of some of the teachers', she explains, 'they just haven't got a clue'. Kelly would prefer her daughter to start off in a private primary school, but she would not choose any of the nongovernment schools in the Southern Industrial Zone. Her husband, who teaches in the public system, is deeply committed to government education and vehemently opposed to private schooling. He calls her a snob, 'because you know I've come from south of the river and now I'm down here and it's a totally different lifestyle, totally different outlook. The kids have a different sort of ideas about things, a different home life to what I had'.[1]

What concerns Kelly most about the students she has taught in the Southern Industrial Zone is their general lack of ambition. If her daughter were to be schooled in the area Kelly would worry that she would not aspire to do anything that Kelly deems worthwhile: 'Down here you're lucky if you graduate school and don't get knocked up beforehand. 'Cause so many of the kids that you know get out of school the first thing that happens is they end up pregnant'.

Despite her husband's deeply held commitment to public schooling, he tends to concur with Kelly and they are seriously considering moving out of the industrial area in order to ensure that their daughter can attend a more acceptable school. They are contemplating enrolling her in a nongovernment primary school. As one who enjoyed her own government school education and who is happy enough to work in such schools, Kelly worries about her apparent hypocrisy. However, she is also aware of the changes that she has experienced: 'Twenty years ago you just went to the local school, but now, we just expect more. Private schools will have better resources and they'll have more competent teachers right throughout because they are able to weed out the undesirable teachers and the undesirable kids'. Her conclusion: 'if I want to give my daughter every opportunity I will be hypocritical.'

The Interview as Fieldwork

Whatever the merits of arguing that anthropology is defined more by its commitment to pursuing a 'generous, comparative but nevertheless critical understanding of human being and knowing' (Ingold 2008: 69), in practice, anthropology is more often than not apprehended and represented as a fieldwork-focussed discipline. Moreover, it remains a discipline deeply committed to 'the aesthetics and the regulative ideals of the Malinowskian paradigm of research' (Marcus 2009: 2).

That said, Malinowski understood his endeavour to be the gaining of a 'clear idea of the metaphysical nature of existence' (Cohen and Rapport 1995: 11–12), something Cohen and Rapport argue is best apprehended by getting inside people's heads through *listening* to them. Listening to people's notions is how Holy and Stuchlik (1983: 22–35) describe this significant component of the anthropological project, a project committed to comprehending the forms these notions have in a person's imaginary, the meanings they hold for them and the uses to which they are put or might be put in ensuing action.

Interviews conducted with an 'ethnographic imaginary' (Forsey 2010b) commit the researcher to understanding the lived experience of the participant/interlocutor by asking about and listening closely to the beliefs, the values, the material conditions and structural forces that underwrite the socially patterned behaviours of all human beings, along with the meanings people attach to these conditions and forces. We argue that when we conduct so-called ethnographic interviews, many of the idealized attributes of participant observation can be achieved. As Kelly helps illustrate, we can hear from our participants their insights about the gap between what they say and what they do; it is not just the researcher who notices these things. In many instances she will not be able to, certainly not in the way that the person in question does. By virtue of the fact that we asked focussed, systematic and searching questions and that Mary and Kelly had granted us licence to do so, these interviews reveal much about the real lives of those whom we meet. Though both interviews have been extracted from larger data sets to which they contribute, material which in part derives from participant observation, our readings of them draw not only on this bigger picture, but also on parallel published studies. Approached in this way, they offer a depth of understanding and engagement usually not achievable in more ordinary face-to-face encounters.

Hockey has already argued that interviews reflect and replicate the realities of social interactions that are often 'spatially dislocated, time-bounded and characterized by intimacy at a distance' (Hockey 2002: 211; cf. Passaro 1997). They are appropriate ways of participating in so-called Western lives. As the two examples canvassed here demonstrate, interviews can show the contradictions that in part typify people's lives. Both Mary and Kelly explored the limits of what can be said in such a context and were, in their different ways, seeking to transcend the categories of either commonsense, or materialist thinking, or social class divisions. Moreover, the reflexivity evidenced in each interview points towards the way in which different aspects of an individual's identity (the 'supernaturalist' and the 'materialist'; the teacher and the parent) not only became accessible to the anthropologist, but also, how these 'aspects' engaged in dialogue with one another in the course of the interview. We do not, therefore, have to observe them to know about them; people are very capable of 'showing' us at least some of the intricacies of their lives through what they tell us through projects of engaged listening.

Conceivably, we could go deeper and wider into the topic with individual participants by hanging out with them for extended periods, which would give us some different and very useful insights into natural burial and school choice. To do this would reflect an anthropological commitment to holism, which is at once a virtue and a problem. We can never fully know a subject and to pursue our topics in this sort of manner is impractical in many instances; it can also be enormously inefficient. Like it or not, current university structures require greater speed of us in our research endeavour than traditional fieldwork practices allow (see Faubion 2009). However, often it is simply not possible to chase down our quarry through participant observation, and regardless of the practicalities, both the natural burial and the school choice projects suggest a case for gathering a spectrum of ideas and experiences across a broad spatial range as another form of anthropological holism.

Interviews allow us to get 'inside people's heads' for a while, a doubtful endeavour in the eyes of those who argue that interviews offer opportunities for people to either lie or to present themselves in the best possible light. This scepticism ignores two dimensions of the interview project. First, as the cases of Mary and Kelly exemplify, dealing with the loaded uncertainties of spiritual life and educational priorities is a process that is arguably more internal than external. The aim of the interviewer is to intercept that process, to engage with it 'on the wing'. What we aim to achieve as anthropologists is an understanding of how social life is negotiated, how it unfolds over time. Second, it is our contention that most who participate in social research interviews take and indeed welcome the opportunity to reveal the processes that constitute an authentic interior self as best they can. Indeed, in our experience, they are often scrupulous about this. Research participants often close with a comment expressing concern that they have not been helpful enough, which reflects concerns about not articulating their ideas, beliefs and values clearly enough. We believe that the people who volunteer their time to meet with us do so because they share our commitment to increasing understanding of social processes. They accept the value of social research and quite possibly participate in the process out of a sense of a civic commitment to enhancing knowledge.

As we close off this chapter, we wonder what might happen if we anthropologists were more precise with our terms. If we recognized that regardless of how we arrive at our data, anthropology is the critical appreciation of humanity in all of its complex glory, that ethnography is a documentary product capturing the dynamic interactions of a particular people in a particular time and place (or places), and that participant observation is but one way to arrive at ethnographic knowledge, might this open up the space for a better, more inclusive practice?

Anthropology is not ethnography is not participant observation. And as anthropologists, we know the importance of understanding what people do in the practice of social life. We realize that the three-part equation is not going to disappear anytime soon and, as long as this is the case, we are compelled to make the case that interviews can, and do, allow us to produce the sorts of knowledge any reasonable anthropologist, no matter how grudgingly, should be willing to call ethnographic. The interview is an important form of participatory research and as such deserves to be considered as anthropological as any other forms of engaged investigation.

Note

1. 'South of the river' is a local expression that historically at least was suggestive of some of the more affluent suburbs of Perth.

References

Back, L. (2007), *The Art of Listening*, Oxford: Berg.

Becker, H. and B. Geer (1957), 'Participant Observation and Interviewing: A Comparison', *Human Organization*, 16(3): 28–32.

Bennett, G. and K. Bennett (2000), 'The Presence of the Dead: An Empirical Study', *Mortality*, 5(2): 139–57.

Bull, M. and L. Back (2003), 'Introduction: Into Sound', in M. Bull and L. Back (eds), *The Auditory Culture Reader*, Oxford: Berg, 1–23.

Clifford, J. (1986), 'Introduction: Partial Truths', in J. Clifford and G. E. Marcus (eds), *Writing Culture: The Poetics and Politics of Ethnography*, Berkeley: University of California Press, 1–26.

Coffey, A. (1999), *The Ethnographic Self*, London: Sage Publications.

Cohen, A. and N. Rapport (1995), 'Introduction: Consciousness in Anthropology', in A. Cohen and N. Rapport (eds), *Questions of Consciousness*, ASA Monographs 33, London: Routledge, 1–18.

Crang, I. and M. Cook (2007), *Doing Ethnographies*, London: Sage Publications.

Efferson, C., M. Takezawa and R. McElreath (2007), 'New Methods in Quantitative Ethnography: Economic Experiments and Variation in the Price of Equality', *Current Anthropology*, 48(6): 912–19.

Eyles, J. (1988), 'Interpreting the Geographical World: Qualitative Approaches in Geographical Research', in J. Eyles and D. Smith (eds), *Qualitative Methods in Human Geography*, Totawa: Barnes & Noble, 1–16.

Faubion, J. (2009), 'The Ethics of Fieldwork as an Ethics of Connectivity, or the Good Anthropologist (Isn't What She Used to Be)', in J. Faubion and G. Marcus (eds), *Fieldwork Is Not What It Used to Be: Learning Anthropology's Method in a Time of Transition*, Ithaca: Cornell University Press, 145–66.

Faubion, J, and G. Marcus (eds) (2009), *Fieldwork Is Not What It Used to Be: Learning Anthropology's Method in a Time of Transition*, Ithaca: Cornell University Press.

Forsey, M. (2008), 'No Choice but to Choose: Selecting Schools in Western Australia', in M. Forsey, S. Davies and G. Walford (eds), *The Globalisation of School Choice?*, Oxford: Symposium Books, 73–93.

Forsey, M. (2010a), 'Ethnography and the Myth of Participant Observation', in S. Hillyard (ed.), *New Frontiers in Ethnography*, Studies in Qualitative Methodology, Vol. 11, Bingley: Emerald, 65–79.

Forsey, M. (2010b), 'Ethnography as Participant Listening', *Ethnography*, 11(4): 558–72.

Forsey, M. (2012), 'Individual Interviewing', in S. Delamont (ed.), *The Handbook of Qualitative Research in Education*, Cheltenham: Edward Elgar.

Gans, H. (1999), 'Participant Observation in the Era of "Ethnography"', *Journal of Contemporary Ethnography*, 28(5): 540–8.

Giddens, A. (1990), 'Structuration Theory and Sociological Analysis', in J. Clark, C. Modgil and S. Modgil (eds), *Anthony Giddens: Consensus and Controversy*, London: Falmer Press, 297–315.

Gramsci, A. (1985), *Selections from Cultural Writings*, London: Lawrence & Wishart.

Gupta, A. and J. Ferguson (1997), 'Discipline and Practice: "The Field" as Site, Method and Location in Anthropology', in A. Gupta and J. Ferguson (eds), *Anthropological Locations: Boundaries and Grounds of a Field Science*, Berkeley: University of California Press, 1–46.

Hockey, J. (2002), 'Interviews as Ethnography? Disembodied Social Interaction in Britain', in N. Rapport (ed.), *British Subjects: An Anthropology of Britain*, Oxford: Berg, 209–22.

Holy, L. and M. Stuchlik (1983), *Actions, Norms and Representations: Foundations of Anthropological Inquiry*, Cambridge: Cambridge University Press.

Howarth, G. (2007), *Death and Dying: A Sociological Introduction*, Cambridge: Polity Press.

Iles, J. (2009), 'Lest We Forget: Calling on the Dead to Remember the Living', Paper presented at the Death, Dying and Disposal Conference, University of Durham, 9 September.

Ingold, T. (1992), 'Editorial', *Man*, 27(4): 693–6.

Ingold, T. (2008), 'Anthropology Is Not Ethnography: Radcliffe-Brown Lecture in Social Anthropology', *Proceedings of the British Academy*, 154: 69–92.

Leach, E. (1961), *Rethinking Anthropology*, London: Athlone.

Marcus, G. (2009), 'Notes Towards an Ethnographic Memoir of Supervising Graduate Research through Anthropology's Decades of Transformation', in J. Faubion and G. Marcus (eds), *Fieldwork Is Not What It Used to Be: Learning Anthropology's Method in a Time of Transition*, Ithaca: Cornell University Press, 1–34.

Miller, D. (2008), *The Comfort of Things*, Cambridge: Polity Press.

Nespor, J. and J. Barylske (1991), 'Narrative Discourse and Teacher Knowledge', *American Educational Research Journal*, 28(4): 805–23.

Okely, J. (1996), *Own or Other Culture*, London: Routledge.

O'Reilly, K. (2009), *Key Concepts in Ethnography*, London: Sage Publications.

Passaro, J. (1997), '"You Can't Take the Subway to the Field!": "Village" Epistemologies in the Global Village', in A. Gupta and J. Ferguson (eds), *Anthropological Locations: Boundaries and Grounds of a Field Science*, Berkeley: University of California Press, 147–62.

Rabinow, P. and G. Marcus, with J. Faubion and T. Rees (2008), *Designs for an Anthropology of the Contemporary*, Durham: Duke University Press.

Rapport, N. (1991), 'Writing Fieldnotes: The Conventionalities of Note-Taking and Taking Note in the Field', *Anthropology Today*, 7(1): 10–13.

Silverstone, R., E. Hirsch and D. Morley (1991), 'Listening to a Long Conversation: An Ethnographic Approach to the Study of Information and Communication Technologies in the Home', *Cultural Studies*, 5(2): 204–27.

Stocking, G. (1983), 'The Ethnographer's Magic: Fieldwork in Anthropology from Tylor to Malinowski', in G. Stocking (ed.), *Observers Observed: Essays on Ethnographic Fieldwork, History of Anthropology*, Vol. 1, Madison: University of Wisconsin, 70–120.

Trow, M. (1957), 'Comment on "Participant Observation and Interviewing: A Comparison"', *Human Organization*, 16(3): 33–5.

Warner, M. (1996), *The Inner Eye: Art Beyond the Visible*, National Touring Exhibitions, South Bank Centre.

Wood, P. (1997), 'Ethnography and Ethnology', in T. Barfield (ed.), *The Dictionary of Anthropology*, Malden: Blackwell, 157–60.

–3–

Finding and Mining the Talk: Negotiating Knowledge and Knowledge Transfer in the Field

Lisette Josephides

To Rimbu (1947?–2011)

This chapter reflects on how anthropologists collect, record and analyse field data in the process of creating academic knowledge. Drawing on my ethnographic fieldwork in the New Guinea Highlands, I develop an argument by posing three main questions: First, what do ethnographic techniques of knowledge-transaction intend to elicit? Second, how is knowledge transacted through them? Third, what are the ethical and epistemological implications of subsequent intellectual activity, postfieldwork, that 'mines' the talk and turns the interview into ethnographic and theoretical knowledge with a designated place in the anthropological corpus and beyond?

I start from the premise that ethnography tells a story that is new. Since *ethnography* is the name that anthropologists have given to the coherent and holistic accounts they construct out of their fieldwork, the premise seems reasonable. Classical ethnographies were presented as descriptive practices with substantial 'invention' in terms of theory, contextualization and interpretation. Now ethnographies tend to be seen largely as reflexive practices. In David Stark's coinage (cited in Ong and Collier 2005: 7) *reflexive practices* referred to the practices of managers, who subjected the organizational model of their firm to critical questioning. In the case of the ethnographic monograph, the text itself becomes a reflexive critique of its own foundations, practices and achievements. This stance, unavoidable since the 'critique of representation' challenged anthropological claims of descriptive neutrality (Clifford and Marcus 1986), now extends to the critical reflections of those studied; in my own ethnography I report on how local people consciously reflect on and question their cultural practices (Josephides 2008a). Ethical considerations are an inevitable part of these reflexive practices, as I argue later in this chapter.

In my investigation of the questions that open this chapter I draw on the work of Bernard Williams, an analytic moral philosopher who (unlike many other philosophers) starts his investigation from what *is* rather than what ought to be ((1985)

2006: 198). He warns against the dangers of conceding to abstract ethical theory the monopoly of providing intellectual surroundings for ethical ideas, and proposes instead that we start from a 'concrete sense of a particular ethical life' (Williams (1985) 2006: 197), a social and ethical life that must exist in people's dispositions (201). Some versions of moral philosophy, Williams argues, propagate a false image of how reflection is related to practice ((1985) 2006: 198) when they assume that 'reflection is a process that substitutes knowledge for beliefs attained in unreflective practice' (152). This is the 'objectivist view' that holds that first we believe and then we attain knowledge through reflection. For Williams, by contrast, a particular ethical belief, though itself an object of knowledge at the unreflective level, will 'not yield other ethical truths directly' ((1985) 2006: 154), however much the holder of that belief ('agent') may reflect upon it. This is because *having* those beliefs is what characterizes the agent's life as excellent; and since the beliefs are not about her or his or other people's dispositions or life, but about the social world (Williams (1985) 2006: 154), self-reflection will not add to ethical truths. The fieldwork context I describe in my work, in which Kewa people negotiate their ethical positions in the context of interactions underlined by ethical dispositions, precisely demonstrates Williams's argument.

This striking convergence between Williams's moral philosophy and my ethnographic findings encouraged me to test the similarities further by pairing my three questions on ethnographic techniques and knowledge-transaction with Williams's three hopes (or 'optimistic beliefs') for ethical thought. Though their denotation as 'hopes' expresses their wishful nature, resting on optimistic assumptions, the assumptions become more robust when Williams reveals them to be 'compressed into a belief in three things: in truth, in truthfulness, and in the meaning of an individual life' (Williams (1985) 2006: 198). These hopes have methodological as well as theoretical and analytic implications. I apply them to the different stages of the conversion of fieldwork into ethnography and theory, by linking 'truth' to my first question, 'truthfulness' to my second, and 'individual life' to my third. Thus my three questions, combined with Williams's three optimistic beliefs, look something like this:

First, what are ethnographic techniques and practices of knowledge-transaction intended to elicit? Echoing Williams, I would answer that they seek 'some reflective social knowledge, including history', that commands assent ((1985) 2006: 199)—what ethnographers might call baseline ethnographic data. Though Williams accepts that science is capable of at least objective truth, he insists that it matters more to extend notions of objective truth to this 'social understanding' if our hopes for self-understanding are to be realized ((1985) 2006: 199). This theoretical stance, which takes truth to refer to a sort of negotiated social knowledge, is elaborated through relevant ethnography.

Second, how is knowledge transacted through these ethnographic practices? The ethnographic focus in section 2 is self-narratives. They best exemplify the human dispositions on which, according to Williams, ethical thought rests. Not unlike

Bourdieu's (1977) habitus, these dispositions work by accepting certain ethical statements rather than showing the truth of those statements (Williams (1985) 2006: 199). Consequently, only through reflective living and as the result of a process can one discover how to combine reflection, self-understanding and criticism with truthfulness to a self or society (Williams (1985) 2006: 200). Truthfulness, then, is the ability of a claim about the world to stand up to reflection (Williams (1985) 2006: 199). In the case of ethnography, 'reflection' is an activity carried out both by the ethnographer and the subjects of ethnography. This double reflection is exemplified in the analysis of the self-narratives.

Third, what are the ethical and epistemological implications of postfieldwork intellectual activity, which analyses, synthesizes and writes up the ethnography, seemingly no longer in conjunction with local input? The ethnographic focus in this section is 'virtual returns', the ethnographer's later reflections and realizations, but with continuing attention to the revelations of self-narratives. This focus brings to the fore the primacy of the individual and of personal dispositions (Williams (1985) 2006: 201), thus stressing, with Williams and in line with Abu-Lughod's 'tactile humanism' (1993), the meaning of an individual life for ethical thought. 'Virtual returns' is the argument that the ethnographer may leave the field, but the field never leaves the ethnographer.

The discussion of these three questions is preceded by a brief consideration of two points: the process of being placed in the field and a description of my field techniques.

Being Placed in the Field

Any technique of knowledge in a fieldwork situation has at least this prerequisite: the ethnographer's placement within a local system of relations from which a baseline of shared understandings can be established. All aspiring anthropologists endeavour to achieve this placing, which transforms them from strangers into subjects, persons connected to other local persons, and determines how they are treated. This transformation cannot reasonably be expected of journalists, whose mode of operation is dictated by other considerations. But being placed in the field as an encounter with the other has implications for ethical relations from which journalists are not exempt. The philosopher Levinas (1969) has described how the encounter with the other calls forth the ethical stance in me ('me' standing for ego in Levinas's usage) in an operation familiar to anthropologists, whose ethnographic fieldwork gives rise to a questioning of the tendency to take their own culture for granted (Josephides 2010). But the encounter should not lead to identification. For Levinas alterity is the irreducible difference of the other, and respect for alterity, which language and communication allow us to leave intact, is an essential part of being human (Levinas 1969: 43). The balance between respect and respectful distance can be difficult to achieve for anthropologists.

I first embarked on fieldwork among Kewa speakers in the southern highlands of Papua New Guinea in 1979, using the classical method of participant observation. Papua New Guinea had become an independent nation in 1975 and the astonishing rate of changes experienced by people—political, technological, cultural and religious—was best expressed in the title of a book published by a statesman a little before independence: *One Thousand Years in a Lifetime* (Kiki 1968). On my first exploratory trip to the area Rimbu invited me to live in his village, conferring on me the kinship title of sister and thus creating for me the identity of a situated social self complete with moral and social aspects. (Ricoeur (1981) describes this as appropriation in his discussion of the hermeneutical circle.) Rimbu had made himself my brother, and as a result I was able to make him and other villagers into ethnographic personages. Though Rimbu's action made my stay possible, it did not mean that he and the rest of the villagers now knew how to treat me. On one occasion I heard Rimbu schooling other villagers in how to approach my house:'You shouldn't go right up and knock on the door', he said, 'she might be busy working. Come up and look through the windows first. If she is in the kitchen or in the study, you know she is busy. But if she is just sitting in the big room, knock on the door.'

When Rimbu himself saunters towards the house and looks through the window from a distance, contriving to appear as if he were going somewhere else and just happened to look in, the comical aspects are irrepressible. At the same time he coughs artificially, politely and loudly, quite a feat considering how tricky it is to be polite and loud at the same time. But while he coughs and almost chokes, he is negotiating an appropriate etiquette. Not only is he eliciting information on how to behave correctly in the circumstances; he is also informing me what he means by these antics. Of course, his curiosity and interest in exploring new terrain are already part of an agenda concerned with his own prestige and importance in the community. From Rimbu's point of view I was his recalcitrant as well as his magical sister. (Magical persons in Kewa myths are recalcitrant; they vanish when someone displeases them—see Josephides 1982, 1995, 1998.) A sister is a crucial though not always publicly visible source of wealth. While Rimbu was keen to impart to me the 'objective' knowledge of his culture, and was always ready to mediate with others by using his social and political skills and his extraordinary understanding of human psychology, he was not willing to let me 'go it alone'. When he stayed away to show his displeasure I felt his absence keenly. He was aware that he was a gatekeeper, and I was conscious of the value of his gatekeeping.

Nonetheless, sometimes I resisted what I experienced as Rimbu's forceful attempts to appropriate my very personality by rerouting all my relationships so that they passed through him and taking personal credit for everything I did. Like him, I wanted contradictory things: to be his sister and enjoy his guidance and protection, to benefit from his coaching in how to behave in particular social encounters, to have him keep at bay people I did not wish to see with petitions I did not want to hear; but also to be free to develop independent networks and be an influential woman in my own right. My confidence in my ability to juggle all these wishes and roles was often uncertain, and inevitably Rimbu and I had a few stand-offs.

It may be objected that, as an ethnographer, I was in the field on sufferance and had no right to claims for my own personhood. But the whole basis of my ethical argument is that truth in ethnography is founded on personal relations developed in the field. As Rabinow has argued, the care of the self is an essential aspect of living a moral existence (2003: 10). One cannot neglect one's ethical self if one is to live an ethical life. Moreover, Rabinow describes how, in the case of classical Greece, the care of the self was highly social, being 'oriented from the self outward to others, to things, to events, and then back to the self' (2003: 10). Following this trajectory, Kewa people, probably like people elsewhere, withhold respect for a person who acts without self-respect.

A frequent barometer of my relationship with Rimbu was the water drum I had installed for the villagers' use. Rimbu appropriated this drum from the beginning by fitting it with a padlock which he locked whenever he was angry with them or with me. That way they had to ask him (or me) for water. His action annoyed me; first because I had intended the drum to be a gift to everyone, and second because it became necessary for me to deal with a flow of requests. My discomfort was exactly what Rimbu wanted to achieve, to bring home to me my dependence on his help and protection. As can be seen, my positioning did not give clear guidelines as to how I had been socialized or how I should be treated. Nonetheless, it made me an accepted person with an approved status and support for my fieldwork. From this position I gathered the knowledge that I then wrote up as ethnography.

Field Techniques

Like many other anthropologists, throughout my fieldwork I was in a permanent state of high alert, in thrall to everything I observed and experienced. My response was in part romantic, in part stimulated by my anthropological training and preparation. As I repeat in my writings (e.g. 1985, 2008a,b), I had come to the furthest place on earth, yet nothing there seemed alien to me. My 'training', consisting of reading wonderful ethnographies and accounts of fieldwork (no methods courses being offered in those days), had filled me with excited anticipation. On arrival in the field, the smallest thing seemed to me innately and intensely interesting, meaningful, potentially crucial, and it must be recorded—written down or photographed—before it was lost forever. A frenzied feeling of retrieval gripped me, as if I were experiencing everything for the first and last time. Malinowski (1926) gave us a word for this plenitude that familiarity put at risk of imminent oblivion: *imponderabilia.* All exchanges seemed to me wondrous transactions, containing precious nuggets of knowledge in condensed form. This initial awe of Geertzian (1973) cultural texts (though not then recognized as such) which once analysed can reveal everything about a culture, or Blake's synecdoche of a world in a grain of sand, gradually gave way to Ricoeurian appropriation. Fieldwork disclosed this phenomenological being-in-the-world through relationships that take the ethnographer to understandings beyond those previously held, giving ethnography the form of a projection of the world rather than alienation from it. The projection, nonetheless, is always through a process of objectification, as the ethnography itself is undoubtedly an object (see Josephides 2008a,b).

Having been placed as a member of a family and a clan, my techniques included participant observation (observing people's actions, listening to their talk, asking questions, participating in their lives); interviewing with prepared questionnaires; confidential nightly 'debriefings' with Rimbu; and the collection of life stories. After Carrithers (1992), I call life stories 'maximal narratives' and all the other exchanges 'minimal narratives' (Josephides 2008a,b).

The Kewa people of the New Guinea Highlands are indefatigable verbal negotiators. 'Finding the talk' occupied much of their time, and the pursuit suited my own philological tendencies and fondness for words. In Melanesian Tok Pisin, the lingua franca of the region, 'seeking' and 'finding' are rolled into one. *Mipela painim tok* means 'We are trying to establish what the problem is', or the best way to express it, or to interpret the situation, or to find a solution. 'I'm looking but can't find it' is expressed as *Mi painim tasol nogat* ('I'm searching but it isn't there'), and 'I've found it!' is *Mi painim pinis,* which is also the past tense. When some clansmen on a visit to my clan (the Yala) carried on as usual, not 'coming out with the real meaning' of their talk but instead beating about the bush in metaphoric language, Michael, a Yala man, expressed his frustration in metaphoric speech: 'All the time you talk, it's just like hitting a box; we don't know what's inside.' Michael was 'finding the talk', which the clansmen were then forced to reveal. Several metaphors are at play here: the visiting clansmen were eliciting their hosts' intentions by 'hitting the box', from whose resulting sound they would glean a meaning (what's inside the box); Michael read their pussyfooting as hiding their intentions, the box in this case being the screen for their real words. My own (English) metaphor of 'beating about the bush', meaning a sort of cautious equivocation or prevarication, catches the aspects of the metaphor that allude to 'eliciting talk'.

In these conditions of active meaning-seeking, Kewa local knowledge is constantly negotiated and made explicit through a series of implicit claims expressed both in everyday talk and in life stories (minimal and maximal narratives respectively). For local people seeking to externalize their lives as data for knowledge-transfer, particularly in a changing world, life stories emerged as the best form of extended discourse; for the ethnographer, they provided both content and form for understanding Kewa lives, practices and selves. The three substantive questions will develop these points further.

1. What Do Ethnographic Techniques of Knowledge-transactions Intend to Elicit?

In response to this question, Williams might say that such knowledge-transactions intend to elicit 'truth that reflects social understanding' ((1985) 2006: 199).

Following Williams, I take 'truth' in this context to refer to an account of social knowledge 'that can command unprejudiced assent' ((1985) 2006: 199)—or achieve a degree of reasonable agreement. Ethical theory needs such social understanding for any self-understanding to be realized ((1985) 2006: 199); and ethnography likewise could not exist without its foundation in social knowledge. Ethnographic techniques are intended to elicit knowledge about people's lives, their practices and understandings, as truths that reflect this social understanding. Though it may seem superfluous to construct arguments for the reality of an ethnographic baseline—'the value of observing life as it is lived and recording talk as it is spoken' (Josephides 1998: 139)—it is a necessary corrective to the perspective (often mine) that the ethnographic encounter creates new contexts. Some acts of observation are less constructive than others of what is being observed, and ethnographies also record local discourses that are not concerned with the communicability of the ethnographic process. The truth in this case refers to local social knowledge as it relates to the lived context of those studied, which may include relations with the ethnographer; but it should not pursue lengthy scenarios of the ethnographer's frustrations.

The techniques discussed in this section are 'minimal narratives', especially interviews with prepared questionnaires and Rimbu's nocturnal reports. On the few occasions when I attempted to conduct formal interviews I found myself being interviewed instead and my questions directed back at me. Early on as part of my PhD proposal I developed a basic questionnaire, which I faithfully administered to a few people in the field. Kewa respondents turned every question into a debating point. Rather than give straight answers, they wanted to know first what answers I might give from my own experience back home and then presented their answers in a comparative light, illustrating the differences in our experiences. In response to a question that concerned marital arrangements, Mapi, a local big man with a complex relationship to Rimbu, being at once his 'senior brother' to be emulated and a rival in the big man stakes, attacked me with the following retort: 'Are your wives unsupportive, your children disobedient?' He was insisting on an acknowledgement of a different practical reality between our actual lived experiences, which made our situations incommensurate. Our different living conditions, he assumed, led to different interpersonal, social and political relations. It is important to note that the difference he was stressing was practical, to do with social arrangements, rather than any ontological reason concerning different kinds of persons. These are the realities denoted by Williams's ((1985) 2006) phrase about 'truth that reflects social understanding'; in Mapi's case, a critical awareness of his own practical situation in a 'hypertraditional' society where he can still exercise judgement ((1985) 2006: 142; see also section 3 of this chapter).

What particularly characterized the interviews was that they did not just set up a (momentary) relationship between interviewer and interviewee. They were conducted in full view of others and had local consequences. This public aspect was not the result of a decision on my part but simply the normal way that forms of interaction are conducted in the area, not in conspiratorial privacy but in open debate. As in the case of self-narratives, the public nature of these exchanges inevitably meant that understandings were challenged and negotiated, demonstrating a different interview context from normal journalistic practice. On one occasion following an interview with Mapi's father on traditional and historical warfare, Rimbu insisted on bringing his own father to 'correct' Mapi's father's account, which he claimed was inaccurate. Clearly the question here concerned who had the right to speak and the knowledge from which to speak. More often than not interviews became group debates in which local people staked their own claims and negotiated until they reached a shared understanding, at least for the time.

An important feature of my fieldwork was the state of 'permanent interview' with Rimbu in his end-of-day reports, when he came to my house to give me a full account of his version of what had happened in the village that day. It was 'conversation with a purpose' (Robson 1993: 28), but its purposes were multifaceted and not immediately obvious. Rimbu was quite simply my hotline, my social and cultural broker. He imparted to me aspects of his world with its truth that I came to call social knowledge, long before I had read Williams on social understanding. But he also negotiated power by mediating with others, rather than simply providing information for me. Establishing an ethnographic baseline thus often entailed an evaluation of data offered in competitive storytelling sessions, as the example of Mapi and Rimbu's fathers demonstrated.

Many changes occurred in my relations with people over the long years of my fieldwork. The contexts of our meetings and the dialectics and ethics of knowledge shifted for all of us. On return trips I was treated as a relative who had a right to be there and was addressed as 'auntie' by a generation of adults who were children at the time of my first fieldwork in 1979. The changing nature of ways of life meant that the many ethnographic understandings had to be reestablished and facts and trends assembled anew. But practices of knowledge-transaction were open-ended. Rimbu continued to be my hotline and others continued with their bids to replace him as a matter of personal prestige.

The most remarkable change occurred in 1993, when I returned to the field with Marc Schiltz, my husband and fellow anthropologist. The tables were then turned entirely, and we became the informants to be interviewed. People fell on us like desert nomads on an oasis. Alas, it was a mirage and we could not satisfy them. Though they turned to us full of questions, we did not have the knowledge and wisdom of our 'place' as they had of theirs. Typical questions that exercised people's imagination and stoked their fears concerned space travel, weapons of mass destruction, the Second Coming, and details about the life of Christ. It was difficult to ignore the heightened levels of religious activity. 'We're always in church', people would say, 'we never rest [*Mipela ino save malolo*]'. When they asked what Christ looked like they were bewildered and dismayed by my response that they could imagine him any way they liked. 'What do you mean, we can imagine Christ any way we want? He came from *your* country; you should know what he looked like. We have no means of imagining him.' There was anger at the suggestion that there is a plane of knowledge where actual realities can be treated as less than real or even interchangeable. According to Kewa villagers, the question concerned a truth that was not their truth in terms of how things actually were.

Two general points can be made with regard to how knowledge was transacted through the interviews. First, as elicitations of knowledge, they took off and resisted the interviewer's concerns. Second, people transacted their own business through them; the interviews had local consequences. One clear conclusion to be drawn from my experience was that I did not control the interview and more generally that I did not control the process of knowledge-acquisition in the field. (This may be the experience of any interviewer; see chapter 1, this volume.) I could not decide what knowledge to acquire, or even recognize what 'knowledge' actually was, without direction from local knowledge-brokers. Nonetheless, it was possible to establish an ethnographic baseline for which there was general assent, although this had to be negotiated through different accounts and its understandings were never final. Local knowledge, far from being taken for granted, was constantly negotiated and made explicit through a series of implicit claims not entirely unlike academic reasoning or polemic (cf. Geertz's 1983 account of local knowledge).

2. How Is Knowledge Transacted through Ethnographic Self-narratives?

While the interviews of the previous section were usually held on the village green, self-narratives were told in my house. The difference in venue did not make them more private, as hordes of people crammed into my house, including children keen for a share of the food I always served. Interlopers also contributed their comments; while one person told her life story inside the house, another responded in agreement or disagreement from the other side of the bamboo wall. People addressed each other through their stories, creating social knowledge through negotiation and reflection while staking their own claims. I welcomed the stories without a thought to how I might use them. In contrast to the narrators, I had no agenda. But when I read the stories much later I found that they fell naturally into three groupings: those of older people, those of middle-aged people, and those of younger married people.

Older people gave their stories as a cultural gloss for how the Kewa in general live, thus elevating themselves to the status of moral persons living the exemplary life (Josephides 2008a: 78–9). By contrast, the stories of younger married people were metanarratives—reflective narratives that no longer took a representative moral personhood for granted (Josephides 2008a: 144), but instead showed how they grappled with a changed world in attempts to establish moral personhood by resisting the alienating effects of an imposed legal and political system. Rimbu's story in particular demonstrated what it meant to be heroic in this context: placing oneself at the centre of the world as it was experienced and attempting to take charge (Josephides 2008a: 137). In a picaresque tale of plantation travel now standing for initiation, Rimbu takes control by counselling against violence at the breakout of a fight and is then consulted solicitously by the magistrate on the severity of the sentence just passed on him. Though in reality the power of self-determination has passed out of the hands of villagers and onto national government structures, villagers empower themselves in these accounts which, at the local level, begin the work of refashioning them as people with a role to play in the modern world.

As word of my interest in collecting life narratives spread, villagers began to turn up at my house prepared to tell their stories. I took notes in longhand and the narrators thoughtfully paused to allow me to complete my writing. As a rule I did not prompt, but asked questions when part of the narrative was unclear or revealed rich veins to be mined. These were 'conversations with a purpose' (Robson 1993) but little privacy. (Only Lari's story was told confidentially; generally women's narratives were restricted to female participation.) Interruptions, promptings and challenges came from other villagers, who turned the narrations into collaborative endeavours for describing experiences to which they were all exposed. The narratives were negotiations among people about the meaning of their lives, but also competitive claims about the truth and meaning of what really had happened.

From a reading of the narratives (in Josephides 2008a) one can readily see that they are themselves reflections on the lives and worlds of the people who tell them. Rimbu and Lari, husband and wife, told the most poignant stories. Lari's story is especially dramatic, beginning with her adventures as a sixteen-year-old, when her father pulled her out of school to marry her off. She first ran to the priest and asked to be baptized, but he was prevailed upon to defer her baptism until after she was married—when her hope had been that it would delay marriage, which she was even prepared to take the veil to avoid. But her real wish was to continue in school. So she ran from relative to relative, as each of them either supported or betrayed her, until eventually the inevitable came about. As Lari's own account is graphically detailed, I give below my summing up of her sentiments in my words.

> Lari's young life opens on a landscape of exciting promise, which the threat of marriage cruelly shatters. She recalls the events surrounding this period with doom-laden precision. Forlorn and frustrated, she escapes into the dark, elemental bush, lashed by torrential rain, her every return to the domestic sphere endangering her anew. She breaks the cross in an act of defiance, but also to symbolise her cloven self—being promised one life and delivered into another. Rather than being chosen by God, she is abandoned by his priest. (Josephides 2008a: 139)

Reflecting on that world, Lari, as she tells her story, remarks how hard a woman's life is, punctuated by constant childbirth. With the benefit of hindsight she reflects on her own life critically, and her part in it as the active part of a person who is never duped, but is always in control, even when overpowered.

A major function of all the narratives was to organize lives retrospectively, integrating experience into memory as consciousness. Because a life story is never the story of one person but entangles many lives together, thus speaking and making claims for others, it has moral implications. As modes of communication, the stories exchange experiences of practical wisdom, make claims, seek approval and feedback. In telling them, people are offering up their descriptions or claims about the world to general scrutiny and reflection. The thick ethical concepts that Williams discusses are found in them all as transformations (or versions) of the paradigmatic Kewa lives appearing in the narratives of the older generation. As mentioned earlier, truthfulness for Williams rested in human dispositions to accept certain ethical statements—'thick ethical concepts'—rather than in showing the truth of those statements ((1985) 2006: 199). The word *thick* should not be confused with Geertz's 'thick description' (Geertz 1973), which refers to accounts that seek to refine and deepen their interpretations by explaining context as well as behaviour. Here 'thick' denotes the more general or basic orientation of a disposition. This understanding is in line with the negotiated truthfulness of the eliciting strategies that I encountered in Kewa exchanges, where the question is whether a certain claim is acceptable until it is 'unseated' by another. As Williams puts it, all claims in principle are 'open to being unseated by reflection', but are honoured until that time, and for that reason their claim to truth cannot reasonably be denied ((1985) 2006: 200). Though the reflection that concerns me here is in the intentionality that underlies the eliciting and negotiating strategies of the people whose lives are being described, it goes without saying that the ethnographer is always expected to reflect deeply on the knowledge that is being transacted.

The understanding I gained of the Kewa owed less to my interpretation of their interviews or life stories, and more to the attention I paid to what the people themselves were doing through their self-narratives and other accounts. They elicited knowledge that resisted the ethnographer's concerns and served as arenas for people to transact their own business. Williams's requirement that truthfulness to an existing self or society must be 'combined with reflection, self-understanding, and criticism', and furthermore that it can be discovered only through reflective living and as the result of a process ((1985) 2006: 199–200), is met in the Kewa case, as Lari and Rimbu's stories illustrate. People here genuinely expose to scrutiny their claims about their world and their place in it in earnest attempts to establish viable ethical answers to questions that plague their changed world. As readers and observers, we become aware of how social knowledge is created and made explicit in these narratives.

3. What Are the Implications of Turning Fieldwork into Ethnographic and Theoretical Knowledge?

This section considers the ethical and epistemological implications of the intellectual activity, postfieldwork, that turns its findings into ethnographic and theoretical knowledge, transforming local knowledge into anthropological knowledge (Crandall 2008). I argue that the understandings gained in the field, in combination with the relations developed there, continue to influence subsequent activity that analyses, synthesizes and writes up the ethnography. Once found, the 'talk' is 'mined' through 'virtual returns', 'fieldwork recollected in tranquillity' (Josephides 2008b) and including a catalogue of materials and activities: rereading of fieldnotes and diaries and songs and poems, listening to tape recordings, looking at photographs and watching videos, studying language materials, gazing at artefacts, recalling unrecorded memories and mental snapshots and other imponderabilia, experiencing emotions and having dreams. As I review my materials and reexperience fieldwork, events appear in a completed state, capturing the beginning and end of a process and thus acquiring a systematic structure. Virtual returns remove the depth and uncertainty of time, though they are beset with the uncertainties of interpretation.

In addition to virtual returns, two related points suggest the continuing input from the field context: the quality of the material and the relevance of an individual life.

By 'quality of the material' I mean the kind of material it is in terms of its meaning for those whose life it makes up; how they use it to construct and give meaning to their world; and the qualities that act as constraints in the way it could be 'mined' for meaning by the anthropologist. As mentioned in section 2, my ethnographic accounts often revealed how much the findings I recorded went against my inclinations and my intellectual expectations. This gave the accounts, which had survived my prejudice, the character of 'evidence rather than argument' (Carrithers 1992: 170). They became 'a sort of common property' (Carrithers 1992: 170), not observations which I could easily shape into neat ethnographic accounts but insistent data that could not be ignored. These insights helped me, away from the field, to develop and understand my own material; they also described the eliciting strategies of local people's strategies, which served as public verifications or corrections of their claims.

This leads to the second point, of the relevance of the meaning of an individual life, which Williams believes is crucial to ethical thought if it is to stand up to reflection. People's self-narratives, and the way they use them to negotiate understandings, show how robustly they stand up to reflection. We can glimpse here the relevance of 'an individual life' (Williams (1985) 2006) for the construction of an ethnography as something new. Encouraged by these narrative exchanges, people constructed new lives and new selves.

A distinction should be made between the changed consciousness of the ethnographer and that of the local narrators. Though I record a change of consciousness in them in relation to their culture, in that they no longer think of themselves as possessing a representative Kewa moral personhood (Josephides 2008a: 144), this change was not induced or produced by my invitation to tell their stories. Rather, it was a response to the larger changes in their world of which I was a small part and sometimes a mere representative. Conversely, the changes in my consciousness were directly caused by my relations with the Kewa people and their stories. Far from finding a ready-made theoretical framework for understanding my fieldwork in my prior philosophical studies, my interest in phenomenology developed in that encounter.

During the fieldwork and writing-up stages, the 'text' is what the ethnographer observes and interacts with, the culture as it is lived. The ethnography is the hermeneutical interpretation which, once written, becomes a text open to further interpretation by others. Ricoeur defines explication as being midway between construction and description, and this is what the ethnographic monograph offers (1981: 126). As ethnographers we do not appropriate an alien experience, or even the culture of the people, so that we may invent it or them (pace Malinowski 1926); what we make our own is a projection of the world, a mode of being-in-the-world that our fieldwork discloses. For the ethnographer, who has internalized it, this is a complete world, though it may be kept as an internalized pocket in time.

The written ethnography, constructed from interviews, life narratives, observations and virtual returns, also becomes part of a library that invents identities which confront people as reifications of what they are. It is always in danger of becoming part of the corpus that Mudimbe (1988) termed *the colonial library*, which distorts, alienates and expropriates by describing colonized people as constituted by a knowledge that objectifies them. But it may also allow people's stories to communicate as lived narratives with wider relevance. My hope is that beyond the Kewa context their ethnography, constructed with their active and vital participation, may bring to life the interplay between personal strategies and social meanings and the necessity to retain a vigilant watch over our own self-presentation and treatment by others. When I wrote that the Kewa use narratives to 'exchange experiences of practical wisdom, to make claims and to seek feedback' (Josephides 2008a: 222), this statement did not arise simply from Kewa ethnography as a locally specific observation. It was a general statement that reflected my expanded insight into the ethnography resulting from all the 'returns', both actual and virtual.

The conclusion I draw in this section is that ethnography—understood as the amalgam constructed from observation, interviews and life stories—tells a story that is new. This point does not contradict the argument in section 1, which insisted on the reality of an ethnographic baseline. The fieldwork encounter creates new contexts, but primarily it is a vehicle for new understandings by disclosing a mode of being-in-the-world. Its openness allows nuanced expressions and interpretations, from the anthropologist and the local people, and negotiated meanings can be seen in the strategies of both. The text constructed on the basis of all these field techniques is a reflection—it reflects upon—a practice in the field. It is always a process of objectification, being an object. That is how ethnography can be true, truthful and reflect the meaning of an individual life.

Being grounded in the accounts of the meanings of individual lives, my analysis of people's self-narratives demonstrates the further claims made by Williams—that the continuing possibility of a meaningful individual life does not reject society, though the content of the dispositions (as depositories or containers for social or ethical life) differs between societies ((1985) 2006: 201). With this argument Williams accounts for cultural differences, but also leaves room for underlying universals. The last point is fleshed out in his discussion of an imagined 'hypertraditional' society whose 'thick ethical concepts'—embedded in culture and everyday beliefs and practices and normally the basis of action—'track the truth' by leaving local people free to replace a judgement not supported by practical or empirical circumstances ((1985) 2006: 142–4).

Conclusion

Williams argues that the modern tension in ethics is between reflection and practice ((1985) 2006: 137). The same can be said of the ethnographic text: it is a reflection on practice and experience in the field, and reflection always makes something other of practice and experience than they were in an unreflected form. The question of 'truth' arises in that transformation. Insofar as ethnography is more than the recording of the actions, words and practices of those who are the subject of study, how can it be justified, legitimated and confirmed in its 'truth' value? Williams's three hopes for ethical thought provided a template for investigating the extent to which the ethnography is 'true': that it reflects social knowledge, that it stands up to reflection, and that it takes into account the meaning of an individual life. Ethical theory, Williams concludes, cannot do without social knowledge, and 'truth' here refers to an understanding of this condition while complying with it. The truth of ethnography can be related to the points Williams makes, but also depends on the quality of the relationship.

During my fieldwork, interviews and the collection of life stories were a series of translations at different levels, involving three languages (Kewa, Tok Pisin, English), three generations and several knowledge-brokers. Because these transactions could never be entirely one to one or confidential, they had local consequences beyond the relationship between interviewer and interviewee. As elicitations of knowledge they constantly pulled away from the ethnographer's express concerns, eventually transforming those concerns. People turned them into debates for staking claims and negotiating understandings among themselves, speaking past the ethnographer who became the pretext or even the facilitator for these exchanges. This shift in perspective was not immediate, but occurred as part of the process of appropriation described by Ricoeur.

For Rapport (all references from chapter 1, this volume) the interview is a hybrid form, a mode of social interaction whose 'restricted code'—as 'nonroutine, purposive and bounded'—allows it to elaborate on what is not yet known and is not conventionally expressed. As a 'mini-relationship' it works by means of a 'dialectic or incremental zigzag' that is 'reciprocal, complementary, collaborative, emergent, or distorted'. Rapport concludes, following an interview with a man whose utterances were strongly guided by his own 'purposiveness', that the interviewee could be said to be conducting an interview with himself, with the ethnographer as the audience.

Rapport's characterization of the interview as a kind of snapshot of the workings of everyday exchange, on which it simultaneously shines a light, can be extended to Kewa people's exchanges among themselves. The ethnographer is the facilitator on these occasions, acting as host and caterer for the storytellers whom she has invited to tell their stories. But each individual storyteller is not conducting an interview with herself or himself, as in Rapport's account; rather, they are all negotiating understandings with one another. Though it would be too much to claim that Rimbu's 'main talking-partner was himself', to some extent he *was* conducting an internal conversation, in which we 'glimpse the tensions, the distance, between forms and meanings', and the distortions, and always the desire to enable the formal niceties of exchange to continue (Rapport, Chapter 1, this volume).

My field techniques have included participant observation, conversations (with a purpose), interviews of varying degrees of formality, nightly reports (with a purpose?) from a major gatekeeper and life stories. Following my discussion, what can be said about the interview and its place in the ethnography? My work suggests that the interview is a flexible tool that does not have to be defined by journalistic standards, whether in terms of form, content or ethics. Formal or informal, structured or unstructured, with or without the element of group dynamics, it is always transformed by the interviewees as something for their own use. They taught me, the ethnographer, to downplay my role in the interpretation of the materials, especially when 'virtual returns' suggested that anthropologists never really leave the field and are incapable of writing their ethnography without its pull. From this perspective fieldwork may be seen as a permanent interview, forcing anthropologists to listen and pursue knowledge in a particular way. This means that the most rounded accounts result from many different forms of data collection—a comment reminiscent of Lévi-Strauss's claim about the necessity to collect different versions of one myth, when each version is seen as a mirror showing a different part of a room that can be viewed only through the mirrors arranged within it (1963: 217).

References

Abu-Lughod, L. (1993), *Writing Women's Worlds*, Berkeley: University of California Press.

Bourdieu, P. (1977), *Outline of a Theory of Practice*, Cambridge: Cambridge University Press.

Carrithers, M. (1992), *Why Humans Have Cultures*, Oxford: Oxford University Press.

Clifford, J. and G. Marcus (eds) (1986), *Writing Culture*, Berkeley: University of California Press.

Crandall, D. (2008), 'The Transformation of Indigenous Knowledge into Anthropological Knowledge: Whose Knowledge Is It?', in N. Halstead, E. Hirsch and J. Okely (eds), *Knowing How to Know: Fieldwork and the Ethnographic Present*, EASA Series 9, Oxford: Berghahn Books, 38–54.

Geertz, C. (1973), *The Interpretation of Culture*, New York: Basic Books.

Geertz, C. (1983), *Local Knowledge: Further Essays in Interpretive Anthropology*, New York: Basic Books.

Josephides, L. (1982), 'Kewa Stories and Songs', Special Issue, *Oral History*, 10(2).

Josephides, L. (1985), *The Production of Inequality*, London: Tavistock.

Josephides, L. (1995), 'Replacing Cultural Markers', in D. de Coppet and A. Iteanu (eds), *Cosmos and Society in Oceania*, Oxford: Berg, 189–211.

Josephides, L. (1998), 'Biologies of Social Action: Excessive Portraits', in V. Keck (ed.), *Common Worlds and Single Lives: Constituting Knowledge in Pacific Societies*, Oxford: Berg, 137–67.

Josephides, L. (2008a), *Melanesian Odysseys*, Oxford: Berghahn Books.

Josephides, L. (2008b), 'Virtual Returns: Fieldwork Recollected in Tranquillity', in L. Chua, C. High and T. Lau (eds), *How Do We Know? Evidence, Ethnography, and the Making of Anthropological Knowledge*, Newcastle: Cambridge Scholars, 179–200.

Josephides, L. (2010), 'Cosmopolitanism as the Existential Condition of Humanity', in N. Rapport and H. Wardle (eds), 'A Cosmopolitan Anthropology', Special Issue, *Social Anthropology*, 18(4): 389–95.

Kiki, A. M. (1968), *One Thousand Years in a Lifetime: A New Guinea Autobiography*, Melbourne: F. W. Cheshire. (Recorded by Ulli Beier).

Levinas, E. (1969), *Totality and Infinity*, Pittsburgh: Duquesne University Press.

Lévi-Strauss, C. (1963), *Structural Anthropology*, Vol. 1, New York: Basic Books.

Malinowski, B. (1926), *The Argonauts of the Western Pacific*, London: Routledge.

Mudimbe, V. (1988), *The Invention of Africa: Gnosis, Philosophy, and the Order of Knowledge*, Bloomington: Indiana University Press

Ong, A. and S. Collier (2005), 'Global Assemblages, Anthropological Problems', in A. Ong and S. Collier (eds), *Global Assemblages: Technology, Politics, and Ethics as Anthropological Problems*, Oxford: Blackwell, 4–21.

Rabinow, P. (2003), *Anthropos Today*, Princeton: Princeton University Press.

Ricoeur, P. (1981), *Hermeneutics and the Human Sciences*, ed. and trans. J. Thompson, London and Paris: Cambridge University Press and Editions de la Maison des Sciences de l'Homme.

Robson, C. (1993), *Real World Research*, Oxford: Blackwell.

Williams, B. ((1985) 2006), *Ethics and the Limits of Philosophy*, London: Routledge.

Part II
Interview Techniques

–4–

The Autobiographical Narrative Interview: A Potential Arena of Emotional Remembering, Performance and Reflection

Maruška Svašek and Markieta Domecka

Introduction

This chapter critically explores the autobiographical narrative method developed by German sociologist Fritz Schütze.[1] We argue that the methodology can uncover domains of psychosocial experience that may be hard to reveal using other interviewing techniques. The method includes a close analysis of interview transcriptions, distinguishing particular textual, performative and affective dimensions of self-narration. It can provide valuable insights into the ways in which personal experiences and emotional trajectories, partially shaped by kinship dynamics, socioeconomic and political processes, can influence identity development and the formation of life attitudes.[2] As will become clear in this chapter, the method also frequently generates a useful reflective space for interviewees, allowing them to express, communicate and work through painful or confusing past experiences. This is less likely to happen using structured and semi-structured interview techniques, where frequent questions by the interviewer can hamper a process of deep inner reflection.

Emotional remembering in the autobiographical interview context can be experienced by narrators as a potentially transformative process. New insights can be generated through 'biographical work', understood as

> reflection about alternative interpretations of one's life course tendencies, self-critical attempts of understanding one's own misconceptions of oneself and self-chosen or self-erected impediments, assessment of the impediments superimposed by others and by structural conditions, [and] imagining future courses of life that support the overall gestalt of the unfolding biographical identity. (Schütze 2008a: 6)

The analysis will take a processual approach to subjectivity, regarding individuals as dynamic thinking and feeling bodies who experience and project changing, at times contradictory, notions of self. Moving through space and time, people commonly face familiar and new situations, experience loving and hostile environments and deal with conflicting loyalties and demands. Negotiating, improvising, experimenting and adapting, they take on contextually specific identities, emphasizing and underplaying particular aspects of their being; they may also be forced into unwanted positions, a process that, in extreme circumstances, can cause deep traumas. As will become clear in this chapter, when asked to talk about their lives, ambiguities around self and specific others may appear in autobiographical accounts and are sometimes addressed by autobiographical narrators through reflective argumentation. Evaluative processes of subjectivity may create temporarily integrating perspectives of existential wholeness (Ewing 1990: 261), and can feed self-conscious decisions about future actions (cf. Cohen 1994).

Schütze's biographical method, used in the analysis in this chapter, provides clearly defined instructions regarding the autobiographical storytelling process. Interviewees are asked to choose a location for the interview to assure that they feel at ease. In our experience, the interview itself takes normally between one and two hours. The lead up to it and unrecorded communication afterwards can give additional clues about interviewees' self-perception and needs to be included in the analysis. Commonly, interviewees have not previously practised telling their life stories. While certain passages will have been told and retold prior to the interview, unless someone is trained to do so, it is virtually impossible to reproduce a prepared, well-rehearsed script of the whole life history. As a result, narrators can surprise themselves, addressing issues they had not planned or expected to discuss.

Before the interview starts, the interviewer explains the general theme of the research but points out that, in telling his or her life story, the interviewee may mention anything that has made him or her into the person he or she is today. Crucially, interviewees are told that they may take as long as they feel is necessary to tell their story. During the first phase of the autobiographical narrative interview, the interviewer does not intervene in the narration and provides only limited, mostly nonverbal, responses. Once the interviewee indicates that the story is finished (this narrative fragment is called a 'coda'), the interview moves to a second stage, when some additional questions concerning the interviewee's biography are asked in reaction to themes the narrator has brought up in the first phase of the narration. During the third and last phase, the researcher asks about motives for certain decisions and poses more explicit questions relating to the theme of the research project.

To distil a metanarrative of dynamic subjectivity from interview material, the life story is transcribed in detail. Various text features are distinguished, including different communicative schemes of presentation (narration, argumentation and description), silences, hesitations and passages that mark the beginning and ending of the segments of the story. These are regarded as important ordering principles that can throw light on the dynamics of self-perception, self-projection, personal experience and transformation. (Table 4.1 provides an explanation of some transcription signs.) Autobiographical narrators are also challenged by three types of constraints

Table 4.1 Transcription Notation

Transcription Notation	***Description***
-ehm-, -hmm-	Hesitation marks.
. . . and . . .	Shorter pauses.
((pause 2s))	Longer pauses.
((smiling)); ((laughing)); ((coughing)); ((crying))	Nonverbal expressions.
(ironically till *)	Changes of tone: the point where the tone changes (*).
(fair?)	a word or expression which can't be easily recognized.
It was <u>*really*</u> important.	Emphasis.
It was pos#	Interruptions.
You- you need to be aware	Repetitions.

that force speakers to order their narratives, namely the need to condense, to go into details and to close textual forms (Schütze 2008a: 16). The need to condense refers to the impossibility to 'tell everything'; the narrator is driven to tell only what is relevant to the overall meaning of the story. The constraint to go into details means that narrated events have to be linked to other events that, in the view of the narrator, belong to the same chain of experience. This implies that the narrator often needs to explain more than initially intended about certain issues. The constraint to close textual forms leads narrators to make finishing statements about past events before moving on to accounts of other events, potentially making new connections. The three constraints are in competition during autobiographic storytelling; only when stories have been told repeatedly can the succession of narrated events be harmonized and polished (Schütze 2008a).

This chapter focusses on self-narratives by two migrant women, conducted as part of a large research project on identity formation in Europe,[3] who at the time of the interviews resided and worked in the United Kingdom. The first interview was conducted by Maruška Svašek with a Dutch woman of Dutch-Surinamese descent who had moved to the United Kingdom. The second interview was conducted by Markieta Domecka with a Polish woman who had also migrated to Britain. The two interviews were selected because of interesting similarities and differences. Both women dealt with difficult relationships and had to negotiate a place for themselves as migrants in the United Kingdom. Premigration emotional discourses, practices and embodied feelings that had shaped earlier identification processes continued to affect their postmigration subjectivity (cf. Svašek, forthcoming). An examination of the ways in which the women used contrast sets, a common feature in autobiographical narratives, and the ways in which the three previously mentioned constraints shaped their storytelling sheds light on these dynamics.

Situating Schütze's Approach

This section discusses various approaches to biographical interviewing, situating Schütze's approach in a wider methodological field. First, a distinction can be made between realist and constructivist understandings of biography. Within the realist approach, represented by Daniel Bertaux (1981, 2003), J. P. Roos (2000) and others, biography is treated as an integral part of social reality directly reflecting people's thoughts, plans and actions. According to Schütze, however, the assumption that narratives would simply mirror social and personal reality leads to misunderstanding regarding the empirical grounding of biographical analysis (Schütze 2008a: 12).

The second approach treats biographical narrations as pure constructions; it is assumed that biographical accounts can be freely made up and changed depending on the ongoing situations of presentation. Constructivists argue that narratives are performances fully dependent on the interview situation and certain characteristics of the interviewer, such as gender, age and cultural background. While the impact of researchers on fieldwork dynamics cannot be denied (Bryman 2001; Bryman and Burgess 1999; Burgess 1991; Domecka, forthcoming; Szlachcicowa et al. 2006), the more extreme constructionist view deprives autobiographical narration of its pivotal epistemic power (cf. Schütze 2008a: 12). It is of course important to acknowledge that autobiographical narration has a performative dimension. Life stories are at least partially consciously staged and directed, as both narrator and investigator look for moral lessons and a sense of coherence (cf. Chamberlayne et al. 2000; Miller 2005). According to Schütze, however, autobiographical storytelling 'should not be seen just as a freewheeling and flexible course of textual invention of the narrator' as crucial life experiences that have shaped people's psychological make-up cannot but influence the deep structure of the narrative (2008a: 14). As Margaret Archer similarly argued, we are not subjectively free to make what we want of the past, constructing our biographies along story lines as we please. 'We bring to the present the objective results of our previous commitments. The "deposited" features are real and impose serious limitations upon narrative freedom because any re-telling of the past has to account for them' (Archer 2003: 126).

Fritz Schütze began developing the autobiographical method in the 1970s. It is in numerous ways different to the biographic-narrative-interpretive method (BNIM), a method established and popularized in the British context by Tom Wengraf and Prue Chamberlayne in the 1990s. As the technique of interviewing is quite similar in both approaches—first there is a self-governed storytelling uninterrupted by the interviewer which is then, after the coda, followed by internal and external questions—the analytical procedures are slightly different. In comparison to Schütze's method, BNIM is less focussed on the sociolinguistic textual structures of the biographical interview. Following the work of Gabrielle Rosenthal, the latter makes a distinction between *lived life* and *told story.* In Schütze's approach, by contrast, the emphasis is put on the identification of 'process structures' (individual and institutional action schemes, trajectories of suffering and metamorphoses) that are thought to generate insights and enable understanding. In this chapter, the analysis of fragments from two autobiographical narratives will identify some of these process structures.

Limitations: Short-term Interaction, Specific Assumptions, Ethics

Before presenting the analysis, some of the method's restrictions must be addressed. The first deals with the relative brevity of the research encounter. Limiting one's methodology to autobiographical narration alone, as is especially common in sociology (cf. Bertaux 1981; Chamberlayne et al. 2000; Humphrey et al. 2003), means that researchers meet interviewees only once or twice, interacting for a few hours as the autobiographical story is told. While such brief encounters frequently result in highly elaborate autobiographical stories that generate useful insights, the approach lacks the advantage of long-term ethnographic fieldwork. In the latter case, researchers spend weeks, months or even years in specific communities or visit and revisit individual informants throughout a substantial period of their lives. Lengthy and frequent interactions in the field provide plenty of opportunities to use a variety of research methods, from participant observation through informal chats to semi-structured and structured interviews (Bryman 2001; Burgess 1991). Evidently, a long-term multimethod approach produces a perspective on people that strongly differs from the autobiographical perspective; while in the latter case, individuals are portrayed as narrators who try to make sense of their individual life trajectories, in the former, they are framed as active beings-in-the-world, engaging in different types of sociality in different times and places.

A second problem stems from the fact that the task of autobiographical narration may not make sense to people unfamiliar with performative genres of one-to-one self-disclosure, so may be entirely inappropriate and unproductive in certain settings (cf. Tonkin 1992). The method also projects specific assumptions about the process of interpersonal communication and about selfhood as the focus of reflective narration and the construction of the protagonist (see Moretti 1987). Having used the methods in various projects, we have noticed that people who have direct or indirect knowledge of counselling practices, those with an interest in family history and migrants who have had to suddenly adjust to different life situations and have conceptualized their lives in terms of chapters 'before' and 'after' migration have tended to find it easier to respond to the task than other groups. There may also be personal reasons for why some interviewees find it easier to tell their story; some are simply more talkative than others, and others may find easier rapport with a particular interviewer because of shared gender, ethnic background or for other personal reasons. We have both been confronted with situations in which informants found it hard to engage in a monologue and demanded to be asked specific questions. While the method did not really work in such situations, these occasions stimulated our reflection on the requirements posed on the narrators and the conditions facilitating and impeding autobiographical narration.

A third problem has to do with research ethics. As is common practice in social science research, autobiographical narrators are always assured anonymity (Driessen 1998; Spradley and Rynkiewich 1976); yet the nature of the produced data, consisting of detailed information about a person's life course, challenges the idea that anonymity can be easily guaranteed. An additional ethical problem stems from the rather particular emotional dynamics of autobiographical rendering, where painful memories may come up, sometimes quite unexpectedly. Interviewees may not just remember but also reexperience past suffering (Svašek 2008), and may feel uncomfortable when they are unable to suppress intense feelings in the interview situation (Kaźmierska (2004) 2005). While the option of withdrawing at any time from the research is always given prior to the interview, the risk of unwelcome emotional discomfort cannot be fully avoided.

With regard to our own use of the method, we have dealt with these problems as follows. Concerning the problem of short-term interaction, we selected our informants with care. We were both familiar with the migrant communities of our interviewees (MS being a Dutch migrant and MD being of Polish descent), and MS had known her interviewee for a number of years. As adult women brought up in European urban environments, both interviewees were familiar with narrative genres of self-development, and assured us after the interviews that they had willingly shared their stories. We anonymized the narratives, leaving out and changing various details. When both women cried during their accounts, we showed empathy and told them that they could stop the interview session and withdraw from the project altogether. We took the time to have lighter conversation after the end of the recording, and rang them the day after the interview, checking how they felt and making sure that they were still happy for us to use the material.

Meeting Loes

I (MS) first met Loes in 2003 in Bridgetown when participating in an event organized by Bridgetown's Association of Dutch Migrants. She had been the main drive behind the establishment of the organization and took a very active role during the event, welcoming the public and leading the singing of the Dutch anthem. She was very confident and laughed easily, and seemed to be a sociable person with a bubbly personality. Her performance and involvement with the association suggested strong identification with her Dutch background and a keen interest in Dutch national traditions. Reflecting the multiethnic composition of the Dutch population, her light brown skin colour showed that she was of mixed descent.

In 2008, having met her on several occasions during the previous five years, I asked her if she would be willing to cooperate in autobiographical life story research for a project on migrants who had moved from one EU state to another. She happily agreed. When I rang her to make the appointment, she promised she would make me lunch and asked whether I drank cappuccino. A few days later, I approached a large, free-standing house situated in the countryside. Loes opened the door with a smile, dressed in a colourful flowery top. I kissed her and her husband Jan three times on their cheeks, laughing about this Dutch tradition. Loes prepared the meal and served me coffee, and when I said that 'this must be the promised cappuccino', Jan remarked with an ironic tone in his voice, 'Did she send you a list?' With an apologetic tone of voice, Loes explained that, as she was such a busy (*druk*) person, she was forced to make structured plans and to-do lists. She commented that all that planning had positive and negative sides. 'You can do a lot'; 'I get confused when things go differently as planned'; 'I need to be in control'; but 'planning everything means that you are not flexible or open for sudden change'. As will become clear, her preinterview remarks alluded to a personal need to deal with deeply rooted feelings of insecurity and nonbelonging that were expressed and commented upon in the autobiographical account that followed.

Dealing with Mixed Descent

While we had spoken in our mother tongue before the start of the interview, we decided to switch to English for the sake of the recording. Although her command of the language was not perfect, she felt comfortable using it. Only occasionally, when looking for a word, did we switch back to Dutch.

In Loes's story, the urge to work through difficult issues came out in three major narrative themes that wove through her two-hour account. In order of appearance, the first concerned her mixed parental background; the second her difficult relation with her father; and the third, ambiguous feelings about her skin colour. Loes explained that she had had a Dutch father who had met her Hindustani mother in Suriname, where he had been stationed as military officer in the late 1940s. At the time, Suriname was a Dutch colony. In 1950, the couple decided to settle in the Netherlands, where Loes had been born. Loes talked about her mixed ethnic background in terms of tensions, dualities and contradictions. She started off saying that her paternal grandparents had not agreed with their son's marriage because his wife of choice had been 'a *real* Surinamese' (i.e. not white) and was therefore 'lower class'. Their perception of their daughter-in-law had of course been strongly influenced by racist colonialist discourse based on evolutionist assumptions.

Loes and her siblings, who grew up in the Netherlands in the 1950s and 1960s, faced a dualistic upbringing. In Loes's words, their parents had decided that their children should become 'as Dutch as possible' and should not be 'brought up with [Surinamese] culture'. They 'always kept the Surinamese language as a secret language' and cooked Dutch food, 'potatoes'. She had, however, still been raised 'partly

Surinamese and partly Dutch'; friends of her mum introduced her to Surinamese food, and her parents promoted 'Asian family values', which meant that she felt differed from her Dutch friends. It is important to note that her parents' notion of Surinamese culture was strongly influenced by an elitist colonialist vision of 'being cultured'. In her self-narrative, she used contrast sets to oppose, compare and evaluate habits instilled by her parents. Ambiguously framed as an example that was both 'important' and 'maybe funny', the following interview fragment alludes to the impact her parents' rules had on her social and emotional habitus, ingraining a sense of 'good behaviour' but also producing deeply felt resistance.

Loes (L): ((swallowing)) But we can see /ehm/ ((swallowing))—with my parents—I give you, oh I would give you some example how we have been raised up, that is important\ this is important and maybe funny\. /Ehm/ ((slow)) my dad and mum had special rules on how to lay the table down.

Maruška (M): Yeah.

L: We all had our own cutlery—all different—(((reporting))) '*don't* make a mistake, *don't* accidentally—use my dad knife and fork or', and there's all little signs (and) you know exactly, but they had also their own cups/.

M: -Mm hmm-.

L: 'Don't make a mistake with that', they would be so cross. Then we have table manners, were quite strict. We were not allowed, and a funny thing is, I raised my, I, I always thought#

M: #-mm-.

L: And always...said to myself ((quiet till +)) my children, I will raise them up totally differently (+). But my parents have (raised us well), we never were allowed to touch the food with our hands.

M: -Mm hmm-.

L: So as small we were—knife work and everything, we were very skilled, even with the, the, the, the toughest chicken or whatever.

M: -Mm hmm-.

L: ((deep breath)) And you think you can be *free* of it...but when you raise up—I am, and, and, and give example, yesterday I had here a party/ and I was *so* disgusted that the people were eating with their hands the little sausages, and, and were so greasy/. And I *have* to pull myself together and I said, 'listen I have forks there, and I have the napkins there' (((excitedly))) but nobody took the fork and the napkins/.

((Laughing))

L: And... but you have been, it is just you're *programmed.*

The narrative fragment is full of contradictions, constructing several competing selves (cf. Ewing 1990: 253). The first lines show the perspective of Loes as a child, scared to break her parents' rules while at the same time proud of her acquired skills. The second perspective introduced in the narrative is that of a child who feels resentment and decides to do things differently. The third voice in the story is an adult who expresses dissatisfaction with her inability to liberate herself from her upbringing. The last speaker is Loes as an adult who, only recently, was unable to suppress the embodied habitus of disgust instilled by her upbringing. Realizing the complexity of her own subjectivity, in the next utterance, Loes turned more directly to me, distancing herself from all previous voices through somewhat nervous laughter, a statement about the usefulness of biographical reflection, and a dual labelling of the situation as both 'funny' and 'awful'. She concluded the narrative section, saying that, 'it's good to talk about it because you analyse yourself why you are like that.'

Ambiguity Towards Her Father

The second major theme in Loes's interview was her relationship with her father. Two minutes into the interview, she introduced the topic, and the fact that she frequently returned to it throughout the interview demonstrated the emotional intensity of her feelings. She began explaining that 'my dad, he was a soldier, ((slowly)) he raised up as—/ehm/ little soldiers. It was really tough to have a father who is a soldier.' She mentioned that 'His punishments were—severe'; later in the interview she recalled bruises she had had to hide at school. Opposing 'dad' to 'mum', who 'towards me, she always, you know, make me feel good', she said:

L: But dad/, because we didn't saw him so much, he was the guy of you know, 'yes is yes, no is no', but he took it *so* seriously\.

M: -Mm hmm-.

L: So *even*—if he thought you did something bad (-) you were not allowed to defend yourself. You couldn't even / say, 'but dad, I didn't do it'. If you say, 'but dad', he hit you.

M: -Hmm-.

L: Another thing ((sighing)) doing your homework. It was bad if dad would help you with your homework because for ((slowly till +)) every wrong answer he had the knuckle and hit you on your hand ((+)) until your hand (had been cut) like that. Those things are ((deep breath))... it's still painful.

Remembering her suffering, she also used the opportunity of the interview to bring things into perspective through emotional distancing and empathy. Trying to understand her father's point of view, she suggested his parents had raised him in the same tough manner. In deep thought, her eyes fixed on a point in the distance, more directed at herself than at me, she stated that there had been other sides to her father.

L: but on the other hand it was a man ((slowly till +)) who knew so much about politics, culture. Dad was a man who had a dose of humour (+). I remember if friends came home—eh—my dad was very talented with singing. He had a beautiful voice and music/. So we kids, (((fondly))) I can remember as a child that when friends or family came there was always music/.

M: -Mm hmm-.

L: They brought their guitar and so on. So as child it was lovely and we would dance and... ((swallowing)) it's, it's strange, now I'm talking about the past, it's always a *very*/happy and a very *sad*\side.

Later on in the interview, however, she gave more details about her father's aggressive behaviour and his inflexibility, describing the latter as something she recognized in herself. Describing her fear for the lasting psychological effects of her father's behaviour, she concluded that her mother's loving behaviour had saved her from internalizing feelings of inferiority. Pointing at some self-help books on her bookshelves, she argued that parents' negativity could have a detrimental effect on the psychological development of their children, making them feel 'stupid'. She had escaped, as she had 'never felt [stupid]', but had 'felt more *rebellious*'. Tellingly using the present tense, she stated, 'I want to *prove* the opposite to my dad.' Reflecting further, she noted that she was actually proving herself all the time, and added that she 'just realized now' that, although she was 'quite successful' it 'cost a lot of effort'. This newly gained perspective on her life brought her to tears.

Dealing with Physical Appearance

While experiences of having a light brown skin colour, black hair and dark brown eyes did not come up in the first part of the interview, Loes discussed this in various ways in the second phase of the interview. Discussing her mixed-race background, she described her ambiguous feelings.

L: and this is really funny, I see myself really as white.

M: -Mm-.

L: Isn't that funny?

She explained that she did voluntary work with newly arrived migrants in her local area, migrants who looked quite similar to herself. Yet she saw herself as 'different'. Opening this perception up for biographical reflection, she said,

L: Isn't that weird?

M: -Mm hmm-.

L: And I just thought, 'listen, the outside world is seeing you *exactly* the same', because I have the same colour#

M: #-mm hmm-.

L: #but I don't feel that way.

M: -Mm hmm-.

L: And I said to [my husband], isn't it strange that I see, if I'm talking with them I see them so totally different, I don't... I feel with them because ((swallowing)) I know a lot about the culture, how to talk because we have a totally different way of approaching. What we do is a lot, if we talk to each other, a lot of touching.

Interestingly, in the fragment she moved from an I-position as someone different from the dark-skinned migrants, first to an I-position of empathy, and subsequently to a we-position, classifying herself as part of the group, sharing a warm and intimate (non-Dutch, non-UK) way of behaving and talking. She added that she had learnt from the migrants' readiness to support each other, something that had reminded her of her parents' emphasis on family values. Evaluating this, she moved back to an I position; 'it is beautiful what I see in that community.'

She argued that her ambiguity about her colour was rooted in her father's refusal to acknowledge that in Holland, his children were often perceived as 'foreigners' because of their skin tone. Connecting accounts of her own and other migrants' experiences of discrimination in Northern Ireland and personal confrontations in the Netherlands, Loes tried to overcome her unconscious denial.

The analysis of Loes's self-narrative makes clear that 'Europe' is a changing territorial space of global reach that, as part and outcome of colonial processes, has been discursively constructed as a 'white zone'. It also demonstrates that 'Europe' is nevertheless a multiethnic space where racial tensions frequently flare up but where people of different ethnic origins also intermarry, have children and identify with European national identities. In addition, it shows that while countries with EU membership allow EU nationals to relocate within EU borders, this does not ensure a warm welcome. Loes, in this context, is a fascinating example of a person who, while passionately defining herself as a 'Dutch national', is faced with ambiguities regarding her identity and national belonging. The use of the autobiographical method did not only demonstrate how these issues were brought to life through narration, but also uncovered deeper psychological mechanisms hard to explore through other methodologies. A close analysis of her verbal reflections created an insight into the ways in which claims to and experiences of self were partially rooted in insecurities and a compulsion to constantly prove herself. As is frequently the case with biographical interviews when narrators consciously create 'the end of the story', she addressed this pressing matter in the last lines of our conversation. After telling me that she always thanks God for the life she is able to live before she goes to sleep, she repeated something she had reflected on during the interview. She said she found it hard to relax, to know her limits, to say to herself, 'Loes, it is now enough.'

Meeting Monika

I (MD) contacted Monika via a common friend who used to work in the same pub as Monika's husband. When I called her, I explained the purpose and the character of the interview. She was a bit shy at the beginning but then agreed eagerly, treating the interview as a way of 'helping a friend of a friend'. She needed some time to arrange everything at home and then called me again proposing to meet at my place on a weekday in the afternoon.

On that day Monika called me to apologize and to say she would be a bit late as she was very busy with her kids. Waiting for her, I prepared something to eat. Knowing that she worked very hard and had four children, I expected a tired-looking woman. Instead, she was very attractive and self-confident, very direct and full of energy, with her hair nicely done, full make-up and elegant clothes. She had come to my place by car. I proposed that we have some 'late lunch' together, and while she kept repeating that she was on a diet, I convinced her to have some asparagus soup with me, followed by coffee and fruit. She told me a bit about her life in Belfast and about our common friend, and the atmosphere was relaxed. As we were chatting, I told her a bit about myself and about the research project and explained what kind of interview it was going to be, stressing that she was free to tell me anything she liked about her life. I asked her to choose those moments and experiences which were important to her.

Commenting on the task ahead, Monika said that it was 'very difficult', explaining that 'there are some things in my life// there are some facts, which are very significant to me, very important to me, but I don't really want to talk about them'. Confirming the ethics of qualitative research, I assured her that this was no problem as it was up to her to decide how much to tell me. Struggling with where to start, she repeated: 'It's difficult, you know', and asked: 'How should [the story] look like? From the very…embryo?' I suggested some options, saying she could start from the moment she was born, or from her earliest memories, or from the moment she liked most, and indicated that she could go through all the life stages until the present moment. I explained I would not interrupt or make any comments and would ask her a few questions after she had finished her story. At this point Monika started her narration.

Dealing with Difficult Family Relationships

The interview took three hours and was conducted in Polish as this was our mother tongue. In Monika's life story, troubled family relationships and related issues of nonbelonging and her need to escape were the leading themes. Her later decision to move abroad was a direct consequence of those three biographical problems. The fact that she started her story talking about her troubled relationship with her family indicated its crucial importance to her personal development and psychological make-up. Monika introduced her father, mother and sister one by one and commented on the roles they had played in her life.

Monika (Mo): Oh God! All right then. I don't remember much of my childhood. At all…almost nothing…Rather nothing. I know only that -mmh- my dad went to the States very early. Very, very, very early, thirty-four years ago. So, all in all, I didn't see him much, maybe a year, maybe a bit less. And I was living with my mum-terrorist ((a short nervous laughter)) who…who probably /eh/ ((sighing)) how to say it…((pause, 3s)) she probably wanted to get off her unfulfilled, I don't know, dreams…I don't know why…maybe that's because she was alone, she was left alone ((pause, 2s)) she was getting it off on me slightly.

Markieta (Ma): -mmh-

Mo: And…I have a sister three years older than me. And certainly she's the favourite one, she's the darling. The whole life, everything's been for her. She's the nicest one, the most beautiful one. And me, I didn't care at all. (((quietly till +))) I don't give a damn (+).

In this preamble, the passage set the stage for the rest of the narrative, a story of continuous suffering. At the end of this passage she tried to deny her feelings of hurt, saying: 'I don't give a damn', but the rest of her narrative showed that her childhood traumas, spilling over into her adult life, remained unresolved.

Fritz Schütze observed that the themes brought up at the beginning of autobiographical narratives often unveil major concerns that will shape much of the overall life story (2008a: 19). In Monika's case, feelings of reproach and anger about painful family relations were the narrative leitmotif. Interesting, the phenomena already present in the preamble are normally expressed even more explicitly in the coda. As we will see later, Monika finished the account of her life with a similar assessment of her painful family relationships as she started with, comparing the past and the present and summing up her life as 'hell on earth'. While she had originally planned not to dwell on very personal aspects of her life, including painful memories, her narrative was full of background constructions in which concrete examples of verbal and nonverbal aggression were given in great detail, in direct speech and with a strong emotional charge. As with Loes's interview, additional indicators of the emotional intensity of her remembered and reexperienced memories were also para-verbal expressions, such as sighing, quick nervous laughter and numerous pauses. Similar to Loes, Monika uses laughter to distance herself from painful memories and to release tensions appearing in the course of the narration.

Due to endless family conflicts, Monika perceived her childhood as unhappy, as something she did not normally like to think about. She stated: 'Nothing good happened to me during childhood, nothing I'd like to remember.' She introduced many contrast sets, placing herself in opposition to her sister, her mother and mother-in-law. In one of her numerous argumentative commentaries, she said: 'I was always the inferior one and I was always treated in a terrible way.' This unequal treatment became even more apparent when both Monika and her sister got pregnant and both needed some help. At this point, the narrative constraint to go into details resulted in a background construction nested within the main narrative line. After two pauses of two seconds each, she recalled her sister's pregnancy and described how they had lived together in the same house, but in two separate tiny flats. Feeling that she needed to give even more details to make herself understood, she said:

Mo: Ah, I'll go back to something earlier, there was such a situation that... my sister had been living for a month, I guess, a month, before she went to the States and I got to know about that unfortunately when she was already in the States that she was in the States. She was working in the mornings and once I got so nervous because I was knocking on her door, and knocking, and knocking and no one was responding. We were living in one tenement building, a private one. There were only... it belonged to my mum and her sister. And her sister was living in one half and we were living in the second half. So I rushed to her, I ran there and I say—'Tell me where my sister is' and she started laughing—'So you don't know anything? She's in America.' It was as if I got a slap in the face, I swear. Just... well, I don't know, I felt... *again* in my life I felt terrible. And I asked her—'Why? Why no one told me?' She just shrugged it off saying that my mum decided that if she had told me, I'd have called the airport and said that she was smuggling some, I don't know, drugs or something and she would have had to stay. Only one reaction—I turned on my heel and just a *regular war* started between me and my family.

Recalling the events, Monika was visibly and audibly furious and disappointed, reliving her past emotions. The memory of her sister moving to the United States evoked a series of other negative memories and comments. 'I remember only the worst moments that happened to me', she said, 'in fact nothing nice happened to me.' In Schütze's terminology, this utterance can be classified as a supra-segmental demonstration marker, indicating a change from one process structure to another. It was followed by a pause of two seconds, a brief attempt to start a sentence ('And... I remember that'), then two more pauses of two and three seconds, followed by another background construction nested in the previous one. It was a detailed account of her most painful experience:

Mo: I was highly pregnant and my sister with my mum in the other room, in the one she didn't make available to me... they were drinking alcohol with my sister, having good fun and they didn't even invite us, even for a biscuit, neither me nor my husband, they just kicked us out. And I remember that I was so tired with all of this, this// that drinking, and that party, and that noise. I wanted to go to bed, so I couldn't stand it anymore and I went there. And I remember I took their bottle and... and took this bottle and went back to my room. They ran after me and... and it's going to be the worse ((faster till +)) I guess the very worst memory of my life connected with my mum (+) that... she jumped after me and I already told her that 'You know, it's enough, just stop drinking that alcohol because I can't stand it anymore.' And I threw this bottle, it broke and she was probably a bit tipsy and she stepped on a piece of glass, she cut her leg. And I kneeled down, I leaned on my arms because I wanted to sweep it off and then so *terribly* ((with feeling till +)) she kicked me *in my belly* (+) I was in the eighth month of pregnancy, she kicked me so badly that I landed in a hospital. And... and that's what I will never forget her.

This highly emotional narrative segment was followed by an argumentative global assessment of the relations with her mother, comparing past and present, and concluding that 'a mother should not behave like that.' She stated that, although now they lived in different countries, she still felt 'emotionally maltreated' by her mother, a feeling she 'can't cope with it', that made her hate her mother.

At this point in the narrative, she started with what Schütze calls a 'pre-coda argumentation', an evaluative statement leading to an assessment of the overall narrated life. In Monika's case, all the significant members of her family and family-in-law were critically assessed. She explained that when her fourth baby was born, her mother-in-law came to visit them in the United Kingdom, and there was a big quarrel, ending when Monika threw her mother-in-law out of the house. She explained that she didn't want to be 'ruled by her', and said that she had 'her own principles'. She claimed that in the end, she always achieved what she aimed for. She then described how, in an attempt to overcome past tensions, she had invited her parents to stay with her in the United Kingdom for ten days. The visit turned out to be 'the worst days of her life'. Closing the content of the autobiographical story and refocussing the attention to the actual 'here and now', she reflexively wondered whether all family conflicts had been her fault. She admitted it had always been difficult for her to adjust to other people, but at the same time pledged that she would never let anybody treat her badly any more. Summing up, she noted that 'life hasn't been great', and had in fact been 'hell on earth'. Nevertheless, she said she was doing her best and hoped to be a better mother for her children than her mother had been for her.

Discussion

These stories demonstrate that the autobiographical interview method has the potential to generate a space for emotional remembering, deep reflection and self-performance. Both women struggled with unresolved issues, and the emotional intensity of their autobiographical work was clearly signalled by the use of linguistic contradictions, hesitations, self-corrections and crying. While Monika announced at the start of her interview that she was not keen on revealing anything about herself, once having started the story, she discussed many unresolved traumas. By contrast, Loes expressed no reservations about talking about her life, but still surprised herself when reflecting on old problems in new ways. Loes's autobiographical narrative work approximated a counselling session in which the client relives painful past events and reflects on their negative impact on self-experience and personal development (Rosenthal 2003). Fear of failure and a constant need to prove herself came out as dominant themes. She frequently seemed to talk to herself—as it is often the case in this type of interview situation—trying to understand the reasons for her own insecurity. Crucially, for the argument of this chapter, her insecurity was not apparent when seeing her perform in public or when talking with her on a previous occasion about Dutch society and her life in the United Kingdom; in such communicative contexts she seemed very confident. It was clearly the autobiographical method that brought her other side to the fore.

In Monika's case, unresolved biographical problems related to her family situation, especially the mother–daughter relationship, became apparent. These problems were a constant source of suffering and therefore constituted the leitmotif of her autobiographical recollection. After blaming her family context for all the difficulties in her life, clearly indicated by numerous argumentative passages appearing throughout the whole narrative part of the interview, Monika reflected on alternative interpretations of her life course tendencies towards the end of the interview. She assessed the troubled relationships she had with her mother, sister and mother-in-law, argued she could not accept certain types of behaviour but also suggested that perhaps she had a 'difficult character' herself, so that some of her problems could have been generated by her inability to adjust to other people. While this reflection was not well developed (it was followed by a pause and the type of justification similar to her previous argumentative commentaries), it showed potential for further biographical work.

Both women had an ambiguous sense of belonging to their country of origin, something they dealt with in their discussions. To Loes, 'Dutch culture' was an object of strong desire, a feeling informed by the complexities of her multiethnic background, her upbringing and experiences of discrimination. The biographical interview created an arena in which to contrast conflicting experiences of ethnic and national belonging that challenged her identity as a mixed-race person. To Monika, 'Poland' was a place of extreme nonbelonging due to her problematic family relationships and the fact that she had felt abandoned when relevant others, in particular her father and her second husband, had left the country. For both women, whilst the United Kingdom offered the potential of a new home, their sense of postmigration well-being was informed by both pre- and postmigration emotional experiences. The interview allowed them to place these experiences in one overall story, as moments that, while marking different stages in their lives, were also related. The task of telling their story inspired them to evaluate these connecting pasts and reflect on the future.

Conclusions

As with any methodology, the autobiographical narrative method should not be fetishized and is ideally used in combination with other research methods. It is a research tool that does not always work and needs to be used reflexively, dynamically and with caution. The analysis has shown that, when analysing autobiographical narratives, it is essential to acknowledge complexity, inconsistency and ambiguity and to examine the fluctuating emotional intensity of the narrative performance as an important analytical focus. Comparing the two stories of childhood suffering and migration, we reconstructed the link between the dynamics of the autobiographical narrative interview situation and the structure of biographical experiences, as indicated in different communicative schemes of presentation, background constructions and other formal features. We also compared the two narrators' engagement with biographical work, as they remembered particular life episodes, spoke about unresolved psychological problems and imagined alternative trajectories and interpretations that projected various desires (cf. Crapanzano 1980: 10).

The richness and depth of autobiographical material combined with meticulous analysis allowed us to go beyond the initial conceptualization of the Euroidentities project. We interviewed Loes and Monika because they fitted very well our 'transnational workers' sensitized group.[4] The analysis of their autobiographical narratives, however, opened up a whole range of new important issues. Loes, dealing with her mixed ethnic background, feeling white but at the same time being challenged as Dutch or European because of her light brown skin, demonstrated how colour-sensitive Europe is. The case of Monika, on the other hand, showed us how European migration may be conditioned by the need of escaping individual and family problems to a much larger extent than by any other factors. Going abroad, initially thought to be a way of leaving behind all the painful relationships, may not turn out to be a solution. Crossing the borders, one still carries along all the unsolved problems, which sooner or later will have to be addressed and worked out biographically.

Taking the limitations of the biographical method into account, we strongly believe that the method can be imported into mainstream anthropology. Ideally in combination with long-term fieldwork, historical analysis and, if relevant, statistical analysis, it confronts the readers of our ethnographies with individuals in all their psychological complexity.

Notes

1. Schütze began developing this method in the 1970s; for more recent publications in English, see Schütze (1990) 1992, 2003, (1984) 2005, 2008a,b.
2. According to Atkinson 'in the telling of a life story, we get a good sense of how and why the various parts of a life are connected and what gives the person meaning in life. There may be no better way to answer the question of how people get from where they began to where they are now in life than through their life stories' (Atkinson 1998: 20).
3. This was a three-year (2008–11; see also Miller 2012) Framework 7-funded project entitled 'Euroidentities'. For more details see http://www.euroidentities.org/.
4. At the beginning of the Euroidentities project, five sensitized groups were defined as those who might be more exposed to European legislation and European frame of reference: 'educationally mobile', 'transnational workers', 'farmers', 'cultural contacts' and 'workers in civil society organisations'. During the analysis two other groups turned out to be significant as well: 'external to Europe' and 'transcultural intimate relationships'. For more details see http://www.euroidentities.org/Workpackages/.

References

Archer, M. S. (2003), *Structure, Agency and the Internal Conversation*, Cambridge: Cambridge University Press.

Atkinson, D. (1988), 'Research Interviews with People with Mental Handicaps', *Mental Handicap Research*, 1: 75–90.

Atkinson, R. (1998), *The Life Story Interview*, Qualitative Research Methods, Vol. 44, London: Sage Publications.

Bertaux, D. (ed.) (1981), *Biography and Society: The Life History Approach in the Social Sciences*, London: Sage Studies in International Sociology.

Bertaux, D. (2003), 'The Usefulness of Life Stories for a Realist and Meaningful Sociology', in R. Humphrey, R. Miller and E. Zdravomyslova (eds), *Biographical Research in Eastern Europe: Altered Lives and Broken Biographies*, London: Ashgate, 39–51.

Bryman, A. and R. Burgess (eds) (1999), *Qualitative Research*, London: Sage Publications.

Bryman, A. (ed.) (2001), *Ethnography*, London: Sage Publications.

Burgess, R. (1991), *In the Field—An Introduction to Field Research*, London: Routledge.

Chamberlayne, P., J. Bornat and T. Wengraf (eds) (2000), *The Turn to Biographical Methods in Social Science: Comparative Issues and Examples*, London: Routledge.

Cohen, A. (1994), *Self-Consciousness: An Alternative Anthropology of Identity*, Oxford: Routledge.

Crapanzano, V. (1980), *Tuhami: Portrait of a Moroccan*, Chicago: University of Chicago Press.

Domecka, M. (forthcoming), *Manoeuvring between Opportunities and Constraints: The Actors of Polish Business Field in the Time of Transformation*, Leuven: The Catholic University of Leuven Press.

Driessen, H. (1998), 'Introduction: Trends, Genres and Cases in Self-Revelation', *Focaal*, 32: 7–13.

Ewing, K. (1990), 'The Illusion of Wholeness: Culture, Self and the Experience of Inconsistency', *Ethos*, 18(3): 251–78.

Humphrey, R., R. Miller and E. Zdravomyslova (eds) (2003), *Biographical Research in Eastern Europe: Altered Lives and Broken Biographies*, London: Ashgate.

Kaźmierska, K. ((2004) 2005), 'Ethical Aspects of Biographical Interviewing and Analysis', in R. Miller (ed.), *Biographical Research Methods*, Vol. IV, London: Sage Publications, 365–76.

Miller, R. (ed.) (2005), *Biographical Research Methods*, Vol. I, II, III, IV, London: Sage Publications.

Miller, R. (ed.) (2012), *The Evolution of European Identities: Biographical Approaches*, Basingstoke: Palgrave Macmillan.

Moretti, F. (1987), *The Way of the World: The Bildungsroman in European Culture*, London: Verso.

Roos, J. P. (2000), *Reality or Nothing: False and Repressed Memories and Autobiography*, http://www.mv.helsinki.fi/home/jproos/falsememory.htm, accessed 10 February 2010.

Rosenthal, G. (2003), 'The Healing Effects of Storytelling: In the Conditions of Curative Storytelling in the Context of Research and Counselling', *Qualitative Inquiry*, 9(6): 915–33.

Schütze, F. ((1990) 1992), 'Pressure and Guilt: War Experiences of a Young German Soldier and Their Biographical Implications', *International Sociology*, 7(2–3): 187–208.

Schütze, F. (2003), 'Hülya's Migration to Germany as Self-Sacrifice Undergone and Suffered in Love of Her Parents, and Her Later Biographical Individualisation: Biographical Problems and Biographical Work of Marginalisation and Individualisation of a Young Turkish Woman in Germany. Part I', *Forum Qualitative Sozialforschung/Forum: Qualitative Social Research*, 4(3), http://www.qualitative-research.net/fqs-texte/3–03/3–03schuetze-e.htm, accessed 5 March 2007.

Schütze, F. ((1984) 2005), 'Cognitive Figures of Autobiographical Extempore Narration', in R. Miller (ed.), *Biographical Research Methods*, Vol. II, London: Sage Publications, 289–338.

Schütze, F. (2008a), 'Biography Analysis on the Empirical Base of the Autobiographical Narratives: How to Analyse Autobiographical Narrative Interviews', Part I, INVITE—Biographical Counselling in Rehabilitative Vocational Training. Further Educational Curriculum. EU Leonardo da Vinci Programme, www.biographicalcounselling.com/download/B2.1.pdf, accessed 4 March 2008.

Schütze, F. (2008b), 'Biography Analysis on the Empirical Base of the Autobiographical Narratives: How to Analyse Autobiographical Narrative Interviews', Part II, INVITE—Biographical Counselling in Rehabilitative Vocational Training, Further Educational Curriculum, EU Leonardo da Vinci Programme, www.biographicalcounselling.com/download/B2.2.pdf, accessed 4 March 2008.

Spradley, J. and M. Rynkiewich (eds) (1976), *Ethics and Anthropology: Dilemmas in Fieldwork*, London: John Wiley & Sons.

Svašek, M. (2008), 'Who Cares? Families and Feelings in Movement', *Journal of Intercultural Studies*, 29(3): 213–30.

Svašek, M. (forthcoming), 'Narrating (Migrant) Belonging: Emotions and Performative Practice', in A. Grønseth (ed.), *Being Human, Being Migrant*, Oxford: Berghahn Books.

Szlachcicowa I., M. Domecka and A. Mrozowicki (2006), 'Zwischen Tradition und Postmoderne: Die Improvisierte Modernisierung in Westpolen', in P. Alheit, I. Szlachcicowa and F. Zich (eds), *Biographien im Grenzraum: Eine Untersuchung in der Euroregion Neiße*, Goerlitz: Neisse Verlag, 265–444.

Tonkin, E. (1992), *Narrating Our Pasts: The Social Construction of Oral History*, Cambridge: Cambridge University Press.

–5–

Eliciting the Tacit: Interviewing to Understand Bodily Experience

Georgiana Gore, Géraldine Rix-Lièvre, Olivier Wathelet and Anne Cazemajou

Introduction

This chapter espouses a phenomenologically informed cognitive anthropology and focusses explicitly on bodily experience. We argue that, when investigating the practical knowledge necessarily at play in bodily practices in a particular situation, special interview techniques are required. Our aim is to elucidate the reasons underlying this and to present two techniques used in three French ethnographically based studies, the focus of which are the seemingly unrelated activities of cooking, rugby-refereeing and learning yoga in order to dance, all entailing, however, bodily techniques and practical knowledge for their effectivity.

The three studies share a number of premises which we highlight rapidly before outlining the tenets of a cognitive anthropology of bodily practices.

In keeping with most contemporary ethnography, all three studies adopt a reflexive approach that acknowledges the situatedness of the production of anthropological knowledge not only in the ethnographic encounter construed dialogically (Bakhtin and Emerson 1984; Bakhtin 1990) as a process of co-construction, but also in its textualization. In order to avoid the postmodern pitfalls of subjectivism and to provide some means of *a posteriori* verification, the studies include an account of the conditions of production of anthropological knowledge in the final rendering (Kilani 1994). Moreover, in acknowledgement of the thorough-going reflexive nature of anthropology, each study orders and implements, in a singular manner, the methodological techniques in which the interview is central.

This reflexive stance necessarily entails a categorical rejection of any remnants of positivism, which Willis (1980) highlighted as intrinsic to the naturalistic posture of participant observation. This in part explains why observational techniques, whether participatory or using audiovisual media, are conceived as inappropriate for the study of practical knowledge, the know-how mobilized by cooks (domestic or expert) and rugby referees or appropriated by dance pupils. Such observational techniques, even as sophisticated as those developed by Grasseni to hone 'skilled vision' (2008), are useful to gain a general understanding of the field, as are conventional interview techniques.

However, to access the tacit knowledge and its constitution that practitioners embody in the course of their activities generates special methodological questions since it can neither be observed nor explicitly formulated. While an apprentice-style method, used by over half of the contributors to Marchand's (2010) special issue of the *Journal of the Royal Anthropological Institute* on *Making Knowledge* of 'legitimate peripheral participation' (Lave and Wenger 1991) or a thoroughly reflexive embodied ethnography (Retsikas 2008) may enable the researcher 'to share the same lived experience from an "adjacent" position' (Grasseni 2008: 152), there are situations in which these stances are simply impossible.

Despite our emphasis on the dialogic and the discursive as a productive means of understanding practical knowledge, we recognize the embodied and situated nature of the ethnographic exchange. We do not concur, however, with the orientation that takes the anthropologist's body and movement as a privileged source of knowledge (Retsikas 2008; Skinner 2010; Sklar 2006), since we consider that anthropological knowledge results from a negotiation of points of view and an objectification of the tacit. However, Skinner's insistence on a nonintrusive antipositivist and antiorientalist stance which counters 'the traditional "rape research model" in the social sciences of field penetration and withdrawal' (2010: 124) should be taken as a methodological proviso. Indeed, 'being affected' may even be, as Favret-Saada (1990) insists, a precondition for anthropological understanding though not a substitute for it.

Moreover, these approaches, even if phenomenologically inspired, do not give access to the actors' first-person accounts, which we consider crucial to understanding embodied cognition. Indeed, one of the trickiest issues concerns how to generate these first-person accounts in which our interlocutors must focus veritably on their own actions and experience in a phenomenological stance (Piette 2009), and the logic which gives rise to these, without resorting to postrationalized representations of action or experience. The two techniques that have proved adequate for the task are self-confrontation with video film (Theureau 1992) and the explicitation interview (Vermersch 1994). The chapter, therefore, focusses on these and the epistemological issues raised by their application by grounding them in the three previously mentioned studies.

A Cognitive Anthropology of Bodily Practices

Beginning mostly as an anthropology of the structure of the mind and its extension within the world (see d'Andrade 1995 for an overview; Sperber 1996), cognitive anthropology has tended to pay scant attention to the body, unlike in philosophical and artificial intelligence writing where the body has gained a certain status (Clark

1997; Lakoff and Johnson 1980; Shapiro 2011). With the exception of some prominent authors, such as Tim Ingold (2000) and his rereading of James Gibson's concept of affordance, and the other contributors to the RAI special issue (Marchand 2010), embodied cognition in anthropology has remained largely underexploited, just as the quality of the mind-body connections has remained unclear, often owing much to Bourdieu's notion of *habitus* (1990). In line with the discourses about embodied cognition in philosophy, the aforementioned authors mostly adopt phenomenological approaches and conceptually favour the sensory regime. This is particularly true of some of the founding essays in the anthropology of the senses, notably Thomas Csordas's work on bodily knowledge (also inspired by Bourdieu's notion of *habitus*) and its rereading by David Howes (1993), which gave rise to a definition of sensory knowledge. These authors have drawn attention to the ill-defined status of the body in cognitive anthropology (Shapiro 2011) and laid emphasis on experience as a means to gain a deep knowledge of embodied cognition.

In contrast with the dominant vein in cognitive anthropology, our common approach focusses on bodily practices as they unfold by questioning the knowledge which underpins these. We aim to study 'the cognitive foundations of experience,…what an actor does but also the knowledge which is mobilised during his activity' (Rix and Biache 2004). The object of inquiry is not experience as it is conceived, but the experience close to that which is actually occurring in, through and during an activity; and the fundamental question may be summed up as: What drives the actor to act as he or she does at the very moment of acting? It is therefore the effectivity of bodily practices that we study and not the prescriptions, the justifications or the discourses concerning the realizations, whether of professional chefs, rugby referees or dance teachers and pupils. The primary aim of the various interview techniques that we discuss is to enable the researcher to document the processes at work during the emergence and course of a practice.

The premise of our approach, derived from Merleau-Ponty's phenomenology (1942), is that no rupture exists either between body and mind, or between the subject and his or her world. Meaning is conceived as embodied and cannot be detached from the practices as they are realized in particular situations. Access to this dimension of experience, which may be considered as prereflective and not immediately verbalizable (Petitmengin 2007; Vermersch 1994), paradoxically requires its explicitation which relies on an effort of reflection made possible by the faculties of consciousness: that is 'the power that the subject has of targeting himself' (Merleau-Ponty 1988: 408) enables him or her to render explicit his or her implicit, syncretic, prereflective lived experience. Verbalization is therefore the means by which the actor's experience is rendered intelligible. Moreover, this does not preclude the contextual dimension of the activity insofar as actions cannot be dissociated from 'the concrete circumstances in which they unfold' (De Fornel and Quéré 1999: 119). However, given that no homology exists between acting and saying, and verbalization necessarily produces a form of 'emplotment' (Ricoeur 1983)—a narrative reordering that introduces a logic or causality in the succession of events and through which the actor confers his or her own coherence on action—we acknowledge that experience may never be rendered explicit as it was lived and is, in a sense, always lost. This implies, therefore, that in the dialogic relationship of interviewing, explicitation always occurs according to a particular perspective. On one hand, this is determined by the researcher who chooses the interview technique and guides the focus and course of the interview in accordance with his or her research object; on the other, it is the interlocutor who chooses the salient and meaningful moments of his or her activity and creates the narrative structure.

Interview, Object and Field

Self-confrontation from video film and the explicitation interview, the techniques which are the focus of the chapter, are next presented in relation to the empirical studies undertaken in order to demonstrate what makes them especially productive for the study of practical knowledge.

Study 1. Perceptive Judgement in Professional Culinary Activity

Cooking, like many practices using hands and tools, is often reduced to its gestural dimension even by experts themselves. In the case of an industrially applied ethnographic study, Wathelet aimed to understand how culinary tasks are performed in professional and domestic settings. Preliminary interviews with professional cooks and students graduating from the Paul Bocuse Institute, a French culinary school training future upmarket restaurant managers, highlighted the potential role of perceptive judgement in culinary activity and the tension between two competencies often contrasted by anthropologists: planning and improvising. If interviews demonstrated that gestures and good hand movements are key elements for understanding apprenticeship—learning how to use a professional knife to cut vegetables into regular pieces is the first lesson provided, with the explicit goal of erasing familial culinary habits and of forming a new professional background of body movements and rhythms—the ability to understand and undertake the material transformation of ingredients during the culinary activity relies on a larger variety of skills, including perceptive ones.

To describe them, our approach draws upon cognitive ethnography. This describes how information is stored, distributed and processed when actors voluntarily transform the material organization of a cooking task (Conein 1990, 2004; de Léon 2003a,b) and aims to capture the embodied dimension of cognition by showing how the body mediates judgements (Hernandez and Sutton 2003; Sutton 2006; Sutton and Hernandez 2007; Patel 2008; Sennett 2008). However, by describing categories of skills and ephemeral material configurations, the temporal dimension of action—which appears to be overtly described as central during interviews—tends to disappear. Moreover, using videotaping of behaviours and comments within the situation or participant observation, those analyses focussed on gestures and rather general feeling instead of the situated subjective dimension of the activity. As a consequence, descriptions are functional—connecting some body movement or category of perception to a category of judgements, as in the ethnographic account of professional pastry made by Krina Patel (2008).[1] As a consequence, how judgements are made and how they follow each other remain outside the scope of investigation. Those two dimensions (temporality and subjectivity) are, however, extremely relevant to understand how the cook and the ingredients engage in dialogue, in a never-ending process of transformation implying successive judgements about sensory qualities.

To gain access to this level, a video interview method was used connecting the elicitation strategy of self-confrontation—by showing video excerpts of their activity to informants—with the phenomenological techniques of interviewing developed by Vermersch (1994). To make explicit what has been lived, instead of shared and standardized knowledge, Wathelet focussed on *how* people actually experience their embodied actions and more specifically how perceptive cues are created to allow fine judgements. Each recipe was filmed using three views. By using the one with the smallest angle, which focussed on the hotplate, hands and top of the cook's body, informants' attention during the interview was more easily directed to their feelings instead of the general rules of actions, as in the head-mounted camera situation (but without its movement) developed by Rix-Lièvre in the next case study.

One of the major findings of the study is that perceptive judgements are organized within the realm of a cognitive trail, which Wathelet named a *perceptive pathway.* Interviews made salient that perceptive judgement is needed to deal with the shift between two operations or acts within the culinary activity. What follows is an example. After having been told that the rise in temperature was a critical piece of information at that specific moment in the process, the ethnographer asks: 'How do we see the temperature rising?' The chef replies: 'We always see a little…The ingredients always start to gain colour at the edge. It's there that you can see it [in the video excerpt]: it's starting to become a little overheated; we need to be wary, we need to reduce the temperature.' The ethnographer, after stopping the flow of images, shows a specific locus in the video and asks: 'Is it the colour at the edge of the ingredient?' The chef responds: 'Yes, the edge. It's always that whatever the ingredient.'

Video is first used as a tool to remember what has been performed, but is also a communicative artefact allowing a process of mutual attunement of sensory abilities—those of the chef and of the ethnographer. By sharing temporarily some perception, the ethnographer is able to gain a better knowledge of the cognitive process underlying the perception itself. In this case, we know about the frequency of the judgement, its level of confidence and its dependency on the specific ingredients.

Most of the time, sensory judgements are described selectively, in the form of remarks when describing action occurring in the video. Descriptions are then shorter, but become consistent when considered together. For instance, the study highlights the role of the process of waiting for relevant transformation at certain specific steps of the culinary process. For example, chef E, a teacher at the Paul Bocuse Institute, stated: 'When I see that [onion] start to brown lightly, then I know that...' Chef B, the former head of a two-star Michelin restaurant, told Wathelet: 'I knew I wasn't in a hurry; I saw my butter was melting down slowly. Besides, you can see it, we can see it simmering as it should be.'

Analysis of these interviews provides the ethnographic description of how the sensory modalities or their combination are used to produce specific judgements (like the sound of butter to define the temperature of the pan and then the perfect moment to introduce meat). Among other relevant findings, it appears that most of the sensory cues are created instead of passively perceived. This means that this sensory information is expected, implying a cognitive gesture of paying attention to something specific. In the two short excerpts cited earlier, we understand the role of sensory judgement in the process of building confidence about the quality of the process. We also gain a knowledge of the kind of sensory cues needed to do so. And more important, unlike in classical interviews based on general experience or revised ones of prior experience, we start to understand how attention drives perception by selectively focussing on some awaited transformation of food materiality.

These micro-expectations are key factors in the process of controlling food transformation in a professional kitchen as much as in the task of time management of staff in a restaurant. They give shape to sensory pathways, the parameters of which define what is acceptable. Chef A, Best Craftsmen of France, stated:

> Someone who's going to start his piece of meat, I can see he's doing it; but if I don't hear the noise of cooking, I know there's something wrong. Even if I didn't see it, because he did it behind my back, there'll be a sort of reflex that tells me: 'there's a mistake somewhere'. Smoking oil, burning butter, we know we're on the wrong tack.

Study 2. A Study of Expert Rugby Referees' Practical Knowledge: Contributions of Subjective Re Situ *Interviews*

Rix-Lièvre's research focusses on the cognitive basis of the rugby referee's experience (Rix 2005, 2007). The referee's activity, often reduced to the application of rules, is studied as a decision-making process. In order to understand what a referee really does and lives during a match, Rix-Lièvre proposes a novel perspective that does not separate act and judgement. Refereeing is not a cold mental process; it is complex practice. From different propositions concerning a judge's activity (Perelman 1990; Ricoeur 1995), referees' judgement acts are defined as bodily or linguistic manifestations that show players and impose upon them what is possible during a match. From an anthropo-phenomenological perspective, acts are embodied and spontaneous meanings (Merleau-Ponty 1942). As we argued earlier in the chapter, direct consciousness and practical knowledge only exist 'in act'. In order to study the cognitive basis of rugby referees' experience, we have to come close to this kind of meaning, especially when they show and impose what is possible in a moment of the game. This presupposes that each referee must be assisted in rendering explicit his or her lived experience during the course of the match. As in Wathelet's case, it is a new orientation to lived experience that supposes a new methodology: rules, gestures, planification and so on, that is to say generalities, are not sufficient to understand practices.

In order to study how the referee spontaneously constructs, shows and imposes what is possible, two specific points have to be taken into account. First, the referee's activity is a public one. It is impossible, therefore, to ask him or her about his or her lived experience, about what is important, about know-how during the match, that is to use apprenticeship techniques. We have to wait to the end. Then, there are many moments in which he or she shows the players something and imposes this upon them. All these moments are different, so the researcher is interested in how, each time, he or she spontaneously makes explicit what is possible despite the fact that it is very difficult for him or her to return to a particular moment in its singularity and to go through the same process for each and every match situation. So video is the means chosen in order to specify, during the interview, each moment the actor, about which he or she is invited to render explicit his or her own lived experience. Second, video is usually used by referees for postmatch autoanalysis or evaluation. Therefore, when watching the video, most of their discourse is a justification: they watch the match as a spectator or a supervisor. This means that there is a limit to using video: it tends to place, during the interview, the referee not in his or her subjective position as actor, but in that of spectator—it is the same for the researcher who watches the recording, as a usual sports video places him or her as spectator. In order to use the advantages of video while taking into account these difficulties, Rix-Lièvre proposes another kind of video recording, a perspective closest to the referee's during the match. He or she is equipped with a head-mounted camera permitting a closeness to his or her subjective perspective in the situation. It is this film that serves as the basis for the self-confrontation interviews, called *subjective re situ* interviews (Rix and Biache 2004; Rix and Lièvre 2008; Rix-Lièvre 2010). This interview takes place as soon as possible after the match and it mobilizes the head-mounted video from the beginning of the match to foster an experiential immersion (Omodei et al. 1997: 142). It begins by requesting that the referee talk, with as much detail as possible, about what he or she experienced during the event that the video is showing. The referee or researcher can stop the video as many times and for as long as is necessary to allow the referee to describe what makes sense for him or her. Throughout the interview, watching the video enables the referee to be focussed, accompanied and brought as close as possible to the dynamics of his or her actions. It thus helps him or her to make his or her experience explicit. This interview, therefore, favours a sharing of the experience that allows the researcher to understand what makes sense for the referee at the moment he or she is refereeing and to approach the subjective side of his or her practice.

Referee (R): Number 5, there's 5, number 5 was in front of the kicker, I explained to him he was offside in front of the kicker, and he went on advancing, so I ticked him off because he hadn't made the effort to stop and go back because he was offside.

Researcher (C): And, you stay next to him? You stay…And, you're next to him; the kicker hasn't passed…

R: That's it, I do, I do because if there's a problem, he's going to create it, because he's in front of the kicker! There you are, OK, he kicks, number 5, number 5, the others make the effort to stop, number 5 keeps going, keeps going…And he's going to tackle, and he's going to tackle, so he's going to stop the blacks from playing on, so I return to the initial foul.

C: So, '5, you're in front', he won't listen…You say it again!

R: Yes, yes…

C: It's number 5, you say it again because it's him? Or…

R: Ah, he has to feel guilty, he has to feel guilty because, because despite being warned, he…he didn't make the effort to stop and start again, and wait to be back onside, so he…He has to feel guilty, he has to be blamed, what foul he's done etc…

This excerpt shows how the referee makes explicit what is at stake for him during this moment. He does not explain a passive application of rules or general principles of what to do when someone kicks; he describes what and how he constructs, what he shows to and imposes on this player, and how he does so.

These investigations have produced data enabling the researcher to understand the cognitive dimensions of referee's activity as produced *in situ*. From this material, three kinds of judgement act were identified. These are three different relations between the referee and the players' actions, three manners to construct, to show, to impose what is possible and three kinds of 'things' imposed. Judgement acts are neither reactions to an environmental configuration nor standard ways of grasping one specific passage of play. These cannot be put into the same category as faults. The referee can impose upon players to continue playing.

The results produced by the possibility of coming close to the referee's lived experience through *subjective re situ* interviews have led to a discussion of classic conceptions of referee activity. Because a judgement act is descriptive and performative, it is possible to conceive that the referee co-constructs the course of the play bringing players into his or her own rugby world. The game's rules provide the possibility for this co-construction insofar as they establish the referee's power over the play and constitute the necessary common values between referee and players for mutual coordination.

Study 3. Researching Subjective Experience in a Contemporary Dance Class: The Explicitation Interview

Anne Cazemajou's study investigates the transmission of bodily experience in a contemporary dance class and the various means by which the amateur adult pupils make sense of the teacher's instructions.[2] From the pupils' leads during explicitation interviews, the research has come to focus on the long preparatory work based on Iyengar yoga, which takes up the first two-thirds of the class. The specificity of this work is that it is mainly based on injunctions to do and to feel and on 'descriptions in terms of kinaesthetic sensations' (Goldfarb (1990) 1998: 130), as we see from the following audio transcription from a video recording of a workshop. The teacher is giving instructions as to how to practise a pose called *dandasana.* The pupils are sitting on their mats with their legs together and extended forward with feet flexed. The hands, in an inverted cup position on both sides of the pelvis, push against the floor so as to straighten and lengthen the spine. 'Carefully press the legs downwards, the spine upwards. Now pull the ischia on the floor, but also towards the outside and far from you. And now press the sacrum towards the inside of the body, and the upper edge of the sacrum you have to pull it upwards.' The teacher continues during a whole body stretch while lying on the floor with the arms extended above the head: 'Turn the thighs towards the inside and start to feel how it allows even more stretching of the lumbar spine towards the hands.'

The aim of the research is to understand how the pupils come to insert this descriptive and prescriptive dimension of the exercises into a subjective bodily experience, the stakes of which are obvious for them. It is the nature and the modes of construction of this bodily experience that are at the centre of the inquiry.

If video documentation, as well as observation, show us pupils involved in an activity with a certain intensity, who manifest a deep concentration and are *trying to do* what they are enjoined to, in no way do these methods enable us to know what they are actually doing, to understand the process of the work, how the pupils go about answering the instructions and how the various explanations and numerous injunctions and descriptions in terms of kinaesthetic sensations resonate. But can interviews give access to such private data?

As Pierre Vermersch remarks, 'what comes first' in a conventional interview are 'generalities, loads of anecdotes shot through with my implicit theories' (1996: 2). This kind of generalization, even if interesting in the sense that it gives information about how the interviewee perceives his or her activity, is also 'what he or she thinks he or she is doing—which is not necessarily what he or she is really doing' (Vermersch 2000: 5). Indeed, all action—and lived experience in general—is autonomous, in the sense of prereflective, implicit knowledge. So, in order to bring this tacit knowledge to light, the explicitation interview (Vermersch 1994) was considered the best technique.[3]

This technique requires that the interviewer guide the interviewee towards the descriptive verbalization of the lived experience of the action, which is closely linked to the other dimensions of lived experience, namely emotions, senses and thoughts. In order to obtain this specific verbalization, the focus has to be, in the case of a recurrent activity such as a dance lesson, on a specific lived moment of the class, the choice of which is left to the interviewee. Every interview began with the same open question for each pupil: 'What I suggest to you, if you agree, is to take your time in allowing a moment of the dance class, which has interested you, to return'.

After this opening question, the pupil was left to tell the context of the moment he or she chose, until the ethnographer was sure that a specific moment had been found and that the interviewee was reliving it, displaying what Vermersch calls an 'embodied discourse position' (Vermersch 2009). When the main point of the moment chosen by the interviewee had been reached, Cazemajou began to 'elucidate', which is the very purpose of the explicitation interview and which consists of 'bringing to light the unfolding of the action to a given degree of subtlety of the description' (Vermersch 1994: 120). A premise of the technique is that all action is made up of elementary operations of identification and execution, sequentially organized. However, the information provided by the interviewee is often too brief in relation to that which the interviewer wishes to understand. This is why the interviewer will have to 'fragment' this information using a very specific guidance technique and a series of cues echoing the words used by the interviewee. Such key cues include: 'What are you are doing when you…?', 'How do you know that…?', 'How do you manage to…?', 'What happens to you when you…?', 'How does it feel?' and 'Is it important for you?' These cues focus on the structure, never on the content, and allow the researcher to question without inducing the answers. Moreover, in establishing a rhythm of questioning, they get the interview going and allow the interviewer to fragment the description so as to reach a sharper level of detail and to delve further into the 'granularity' of the experience.

It is due to that level of detail and to that granularity that Cazemajou was able to understand how the pupils' bodily experience was constructed through the ongoing intensity of the work. Indeed, the pupils insist, in the interviews, on the 'many things to do and to think' in the class, showing how the ceaseless reiteration of instructions imposes a real rhythm of work. It is in this sense that a pupil evokes a sensation she had: 'I don't know what happened at the level of the femur or the muscles, but I, a consciousness…as if suddenly a curtain was falling and that I was discovering a thing but it was incredible this sensation…' It is interesting that she mentions afterwards that this happened 'following a certain number of exercises where we had well worked the legs, so... progressive awakening of consciousness'. Describing the exercise out of which this 'incredible sensation' emerged, she stresses 'the energy it requires', 'the work', 'the concentration' and so on. She explains: 'I make the exercise last.' As Cazemajou asks her for precisions, she adds: 'Always this effort, of flattening the leg on the floor, of stretching the back, of, of straightening up... ' So it is after repeated efforts to respond to the teacher's instructions, when the pupils say they 'cannot let go', that something ends up by giving way and opens onto a new experience. It is the moment when pupils, in their own words, can 'let go of the body' and 'really enter the movement', leaving the efforts for a 'mechanical mode' to take over. At this point, when the sensory relation reverses and when the pupils are taken into what they try to sense, immersing themselves into 'the music of movement', they report being 'totally conscious', 'alive', 'really in their body'. The core experience of this yoga work can thus be seen, following Merleau-Ponty (1945, 1964), as the very experience of perception, which the pupils describe, in terms astonishingly close to those used by the philosopher, as an experience of depth.

The Two Techniques: Differences and Shared Presuppositions

Differences

The most salient difference between these techniques concerns the reliance or not on audiovisual traces as aids to the verbalization of the interviewee's actions. The explicitation interview is based upon the actor producing his or her own affective trace through a process of memory recall, while self-confrontation relies upon a video trace. The explicitation interview thus requires a particular cognitive orientation in relation to the memory of an action or event. Self-confrontation interviews proceed, rather, through the literal confrontation of the actor with the traces of his or her own activity; this represents both a constraint and an asset when researching a particular practice (Rix-Lièvre 2010). It is a constraint insofar as the interview can only be undertaken in a moment of which the actor or researcher has a trace, more often than not a video recording, and an asset insofar as the latter constitutes an addition to the other materials (fieldnotes, photographs and so on) that contribute to the analysis of that moment of the activity.

The second difference concerns the way in which the interview is conducted by the researcher and the means used to control the relation between the interviewee's verbalizations and the actions to which they refer. It is indirectly controlled in the explicitation interview insofar as the researcher uses as indices the orientation of the interviewee's gaze, the rhythm of his or her speech, the grammatical tense and the person (first, second or third person singular) used. In the self-confrontation interviews, the control is more direct as, by means of the trace, that is the video recording of the action, the interviewee may be brought back to the effective unfolding of the action.

Shared Presuppositions

Although self-confrontation and the explicitation interview grant access to subjectivity through different means, they arise from a number of presuppositions which we briefly outline. First, we assume, as already mentioned, that practice is embedded in its context, which implies that action and its cognitive dimension cannot be dissociated from the situation (Garfinkel 1967; De Fornel and Quéré 1999; Suchman 1987; Hutchins 1995). Moreover, it is effective and singular actions as they unfold in a particular physical and human framework that must be studied (Suchman 1987). It is, therefore, the knowledge at work in a given moment that must be grasped in the ecological situation as in ethnographic research or in a semi-experimental set-up, which recreates that situation.

Second, exterior observation is not sufficient to account for a person's activity. It is important to consider his or her particular way of living, of perceiving, of making sense of his or her situation, that is to take into account his or her own world. The difficulty lies in the fact that the subjective side of practice stems from an embodied meaning, from 'significant real-life sets' (Merleau-Ponty 1942: 179), from knowing-in-action (Piaget 1974). Practice 'conveys an ante-predicative prelinguistic meaning' (Dauliach 1998: 309) similar to 'pre-reflective awareness' (Vermersch 2003: 71). In spite of the unarticulated nature of practical knowledge, it is important to address these elements.

The third postulate concerns the actor who is considered a reflective practitioner endowed with the possibility of recognizing his or her own activity from a new perspective. The phenomenological premises underlining 'the power the subject has to set sights on himself or herself' (Merleau-Ponty 1988: 408) establish the possibilities the actor has to explicate his or her experience (Dauliach 1998; Vermersch 2003, 2004). To do so, experience must 'become the object of conscious awareness' (Vermersch 1999: 34), which is not a position that is spontaneously adopted, but must be encouraged by a method (Theureau 1992; Vermersch 1994). Since informants tend to use abstract knowledge in order to describe their actions (Lave 1988), the method developed must constitute an aid to return to, to reflect upon, the intended action and to verbalize such action. However, this interview method may not take place during the action as a reflection disturbs and modifies the action.

The actor's return to his or her own activity consummates the passage from an act to a linguistic activity about this act. An epistemological break thus takes place: knowing-in-action and discursive knowledge concerning it are not of the same nature.

Conclusion

If intersubjectivity is often highlighted as a key dimension of the ethnographic method, our aim in this chapter has been to show that the understanding of subjectivity is far from a natural benefit of the ethnographic encounter, but relies on dedicated techniques. Video devices coupled with specific modes of interviewing are currently available to ethnographers to go further into the description of the subjective, the cognitive and the embodied dimensions of human experience. This short introduction features some of their key advantages such as their ability to add knowledge of informant' subjectivity to participant observation and to extend to the bodily the dynamic recollection of an experienced situation. Of course, these techniques also have strong limitations by being situational, that is of being necessarily linked to a lived situation available both to observation and recollection, and they often (but not always) need to be used in conjunction with long-term fieldwork. Notwithstanding this, as methods already much discussed and well developed in several scientific communities (such as those of ergonomists and educators), we believe that they are key tools for the further development of anthropology. As regards the study of so-called tacit knowledge, they are certainly powerful means to help us to understand how cognition is culturally embedded, situated and distributed by social actors.

Notes

1. In her study, she highlights the several 'standard' units of measurement recorded in the baker's body (pressure, amount of force to squeeze, etc.), describes their functional aim, but does not connect them to the flow of activity and to their phenomenal qualities.
2. The classes are given by Toni D'Amelio at the Peter Goss School in Paris. Pupils, who have been attending for a few months to ten years, take two or three classes a week and several intensive week-long workshops a year.
3. This technique requires special training, which Cazemajou undertook, as well as the practice required to hone all interview techniques.

References

Bakhtin, M. (1990), *Art and Answerability: Early Philosophical Essays*, ed. M. Holquist and V. Liapunov, trans. V. Liapunov, supplement trans. K. Brostrom, Austin: University of Texas Press.

Bakhtin, M. and C. Emerson (1984), *Problems of Dostoevsky's Poetics*, Theory and History of Literature, Vol. 8, Minnesota: University of Minnesota Press.

Bourdieu, P. (1990), *The Logic of Practice*, Stanford: Stanford University Press.

Clark, A. (1997), *Being There: Putting Brain, Body and the World Together*, Cambridge: MIT Press.

Conein, B. (1990), 'Cognition située et coordination de l'action. La cuisine dans tous ses états', *Réseaux*, 8(43): 99–110.

Conein, B. (2004), 'Cognition distribuée, groupe social et technologie cognitive', *Réseaux*, 124(2): 53–79.

D'Andrade, R. (1995), *The Development of Cognitive Anthropology*, Cambridge: Cambridge University Press.

Dauliach, C. (1998), 'Expression et onto-anthropologie chez Merleau-Ponty', in R. Barbaras (ed.), *Merleau-Ponty. Notes de cours sur l'origine de la géométrie de Husserl, suivi de Recherches sur la phénoménologie de Merleau-Ponty*, Paris: PUF, 305–30.

De Fornel, M. and L. Quéré (1999), *La logique des situations*, Paris: EHESS.

de Léon, D. (2003a), *Actions, Artefacts, and Cognition: An Ethnography of Cooking*, Lund University Cognitive Studies, Vol. 104.

de Léon, D. (2003b), *The Cognitive Biography of Things*, Lund University Cognitive Studies, Vol. 103.

Favret-Saada, J. (1990), 'Être affecté', *Gradhiva*, 8: 3–9.

Garfinkel, H. (1967), *Studies in Ethnomethodology*, Englewood Cliffs, NJ: Prentice Hall.

Goldfarb, L. W. ((1990) 1998), *Articuler le changement*, Paris: Editions du Temps Présent.

Grasseni, C. (2008), 'Learning to See: World-Views, Skilled Visions, Skilled Practice', in N. Halstead, E. Hirsch and J. Okely (eds), *Knowing How to Know: Fieldwork and the Ethnographic Present*, EASA Series Vol. 9, Oxford: Berghahn Books, 151–72.

Hernandez, M. and D. Sutton (2003), 'Hands That Remember: An Ethnographic Approach to Everyday Cooking', *Expedition*, 45: 30–7.

Howes, D. (1993), *Sensual Relations: Engaging the Senses in Culture and Social Theory*, Michigan: University of Michigan Press.

Hutchins, E. (1995), *Cognition in the Wild*, Cambridge: MIT Press.

Ingold, T. (2000), *The Perception of the Environment: Essays on Livelihood, Dwelling and Skill*, London: Routledge.

Kilani, M. (1994), *L'Invention de l'Autre: Essais sur le discours anthropologique*, Lausanne: Payot.

Lakoff, G. and M. Johnson (1980), *Metaphors We Live By*, Chicago: University of Chicago Press.

Lave, J. (1988), *Cognition in Practice: Mind, Mathematics, and Culture in Everyday Life*, Cambridge: Cambridge University Press.

Lave, J. and E. Wenger (1991), *Situated Learning: Legitimate Peripheral Participation*, Cambridge: Cambridge University Press.

Marchand, J. (ed.) (2010), 'Making Knowledge', special issue of *Journal of the Royal Anthropological Institute*, 16 (s1).

Merleau-Ponty, M. (1942), *La structure du comportement*, Paris: PUF.

Merleau-Ponty, M. (1945), *Phénoménologie de la perception*, Paris: Gallimard.

Merleau-Ponty, M. (1964), *Le visible et l'invisible*, Paris: Gallimard.

Merleau-Ponty, M. (1988), *Merleau-Ponty à la Sorbonne. Résumé de cours 1949–1952*, Dijon-Quetigny: Cynara.

Omodei, M., A. Wearing and J. McLennan (1997), 'Head-Mounted Video Recording: A Methodology for Studying Naturalistic Decision Making', in R. Flin, E. Strub, E. Salas and L. Martin (eds), *Decision Making under Stress: Emerging Themes and Applications*, Aldershot: Ashgate, 137–46.

Patel, K. (2008), 'Thinkers in the Kitchen: Embodied Thinking and Learning in Practice', *Scienze Gastronomiche*, 4: 87–97.

Perelman, C. (1990), *Ethique et droit*, Bruxelles: Editions de l'Université de Bruxelles.

Petitmengin, C. (2007), 'Towards the Source of Thoughts: The Gestural and Transmodal Dimension of Lived Experience', *Journal of Consciousness Studies*, 14 (3): 54–82.

Piaget, J. (1974), *Réussir et Comprendre*, Paris: PUF.

Piette, A. (2009), *L'Acte d'Exister: Une phénoménographie de la présence*, Marchienne-au-Pont: Socrate Editions.

Retsikas, K. (2008), 'Knowledge from the Body: Fieldwork, Power and the Acquisition of a New Self', in N. Halstead, E. Hirsch and J. Okely (eds), *Knowing How to Know: Fieldwork and the Ethnographic Present*, EASA Series Vol. 9, Oxford: Berghahn Books, 110–29.

Ricoeur, P. (1983), *Temps et récit. Tome 1: L'intrigue et le récit historique*, Paris: Seuil.

Ricoeur, P. (1995), *Le Juste*, Paris: Seuil.

Rix, G. (2005), 'Typologie des actes de jugement de l'arbitre de rugby expérimenté', *Science et Motricite*, 56(3): 109–24.

Rix, G. (2007), 'Le 31ème homme: Un garant de la culture du rugby à XV', in J.-Y. Guillain and P. Porte (eds), *La planète rugby. Regards croisés sur l'ovalie*, Paris: Musée National du Sport et Atlantica, 331–50.

Rix, G. and M. Biache (2004), 'Enregistrement en perspective *subjective située* et entretien en *re situ subjectif*: Une méthodologie de constitution de l'expérience', *Intellectica*, 38: 363–96.

Rix, G. and P. Lièvre (2008), 'Towards a Codification of Practical Knowledge', *Knowledge Management Research and Practice*, 6: 225–32.

Rix-Lièvre, G. (2010), 'Différents modes de confrontation à des traces de sa propre activité. Entre convergences et spécificités', *Revue d'anthropologie des connaissances*, 4(2): 357–76.

Sennett, R. (2008), *The Craftsman*, London: Penguin Books.

Shapiro, L. (2011), *Embodied Cognition*, London: Routledge.

Skinner, J. (2010), 'Leading Questions and Body Memories: A Case of Phenomenology and Physical Ethnography in the Dance Interview', in P. Collins and A. Gallinat (eds), *The Ethnographic Self as Resource: Writing Memory and Experience into Ethnography*, Oxford: Berghahn Books, 111–28.

Sklar, D. (2006), 'Qualities of Memory: Two Dances of the Tortugas Fiesta, New Mexico', in T. J. Buckland (ed.), *Dancing from Past to Present: Nation, Culture, Identities*, Madison: University of Wisconsin Press, 97–122.

Sperber, D. (1996), *Explaining Culture: A Naturalistic Approach*, Oxford: Blackwell.

Suchman, L. (1987), *Plans and Situated Actions: The Problem of Human-Machine Communication*, Cambridge: Cambridge University Press.

Sutton, D. (2006), 'Cooking Still, the Senses, and Memory', in E. Edwards, C. Gosden and R. Phillips (eds), *Sensible Objects: Colonialism, Museums and Material Culture*, Oxford: Berg, 87–120.

Sutton, D. and M. Hernandez (2007), 'Voices in the Kitchen: Cooking Tools as Inalienable Possessions', *Oral History*, 35: 67–76.

Theureau, J. (1992), *Le cours d'action, analyse sémiologique: Essais d'une anthropologie cognitive située*, Berne: Peter Lang.

Vermersch, P. (1994), *L'entretien d'explicitation*, Paris: ESF.

Vermersch, P. (1996), 'Pour une psycho-phénoménologie', *Expliciter*, 13: 1–6.

Vermersch, P. (1999), 'Introspection as Practice', *Journal of Consciousness Studies*, 6(2–3): 17–42.

Vermersch, P. (2000), 'Approche du singulier', in J. M. Barbier (ed.), *L'analyse de la singularité de l'action*, Paris: PUF, 239–56.

Vermersch, P. (2003), *L'entretien d'explicitation: Nouvelle édition enrichie d'un glossaire*, Paris: ESF.

Vermersch, P. (2004), 'Prendre en compte la phénoménalité: Propositions pour une psycho phénoménologie', *Expliciter*, 57: 35–45.

Vermersch, P. (2009), 'Describing the Practice of Introspection', *Journal of Consciousness Studies*, 16(10–12): 20–57.

Willis, P. (1980), 'Notes on Method', in S. Hall et al. (eds), *Culture, Media, Language*, London: Hutchinson, 88–95.

–6–

Difficult Moments in the Ethnographic Interview: Vulnerability, Silence and Rapport

Anne Montgomery

Charles Briggs points out that 'the commonsensical, unreflexive manner in which most analyses of interview data are constructed' (Briggs 1986: 102) is the 'single most serious shortcoming relating to the use of interviews in the social sciences' (ibid.). This chapter offers my reflection upon a difficult and challenging moment in one of my own ethnographic interviews in a study exploring how narratives of risk and trust are constructed by sufferers and lay caregivers of myalgic encephalomyelitis/ chronic fatigue syndrome. This difficult moment, I believe, came about as a result of my silences and inadequate rapport in the interaction of the interview which made my participant vulnerable in particular ways that she would not have been had she not agreed to speak with me about her illness experience.

This difficult moment has caused me to reflect on at least two aspects of the ethnographic interview. First, in the physical space of my participant's living room, where we shared refreshments and small talk, I considered myself to be, and positioned myself as such to her, someone with whom she could be comfortable sharing the story of her illness. Back then, even though a novice researcher, I was aware of the 'co-authored' (Williams 1984: 181) construction of the interview. I understood that both she and I were coparticipants in the construction of this interview and my role as a listener was to 'take an active part in its [the story] construction in order to be able to understand what it is all about and how it can be expected to develop' (Hyden 1997: 60). However, I failed to adequately take into account the cultural ways of thinking that work their ways into the coauthored narrative of the interview in ways which 'allow and constrain what is said and how it is expressed' (Bury 2001: 278); and in this example, a difficult moment was created.

Second, my reflection has shown me how such difficult moments may be concealed through the transcribed textual representation of the narrative in published accounts of the resulting research. My reflection around such moments thus compels me to consider both macro- and microscopic issues; that is, how cultural ideas work their way into the finely coordinated interactional work of coparticipants in a research interview.

I will begin the chapter by outlining what I mean by silence, rapport and vulnerabilities in the ethnographic interview. Next, I will describe my own difficult moment through using two transcriptions, though differently detailed, of the same one minute of interaction from the relevant research interview. I will describe the process that transforms the, often audio or video recorded, interaction of the interview into its textual representation in a transcription. I will show how a more detailed transcription has demonstrated potential to help in the interpretation of interview data (Hepburn and Potter 2003: 187) and hence also potentially help to address the concern that troubles Briggs as it allows me to reflect on why this particular one moment of interaction was difficult. Finally, I will show how Sinding relied keenly on her observational notes to examine her own difficult moments (Sinding and Aronson 2003). My intention is to provide examples of difficult moments that may inform reflection on the day-to-day experience of the ethnographic research interviewer.

Silence, Rapport and Vulnerabilities

As researchers, part of our ethical duty of care in the qualitative research interview is to prevent harm to our participants. Research ethical committees imply that 'all manner of harm to research participants can be anticipated, the appropriate salve identified in advance of fieldwork and retrieved at the difficult moment' (Sinding and Aronson 2003: 96). However, often 'difficult' moments only become apparent in the unfolding interaction of the interview or in the conduct of the fieldwork and this calls for constant consideration of harm along the research process. The issue of power, especially its imbalance, in the research interview is never far away from ideas of what may cause harm to participants (Edwards and Mauthner 2002; Sinding and Aronson 2003; Liamputtong 2007). David et al. (1994) imply that the qualitative interview, in its various forms (see also Rapley 2003), is beneficial in reducing the power imbalance over more structured research methods. However, Sinding and Aronson reflect on how the power researchers bring to and exercise in qualitative interviews may impact the process of those taking part in the interview, jointly creating what they call 'liveable stories' (2003: 115), that is stories which can be lived with after the researcher has gone. They suggest that causing 'harm' may occur when participants are made vulnerable to perceiving failures in their lives and that those who take part in research ought to be able to live easily with the stories that they tell and not feel worse about any aspect of their life or experience as a result of taking part in research. Some movement towards reducing the imbalance of power can be seen in the change in understanding of how interview data are produced and the role of rapport in that production.

While much has been and will be said about the qualitative interview, there are two major ways in which its data have been understood: as a resource and as a topic. Interview data as a resource sees data as more or less reflecting the interviewee's reality outside the interview, while interview data as a topic sees the data as more or less reflecting a reality jointly constructed by the interviewee and interviewer participants (Seale 1998; Taylor 2001; Charmaz 2002; Rapley 2003). Interview data as a resource represents what many conventional social science perspectives assume; that the interviewee has preexisting knowledge (beliefs, attitudes, experience, perspectives) that the researcher has to 'get' in order to produce the 'data' (Baker 2004). These data are then analysed by the interviewer/analyst by seeking 'themes' in the content of what is said by the interviewee. The accomplished interviewer will position himself or herself in a way, i.e. as a friend, a professional, as someone who cares and can be trusted, in order to encourage the interviewee to speak openly and truthfully. This positioning is described as building rapport:

> Becoming trusted and seen as someone with whom research participants are comfortable spending time, talking, and sharing their lives is called 'establishing rapport'. In order for a researcher to truly understand the world from the perspectives of those being studied and to see how persons being studied think about their world it is critically important for rapport to be established. (Miller and Tewksbury, in Liamputtong 2007: 56)

The perspective of interview data as a resource has been considerably criticized by those understanding interview data as a topic. Much of this criticism stems from highlighting that the interview is an interactional event in which each of the participants 'mutually monitor each other's talk' (Rapley 2003; see also Seale 2004; Silverman 2001; Holstein and Gubrium 2004; Baker 2004) to create accounts of events. However, there has also been significant criticism of 'how researchers *represent* their participants' stories and bring the reader into the written narrative' (Charmaz 2002: 303, emphasis added), with the attendant potential to 'mask rather than illuminate' the meaning of the teller's story (2002: 303). This is of particular importance because of the sociological and anthropological reliance on the representation of narrative data for explanations of everyday phenomena (Williams 1984; Atkinson 1997; Atkinson and Silverman 1997; Hyden 1997; Bury 2001).

One issue of interest is that of 'silence', and particular attention has been paid to its significance in accounts both of violence in Northern Ireland (Donnan and Simpson 2007) and of the chronically ill (Charmaz 2002). Donnan and Simpson argue in the context of victims' suffering that to some extent silence is 'a matter of context, of disposition and of opportunity' (2007: 7) and Charmaz argues that silences may 'reflect active signals—of meanings, boundaries and rules' (2002: 303). These authors recognize how the embodied experience of the teller of the story is specific to a historical, political or cultural context in which silences emerge, either 'self-imposed or imposed by others' (Donnan and Simpson 2007: 6). Thus it can be seen that the issue of power and external context is significant in understanding silence. Silence, as an interactional feature in the qualitative interview resulting either from interviewer power or from the potential of the broader cultural context to work itself into the interactional context of the interview in such a way that may cause harm or vulnerability to participants, has been insufficiently addressed (although see the discussion by Charmaz (2002) on the reflexivity of the researcher). As argued earlier, silences are often masked in the representation of the narrative account in published texts, and difficult moments, such as the one I will shortly describe, are not often explored by interactional features such as silences.

Key to the interview data as topic perspective is that the account that *is* created is an outcome of the context of the event in which it is produced, i.e. the interview. Recognizing this, however, does not exhaust the consideration of what counts as relevant context (see Wetherell 2001). Poland and Pederson (1998) argue that methodologies such as participant observation, with its ability to generate explicit insights about the context in which talk occurs, and is shaped by, may be better placed than the interview, though not guaranteed, to produce a rich understanding of the meaning of talk. Therefore, in order to understand why stories are created in the way that they are, there ought to be a greater consideration of multiple contexts which includes at least the interactional context of the naturally occurring talk (the uhms, ehs, rights, silences, emphasis, overlapping speech, laughing, shouting); the immediate proximate context of the interview setting, including for example the number and identity of participants in the interaction and the location of the interview; and the 'discursive surround' of the broader context, i.e. historical, cultural, political messages of how one ought to behave or think (see Baker 2006; Wetherell 2001).

The interaction in the qualitative interview has often been described as a conversation. However, because participants interacting in everyday conversations behave in a different way to how they behave in an interview, Rapley, among others, argues that though it may be 'conversation*al*' (2003: 26, emphasis in original), an interview cannot be considered to be a 'naturally occurring' conversation. This has not prevented the interview being analysed by using some of the transcription conventions of conversation analysis in order to shed light on the interactional context of the interview as, for example, in the discursive action model (Horton-Salway 2001) and discursive psychology (Edley 2001). However, these transcription conventions are limited; while they show how the interactional context plays out, they are silent regarding the immediate context of the setting and the discursive surrounds. Nonetheless, they are useful in this chapter as they provide a means to examine the finer details of the interactional context of my difficult moment, so that I may reflect more ably on why I believe I responded inadequately to my participant in this moment.

Silverman argues that we live in an 'interview society' (2001: 160), by which he means that interviews have become increasingly central to the way we, living in the world we live in, make sense of our lives, and there are particular expectations about how the interaction in interviews should proceed. For conversation*al* interaction to proceed, Rapley offers suggestions for what he calls 'mundane interactional "methods" [for] cooperative interviewing' (2003: 25) including 'listening to interviewees talk and following it up with talk about your own personal experience...or your personal opinion or ideas…, or the opinions or ideas of other people [and] whilst listening going "mm", "yeah", "yeah, yeah", alongside nodding, laughing, joking, smiling, frowning' (2003: 25–6). These relate to the ideas of rapport in the Miller and Tewksbury (2007) definition.

The methodological advice implicit in the Miller and Tewksbury definition and other more explicit advice about how a 'good interviewer' should behave in order to 'get' the 'best' data is what Rapley describes as a methodological 'gloss' (2003: 19) of the ideals of rapport and neutrality. He is, of course, not the only one to present a challenge to these ideals as feminist researchers in particular (see Oakley 1981) argue that rapport may be enhanced through personal disclosures by the interviewer. Both Oakley and Rapley talk about ideas of intimate reciprocity, although in different ways. For Oakley, there is 'no intimacy [rapport] without reciprocity' (1981), and reciprocity is given by, for example, personal disclosures, help with housework or conveying the attitude and actions of a helpful friend rather than a researcher. Rapley, on the other hand, doesn't '"*do* self disclosure"' (2003: 25, emphasis in original) just to encourage respondents to be '"more forthcoming"' (2003: 25). His idea of intimate reciprocity is '*just get on with interacting with that specific person*' (2003: 20, emphasis in original), exploring their thoughts and perceptions and sharing yours *if relevant.* He advises that, when analysing the interview, the interviewer should analyse how the actual interaction produced that specific account.

My Challenging Moment and its Textual Representation

I will now set the context for my own difficult moment and show two different transcriptions of the same moment of interaction in my interview. The process that transforms the live conversation*al* interaction of the interview into the textual representation of a transcription is one which Poland (2002) argues is full of opportunities for error: for example, problems with sentence structure, punctuation marks (or lack thereof) and omissions and mistaking of words or phrases for others. Additionally there are interpretive judgements of what to include in the transcription and how best to represent them, or indeed not to represent them, for example in/out breaths, silences, emphasis, and uhms, ehs, mmms (Poland and Pederson 1998). To this end Agar suggests that transcriptions can 'represent minute phonological detail, or they can be edited into clean spoken prose' (1987: 211). That the latter is more readable than the former there is no doubt, but Hepburn and Potter suggest that although attending to the phonological detail presents a less readable transcription, the researcher has 'a closer record of what actually went on rather than a record that suggests something else went on!' (2003: 187). Making transcriptions closer to the heard conversation helps the analyst to interpret the participant's story more than is possible through attending only to the words. When interviews are transcribed in this way they can be seen as spaces of '*finely co-ordinated interactional work in which the talk of both speakers is central to producing the interview*' (Rapley 2001: 306, emphasis in original).

My data are taken from my MSc study, *Believing in ME: Narrative Constructs of Risk and Trust in the Context of Disbelief in Myalgic Encephalomyelitis/Chronic Fatigue Syndrome (ME/CFS) and Declining Trust in Experts* (Montgomery 2008). It explored how narratives of risk and trust are constructed by sufferers and lay care-givers of ME/CFS. Twenty-seven people took part in this study either by one-off individual interview or focus group: six interviews with sufferers; four interviews with caregivers; and one focus group of sufferers. I paid analytic attention to both the *hows* and *whats* of the research process. The analysis of the *whats* provided some evidence that there is cultural disbelief in ME/CFS, informed by 'experts', and that this has consequences for the perception of risk and trust that the participants experienced. The analysis of the *hows* showed that my qualitative interview method allowed participants to 'talk back' (Blumer, in Miller and Glassner 2004: 134) issues of concern to them allowing some redress of the normal power imbalance in social research. There was also evidence of interactional difficulty in the discussion of sensitive issues in one-to-one interviews and it is to this interactional difficulty that this chapter now turns.

Transcription excerpt 1a is a readable transcription taken from an interview with a sufferer of ME. This interview takes place towards the end of the fieldwork when eight interviews, four each with sufferers and carers, and one focus group of sufferers, in which my participant was also a member, had already taken place. The excerpt in question begins in the thirty-fourth minute of a fifty-one minute (and otherwise unproblematic) interview. This excerpt begins with my asking the participant about contexts that make her feel particularly fearful or at risk.

Transcription Excerpt 1a

Interviewer (AM): [. . .] So were there any other times where you felt particularly at risk or you had particular fears, because of your ME, any particular context that made you feel particularly fearful or at risk?

Interviewee (PD): Well, in my intimate relationships with my husband, because there was a lot of, you'd hear on the news or that, or in newspaper features, a lot of marriages breaking up, plus you weren't able, from the physical point of view, you weren't in the position to have full sexual relations at times with your husband. Well most of the time you didn't because it was a matter of weighing up, yes I could, my husband and I could make love, but is it worth it, being totally incapable of doing anything else for the next five days and suffering an enormous amount of pain. And then you had to weigh up, well, if we do make love, it'll give me a wonderful mental boost, that I'm still attractive, I'm still wanted, I still have a role as a wife, and, to pay for that I will have the five days in agony. That was another bit which you can't talk about openly, Anne, because, nobody talks about that side of ME openly. I don't know if anybody else has, in their interviews, talked about that, but certainly in our group.

AM: Well, just what you're saying there, something I am interested in, is the weighing up of the risks, why you choose to have one risk over the other. So that's certainly, that really is very, very appropriate, what you've said.

PD: It's just a matter of, what is it, you know, what is of importance to you. At that time, my husband at that stage, my husband was very good to me all the way through, he never doubted me once [. . .]

It is clear by the content of this excerpt that my participant was sharing something very intimate with me but how that content was delivered to me is masked by how I have represented her narrative in this transcription. Represented as such, the narrative ostensibly exemplifies various benefits of the qualitative interview. For example the participant appears to be providing a reflexive account of her experience and 'talking back' those issues of concern to her. In Lines 18–20 I could be interpreted as showing rapport, as described in many methods texts, as I am telling my participant that I am listening; that what she is saying is something that I am interested in as it matches my idea of what I am there for. In sum I represent myself as a good interviewer and my participant as a good interviewee. However, I, more than anyone, except perhaps my coparticipant, know what was happening in this snippet of interaction and I am fully aware that I did not respond to my participant in the way that she asked me to. Transcription excerpt 1b shows the same excerpt transcribed in more detail using particular transcription conventions (see appendix for details of these conventions).

Transcription Excerpt 1b

AM: [. . .] so were there any (.) other times where you felt particularly (.) at risk or you had particular fears (.) because of (.) your ME (.) any particular context that made you feel (.) eh particularly fearful (.) or at risk

PD: .hhh well I ehm hhh (2.5) in my (.) in my intimate relationships with (.) with my husband (1.3) ehm (1.3) because there was a lot of (.) you'd hear on the news or that or in newspaper features (.).hhh a lot of marriages breaking up (1.0)

AM: right =

PD: = ehm (1.3) plus y-you weren't able (0.4) from the physical point of view (0.7)
you weren't in a position (0.8) to have full sexual relations (0.5) at times (.)
with your husband (.) well most of the time you didn't (0.8) ehm because it
was a matter of (1.0) weighing up (.) ehm (1.0) yes I could (.) my husband and
I could make love (1.6) but (.) is it worth it (1.0) being (1.2) totally incapable
of doing anything else for the next five days
(0.8)
AM: [right
PD: [and suffering (0.8) an enormous amount of pain (1.0).hhh and then you had to
weigh up (0.4) well (1.5) if if we do make love (.) it'll give me (.) a wonderful
(.) mental boost
(1.0)
AM: right
PD: that I'm still attractive (0.8) I'm still wanted (0.5) I still have a role as a wife
(2.7) and (0.2) to pay for that (0.2) I will have the five days in agony (0.6).hhh
that was another (.) bit which y-you can't talk about openly Anne
(0.4)
AM: right
PD: because (0.8) nobody talks about that side of ME openly
(0.5)
AM: ok
(0.9)
PD: I don't know if anybody else (.) has (.) in their interviews (1.3) <talked> about
that (.) but certainly in our [group
AM: [°mmm°
(1.8)
PD: you know =
AM: = well it's just what you're saying there something I am interested in is the
weighing up of the risks (.) ehm why you choose to have one risk over the
other↑ (.) so that that's certainly (.) that
PD: yeah =
AM: = really is (.) very very appropriate (.) what you've
PD: h:ehm[::
AM: [said
(3.0)
PD: .hhh i-it's just a matter of (.) what is it (.) >you know< (.) what is of importance
to you at that [time
AM: [mmm
(1.2)
PD: my husband at that stage (.) my husband was very good to me *all* the way
through (.) he never doubted me (0.6) once [. . .]

There are many interactional features of transcription excerpt 1b but for the purposes of this chapter I would like to note particularly the interaction in Lines 27–42 (see also the comparable Lines 15–20 in transcription excerpt 1a). My coparticipant was sharing something very intimate with me and perhaps, as Line 27 might suggest, this was the first time she had ever spoken about it. Here, she also reaches for a cultural discourse made explicit a short time later in the interview.

Transcription Excerpt 3

PD: you know (.) ehm (.) I don't know why (.) I don't know whether it's just the society we live in↑

(1.7)

AM: right

PD: that you don't talk ((brief laugh)) about sex

In Lines 31–35 she asked me to tell her if anybody else in my research interviews had talked about this intimate issue. My clear understanding of this request was that it represented implicit pleas for help or support from me: Does anybody else share my experience? Am I alone in thinking or feeling as I do? And can you please help me to understand my experience? In my failure to answer these implicit pleas (Line 31: the (1.3) silence; Line 33: my quiet 'mmm'; Line 34: my (1.8) silence and Lines 36–42: my verbal response), I believe that my verbal and nonverbal responses to my participant were inadequate. What follows is my analysis of both how and why this was inadequate.

My Silences and 'Mmm' and Their Role in Interaction

First of all, let me consider my silence in Line 31. Initially, I did not recognize that this silence was 'mine' but after further reflection, I realized that my participant did not need to finish her question with '<talked> about that' as her meaning was clear to both of us in the interaction. After failing to get an answer to her question about whether 'anybody else' I had interviewed in my research had talked about intimate relations with their partners, she then narrows her question to consider those 'in [her] group'. This may have been an attempt to make it easier for me to respond.

I then utter a very quiet 'mmm' overlapping with the last word of my participant's question. Studies of talk in interaction include not only how people speak but how they listen, for example, Gardner (1998) has argued that there are important aspects, such as backchannels, minimal response and receipt tokens, of listening that are largely neglected in language studies. These acknowledgements such as 'yeah', 'right', 'great', 'mmhmm', 'okay' and 'mmm' show the influence that a 'listener in conversation (and other kinds of talk) can have on the talk as a *listener*, i.e. not through contributions to the development of the topic but through minimal feedback' (1998: 204, emphasis in original) and that 'such minimal responses are a significant contribution by conversationalists to the way in which the talk develops' (1998: 205). He further suggests that if such acknowledgements are not used, then the conversation is problematic. What is interesting about his research for making sense of my 'mmm' is that he argues that this is 'a most minimal response to immediately prior talk that allows for any subsequent action…and if it projects anything, then that is something like "let's move on to next matters, as I have nothing to say on the current matter"' (1998: 210). It may be then that my 'mmm' was purposed by me to be heard, and indeed was heard, by my coparticipant in this way.

What follows next is another silence. Poland and Pederson (1998) suggest that silences are an enduring feature of human interaction and as such are a legitimate focus of investigation in qualitative research. They propose that silences may often be 'socially awkward' (1998: 301) and, if used by the interviewer, may create anxiety on the part of the interviewee about how she is being perceived or judged. However, the meanings of silence may be 'varied, contingent and open to (re)interpretation' (1998: 308) and can be used by a skilful interviewer to draw more details from the interviewee. They argue, from a key text on ethnographic interviewing, that silence has been portrayed as either a problem of interviewer rapport or of interviewee recruitment:

> [silence] is seldom considered in its own right as an area of reflection and inquiry. In a classic text on ethnographic interviewing, for example, Spradley (1979) explicitly states that the aim of early interviews in a research project that involves multiple interviews with the same participants is to establish rapport and free-flowing conversation. To that end, he advises interviewers that the first principle of the ethnographic interview is 'keep informants talking' (p. 80). Silence represents a failure on the part of the interviewer to 'draw out' the requisite 'data' from the interviewee, or it represents a troublesome interviewee. From this perspective, silence reflects either interviewer or interviewee inadequacy, for which the remedy is better interviewer training and better selection of 'good' reflective interviewees. (Poland and Pederson 1998: 295)

So how then do I problematize my silences in Lines 31 and 34? Is this, as Spradley suggests, a problem of an insufficiently reflective interviewee or is it the lack of my rapport as interviewer? There is no evidence, either in the detailed transcription or in my reflections on the interaction to suggest the first option is fitting. This leaves, as an explanation, the potential compromise of my preferred identity of being a 'good interviewer' in my failing to live up to the professional obligation to build rapport with my interviewee.

My coparticipant's utterance of 'you know' (Line 35), according to the ideas of Gardner, may be evidence of her 'seeking hearer support' (1998: 219). It is clear to me that she would like me to give her support and not just in a way that lets her know that I've heard her, but that provides answers to her implicit pleas. Finally, in Lines 54–60, I verbally respond to my participant's plea for support in what I realize, then and now, was a very inadequate way. Here, I reproduce my entry in my reflective writing in my MSc dissertation regarding this: 'Given the intimate details of the content of a participant's emic response, why did I, in my exploration and request for extension of her response, do so in a way in which *my* etic concept was framed rather than her emic concept?' (Montgomery 2008). While I do not subscribe to the view represented in many methodology texts of building rapport in order to elicit valid data, the answer to this question may be that I did not, in Rapley's terms of intimate reciprocity, just get on with interacting with my participant, sharing my experiences, thoughts and opinions *as relevant* to the discussion.

Others' Difficult Moments

Sinding and Aronson (2003) both give an account of a research project that describes how what they call 'interview factors (an interview strategy, the interviewer's presence, a line of questioning)' (2003: 96) may intersect with political and discursive surrounds in order to produce 'vulnerability' (2003) on the part of their participants. This vulnerability means that their participants, through the process of participating in the research, are at risk of perceiving 'failures' in their lives. It is interesting that they focus on those things which are not in the interactional context but rather the immediate and historical and cultural discursive context of the interview. They make the connection between the 'power that researchers bring to, and exercise in, interviews' (2003: 95), with causing harm to their participants, and propose that this harm may happen if the participants are made vulnerable to perceiving failures in their lives. Unlike my use of detailed transcriptions to examine my difficult moment, they pay careful attention to their extensive fieldnotes in capturing how they dealt with difficult moments in their interviews and to reflect on how they might deal with future such moments.

I will focus only on Sinding's contribution to their paper. Her research, *Relatives and Friends Providing End-of-Life Care*, explored 'people's experiences of supporting relatives or friends dying of cancer' (2003: 98) in the political context of constraints in the health sector and informal care for people dying of cancer. Her interview strategy was to ask participants to '"tell the story"' (2003: 98) of caring for a person who died, with prompting questions focussing on 'times when the participant found him or herself doing more for the other person and on moments of strain and reward or ease in caring' (2003: 98). Sinding makes explicit that people providing informal end-of-life care do so in a cultural discourse of what it means to have a 'good death' or be a 'good caregiver'. Somebody who dies a 'good death' does so availing of desired medical and spiritual options; acknowledging self as dying; expressing the feelings this knowledge evokes; is accompanied in death; and dies peacefully without pain (2003: 97). A 'good caregiver' is one who enables spiritual and health-care choices easing all pain; receives, prompts and responds to spoken acknowledgements of dying; maintains or creates intimacy with the dying person; and makes the logistical, economic and emotional accommodations home death requires (2003: 97). Sinding suggests these discourses mark minimum standards, falling below which indicates failure in some way.

Furthermore, a discourse such as a 'good death' is often accompanied by common phrases which Wilkinson and Kitzinger argue are 'particularly resistant to question or contradiction... in conversation, they are likely to attract agreement and endorsement' (2000: 803). Such expressions include: '"she didn't suffer", "they did everything they could", "it was for the best"' (Sinding and Aronson 2003: 103). Sinding refers to these as 'consoling refrains' (2003: 103), describing them as 'important social and psychological resources for individuals facing loss' (2003: 115); but perhaps they too are cultural resources drawn upon in response to the cultural surrounds of 'active ageing' and 'a good death' and a 'good caregiver'.

Sinding identified how her interviews, unfolding in particular political and cultural discursive contexts, and her interview strategy exposed her research participants to perceptions of failure in their lives. This left her, as a researcher, unsure and uncomfortable about how to respond and how to position herself in relation to the dominant cultural discourses of kinship, dying, caring and ageing. She observed in her research journal: 'Do "consoling refrains" become untenable—or at least get stretched—by these interviews? After one has spent half an hour describing suffering, surely it becomes less possible to say, "she didn't suffer"–? Am I part of making "bad deaths"?' (2003: 103). Sinding also describes an instance when an elderly male participant realizes, maybe for the first time, that perhaps doctors did not do '"everything they could"' (2003: 103) for his wife and that she need not have died when she did. Here, potential vulnerabilities to her participant were that he not only could no longer easily use this consoling refrain but that he also encountered himself 'as a person he does not want to be—someone who "harbours resentments"' (2003: 104). It is possible that the coparticipant in my interview was left vulnerable to feeling that she was alone in thinking and feeling as she did about her intimate relations with her husband.

Discussion: My 'Encultured Silence'

Having looked at *how* the interactional context of my difficult moment played out, I can perhaps attempt to provide answers as to *why* it played out as it did. Poland and Pederson, in their exploration of potential interpretations of silence on the part of the researcher, suggest an idea they call 'encultured silence' (1998: 298). They define this as 'the inability to hear or be heard because one's life experience is sufficiently different that one does not know the customs and language of a particular social world [of the other speaker]' (1998: 298). However, I wonder if this definition can be turned on its head somewhat. I would like to propose that an 'encultured silence' is one where the life experience of the hearer is sufficiently *similar* so that he or she *does* know the customs and language of the particular social world of the other speaker to the extent that there is an apprehension, resulting in silence, on the part of the hearer. For example, in the brief interaction I described earlier, I am aware of the understanding that my participant and I, and all the others she refers to in her talk, share that in 'the society we live in [...] you don't talk about sex' (transcription excerpt 3). While this is a known meaningful discourse, it was unexpected, by me at least, in this interview and it indicates that neither participant in an ethnographic interview can fully anticipate how a question asked will link with a discursive context and produce vulnerability in research participants. This idea of 'encultured silence' has implications for researchers wishing to use interviews as a method of research inquiry and it encourages reflection upon how cultural or political discourses may play out in the finely coordinated interactional work of the coparticipants in a research interview. Sinding and Aronson propose a number of issues for researchers to reflect upon in their preparation for fieldwork which I summarize here:

- The kinds of experiences that may be culturally relevant to the participant and how participating in an interview might expose the differences between these and an individual's experience as narrated in a research interview
- The ways of talking that participants might have to accommodate their experience within a cultural or political discourse
- How participating in an interview might unsettle these accommodations
- What the interviewer will do when these accommodations are unsettled and vulnerability to failure is exposed (2003: 114)

While these reflections are useful, they indicate that potential discourses can be identified as relevant beforehand and, thus, in a sense then advocate that, as proposed earlier, 'all manner of harm to research participants can be anticipated, the appropriate salve identified in advance of fieldwork and retrieved at the difficult moment' (Sinding and Aronson 2003: 96). What then if, as in my own difficult moment, the researcher encounters a *known* cultural, political or other discourse, but it is one that has an unexpected relevance to your participant and which may produce vulnerability during the interview? Sinding and Aronson identify strategies to contend with this potential situation. First, they build on the notion of 'process consenting' (2003: 109) in order to assess the willingness of the participant to speak about a difficult issue, asking indirect questions; for example, 'I hope you don't mind me asking about...'

or 'you maybe prefer not to talk about…' Second, they suggest abandoning, or at least carefully considering, lines of questioning if the researcher encounters words, gestures or tones that seem to say 'don't go there' (2003: 111). A third strategy is to reflect valued selves back to participants, although this may be problematic as the valued identities most available for affirmation are often embedded in the very discourses and policy contexts implicated in participants' suffering, although this is somewhat resolved by offering a critique of institutional contexts and discourses that give rise to experienced failures. Another strategy is to draw attention to the dominant discourse which may ease the vulnerability produced when personal situations are set against cultural prescriptions, e.g. 'it's so much more complicated and messier than it gets set out to be' (2003: 113). Interviewers could also frame participants' stories as socially important.

Conclusion

In this chapter I have reflected on various difficult moments in interviews in order to illustrate how the broader external cultural or political discursive context of the interview works itself into the interactional context of the interview in such a way that may cause harm or vulnerability to the participants in ethnographic research. I have shown that an examination of discursive surrounds is an issue that researchers ought to consider in their preparation for fieldwork. However, this is not sufficient, as I have also shown that whether or not a researcher is aware of certain discourses, in an ethnographic interview, neither of the coparticipants can fully anticipate how a question asked will link with a discursive context and produce vulnerability in research participants.

References

Agar, M. (1987), 'Transcript Handling: An Ethnographic Strategy', *The Oral History Review*, 15(1): 209–19.

Atkinson, J. M. and J. Heritage (eds) (1984), *Structures of Social Action: Studies in Conversation Analysis*, Cambridge: Cambridge University Press.

Atkinson, P. (1997), 'Narrative Turn or Blind Alley?', *Qualitative Health Research*, 7(3): 325–44.

Atkinson, P. and D. Silverman (1997), 'Kundera's Immortality: The Interview of Society and the Invention of the Self', *Qualitative Inquiry*, 3: 304–25.

Baker, C. (2004), 'Membership Categorization and Interview Accounts', in D. Silverman (ed.), *Qualitative Research: Theory, Method and Practice*, 2nd edn, London: Sage Publications, 162–76.

Baker, P. (2006), *Using Corpora in Discourse Analysis*, London: Continuum.

Briggs, C. L. (1986), *Learning How to Ask: A Sociolinguistic Appraisal of the Role of the Interview in Social Science Research*, Cambridge: Cambridge University Press.

Bury, M. (2001), 'Illness Narratives: Fact or Fiction?', *Sociology of Health and Illness*, 23(3): 263–85.

Charmaz, K. (2002), 'Stories and Silences: Disclosures and Self in Chronic Illness', *Qualitative Inquiry*, 8: 302–28.

David, D., A. West and R. Ribbons (1994), 'Mother's Intuition? Choosing Secondary Schools', in *D845 Study Guide*, Milton Keynes: Falmer Press, Open University.

Donnan, H. and K. Simpson (2007), 'Silence and Violence among Northern Ireland Border Protestants', *Ethnos*, 72(1): 5–28.

Edley, N. (2001), 'Analysing Masculinity: Interpretative Repertoires, Ideological Dilemmas and Subject Positions', in M. Wetherell, S. Taylor and S. Yates (eds), *Discourse as Data: A Guide for Analysis*, London: Sage Publications, 189–228.

Edwards, R. and M. Mauthner (2002), 'Ethics and Feminist Research: Theory and Practice', D845 Generic Course Resource, http://www.open.ac.uk/courses/tasters/d845/objects/d2557.pdf, accessed 7 April 2010.

Gardner, R. (1998), 'Between Speaking and Listening: The Vocalisation of Understandings', *Applied Linguistics*, 19(2): 204–24.

Hepburn, A. and J. Potter (2003), 'Discourse Analytic Practice', in C. Seale, D. Silverman, J. Gubrium and G. Gobo (eds), *Qualitative Research Practice*, London: Sage Publications, 180–96.

Holstein J. and J. Gubrium (2004), 'The Active Interview', in D. Silverman (ed.), *Qualitative Research: Theory, Method and Practice*, 2nd edn, London: Sage Publications, 140–61.

Horton-Salway, M. (2001), 'The Construction of M.E.: The Discursive Action Model', in M. Wetherell, S. Taylor and S. Yates (eds), *Discourse as Data: A Guide for Analysis*, London: Sage Publications, 147–88.

Hyden, L.-C. (1997), 'Illness and Narrative', *Sociology of Health and Illness*, 19(1): 48–9.

Liamputtong, P. (2007), *Researching the Vulnerable: A Guide to Sensitive Research Methods*, London: Sage Publications.

Miller, J. and B. Glassner (2004), 'The "Inside" and the "Outside": Finding Realities in Interviews', in D. Silverman (ed.), *Qualitative Research: Theory, Method and Practice*, 2nd edn, London: Sage Publications, 125–40.

Montgomery, A. (2008), 'Believing in ME: Narrative Constructs of Risk and Trust in the Context of Disbelief in Myalgic Encephalomyelitis/Chronic Fatigue Syndrome (ME/CFS) and Declining Trust in Experts', MSc dissertation, Open University.

Oakley, A. (1981), 'Interviewing Women: A Contradiction in Terms?', in H. Roberts (ed.), *Doing Feminist Research*, London: Routledge & Kegan Paul, 30–61.

Poland, B. (2002), 'Transcription Quality', in J. Gubrium and J. Holstein (eds), *Handbook of Interview Research: Context and Method*, Thousand Oaks: Sage Publications, 629–49.

Poland, B. and A. Pederson (1998), 'Reading between the Lines: Interpreting Silences in Qualitative Research', *Qualitative Inquiry*, 4: 293–312.

Rapley, T. (2001), 'The Art(fulness) of Open-Ended Interviewing: Some Considerations on Analysing Interviews', *Qualitative Research*, 1(3): 303–23.

Rapley, T. (2003), 'Interviews', in C. Seale, D. Silverman, J. Gubrium and G. Gobo (eds), *Qualitative Research Practice*, London: Sage Publications, 15–33.

Seale, C. (1998), 'Qualitative Interviewing', in C. Seale (ed.), *Researching Society and Culture*, London: Sage Publications, 202–32.

Seale, C. (ed.) (2004), *Researching Society and Culture*, 2nd edn, London: Sage Publications.

Silverman, D. (2001), *Interpreting Qualitative Data: Methods for Analysing Talk, Text and Interaction*, 2nd edn, London: Sage Publications.

Sinding, C. and J. Aronson (2003), 'Exposing Failures, Unsettling Accommodations: Tensions in Interview Practice', *Qualitative Research*, 3(1): 95–117.

Taylor, S. (2001), 'Locating and Conducting Discourse Analytic Research', in M. Wetherell, S. Taylor and S. Yates (eds), *Discourse as Data: A Guide for Analysis*, London: Sage Publications, 5–48.

Wetherell, M. (2001), 'Debates in Discourse Research', in M. Wetherell, S. Taylor and S. Yates (eds), *Discourse Theory and Practice*, London: Sage Publications, 381–98.

Wilkinson, S. and C. Kitzinger (2000), 'Thinking Differently about Thinking Positive: A Discursive Approach to Cancer Patients' Talk', *Social Science and Medicine*, 50: 797–811.

Williams, G. (1984), 'The Genesis of Chronic Illness: Narrative Reconstruction', *Sociology of Health and Illness*, 6(2): 175–200.

APPENDIX

The data were transcribed according to some of the conventions developed by Gail Jefferson. A more detailed description of these transcription symbols can be found in Atkinson and Heritage (1984: ix–xvi).

Table 6.1. Transcription Notation

Transcription Notation	*Description*
(0.5)	Length of pause measured in tenths of a second.
(.)	Micro-pause, less than two-tenths of a second.
word↑	very rapid rise in intonation.
°why°	Degree signs: the volume of talk is less than the surrounding talk.
word	Underlining: speaker's emphasis or stress
>word <	Word in > < indicates faster pace than surrounding talk
<word>	Word in < >indicates slower pace than surrounding talk
word=because	Equals sign: words are latched, that there is no hearable gap
wh:::y	Colons: sound-stretching
w[ord [yes	Square brackets: onset overlapping talk
(word)	Word in brackets: the best possible hearing
.hh	in-breath
hh	outbreath

Part III
Interview Cases

–7–

Instances of Inspiration: Interviewing Dancers and Writers

Helena Wulff

Last week my table turned, temporarily. Instead of conducting an interview for my research, I was interviewed for a research project. The interviewer, a young American psychology student, was doing a master's degree at the London School of Economics on work–life balance among women in academia. Sweden, with its extensive policy and laws on equality, is a useful case in point. The interview accentuated for me, however, what we as anthropologists tend to neglect, at least we did before the conference resulting in this volume: the interviewee's point of view. What exactly does the interviewee get out of being interviewed? I was very busy as usual and on the way to the interview, to be honest, slightly bored with the prospect of having to reply to fairly routine questions I did not think would catch my imagination. But it became a really nice encounter over an iPod in my office at Stockholm University, not least as it left me with one or two new insights about my own life and work. My interviewer managed to establish rapport by saying 'I couldn't do this without you', even though I am far from the only woman academic in Sweden. Still, I took her point and agreed to join her inside a Batesonian 'This is interview' frame.[1]

As society changes, so does anthropology. In order to capture contemporary issues, new research techniques are required in addition to traditional participant observation (cf. Melhuus et al. 2010; Faubion and Marcus 2009; Hannerz 2003; Wulff 2002). Interviews are not a new technique, but with increasing diversity in social life as well as new recording devices and computer programs for categorizing interview data, interviewing has developed into an increasingly sophisticated and multifaceted research technique. Interviewing is now a core method in contemporary anthropology which impacts knowledge production in the discipline.

In this chapter, I am interested in the anthropological interview as an instance of inspiration when the interviewer and the interviewee trigger each other into an exchange of escalating states of creativity beneficial for the interviewer's research process as well as for the interviewee in the form of potential new personal or professional insights. When it works, this can be seen as a synergy situation, as the two people involved would not have reached these particular insights independently.

Featuring interview cases from extensive ethnographic research on dancers and writers, this chapter is intended to bring out connections between participant observation and interviews and also to discuss the interviewer's demeanour and design of questionnaires.

Dancers and writers differ when it comes to verbal eloquence and how they talk about their work in interviews. Dancers are trained to talk with their bodies while writers are trained to talk with words, when it comes to speaking about their work as well as doing the actual writing. Both dancers and writers contribute to a contemporary interview society (Atkinson and Silverman 1997; Gubrium and Holstein 2002), as they are frequently interviewed by journalists for newspaper and magazine features and promotional articles, as well as for documentary films, television and radio programmes on the arts. It happens that dancers are interviewed live at dance festivals in front of an audience, while writers appear regularly as interviewees at literary festivals and conferences. Such interviews are often streamed live on the Internet and later broadcast on YouTube. All this interviewing in media means that especially famous writers and dancers acquire a polite, polished attitude to interviewers that the anthropologist has to break through in her search of backstage life in dance studios and writers' workrooms.

What then is inspiration? The concept of inspiration has traditionally been associated with artistry, and as Brogan (1994: 15–16) describes these impulses that lead to creativity: 'Every poet recognizes that during poetic composition material emerges—words, images, figures, rhythms—from sources which lie beyond the pale of consciousness.' Looking back in history, he goes on to talk about the widespread belief that these sources were divine. In the West in classical times, there was also the idea of the muse who would inspire poets. Brogan points to 'the claim that when the god does take possession, the poet enters a state of transcendental ecstasy or frenzy, a "poetic madness" or *furor poeticus.*' But Brogan is eager to bring up a long-standing awareness that inspiration does not come without practice. This highlights 'the importance of craft' or 'the application of effort and skill in the acquisition of technique—practiced, learned, remembered, repeated.'[2] This description parallels scholarly work in general, but above all it captures the process of anthropological interviewing where inspiration can only spring up if the interviewer has been trained, has practised and learnt the skill of interviewing. And if anthropological interviewers and interviewees do not quite get into a transcendental ecstasy, when inspiration strikes, and the interview lifts, 'composition material emerges—words, images, figures, rhythms—from sources which lie beyond the pale of consciousness' and can still appear.

Reaching for Rapport

The crucial point here is that in anthropological interviews, inspiration is relational and a possibility after a 'mutual tuning in' (Schutz 1964: 161) has been taking place between the interviewer and the interviewee. Both parties have to set their mind on this shared task. Still, we as interviewers are in charge and responsible for the subsequent rapport. The fact that rapport in anthropological interview situations can take many forms is exemplified in Skinner's article on an interview he did with a woman salsa dancer with whom he also danced (2010: 114). They established a 'relaxed rapport', but when Skinner asked the woman to comment on his article the year after, she admitted having been trained in counselling technique which resembled Skinner's social science interview training. Skinner (2010: 124) then realized that: 'Before, after—and during the interview, we had been literally dancing around each other.'

Having conducted interviews in six anthropological studies between 1981 and the present,[3] I know that occasionally the rapport between interviewer and interviewee never happens; when rapport happens, it tends to define the interview early on, but it may come later after the interviewer has tried and failed with a number of strategies to reach the interviewee. Interviewing a prima ballerina in Stockholm, I did not get anywhere until I took to one aspect of a counselling technique I had learnt informally from a psychologist friend. Conducting counselling sessions, my friend would reveal a sensitive matter about herself which related to the issue troubling the patient. This would make the patient realize that she or he was not the only one dealing with a situation like that, and so a sense of community and trust would begin to develop. The Stockholm ballerina did not make any efforts to hide that she was blasé, and kept replying without enthusiasm to my questions. As it was something of a scoop to get to do an interview with this prominent ballerina, and thus an important opportunity for my study, it had to be a good, useful interview. While posing my questions, I was trying very hard to think of how to reach her, searching for some common ground. It was when I shared with her what I had learnt about the stage fright university lecturers with large classes can have that she opened up. Inspired by my confession, she started confiding in me about her experiences of vulnerability on stage. Suddenly, we were close, and she talked at great length about how she often felt exposed on stage as 'the audience, they can see what you have inside'. In dancing leading dramatic roles, dancers use their 'emotional memory' (cf. Stanislavsky 1967: 55) of strong feelings such as passion, desire, fear, sadness and grief. The ballerina kept her open and warm approach during the rest of the interview when we moved into questions on other topics.

Inspiration is linked not only to creativity, but also to notions of flow and improvisation as it can initiate both types of situations. Writing about creativity and the difficulty of defining this concept, Ingold and Hallam contrast

> two notions of creativity that can be discerned in early twentieth-century philosophical works. It may be understood, on one hand, as the production of novelty through the recombination of already extant elements, or on the other, as process of growth, becoming and change. The former view posits the world as an assemblage of discrete parts; the latter as a continuous movement or flow. (2007: 16)

Ingold and Hallam acknowledge the role of collaboration in creativity and argue that 'the capacity for creative improvisation is exercised by individuals against the conventions of culture and society. Improvisation and creativity, we contend, are intrinsic to the very processes of social and cultural life' (2007: 19). So is improvisation. Ingold and Hallam appreciate Edward Bruner's suggestion of 'the importance of rules and codes' and that 'we will never understand how culture works, or how it changes, unless we take into account the human capacity for improvisation and creativity' (1993: 26). In other words, people improvise because rules cannot cover every contingency. Just like in musical improvisation, such as jazz (Berliner 1994), and choreographic improvisation (Wulff 1998), improvisation in life—and in interviewing—consists of the slightly changed repetition of an already existing element put into new combinations (see also Cerwonka and Malkki 2007).

So inspiration, creativity and improvisation all lead to the formation of something new out of existing parts, but the important difference between inspiration on one hand and creativity and improvisation on the other, I would argue, is that inspiration is the initial state that can turn into a process of creativity which might include new moments of improvisation. So inspiration can be the start of what John Blacking (1977) famously referred to as transcendental states or peak experiences. During such moments we enter into 'flow' in Csikszentmihalyi's (1992) terminology, when a task—that of an artist, scholar, any craftsman—suddenly becomes effortless as it reaches into new territories.

'If I Could Tell You …'

'If I could tell you what it means, I wouldn't have to dance it', Isadora Duncan is reputed to have said (Middleton 1988: 165). Dance is, of course, mostly nonverbal[4] and has the potential to create and convey circumstances, moods and form that cannot be expressed in the same way, or at all, through words, orally or textually (Blacking 1988; Wulff 2001, 2008b: 75). This is why dancers are trained to talk with their bodies. In the ballet and dance world, this is referred to as 'talking with your feet'; in Ireland, traditional dance is sometimes described in terms of the poetic 'song of feet' (Wulff 2007: 70). During interviews I did with dancers in my study of the transnational ballet world it often happened that the dancer would get up from the table and start illustrating a point he or she was making through a step or a combination of steps. It was also more common than not that the dancer I interviewed would move around while sitting down, flapping arms and lifting legs under the table. Once a male principal dancer I was interviewing over a breakfast table in a hotel on a tour got so excited over a role in a performance we were discussing that he overturned the table, sending coffee cups and croissants flying around the room, to the amusement of everyone present.

My study of career and culture in the transnational ballet world was conducted between 1993 and 1995 with four major ballet companies: the Royal Swedish Ballet in Stockholm, the Royal Ballet in London, the American Ballet Theatre in New York and the contemporary ballet company Ballett Frankfurt in Frankfurt-am-Main (Wulff 1998, 2008a,b). The methodological repertoire included primarily participant observation complemented with interviews and to some extent watching videos used for documentation and promotion in the ballet world. I did participant observation of everyday work: training, rehearsal and performances. In addition, I conducted almost 120 interviews with dancers, choreographers, coaches, directors, musicians, conductors, critics and other ballet people working in the theatres or belonging to fan followings. Interviewing ballet dancers was a specific situation for me, different from interviewing teenaged girls, teachers and youth workers in South London, young Swedes in New York or traditional dancers or writers in Ireland. It was my experience of having grown up in the ballet world that made this difference. I engaged in intense ballet training for fifteen years until I unexpectedly had to stop in my late teens because of an injury. The fact that I went to the same ballet school as some of my interviewees, used to dance with them and thus grew up with them is an unusual aspect of anthropological research. We had a shared past, which meant that I was able to contextualize people and events from their childhood and youth that they talked about in the interviews. So there we were, me asking questions and a dancer responding in an attentive yet flexible tone. Contrary to most other interviews I have conducted, I could sense the dancers' trust and how they reach out for me. There was a give and take and exchange just like in dancing. They were trained in partnering.

Writing about the interview Skinner did with the woman salsa dancer, he notes that it is 'a learning case study' and 'above all, one based around muscle and cerebral memories' for both of them (2010: 11). When I was interviewing ballet dancers, many of them, again, related to me *as if we were dancing a duet* together. For me, Bourdieu's (1977) body hexis was activated, and I was reminded of my bodily memory of having danced classical ballet. It is important that the dancers were aware of this as dancers see themselves as different from other people, often misunderstood. My dancing past made them trust me and accept me as a part of their setting.

Working with Words

My ongoing study of the social world of contemporary fiction writers in Ireland such as John Banville, Colm Tóibín and Anne Enright focusses on work practice, prestige and career patterns, the private versus the public and the local versus the global in a postcolonial age (Wulff 2008c, 2009). I do participant observation at writers' festivals and retreats, literary conferences, book launches, prize ceremonies and creative writing workshops. I also meet the writers on informal occasions. I do in-depth interviews with them and I read their work. Important, I connect participant observation and interviews: a piece of information I first get through participant observation, I then check during the interview, and vice versa; something I learn in an interview, I look for during participant observation in order to confirm and contextualize it.

Even though writers work with words they are not necessarily easier to interview than dancers. In a seminar I gave at Stockholm University on my research on Irish writers at Stockholm University, a colleague asked: 'What has been the hardest part of your research this far?' I had to think awhile before I knew the answer. It is to interview writers with an international reputation. They have been interviewed an innumerable number of times by literary scholars and journalists who do not always come all that well prepared. When I first meet these writers, they radiate a curious combination of being blasé out of assuming that they will have to reply to the same questions all over again and fright that I will reveal sensitive issues or misrepresent them. They are on guard. So I have to make them understand that I will be ethical when I write and not discuss sensitive personal or professional circumstances such as declines in careers or failing to win prizes after having been short-listed. I am pleased that by now I have learnt how to reach them by formulating questions that interest and surprise them rather than the routine questions they expect and to which I can find the answers on the Internet anyway. One example of this was in a hotel bar in Dublin in 2010 when I interviewed John Banville, one of the most prominent and productive award-winning contemporary Irish writers. At age sixty-five, Banville has written seventeen novels, seven plays and one collection of short stories. He has also written four detective stories under the pen name Benjamin Black. Banville turned out to be pleasant and cooperative. This I had not really anticipated as the protagonists in his writings tend to be rather cruel and complicated men, not very nice. He identifies his writing style in terms of 'an Irish tone of voice—grim comedy'. During the interview, he gave the impression of being someone who cared about people around him, certainly his friends, but also colleagues. I already knew from comments in the literary world in Dublin that he had been elected to the Irish arts association *Aosdána* in 1984, but when he could make a living on his novels and journalism he resigned to allow another artist to receive the annuity, the annual income to which members of *Aosdána* are entitled.

After the interview, I wrote in my fieldnotes that 'Banville is actually a kind man who would like to be cruel…' Before the interview, I had been thinking of how to open it, how to inspire him. What would be vital to him? So I started by asking:

Wulff (W): Why do you write?

He was taken aback in amusement and surprise by the seemingly self-evident question. Laughing at first, but getting serious and committed, he replied:

Banville (B): Why do I write? I can't not write, and I've been doing it since I was twelve. I feel reality is not real until it has been put into words.

Later during the interview, when we talked about how he was renewing his style, he came back to why he writes. It seemed as if my opening question had touched a nerve:

B: Why am I doing this? I ask myself. This is no job for a grown man. Why am I doing this? What else could I do? It's my way of filtering the world, fiction. The function of fiction is to illuminate. It's an amazing privilege to earn one's living from writing sentences, words. What is the greatest innovation of humankind? It is the sentence.

For this study on Irish writers it is also necessary for me to hang out with those I have interviewed in different contexts such as literary festivals, readings and book launches. During such participant observation I can drop interview questions or steer the conversation in a certain direction. As Hammersley and Atkinson (1995: 19) remark:

> Interviews in ethnographic research range from spontaneous, informal conversations in places that are being used for other purposes, to formally arranged meetings in bounded settings out of earshot of other people. In the case of the former the dividing line between participant observation and interviewing is hard to discern.

Now the writers are getting used to me turning up here and there (cf. Hannerz 2003), which creates occasions for growing even closer and follow-up conversations. It is only by joining them in the different places around Ireland where they go—and meet each other—that I can fully grasp the nature of their work practice.

Questions and Questionnaires

There are formal versus informal interviews with an open-ended and in-depth approach. Agar identifies the informal ethnographic interview as an interview conducted without 'a written list of questions. Rather, you have a repertoire of question-asking strategies from which you draw as the moment seems appropriate' (1980: 90). An informal interview, Agar goes on, is 'informal because it happens in many different situations':

> You might ask informal questions while working with an informant on a harvest; you might ask during a group conversation over coffee; or you might ask while watching a ceremony.

'If used with tact', he concludes, these questions will not be 'doing any harm to the natural flow of events'.

In earlier studies such as the one on teenaged girls and ethnicity in South London (1988, 1995), I have used a number of different interview types conducted on separate occasions but mostly with the same people. These types of interviews have been social network mapping (Wallman et al. 1980), genealogies three generations deep, time-budgets, school essays, week diaries, life histories (George and Narayan 2001), focus groups interviews (Morgan 2001), as well as surveys. Designing the questionnaires for my studies in the ballet world, on dance and on writers in Ireland, I listed thirty-five questions for each one, planning for the interview to take about an hour. (When asking for an interview with busy people, it is, of course, an advantage to be able to say how long it would take and that this can be shortened.) Among these questions I included topics referring to 'social network' such as 'Who do you hang out with?', 'week diaries' such as 'How did you spend last Wednesday, Saturday and Sunday?' and 'life histories' such as 'Where were you born? Why did you start to dance? What dance school did you go to? Tell me about your career.'

Training in interview technique and how to design questionnaires and surveys seems now to be included in most methods courses. It was already in place at the Department of Social Anthropology at Stockholm University when I was a PhD student. As a part of the preparations for going to the field, the supervisor instructed his or her student both in how to formulate questions and how to act during the interview. During my first fieldwork in South London, I was fortunate to be a part of Sandra Wallman's project on the inner city, the Resource Options Programme, for which I contributed interviews in Battersea. With time, I noticed that it is useful to finish an interview by asking the interviewee if there is anything he or she would like to add. This is often when the most interesting pieces of information come out. Many times, I have also been told very special stories when the interview can be said to be over, as I am being walked to the door or the car.

The fact that my key informant among the writers, Éilís Ní Dhuibhne, besides her over twenty novels and collections of short stories, children's books, as well as plays and poems, has a PhD in Irish folklore and a number of academic publications makes her also a colleague and a friend. This is a case of how interviewing can create mutual close friendship that extends beyond the research. We spend time together both in Dublin and Stockholm as she has family in Sweden. One sign of when a 'friendship like' relationship with an informant/interviewee turns into an ordinary friendship is that there are many zones of intimate information appearing that the anthropologist excludes from fieldnotes and publications. I have interviewed Éilís Ní Dhuibhne with a list of questions three times. The interviews have been characterized by exceptional inspirational moments. As I have known her since I was doing my study of dance in Ireland, I first tried out my ideas for a new study of writers with her. She connected me to people I could do pilot interviews with and to creative writing classes where I could do pilot observations, all of which was most useful for how I developed my research proposal. About a year later, she told me about her next novel entitled *Fox, Swallow, Scarecrow* (2007), which is about the literary scene in

Dublin: 'I've written it very quickly. It just flowed out', and: 'The story is going to be about relationships in the group, the petty catting all the time'. She then confessed that the novel was inspired by my research topic on Irish writers.

With a three-year grant from the Swedish Research Council, I have been able to go to Ireland, every other or third month, for about a week at a time. It was when I did my study of dance in Ireland and questions of memory and mobility that I found myself almost commuting to Ireland for certain dance events. I then began to think of that research as yo-yo fieldwork (Wulff 2002, 2007). In the end I had spent altogether about eight months in the field going to different places in Ireland as this was also multilocal fieldwork (Marcus 1998; Hannerz 2003).

This is obviously becoming an increasingly common way of doing anthropological research. Some field studies demand repeat visits over more than one year to a number of sites rather than one long stretch in one place, when the studies include central events that happen infrequently and may need to be revisited. Going back to the same places in this way over the course of a few years thus provides opportunities for interviews.

Frenzy in the Field

Most of the time, people are cooperative, even flattered by the invitation to be interviewed, but occasionally we are rejected, at least initially. This was the case with one interview I did for my dance in Ireland research. In line with the theme of this volume, which among other things asks 'What exactly is the relationship between the interview and the anthropological text?' I will show how interview data can be embedded in a published text. The following[5] illustrates how an interview is driven forward by moments of inspiration.

Searching for authenticity and tradition in Irish dance, I flew in early September 2001 to Dublin and then on to Galway in the west of Ireland, where I boarded a local bus which took me to the small village of Carraroe on the Connemara coast. The sun had just come out after a spell of rain, making the pastoral landscape shine in the late afternoon light. I watched low walls encircling little green fields and white houses, sheep and horses against a backdrop of the Aran Islands. In Carraroe, I went to the pub An Chistin where the 2001 competition in *sean-nós*, old-style step dancing, was about to unfold. Eight dancers were waiting in another room. The musicians at the side of the stage began tuning their instruments: an accordion, a harmonica and a fiddle that soon came together in catching rhythms.

First out was the previous year's winner, a young girl dressed in blue jeans and so-called step shoes, hard shoes with big heels. She danced very well, executing her steps clearly and confidently, raising the atmosphere in the pub. After her came a man and then a woman, neither of them leaving any particular impression. A little boy about ten years of age took the floor. He danced with a precision and joy that brought down the pub. Two young men appeared, one after the other, filling the stage with their electrifying steps and making the audience scream. And I knew: one of them will win. You know good dance when you see it.

That was when a tall, good-looking man in his fifties dressed in worn casual trousers and a modest shirt went out on stage. He did not wear step shoes, just ordinary shoes with iron plates on the front and back of his soles. The music started and he tilted his head as if he was letting the music stream through his body as he listened to the sound, the clicks, of his steps. Everyone in the pub was completely spellbound by this highly skilled, effortless and exquisite dancing. I have no clear memory of the last dancer, although I have read in my fieldnotes that it was a man dressed in dark clothing who got a loud applause. But it was the man in his fifties with the elegant execution who won the competition. His name was Paraic Hopkins. He was in a class by himself.

The next day I went back to the pub, which opened around noon. I had made interview appointments with Colm, the man in charge of the competition, and with Paraic, the winner. The daylight that streamed in through the small windows made the pub look quite different from the warm semidarkness at the competition the night before: now it was harsh and desolate. Two rugged old men were already drinking at the bar. They offered long, rich stories about local dancing in the past, and when I started interviewing Colm, they were happy to join in, commenting and elaborating on what he was saying. 'Low and fierce' is how good *sean-nós* dancing should be, I learnt. Later Paraic strode in having driven from the small farm where he lived and worked. He sat down and ordered a cup of coffee, which he clutched with his big hands while his eyes were moving quickly around. Something was about to happen that has never happened to me before in the field: he demanded a fee for the interview. 'You will write a book and get money from it', he began and he went on to tell me that when he had taught the president of Ireland to dance or when he had been on television, he had received IR£100. (This was before the Euro was introduced.) I told him that academics do not earn a lot of money on their books and that I had no money to give him.[6] 'When I teach classes', he persisted, 'I get IR£60.' The price dropped, I noted. After some negotiations, when I tried to lure him into talking about Ireland generally, which he refused, realizing that this topic was also a part of my study, he finally urged me to take out my notebook. And so he talked generously and eloquently at great length about his love of music as a child and how he learnt *sean-nós* dancing by watching the old people dance at parties, or 'do a party piece' at weddings, christenings and Christmas parties, and how he would imitate them: 'That's how you get into it, same with *sean-nós* singing. The kids would pick up the words—and that's how the tradition has been kept, handed down from generation to generation.'

He also described the joy of dancing ('When you see somebody who enjoys it, he gets carried away! He's like floating in the air and it is the music that is holding him up!') and about teaching this dance form:

> *Sean-nós* dancing is a natural dance. The old people used to say 'you can't teach it, you can learn it.' You don't let the body do the music. You get the person to listen to the

> music, the music will do the dancing. You don't worry about what the feet are doing. You don't worry about music and time and the feet does their own bit! When I started teaching I couldn't slow down to see the steps. I kept saying no for many years, then I learnt to slow down, now I'm teaching young kids. They picked it up very, very quickly. So they taught me back my own steps!!

We talked for over an hour and then he gave me a lift to the bus stop down the road.[7] I promised to send him my book. It was with mixed feelings of having accomplished a lot during the short span of twenty-four hours, but also with regret, that I headed back to Galway and on to Dublin. Having been touched by extraordinary dancing and stories about dancing, I brought many fond memories. The initial negotiations I had had with the winner before he started talking to me had given me data about multilocal links between the village and wider Irish society, even globally, such as that *sean-nós* dancing had been included at Irish festivals in Boston, Milwaukee, Scotland and the Isle of Man.

Interviews as Instances of Inspiration

We used to consider interviews a complementary method, one that would add data to the main method, participant observation. The relationship between participant observation and interviews is still significant, not least because of new forms of participant observation which, for instance, multilocal and yo-yo fieldwork entails. Important, with a large part of modern social life being enacted behind closed doors, perhaps in front of computer screens, and thus offering fewer opportunities for observable situations, there is a growing dependency on interviews in anthropological research. Interviews can actually constitute the main method in anthropological research, such as in Ulf Hannerz's (2004) study of foreign correspondents. The success of this study, however, had to do with Hannerz's extensive experience of traditional fieldwork. Such experience can provide the anthropologist with a crucial sense for context and an eye for ethnographic detail around the interview.

Inspiration does not happen in every anthropological interview, but when it happens it consists of one or two moments that drive the rapport between the interviewer and the interviewee further. Inspiration is an impulse that moves the interview in an unexpected direction. I would like to wrap up by observing that dancers and writers I study share the experience of being interviewed by journalists, and especially the famous ones learn to perform in a polite but distanced way which I have to bridge in my search for life and work practice behind the scenes. My strategy is to make the interview exciting for them as well, which requires extra research every time. As the interviews are tailor made for each writer, they are also quite different from each other, which mean fewer opportunities for systematic comparison of large materials. In that respect, the interviews are not like conversations.

Dancers and writers differ, however, when it comes to verbal eloquence, and thus how they talk about their work in interviews. Dancers are trained to talk with their bodies while writers are trained to talk with words. When I was interviewing dancers, it was an advantage that I used to dance. There is still a dance sensibility in my body, which the dancers recognized. Also during participant observation:

> Increasingly, I noticed that some of my formulations and observations both about ballet and social life in the theatre 'came back' to me from the dancers. By then I had an idea about who was talking to whom about what, and I was able to trace my comments. Without striving for it, I had given the dancers words by verbalizing aspects of crucial ideas in the ballet world that appealed to them. (Wulff 1998: 1)

Finally, in my research on Irish writers, Deirdre Madden warned me by email before we met that she was 'very reserved' and that she was not sure I would benefit from talking to her. It did not take long before she took over the interview, asking intriguing questions about me and my work. It remains to be seen if this interest will be transformed into a fictionalized anthropologist in one of her novels, perhaps as another instance of inspiration from the interviewee's point of view.

Notes

1. This refers to Gregory Bateson's renowned idea about the so-called metacommunicative message 'this is play', a tacit agreement between two people to play rather than, for example, fight, within a certain frame (1972: 177–9).
2. In addition, Brogan (1994) considers that inspiration has been located in the inner psyche. See also 'Inspiration' in *Princeton Encyclopedia of Poetry and Poetics* (Preminger 1974: 96–7).
3. My first study, which was for my PhD, focussed on teenaged girls and ethnicity in South London (Wulff 1988, 1995), the second on young Swedes' exceptional experiences in 1980s New York (Wulff 1992). Then I moved on to a major study of the transnational ballet world (Wulff 1998, 2008a,b), which led to an engagement with dance and new technology (Wulff 2003). This was followed by another major study, on dance in Ireland and questions of memory and mobility (Wulff 2007), which made me formulate my current research, also major, on Irish contemporary writers and their English-language work (Wulff 2008c, 2009).
4. Contemporary dance might include one or two monologues, dialogues, an exclamation or even song. Written words and sentences appear in dance performances on screens or posters and other materials, and might be moving around, dancing as it were.
5. These are slightly revised sections from *Dancing at the Crossroads* by Wulff (2007) republished here with permission from Berghahn Books.

6. Even though some anthropologists pay for assistance with interpretation and other tasks during fieldwork, it is rare to pay for an interview with an informant. I am uncomfortable with the idea of paying for an interview as it would define the situation as a business encounter with monetary gains rather than one on a human, 'friendship like' level, ideally with a closeness and trust that cannot be bought for money. (In the same vein as 'Money can't buy you love.') The gain for the interviewee would, again, be insights about his or her life.
7. After we had gone through my list of questions, the interview turned into what Robson calls 'a conversation with a purpose' (1993: 228).

References

Agar, M. A. (1980), *The Professional Stranger*, New York: Academic Press.

Atkinson, P. and D. Silverman (1997), 'Kundera's Immortality: The Interview Society and the Invention of the Self', *Qualitative Inquiry*, 3(3): 4–25.

Bateson, G. (1972), *Steps to an Ecology of Mind*, New York: Ballantine Books.

Berliner, D. (1994), *Thinking in Jazz*, Chicago: University of Chicago Press.

Blacking, J. (1977), 'Towards an Anthropology of the Body', in J. Blacking (ed.), *The Anthropology of the Body*, London: Academic Press, 1–28.

Blacking, J. (1988), 'Movement, Dance, Music, and the Venda Girls' Initiation Cycle', in P. Spencer (ed.), *Society and the Dance*, Cambridge: Cambridge University Press, 64–91.

Bourdieu, P. (1977), *Outline of a Theory of Practice*, Cambridge: Cambridge University Press.

Brogan, T. (1994), 'Inspiration', in T. Brogan (ed.), *The New Princeton Handbook of Poetic Terms*, Princeton: Princeton University Press, 15–16.

Bruner, E. M. (1993), 'Epilogue: Creative Persona and the Problem of Authenticity', in S. Lavie, K. Narayan and R. Rosaldo (eds), *Creativity/Anthropology*, Ithaca: Cornell University Press, 321–6.

Cerwonka, A. and L. H. Malkki (2007), *Improvising Theory*, Chicago: University of Chicago Press.

Csikszentmihalyi, M. (1992), *Optimal Experience*, Cambridge: Cambridge University Press.

Faubion, J. D. and G. E. Marcus (eds) (2009), *Fieldwork Is Not What It Used to Be*, Ithaca, NY: Cornell University Press.

George, K. and K. Narayan (2001), 'Interviewing for Folk and Personal Narrative', in J. Gubrium and J. Holstein (eds), *Handbook of Interview Research*, London: Sage Publications, 815–80.

Gubrium, J. and J. Holstein (eds) (2002), *Handbook of Interview Research*, London: Sage Publications.

Hammersley, M. and P. Atkinson (1995), *Ethnography*, London: Routledge.

Hannerz, U. (2003), 'Being There…and There…and There! Reflections on Multi-Site Ethnography', *Ethnography*, 4: 229–44.

Hannerz, U. (2004), *Foreign News*, Chicago: University of Chicago Press.

Ingold, T. and E. Hallam (2007), 'Creativity and Cultural Improvisation: An Introduction', in E. Hallam and T. Ingold (eds), *Creativity and Cultural Improvisation*, Oxford: Berg, 1–24.

Marcus, G. E. (1998), *Ethnography through Thick and Thin*, Princeton: Princeton University Press.

Melhuus, M., J. Mitchell and H. Wulff (eds) (2010), *Ethnographic Practice in the Present*, Oxford: Berghahn Books.

Middleton, J. (1988), 'The Dance among the Lugbara of Uganda', in P. Spencer (ed.), *Society and the Dance*, Cambridge: Cambridge University Press, 165–82.

Morgan, D. L. (2001), 'Focus Group Interviewing', in J. F. Gubrium and J. A. Holstein (eds), *Handbook of Interview Research*, London: Sage Publications, 141–59.

Ní Dhuibhne, É. (2007), *Fox, Swallow, Scarecrow*, Belfast: Blackstaff Press.

Preminger, A. (ed.) (1974), 'Inspiration', in A. Preminger (ed.), *Princeton Encyclopedia of Poetry and Poetics*, Princeton: Princeton University Press, 96–8.

Robson, C. (1993), *Real World Research*, Oxford: Blackwell.

Schutz, A. (1964), 'Making Music Together: A Study in Social Relationship', in A. Schutz, *Collected Papers II*, The Hague: Martinus Nijhoff, 159–78.

Skinner, J. (2010), 'Leading Questions and Body Memories: A Case of Phenomenology and Physical Ethnography in the Dance Interview', in P. Collins and A. Gallinat (eds), *The Ethnographic Self as Resource*, Oxford: Berghahn Books, 111–28.

Stanislavsky, K. (1967), *On the Art of the Stage*, London: Faber and Faber.

Wallman, S., Y. D'hooge, A. Goldman and B. Kosmin (1980), 'Ethnography by Proxy: Strategies for Research in the Inner City', *Ethnos*, 45: 5–8.

Wulff, H. (1988), *Twenty Girls*, Stockholm Studies in Social Anthropology, 21, Stockholm: Almqvist & Wiksell International.

Wulff, H. (1992), 'Young Swedes in New York: Workplace and Playground', in R. Lundén and E. Åsard (eds), *Networks of Americanization*, Stockholm: Almqvist & Wiksell International, 94–105.

Wulff, H. (1995), 'Inter-Racial Friendship: Consuming Youth Styles, Ethnicity and Teenage Femininity in South London', in V. Amit-Talai and H. Wulff (eds), *Youth Cultures*, London: Routledge, 63–80.

Wulff, H. (1998), *Ballet across Borders*, Oxford: Berg.

Wulff, H. (2001), 'Dance, Anthropology of', in N. Smelser and P. Baltes (eds), *International Encyclopedia of the Social and Behavioral Sciences*, Oxford: Elsevier, 209–12.

Wulff, H. (2002), 'Yo-Yo Fieldwork: Mobility and Time in a Multi-Local Study of Dance in Ireland', *Anthropological Journal of European Cultures*, 11: 117–36.

Wulff, H. (2003), 'Steps on Screen: Technoscapes, Visualization and Globalization in Dance', in C. Garsten and H. Wulff (eds), *New Technologies at Work*, Oxford: Berg, 187–204.

Wulff, H. (2007), *Dancing at the Crossroads*, Oxford: Berghahn Books.

Wulff, H. (2008a), 'Ethereal Expression: Paradoxes of Ballet as a Global Physical Culture', *Ethnography*, 9(4): 519–56.

Wulff, H. (2008b), 'To Know the Dancer: Formations of Fieldwork in the Ballet World', in N. Halstead, E. Hirsch and J. Okely (eds), *Knowing How to Know*, Oxford: Berghahn Books, 75–91.

Wulff, H. (2008c), 'Literary Readings as Performance: On the Career of Contemporary Writers in the New Ireland', *Anthropological Journal of European Cultures*, 17: 98–113.

Wulff, H. (2009), 'Ethnografiction: Irish Relations in the Writing of Éilís Ní Dhuibhne', in R. Pelan (ed.), *Éilís Ní Dhuibhne Anthology*, Galway: Arlen House, 245–61.

–8–

'Angola Calling': A Study of Registers of Imagination in the Interview

Madalina Florescu

> The greatest challenge to anthropology is not to read other cultures correctly but to recover disappearing epistemologies.
>
> Hastrup 1995: 43–4

> Collectors are people with an instinct for tactics; in their experience, when they take a fresh town the tiniest antique shop may constitute a fortress, the most out-of-the-way stationer's a key position.
>
> Benjamin (1931) 2009: 165

My chapter is about the context of the interview and its materiality: an audiotape and my memory of what was *not* recorded after the recorder was stopped by the occurrence of an unexpected event. I have tried to shift the focus from the interview as fieldwork experience to the experience of the presence of its trace and to define the connection between traces and the claims made about their meaning as a 'register of imagination'. The articulation of this composite material has been difficult to contemplate partly because of a differentiation that exists in Western culture between the material traces left by inscription and the allegedly nonexistent traces of incorporation (Connerton 1989: 102), which has in turn led to differentiation and hierarchical relation between activities of the mind and bodily practices (1989: 82–3, 101).

This dualism is founded on a linear and unidirectional conception of time according to which renewal can only originate in the future as a transcendental realm. Hastrup (1995) for instance has argued that the ethnographic present serves to lift up the fieldwork experience from biographical and historical time and fix it in theory, thus making it into an example which carries a truth 'that is not outlived when the ethnographer leaves the field' (Hastrup 1995: 25). Temporal distancing then is not to deny others' coevalness but a consequence of anthropological writing itself, which is prophetic to the extent that it transforms an 'old experience' into a 'new theoretical' perspective (1995: 24–5). This stance not only presupposes that writing, or inscription more generally, is the prerogative of a subject in full autonomy from objects, but it also presupposes the finitude of the past.

Contrary to the prophet, the collector conceives of the past as unfinished and a source of renewal (Benjamin (1931) 2009: 162, 169) and in a collection both humans and things have agency. For a collector, 'ownership is the very deepest relationship a person can have with things; not that they live inside him; it is he who lives in them' (Benjamin (1931) 2009: 171). Further, Hastrup's defence of the ethnographic present presupposes that the fieldwork experience is clearly bounded in space, time and social status from the anthropologists' ordinary life. This is also untenable from a collector's point of view since the interpenetration between the collection and the collector is such that the life of one cannot be 'lifted up' from the life of the other: they are not distinct domains and do not have separate durations. The 'presence' of a collection for its owner is therefore not the same as the 'ethnographic present' of an experience whose generalization has alienated it from its original owner so that it cannot be transmitted as an experience.

Collecting is a kind of inscription that differs from prophetic writing. Also, a collection is not a theory of collecting and the particular circumstances in which an object was acquired are part of that object and therefore cannot be 'generalized' beyond an account of the place of that object in a collection. Thus, in a sense, collecting is a reverse process to theorizing: it is the drive to make the world anew by searching for new paths through a time that has *passed*, as opposed to the movement from the particularity of experience to the generality of theory that introduces a break with the past. In sum, there is a fundamental difference between the historical consciousness produced through fixing experience in theory and the historical consciousness produced through fixing experience in things gathered in a collection. And this difference is not reducible to an opposition between 'modernity' and 'tradition'.

Register of Imagination: Towards a Definition

Anthropologists acknowledged long ago that the difficulty of delimiting a relevant field of study is not a methodological shortcoming but the very speciality of the discipline (Devons and Gluckman 1964: 185; Dilley 1999: ix–x). What does it mean, then, to remain 'open minded' to the possibility of having closed (or having been *forced* to close) one's analytical framework at an inappropriate point (Devons and Gluckman 1964: 185; Fabian 1999: 89)? Fabian for instance has suggested that in face-to-face communication misunderstanding can occur at all levels of language: phonological, grammatical, semantic and pragmatic (1999: 86). But it is only after the fact that these misunderstandings can be apprehended and 'corrected' (1999: 89). Thus, a way of being 'open minded' is to return to one's recordings of interviews and listen to them *again* by suspending assumptions about the context in which they occurred, such as assumptions about the language spoken by interlocutors (1999: 88), the gender of the characters in their stories (1999: 89) or the genre of their narrative (1999: 97). The possibility of misunderstanding is therefore an awareness not only of the fact that context is socially produced but that it may not be shared on a full scale. As a communicative subject, then, the researcher engages in communicative practices as someone who does *not* have a priori knowledge of the context that is relevant for their interpretation (1999: 89).

On the other hand are social constraints on how individual researchers can remain 'open minded' in practice given that the practice of anthropology should be seen in its relation to particular life styles (Hastrup 1995: 14). Anthropology seems to be more like a religion that has been formalized as doctrine and which is transmitted through textual learning (Parkin 2007: 52–3). This is why the relation between the institutionalization of anthropology and the practice of anthropology should not lead to greater abstraction and generalization for the sake of simplicity. The fieldwork experience for instance is supposed to be a break with habitual memory, such as the individual researcher's routine assumptions about context (Fabian 1999: 89), which encompass assumptions about and enactments of ideas of appropriate and inappropriate behaviour and speech (Connerton 1989: 73–4). Status differentials among individual researchers matter because some may have incorporated a position of subordination in relation to nation-states and the global economy that others have not. And these differentials tend to be reproduced rather than changed when in the course of fieldwork the imaginary takes over from the break with routine assumptions and habitual memory. This means that the ways in which status differentials affect the production and transmission of anthropological knowledge cannot be described as a difference between consciously held theoretical stances towards the world (Fardon 1985, in Dilley 1999: 9). Among the relevant elements left out of the delimitation of a relevant field of study may be aspects of the researcher's own persona.

Writing in anthropology should not be a pursuit of the transcendence of the social conditions and biographical circumstances of production of anthropological knowledge. If the condition for remaining open minded to what has been left out from a delimitation of the relevant field of study is to suspend routine assumptions, then anthropology as a scholarly discipline should be also open to the possibility of radical changes in consciousness during the fieldwork experience and to the implications that a conscientization of social structures has for the production and transmission of anthropological knowledge outside the framework of the habitual memory of the ethos of a particular status group. Otherwise, the construction of a register of imagination of a realm of potential relevance as well as of relevant potentiality will be predicated on the mnemonics of the researcher's body instead of a new awareness of possible understandings and misunderstandings that results from exposure to the violence that unexpected events can perform on the symbolic order. This leads me to also suggest that the duration of the fieldwork experience should not be measured in absolute units of time, such as number of months or years, but seen as *relative* to the degree of change in the researcher's way of thinking and decisions about what are relevant sources of knowledge. Further, the fieldwork experience does not belong to a finished past, as the hermeneutical tradition would have it, but to an unfinished past, as the collector has it.

Registers of imagination of possibility, then, may be said to depend on the relationship between the historical trajectories of individual researchers' cultural identities, their collection of ethnographic documents and anthropology as scholarly discipline. The notion of register of imagination is thus an attempt, awkward perhaps, to find ways of remaining 'open minded' against the odds of the power of dominant social classifications. I think the best illustration of what I have in mind is Walter Benjamin's description of 'the imaginary world enshrined in collecting' ((1931) 2009: 170) and where the collector's ownership of his or her things is established as a relationship of mutuality whereby the little 'spirits' of the things he or she owns take up residence in the collector while the collector takes up residence in his or her things (Benjamin (1931) 2009: 170–1).

> I must ask you to imagine yourselves with me, amid the disorder of torn-open packing cases, breathing in the sawdust-laden air, the floor around me littered with scraps of paper eyeing piles of books that have only now, after two years of darkness, been returned to the light of the day; I want you, from the outset, to share a little of the mood (not a mournful mood by any means, rather one of anticipation) that they awaken in a true collector. (Benjamin (1931) 2009: 161)

Collecting is not a 'method', for a method presupposes a system of disembodied ideas, like the taxonomy of the natural sciences. The collector's acquisition of an object is unlike that of any other, for it happens by accident. A collector cannot have a priori knowledge of the object he or she is about to acquire, of the circumstances in which the acquisition will happen or of the object's previous owners and which are part and parcel of the object that crosses the threshold of the collection (Benjamin (1931) 2009: 163). A collection cannot be rationalized: its heart remains inscrutable (Benjamin (1931) 2009: 166), it is a place of pitch dark (Benjamin (1931) 2009: 169). What makes objects stick together is not money and expertise but the collector's decision about whether a particular object belongs to his or her collection or not, an ability to perceive the 'new' object in relation to the collection as a whole (Benjamin (1931) 2009: 166). A collection has therefore a known, visible and material side—composed of the objects that have been acquired—and an unknown, invisible and immaterial side composed of the objects yet to be encountered and which exist in an infinite number. This infinity is possible precisely because a collection is not a theory of collecting and its objects are not examples; it is there to speak about fate and chance in a time that has *passed* (Benjamin (1931) 2009: 162). I hope to show in this chapter how the interview can be a way of learning about the 'collections' of memories others inhabit, in particular those who experience the violence of the margins of nation-states. It is an interview from my field study conducted between 2006 and 2007 at the Episcopal House in Luanda, capital of the Angolan nation-state, at the ending of four decades of armed conflict (1961–2002).

The Topic of the Interview: A Heuristic Device

The interview I will describe took place on the afternoon of the 16th December 2006 in the priests' hall (*sala dos padres*) at the Episcopal House in Luanda. The interviewee was an Angolan Catholic priest from Northern Angola and the agreed topic of the interview was children accused of sorcery (*feitiçaria*) that in the official discourse were said to live among 'the Bakongo', a label used to refer to the ethnic group of Northern Angola. The choice of this topic on the other hand had been heuristic. It had been motivated in part by the difficulty of delimiting a relevant object of study in the immediate aftermath of a war while remaining 'open minded', and in part by the need to give a satisfactory answer to my co-lodgers and commensals at the Episcopal House who wanted to know who I was and what I was there for. I reckoned that presenting myself as doing a research (*pesquisa*) on the said topic would help them, and me, to make our copresence somewhat more meaningful and eventually find a common sense. The responses I received, though, were discouraging. I was told for instance that *feitiçaria* was a worthless topic of research, like 'an email without subject or address', like 'a broken glass' or 'an empty bottle', and that I should study 'development' instead. Other responses were more mitigated, saying that it was the duty of bishops to eradicate this sort of backward superstition, which is why priests were not concerned with it. Yet others said that priests who knew something about it were found in remote provinces, not there at the Episcopal House in the capital. There seemed to be something embarrassing in displaying knowledge of what in the official discourse and national media was stereotyped as 'Bakongo cosmology' because it seemed to belong to an African space beyond the confines of the capital and which was not commensurable with Catholic religion and citizenship status. The closer I tried to get to the topic of my research, the farther it seemed to recede.

In the official discourse the topography of *feitiçaria* was an implicit local knowledge of who 'the Bakongo' were and of where they could be found. In the national media of the capital, for instance this implicit local knowledge was encoded in the iconography of the backwardness of 'Bakongo' religion and poverty of 'Bakongo' households. This imagery conveyed a message about the difference between legitimate Angolan citizens and illegitimate 'Bakongo' ways of life that echoed the Portuguese colonial discourse about Africans and in particular African men, who were defined as incapable of 'Catholic love' for their wives and children because of their boorishness (*boçalidade*) (Serra Frazão 1952: 13–14, 17–18). Thus, the postcolonial official discourse reproduced the binarism of the colonial discourse, substituting an opposition between 'legitimate' Angolan citizens and 'illegitimate' subnational ethnic groups for the binarism between the 'legitimate' Portuguese and the 'illegitimate' African ways of life (cf. Herzfeld 2005: 15). This binarism had been the colonial principle of social, moral, juridical and fiscal classification, and this principle had not changed with independence and with the replacement of the Portuguese with African officials.

During colonialism, African men (*indígenas*) were bound by law to provide a certain amount of contract labour because of their putative idleness, and compliance with this requirement—or failure to do so—was inscribed in an identity document (*caderneta*) that the individual had the obligation to always carry with him, ready to show for inspection to an official. In theory, it was possible for *indígenas* to change their status by becoming 'assimilated' (*assimilado*), which meant an equal status to the Portuguese, though assimilation was not inheritable and in the 1950s also became revocable. To obtain the certificate of assimilation the candidate had to demonstrate formal education up to the fourth grade, fluency in Portuguese, Catholic religion, 'good' table manners—such as the use of crockery instead of hands—formal European dress and sufficient economic resources to sustain a 'civilized' lifestyle. These aptitudes would be checked by a test made by specifically appointed officials. The formal education of Africans had further been made the monopoly of Catholic mission schools and Portuguese was the only legitimate language. Portuguese Catholic missionaries were reluctant to live outside the urban settings where the Portuguese population lived, so this formal education was inaccessible to those who would aspire to assimilation insofar as the education available in Protestant mission schools was not recognized by the Portuguese government (cf. Newitt 2007: 77–87). Thus, by the end of the colonial period there was a very small percentage of 'assimilated', also due to the difficulty of assembling the social and economical conditions required to fulfill the change in status (Newitt 2007: 77–87). In practice, 'assimilation' was a privilege of Africans descended from families who had acquired and consolidated an urban residence, fluency in Portuguese and familiarity with Catholicism over the previous four centuries. This deep historical cleavage became the main source of violence throughout the conflict (cf. Newitt 1981: 138–47).

The change in signifiers between precolonial, colonial and postcolonial contexts had facilitated the fixation of this binary opposition as their signified, creating a Janus-like national cultural identity held together by an ambiguous relationship to the symbols of Portuguese culture and Catholicism and which is on a continuum between rueful introspection and violent conflict (Herzfeld 2005: 16). The colonial discourse on 'assimilation'—channelled into the postcolonial present through the war—became the semantic environment (Dilley 1999: 3) in which my research topic was understood and responded to.

On the other hand, my presence also created an ambiguity that allowed for creatively redefining the context of our face-to-face encounter beyond the binarism of the colonial social classification. For instance, I said I had come from London, but my name did not sound 'English', and I also spoke Italian and French with some priests; I looked 'Portuguese', but I spoke Portuguese with a strong accent that was not recognizable in terms of familiar categories of language and identity. In the context of this relation the colonial discourse about 'Africans' could be brought back to speech and articulated with the postcolonial present in a different narrative than the official one. There seemed to be few occurrences for the articulation of a formal enunciation other than the official one about what it meant to live in the margins of the Angolan nation-state (or with the awareness of their existence in proximity rather than distance).

The Angolan nation-state came into being in 1975 when the Portuguese government transferred sovereignty to 'all the people of Angola' after more than a decade of armed conflict between the Portuguese conventional army and a guerrilla movement composed of three organizations: MPLA (Popular Movement for the Liberation of Angola), FNLA (National Front for the Liberation of Angola) and UNITA (National Union for the Total Independence of Angola). The war of decolonization (1961–74), however, did not end with independence or with the end of the Cold War, but continued for another twenty-seven years (1975–2002), adding up to a total of forty-one years of armed conflict with huge imbalances between the experience of the force of arms in the country and in the coastal cities. But in the historical narrative of the ruling party, independence from Portugal in 1975 had been a radical break with the colonial past, a narrative that has become a temporal framework in Angolan studies as well.

The Angolan conflict has been studied in isolation from conflicts in neighbouring countries like the Democratic Republic of Congo and with an emphasis on discontinuity rather than continuity between the war of decolonization and the war that followed. This emphasis is a logical consequence of the analytical construct and study of each of these political organizations in isolation from one another, as if atoms of Angolan nationalism. Thus, stereotypically, the constituency of the MPLA was Catholic urbanites in the capital, Mbundu Methodists in the hinterland of Luanda and to a lesser extent Catholic Bakongos in northwest Angola. The constituency of the FNLA was instead based among Bakongo Baptists with more cultural and commercial ties to the capital of the neighbouring Democratic Republic of Congo than Luanda, and that of UNITA were Ovimbundu Congregationalists in the central and southern highlands. Not only does this classification illuminate connections in the history of Protestant missionary expansion more than in the history of the Catholic Church, but the perspective that tends to dominate in Angolan studies replicates the colonial gaze inherited by the ruling party, a gaze that from within the capital looks eastward and southward to the African interior seen as 'lands at the end of the world' (Brinkman and Fleisch 1999: 38). Although this classification of nationalist movements and the periodization of the war are heuristic conceptualizations, there seems to be nevertheless an enduring conviction in Western scholarship that there actually existed three distinct nationalist movements which 'failed' to create a unified front against the Portuguese and to 'share' power after independence, as if 'relatedness' and 'sharing' implied absence of violence. This perception also reflects the influence of the binarism of the Cold War on scholarly thinking. Less attention has been given for instance to the fate of the FNLA after independence. Its disappearance from mainstream politics, polarized between 'anticapitalist' (MPLA) and 'anticommunist' (UNITA) camps, has made it also disappear from scholarly agendas, a little bit like Eastern Christianities in studies of 'globalization' polarized between Western Christianities and Islam.

The adoption of the narrative of the ruling party as paradigmatic of academic approaches has further contributed to a conflation of 'cultural colonialism' with political and economical colonialism. Yet, as Herzfeld (2005) has cogently observed, 'externally imposed models of cultural superiority…may long outlast the force of arms or wealth that elevated those models to dominance in the first place' (Herzfeld 2005: 17). Thus, in spite of the collapse of Portuguese colonialism as a military and economic power—or precisely because of it—'the assimilated native' continued to be a powerful stereotype of self-promotion alongside the 'the boorish native' as a rueful stereotype of intimate self-knowledge (Herzfeld 2005: 15–16). Perhaps the endurance of these colonial models has also to do with the fact that the Third Portuguese Empire (1926–74) was not territorially compact but more like an archipelago of islands interconnected by the Portuguese language, Catholicism and colonial propaganda about 'five hundred years of uninterrupted Portuguese presence'.

I hope to have given the reader an idea of the cultural and social surroundings in which the topic of the interview was received, understood and responded to at the Episcopal House in Luanda by the designation of the most appropriate person to interview in the form of a priest who had a reputation of 'speaking well' (*falar bem*).

'Speaking Well' about the Cleansing of a Postwar Society

N, the interviewee, was a Catholic priest in his mid forties from a town in Northern Angola, as well as someone with kinship ties to government officials and who had travelled to Portugal, the United Kingdom, Hong Kong and the United States. He had a reputation for having a perspective that would be a match for that of a 'European researcher'. This hierarchical relation between 'global' and 'local', 'modern' and 'traditional', or 'official' and 'unofficial' forms of knowledge is based on the assumption that knowledge reflects the scale of a perspective, and that perspective is directly proportional to the geographical scale of one's physical mobility and to the height of one's rank in a hierarchy of social statuses that guarantees the 'legitimacy' of that outlook (Anderson 1991, in Ferguson and Gupta 2002: 987). The implication is that those whose physical and social mobility is restricted are relatively 'ignorant' and their claims to knowledge of the underside of the production of authorized perspectives 'illegitimate' (cf. Ferguson and Gupta 2002: 990). 'Speaking well' thus meant to be able to speak publicly and legitimately about a topic that was part of official representation.

N: People go about for their survival, in search of their [daily] bread, but generally, those in the north continue to be with the FNLA…whether you like it or not...you can be in the party of the MPLA in the first place [as a public face], but among themselves...people know, and say that 'who is from the North is with the FNLA and who is from the South is with UNITA'.

Madalina (M): The FNLA, how did it start? Who was its founder? [...] the Bakongo origin of the FNLA...

N: It is not the Bakongo origin of the FNLA...those who associated themselves with Holden as president were the first in the whole country who began the fight against colonialism...the MPLA and UNITA came after and according to history many of the MPLA and of UNITA went to the FNLA because it was the first party..., this is the story that is told...but then [after independence] the story took another course, according to the intentions of other parties...like the party in power who wants to turn the story in its favour as if it were the protagonist, but it is not...it is the least spoken party, it is a party with little presence...but then it had the luck of making an alliance [first] with Portugal and [then] with the United States...

M: Mmm...and do you think, now, in relation to *feitiçaria* [...] do you think it is a question of economy or [...] [of] a political representation of those who see themselves as Bakongo?

N: I don't think so...a direct link with politics...there may not be one...in fact there isn't any...[accusations of sorcery against children happen] because we have many families who are very poor, very poor...in the South there are shelters [for demobilized soldiers and displaced civilians], the mentality of our people in the South is very different, it seems they are more patient,...calm...more tolerant and are more habituated to suffering than those in the North, who are more impatient, resolute and swift in finding solutions, so...in a society full of problems they search for answers they cannot find, so they make up their own mind, and send away the children [by accusing them of being sorcerers].

M: Is it true that after children have been taken in a shelter [of the Catholic Church] their families come to search for them?

N: You know, at time this makes me think of the story of Moses...What happened? Moses was put in the water by his mother, who could not kill him, but she kept an eye on the basket, she even knew where the basket would stop...According to the story she did it with a purpose...she knew where Pharaoh's daughter would be, with her maids, so, she went upstream, then she put the basket [on the water] that went with the current exactly up to the point where she had thought it would go [...] but Moses's mother did not leave, she remained there, in proximity, to see how her son was growing up, and when he was grown up they became reconciled [...]. It is the same story...what do parents do? [...] they do not kill [...] the majority send the children away by accusing them of sorcery [...]

To understand the use of Moses's parable to speak about the use of 'sorcery' by those who bore the full brunt of the social consequences of war, N's interlocutor was supposed to know that Pharaoh's daughter was Egyptian and Moses's mother Hebrew, and thus recognize a leitmotif of ethnic cleansing as a strategy to secure subservience—if not loyalty—where rulers and ruled did not share the same religion and legal framework. This in turn meant to recognize religious difference, ethnic cleansing and the problem of the legitimacy of the transgression of the law as the link of resemblance between the society depicted by this biblical story and the postwar Angolan society.

In postwar Angola on the other hand the state did not kill those whose birth and reproduction was considered 'illegitimate'. The new political order was maintained instead through a visual codification of legal citizenship. To use a metaphor: legal citizenship was like the cleansed surface of a rug whose visibility was the only legitimate visibility, but whose underneath hosted the 'dirt' of the traces of the violence that had founded that new legal order—the order of the religion of the state that was not, however, the religion of the whole society. This codification of legal citizenship was thus similar to the colonial codification of society.

The denominations of the political parties (MPLA, FNLA, UNITA) were not 'real' signifiers of power. In common parlance, the significant distinction was between 'Northerner' and 'Southerner', and these stereotypes included both the privacy of the household and the public domain. The northern/southern classification was linked to another one between 'sorcery' and 'luck'. Thus, the international recognition that maintained the ruling party in power stemmed from its 'luck', whereas the power of the FNLA was unofficially recognized to stem from 'sorcery' and to be the actual peg of a postcolonial national identity, but which did not have the 'luck' of international recognition.

The classification in 'North' and 'South' was used to communicate an intimate knowledge of different relations to the authority of the state to decide who was and who was not a legitimate citizen. 'Southerners' were described as those who accepted the religion of rulers and did not transgress the official boundary between legitimacy and illegitimacy. 'Northerners' by contrast were described as those who did not accept the religion of rulers and used 'sorcery' to transgress that boundary, albeit behind a public façade of adherence to the official discourse about national identity and its demarcation of the limit of legal citizenship. This is also why 'Southerners' were seen as poorer than 'Northerners'. 'North' and 'South' were not spatial categories but different religions related to one another through the relation each had with centralized power. They differed in their culturally 'meaningful' life course in the margins of a nation-state. Thus, N 'spoke well' about the relation between the postwar society and state in the sense of being able to articulate and be eloquent about political violence.

The Tune at the End of My Recording

Intonation and rhythm were also important in conveying contextual meaning for they indicated switches to and from official and unofficial discourse. For instance,

N stressed the words 'first party', 'least' in 'least spoken' and 'little' in 'little presence' by stretching their length and lowering the tone of his voice. He then uttered rapidly and with a raised pitch the first syllable in the expression 'but then' (*só que*) in 'but then the story took another course' and 'but then it had the luck'. He also repeated 'very poor' in a low tone, almost a whisper, as if punctuating his speech as well as pondering the meaning of those words. It was also through this acoustic channel—which was not expressive but relatively autonomous from the meanings of words—that links of resemblance were then established between the cultural script of sorcery and Scriptures. Although the recall of Moses's parable was improvised to the extent that it had been triggered by my question, it was a formal improvisation.

He opened the recall with raising the pitch of voice in uttering 'you know' (*sabes*) in 'you know, at times this makes me think of the story of Moses' to then close and insert the digression in the ongoing narrative about unofficial representations of the past and 'sorcery' with the expression 'it is the same story'. It was this same formal procedure that he also used to 'capture' a phone call he received in the course of the interview by relating the occurrence he had just learnt about as yet another illustration, in addition to Moses's parable, of his point that it was better to use 'sorcery' than to be 'very poor'.

The fact that N had with him a mobile phone that was switched on and which he was ready to answer showed that N had accumulated various social roles and was habituated to use a plurality of codes and channels of communication that would define his performance in the interview, not the other way round. It also suggests that from his perspective the code of the interview, although formal, was not on a continuum with the ritual settings of the Catholic religion, such as the Eucharist or confession, for these were settings that excluded a priori the usage of mass media by the priest. His eloquence thus belonged to a genre of speech used to communicate within a religious public space not bounded to Catholicism, and about topics, such as the usage of 'sorcery' to transgress the law of the official religion, that were not easily compatible with Catholic priesthood or with the stereotype of the 'assimilated native'. That which was not 'logically' commensurable became so at the level of the musicality of the context of the communicative event, such as the intonations and rhythm of his voice or the tune of his phone.

It was with reference to this acoustic code that continuity would be created in the course of a communicative event that involved switching back and forth between multiple codes and channels of communication that was also a constant reconfiguration of roles and relations of communication. Thus, when he received the phone call, he switched to a phone conversation for twenty minutes before switching back to the face-to-face communication and establishing continuity by relating the event of that instance of communication to our ongoing conversation.

The call had been made from his home town and it was about the death of a friend and business associate he described as 'full of life' (*jeito*) and whose death had left him without *jeito* too. The deceased had two wives in two different cities that happened to also be in different countries, Angola and the Democratic Republic of

Congo, and sixteen children in the middle. He had died on the road that connected these two ends of his household and which also cut across a national boundary. N said it was a very ugly road that he himself would never had taken.

His narrative of the event of that phone call thus further expanded the horizons of the context of the interview in a similar way to how his digression on Moses had done, creating new connections that added new dimensions. In N's perspective, the phone call had the same kind of agency as my question that had triggered the memory of Moses's parable, revealing the fluidity that for him existed between the cultural script of the conversation on the phone and the Scriptures, like that between 'sorcery' and the Scriptures, this was the fluidity of *jeito*, a cultural concept of power that was the 'wealth' of those who lived and died in the margins of official law, between two nation-states. Thus, to continue to communicate I had to alternate between the roles of addressee and nonparticipating audience.

'Rhythm', Connerton (1989) observed, is 'the privileged mechanism of recall because rhythm enlists the co-operation of a whole series of bodily motor reflexes in the work of remembrance' (1989: 76). Thus, shifting focus from the disjuncture between the technologies used (tape recorder and mobile phone) to the continuity between the face-to-face situation and the communication with his distant home town created by the 'bodily mnemonics' and speech genre one can see the morphology—or 'grammar'—of the communicative event as a whole.

Nineteenth-century travellers to the Loango Coast, for instance, reported that African men in that region had the habit of using small objects sculpted in human shape out of wood called *fetishis* or *manipanchas* to communicate with their distant home towns and that these objects would only convey information about their owners' domestic lives. They would sprinkle the objects with a mouthful of water or brandy, and when the communication began their bodies would be shaken by violent convulsions and contortions amidst unintelligible words (Tams 1850: 197–8). In the equatorial culture of West and Central Africa, communication is not limited to humans but involves all 'animate' beings. This concept of agency further differentiates between 'visible' and 'invisible' aspects, attributing the former to humans and the latter to ancestors.

Not all humans can communicate with ancestors. Communication between the two sides of the 'animate world' is a prerogative of those who belong to the same category of 'container' as ritual objects (MacGaffey 1977: 178). 'Container' people are those who do what they do because of who they are, and they are what they are because of their exposure to the power of the spirits of ancestors in the context of an event. They are therefore those who will speak the 'truth' about that event (i.e. what it meant experientially and emotionally, not its cognitive content) (cf. Boyer 1990: 106). Thus, speaking about the event of the conversation on the phone or speaking about Moses's parable were instances of communication with a realm of the imagination and affectivity that is beyond the realm of sensorial perception, albeit on an ontological continuum with it.

On the other hand there is no one-to-one correspondence between the categories of the equatorial culture and the formal grammar of European languages, such as number or gender. MacGaffey (1977) for instance has observed that in Kikongo 'the semantic segregation of noun classes [e.g. personalized forces vs. ritual objects] is a tendency rather than a rule' and there is no clear distinction 'between cults of personal protection and cults of affliction involving the community as a whole' (MacGaffey 1977: 179). This further suggests that knowledge of these categories cannot be transmitted as cognitive content of verbal communication using Portuguese or English, since the 'grammar' that organizes the production of contextual meaning cannot be deduced from the formal grammar of the language used to speak (Firth 1935: 48).

Ironically, it is the unexpected occurrence of the phone call that made this event into an instance of the transmission of the knowledge of the morphology of the communicative event as a whole, the genre of its performance not bounded to speech. Not expecting the occurrence of the phone call, I interpreted it as an 'interruption' of the face-to-face communication and I stopped the tape recorder. When the conversation finished I did not switch the recorder back on, continuing instead to participate in the face-to-face situation no longer as a 'record player' but as the audience of a storyteller who learns to conceive through listening and imagining what is being talked about. Thus, contrary to Connerton's claim that the incorporation of events, unlike their inscription, does not leave material traces, my own memory of the performance of the interview as a communicative event beyond my tape recording of it was in itself a trace.

The Audiotape of an 'Interrupted' Interview: Endings, Interruptions and Continuity

In preparation for the interview, I had equipped myself with a tape recorder, a ninety-minute tape and two batteries, as well as a notebook with a pen. However, the duration of the tape recording is less than thirty minutes and the recording stops shortly after the tune of my interviewee's mobile phone is heard, muffling his voice as he completes his utterance before answering the call. The ending of the recording on the other hand is not the ending of the tape or of the interview, or of my memory of it. Nevertheless, and for a long time, I considered the duration of this recording to be insufficient for it to have any ethnographic value, partly because of a supposed inseparability between materiality and meaning (Hastrup 1995: 18). Fabian's observation that ethnographers of communication should think dialectically rather than logico-methodologically (1999: 101) has encouraged me to shift my focus from the content of the recording, its 'positive' duration, to its indexicality of what had not been recorded, or 'negative' duration. This leads me to make the claim that if a tape recording can 'correct' misunderstandings of the context in which a communicative practice took place (Fabian 1999: 86), then it can also 'correct' the assumptions about the context where a recording is 'played back'.

This is the context in which ethnographic experience is made into ethnographic evidence (cf. Tedlock 1991: 72, 76). But assumptions about what constitutes ethnographic evidence are not shared. In particular, what evidence can there be of the effort at remaining 'open minded' in the course of communicative events? I would say that the embodied memory the individual researcher has of communicative events should count as 'ethnographic evidence' in spite of its problematic 'objectivity'.

The production of anthropological knowledge, based on ethnographic 'evidence' as it is, depends on ethnographers' cultural backgrounds and hence on their different ways of fixing ethnographic data on material supports and on their preferential usage of some materials to the exclusion of others (cf. Barber 2007: 24–5, 227n11). Thus, the record of the interview has been partially recorded on an audiotape (its visible and objective aspect) and partially incorporated (its invisible and subjective aspect): these two aspects are part of one and the same objectification of one and the same event.

Contrary to Fabian, it is not my decision to begin the recording of a communicative event (Fabian 1999: 91), but my decision to 'end' it that has produced an 'ethnographic document'. In particular, it is a document about the quasi-simultaneity of a plurality of codes and channels used to communicate without explicit verbal markers of 'transition,' such as telling someone one is having a face-to-face conversation with something like 'Would you please excuse me for one moment, I am receiving a phone call, it shouldn't last too long.' This pluralism is like the linguistic pluralism of one individual familiar with a linguistically plural environment where there is no need for making explicit statements about the change of language or code or channel. Participants are expected to be familiar with this pluralism and therefore to keep in touch as it were without an explicit invitation. The ending of the recording signals a cumulative 'switch' in code and medium. Acknowledging the 'ending' as a 'switch' in turn makes visible a fuller spectrum of the codes used in the same form of communication than would have been accessible by relying on one medium (the tape recorder) and one code (verbal). The memory of those present at the event is thus an integral part of the 'ethnographic document'. Thus, the ethnographic document may be seen as an object in the ethnographer's collection, itself a composite of diverse materials and technologies that is the visible and tangible aspect of the memory of a particular context of a situation whose invisible or intangible aspect is the embodied memory of participants to the event.

References

Barber, K. (2007), *The Anthropology of Texts, Persons, and Publics*, Cambridge: Cambridge University Press.

Benjamin, W. ((1931) 2009), *One-Way Street and Other Writings*, London: Penguin Books.

Boyer, P. (1990), *Tradition as Truth and Communication: A Cognitive Description of Traditional Discourse*, Cambridge: Cambridge University Press.

Brinkman, I. and A. Fleisch (eds) (1999), *Grandmother's Footsteps: Oral Tradition and South-East Angolan Narratives on the Colonial Encounter*, Köln: Köppe.

Connerton, P. (1989), *How Societies Remember*, Cambridge: Cambridge University Press.

Devons, E. and M. Gluckman (1964), 'Conclusion: Modes and Consequences of Limiting a Field of Study', in M. Gluckman (ed.), *Closed Systems and Open Minds: The Limits of Naivety in Social Anthropology*, Edinburgh: Oliver and Boyd, 158–261.

Dilley, R. (1999), 'Introduction: The Problem of Context', in R. Dilley (ed.), *The Problem of Context: Methodology and History in Anthropology*, Oxford: Berghahn Books, 1–46.

Fabian, J. (1999), 'Ethnographic Misunderstanding and the Perils of Context', in R. Dilley (ed.), *The Problem of Context: Methodology and History in Anthropology*, Oxford: Berghahn Books, 85–104.

Ferguson, J. and A. Gupta (2002), 'Spatializing States: Toward an Ethnography of Neoliberal Governamentality', *American Ethnologist*, 29(4): 981–1002.

Firth, R. (1935), 'The Technique of Semantics', *Transactions of the Philological Society*, 34(1): 36–73.

Hasrup, K. (1995), *A Passage to Anthropology: Between Experience and Theory*, London: Routledge.

Herzfeld, M. (2005), *Cultural Intimacy: Social Poetics in the Nation-State*, London: Routledge.

MacGaffey, W. (1977), 'Fetishism Revisited', *Africa*, 47(2): 172–84.

Newitt, M. (1981), *Portugal in Africa*, London: Hurst and Co.

Newitt, M. (2007), 'Angola in Historical Context', in P. Chabal and N. Vidal (eds), *Angola: The Weight of History*, London: C. Hurst and Co., 19–92.

Parkin, D. (2007), 'The Accidental in Religious Instruction: Ideas and Convictions', in D. Berliner and R. Sarró (eds), *Learning Religion: Anthropological Approaches*, Oxford: Berghahn Books, 49–64.

Serra Frazão, F. (1952), 'O Adultério e o Divórcio', in *Mensário Administrativo*, no. 53–4, Luanda: Edição da Direcção dos Servicos de Administração Civil, 11–32.

Tams, G. (1850), *Visita às Possessões Portuguezas na Costa Occidental d'Africa*, Porto: Typographia da Revista.

Tedlock, B. (1991), 'From Participant Observation to the Observation of Participation: The Emergence of Narrative Ethnography', *Journal of Anthropological Research*, 47: 69–94.

–9–

The Contortions of Forgiveness: Betrayal, Abandonment and Narrative Entrapment among the Harkis

Vincent Crapanzano

> I have been trying to indicate the extent to which the analysis of a psychological concept, if carried out with the widest objective reference, can expose the precariousness of our delineations of the human condition.
>
> Rodney Needham

In memory of Raymond Firth, certainly one of anthropology's greatest fieldworkers, I would like to recall an 'old tale' he recounts in his essay on bond friendship among the Tikopia (Firth 1967: 108–15). I offer only a brief summary. Two bond-friends went out to net birds. They lowered a sinnet in order to climb down to a ledge where the birds were. One of them, Pa Raropuka, returned earlier than the other, climbed back up, and untied the sinnet, leaving his friend, Pa Fatumaru, stranded. Days later, Pa Raropuka returned, thought his friend was dead—his friend, who had bathed his body with eggs, was covered with flies—and went snaring. Pa Fatumaru climbed up the sinnet and untied it, leaving Pa Raropuka stranded and wailing. He eventually died. Pa Fatumaru, so the story goes, continued snaring birds. Firth's informant concludes the tale: 'But the bones remained there in a cave. My grandfather saw the bones.' The only explanation Firth's informant offers is that Pa Raropuka had tried to get rid of his friend in order to take possession of his family orchard.

Though Tikopia of the 1920s is as remote as one can get from the Harkis—those Algerians, now living in France, who sided with the French during the Algerian War of Independence—Firth's 'old tale' raises several of the themes I explore in this chapter: betrayal, abandonment, revenge, retaliation, storytelling and—singularly absent from Firth's tale (though perhaps not in Tikopian life)—forgiveness and apology.

All of these themes figured in my interviews and conversations both directly, as topics of discussion, and in far more complex ways in the dynamics of my encounters with the Harkis—with their attempts, for example to cast me as their advocate, in their figuring themselves as victims of the French while maintaining their dignity and in considering their interviews testimonies. The Harkis and their children were consumed by their story behind which lay, paradoxically, a silence, that which could not be spoken, an absence, death perhaps. It was in informal conversations rather than in interviews that some of the Harkis, especially their children, were able to talk more freely, though they frequently fell back, defensively, into a testimonial mode. I discuss these conversations and interviews in the Appendix.

Strictly speaking, *Harki* (from the Arabic for military movement) refers to those Algerian civilians of Arab or Berber descent, numbering around two hundred sixty thousand, who served on a contractual basis (without the usual military benefits) as auxiliary troops (*supplétifs*) for the French, but the term is often used loosely for any Algerians who served with the French military or police forces during the Algerian War of Independence.[1] The Harkis have been called *les oubliés de l'histoire* ('history's forgotten'); for, until recently, they have been ignored by both scholars and the press and have lived, for the most part, in abject silence. Although some of the Harkis sided with the French because they believed that Algeria would be better off under them than independent or because they or their fathers had served in the French army, most of them, poor, illiterate peasants, did so because they desperately needed whatever they could earn in an impoverished, war-torn country. Many had suffered at the hands of the militant, often brutal Front de Libération Nationale (FLN), which led Algeria to independence and, according to the Harkis, among others, has been responsible for the chronic violence and dilapidation of the country.

Despite warnings of likely bloodshed from officers who had fought alongside the Harkis, the French government ordered their demobilization after the signing of the Treaty of Evian on 18 March 1962, and sent them, unarmed, back to their villages. The treaty offered them no protection, and in the months surrounding its ratification on 3 July 1962, between sixty thousand and one hundred fifty thousand Harkis were tortured, mutilated and killed by the Algerian population at large. I myself heard stories of Harkis whose throats were cut in front of their wives and children, and there have been reports of others who were impaled, roasted alive or even forced to eat chunks of their own flesh. One man I interviewed was thrown, after being tortured, into a dry well where he was kept for eleven months and fed couscous mixed with sand and blood when he was fed at all.[2] He was never given a change of clothing nor was the well cleaned and his excrement removed. Many of these deaths were instigated by the army wing of the FLN or by the so-called Marsiens (from the month of March—*Mars*); that is those Algerians who suddenly identified with the FLN in March 1962, when they realized it would come to power and wanted to prove their loyalty to it for reasons of self-interest.

Overwhelmed by the arrival in the spring of 1962 of nearly a million *pieds-noirs*, or Algerians of European origin, many of whom supported the OAS (Organisation Armée Secrète; Secret Army Organization), far-right militants who opposed Algerian independence and who had attempted a coup d'état the previous April, de Gaulle's government did almost nothing to halt the bloodbath. As little sympathy as de Gaulle had for the *pieds-noirs*, he had even less for the Algerians. On 16 May 1962, in a now-famous telegram, Louis Joxe, the minister of state for Algerian affairs, prohibited individual efforts to settle Harkis in France, as some officers who had fought with them had tried to do (Jordi 1999: 36–9). Following Joxe's order, fifty-five Harki families who had tried to land in Marseilles were sent back to Algeria where, as many of the Harkis I interviewed insisted, they were massacred. However, despite the efforts of de Gaulle, Joxe and Army Minister Pierre Messmer, 48,625 French Muslims had officially arrived in France by 28 September 1962. It is likely that another sixty thousand were able to make it to France by 1967.

In France, most Harkis were interned in camps, like Rivesaltes near Perpignon and Saint-Maurice-l'Ardoise near Avignon, forced to live in miserable conditions and subjected to abusive discipline and constant humiliation. Many suffered—and continue to suffer—the pathologies associated with abjection: identity loss, anxiety attacks, idées fixes, delusions of persecution, depression, bouts of violence, suicide and, among the men, alcoholism. Their identity was so brutally undermined that many of them have never found firm footing again. Many of those who are still alive are lost in themselves—in a haunting silence. They never talked to their children (or to me for that matter) about their reasons for joining the French and their experiences during the war. Their silence was a leitmotif in all the conversations I had with the Harki children.[3]

Eventually, fourteen thousand families were moved into seventy-five remote forestry hamlets scattered across southern France where they worked on an enormous reforestation project. (The physically and mentally disabled and widows and their children were transferred to the camps at Bias and Saint-Maurice-l'Ardoise.) Although these hamlets were purportedly designed to integrate the Harkis into French society, they served, in fact, to isolate them—to make them invisible, the Harkis like to say. Those who could find work outside the camps, often through personal contacts, left as soon as they could. Many remained, some for more than sixteen years, until, after violent protests by the Harkis and their children, the last of the hamlets was closed in 1978.

Although concentrations of Harkis remain in the south of France, often near the camps where they were interned, and in the industrial north, many Harki families are now scattered across France. They, and to a lesser extent their children and grandchildren, have remained a population apart. Though they have the rights of any French citizen, they find themselves treated as half-citizens: mistrusted, marginalized and often subject to the same virulent racism directed towards immigrant workers. The old Harkis are, for the most part, lost in themselves, their despair and their story, which, paradoxically, they keep to themselves. When they do speak of their past, they focus obsessively and with little elaboration on their abandonment and betrayal by the French.

'Abandonment' and 'betrayal' have become icons of the wounds the Harkis and many of their children have suffered—indignation, humiliation, disorientation, marginalization and, as one of their children put it, 'the loss of a future, any future'. They are also condensations of their all-consuming narrative: one that so insistently frames its subject matter—indeed, the narrator and his or her interlocutors—that there is little room for escape, as I myself often experienced as I listened to them. Their individual stories were subsumed by their collective histories. Turned in on itself, on its reproduction, it seems to lead nowhere. Repeated over and over again, often legalistically, as testimony, it loses its vitality and foreshadows what many of the Harkis and especially their children know but prefer not to acknowledge: namely, that their story, their suffering, will slip out of memory, becoming at best a line or two in a history book. Their desire to perpetuate their story figured significantly in my meetings with them. They looked forward to my informing the English-speaking world of their plight. Harki children often talked to me about how they would tell their children about the Harki experience.

The children, particularly those raised in the camps, have assumed their fathers' wounds and articulate their identity in terms of those wounds. They share, if vicariously, their parents' sense of having been duped. Like their fathers, they are haunted, but not as consumed, by the Harki story. With rare exceptions, they stress their fathers' silence with a sympathy that barely contains their disappointment, their anger even. They cast their fathers as victims, broken men, devalued, dishonoured and emasculated—lost. They often remember them sitting alone or in groups, leaning against a tree or wall, ruminating. Some speak of their fathers' depression, their drinking, their drunken rages, usually directed at them or their mothers. Rarely did they want me to meet their fathers. 'They won't talk to you', they said. 'They didn't talk to us. They're old. Why bother them? Why bring up a painful past?'

However knotted by conflicting emotions, the fathers have to acknowledge their decision to join the French. They can regret, they can justify, they can self-righteously blame the French, and indeed the Algerians, for what they had done to them. However overwhelmed by what Flaubert calls 'the dark immensity of history' and others simply destiny, they have to assume some responsibility (Crapanzano 2009b). But the children can take no responsibility for what they inherited from the cradle. They are doubly wounded—by their own experiences and their fathers' haunting silence. They are tortured by an absence: an unknown they can never know and the imaginative possibilities that ignorance evokes. Unlike most of their parents, some of them have taken an activist stance, forming political associations lobbying for the recognition of the sacrifices their parents made for France, claiming compensation for the losses their parents sustained and demanding an apology for their parents' betrayal and abandonment.[4]

Paradoxically their quest for recognition—the legal and administrative manoeuvers required—perpetuates their marginalized status. They are victims of a stigmatized identity, which they have had no choice but to accept, if only because that identity affords them a means of claiming the recognition and the compensation they believe, not without reason, they and their parents deserve. They are caught in a paradox. To free themselves of this stigma, they have to accept it; to cease being a victim, they have to be a victim. Given the assault on their identity, they do not have the distance to play the victim. Their demands for recognition, compensation and apology have, I believe, to be seen in this light. They cannot simply be dismissed, as some French and Algerians try to do, as playing the system for only material gain. They have, in fact, been given some recognition and compensation, but they have not yet received the apology many of the younger generation believe would restore meaning to their parents' lives and, indeed, to their own. However, as realists, they assume the French will never apologize.

* * *

For forgiveness to occur, the wrongdoers and their victims have to acknowledge the wrongdoing, appreciate each other's perspective and recognize the role it has played in the way they have each configured their individual and collectives lives (as, for example a central trauma, an excuse for inaction, a source of resentment). And, as philosopher Charles Griswold argues, they have to 're-envision' or 're-frame' both the offence and their sense of self (2007: 174). The forgiver has to forswear revenge, moderate rancour and resentment and not vindictively remind the offender of his or her wrongdoing; the offender has, of course, to agree not to repeat the offence or retaliate for having had to apologize. Ideally, the offender should acknowledge the truth of what he or she has done and resist rationalization and self-justification.

Irreversible events of magnitude, like the massacre of the Harkis, always figure dramatically in the self-constitution—the identity—of both aggressors and victims. Paradoxically, forgiving and being forgiven for such tragic events can have a devastating effect on both the forgiver and the forgiven: the rug is, so to speak, pulled out from under them. As Emmanuel Brillet argues, and as I have suggested, were the French (or the Algerians) to apologize for their treatment of the Harkis, the Harkis' sense of self and community (insofar as it is centred on the French refusal to apologize) would be threatened. 'Because all recognition, and a fortiori, that which confers pardon, is at once comforting and a little death [*petit mort*] for a community marked by the proof of disaster', Brillet observes (2001: 4).

I suggested on several occasions in my conversations with the more sensitive Harki children that the only way they could be liberated from the burden they bore as Harkis was by pardoning the French. However, as they knew and I knew, this was impossible for they had no platform from which to proclaim forgiveness. What were they to do? Stand up in front of the Elysée and say, 'La France, je vous pardonne'? One woman said she had thought of this but realized that it was impossible and was, in any case, quite certain it wouldn't work. Another suggested that I was being 'too Christian'. (I had not thought of this.) And other Harkis could make no sense of what I was saying. Forgiveness was simply impossible. 'And if the French apologized?', I asked. It would still be impossible, the Harkis insisted.

Were the Harkis confronted with the paradox Jacques Derrida noted in his essay, 'On Forgiveness': that you can only forgive what is unforgivable (2001: 31–3)? If you are only prepared to forgive the forgivable, Derrida argues, then the idea of forgiveness would disappear. I am by no means convinced of this argument. It is important, as Derrida himself recognizes in Christian terms, to distinguish among different types of sin. I would argue that there is a difference between the conventional forgiveness of—or, more accurately, excusing—those trivial acts, however hurtful they may be, that are taken to be remediable, dismissible or annullable, and the forgiveness of serious ones—the ones Derrida would claim to be unforgivable—which are irreversible. These demand unconditional forgiveness, a forgiveness that, if I understand Derrida, must, in its purity divorce itself from the conditional—'from what is heterogeneous to it, namely the order of conditions, repentance, transformation, as many things as allow it to inscribe itself in history, law, politics, existence itself' (2001: 44–5). The conditional and unconditional are absolutely heterogeneous, irreconcilable and yet indissociable, if forgiveness is to become effective within concrete historical situations. Derrida's aim here is to free forgiveness from its political implication, say, reconciliation, and its insertion in an economy of exchange. It is within the aporetic tension between the conditional and the unconditional that decisions are made and responsibilities assumed.

By referring to 'trivial and serious acts', rather than 'venial and mortal sins', I want to avoid, as best I can, the culturally specific Christian presuppositions of much of the theorizing about forgiveness and the postulation of the requisite spiritual condition (e.g. remorse, contrition, repentance) for its success. It is by no means certain that the apology the Harkis demand of the French requires a real change of heart. They are realists, and they know that the events for which they are asking an apology are irreversible and ultimately unforgivable. Many suspect that, were the French to apologize, their apology would be conventional and ultimately dismissive.

One can, of course, accept an apology without forgiving in return. Think of the expression, 'Oh, forget about it', after someone has apologized for having wronged you. Does it imply forgiveness? Or is it simply an excuse—a way to get on with the business at hand? Griswold suggests, a bit too facilely, that excuses are backwards-looking while forgiveness is forwards-looking (2007: 57). We—in Euro-American culture at least—normally think of an apology in terms of spiritual transformation, forgiving reciprocation and in consequence reconciliation. But, let us suppose that at least some of the Harkis and their children see the apology (*shkir*) as simply an occasion for sparring, for getting the better of the French by forcing them into a humiliating admission by succumbing to the Harkis' demand, for 'internalized' revenge.

It has been argued that reference to inner life does not have the same rhetorical weight everywhere as it does in confessional societies like those of Europe and America. One could argue that the dynamics of mental life, such as forgiving, apologizing, exonerating, showing mercy, vindicating, judging and intending are so highly valued that through metaphorical transfer they come to describe, explain and even legitimate collective dynamics. In the event, I have heard *pieds-noirs* seriously question the existence of inner life among the '*indigènes*'. This position reflects the stress on the raw, instinctual nature of the native—a view that was current in North Africa during the colonial period, thanks in part to Antoine Porot, the chief of psychiatry at the University of Algiers, who claimed to find cervical—anatomical—evidence for it (Berthelier 1994: 84, 71–85). Such views are, of course, intolerable. Not only do they reflect cultural arrogance and pernicious racism, but they fail to distinguish between psychic reality and the rhetorical use of that reality in figuring other domains like the social, political and legal.

Despite Koranic stress on knowledge of the heart, the old Harkis, in my experience, do not generally give rhetorical weight to the expression of inner experience. Many of their children, raised in France, are, as I found in my interviews and conversations, more open to revealing and metaphorizing their inner feelings. I suspect that the old Harkis' lack of stress on the inner life can be related to the Harki experience itself (Crapanzano 2008); in part to the belief that it is only Allah—not human beings—who has the power of forgiving the repentant; and in part, to the old Harkis' stress on the manly virtue of *sabr*: that is patience, endurance, forbearance, resignation, submission and even renunciation (Wensinck 2009). For the Harkis, *sabr* is best understood as suffering the blows of fate in silence. Their children do not, in my experience, give the same value to silence and forbearance.

A number of writers have understood forgiveness as an exchange, most often referring to Marcel Mauss's essay on the gift, in which the French anthropologist refers to the reciprocal obligations (give, receive, return) in any exchange system and the power that resides in the gift itself (Brillet 2001). It has often been noted that, etymologically, 'gift' and 'forgiveness' are related to each other in many Indo-European languages: gift/forgiving, *dono/perdono*, *Geben/Vergeben*, etc. But can a gift and forgiveness be equated?[5] Paul Ricoeur argues that, although both giving and forgiving are bilateral and reciprocal, their insertion in analogous circles of exchange precludes distinguishing between forgiveness (*pardon*) and payment (*rétribution*) which, he claims, equalizes the relationship between the two parties in the exchange (2000: 624). To distinguish the two, he suggests (in Christian fashion), it is necessary to turn to the 'radical commandment to love one's enemy without return' [without expecting anything in return, *sans retour*]. This 'impossible commandment' appears to be the only one that can rise 'to the height of the spirit of apology' [*seul à la hauteur de l'esprit de pardon*]. 'The enemy does not ask for pardon; it is necessary to love him as he is.' But must all demands for forgiveness demand unconditional love? Must forgiveness be distinguished from retribution only in spiritual terms? Can it not be simply a formula for realigning the forgiver and the forgiven? Must any act of apology be inserted in a system of exchange? Or is a single exchange sufficient for forgiveness?

Ricoeur's model of exchange ignores risk. Even the most conventionalized exchanges are dangerous. The gift (like an offence) can be conceived as a challenge demanding a response, as Pierre Bourdieu suggests in his discussion of the dialectics of honour among the Kabyles. Bourdieu speculates: 'Perhaps every exchange carries in itself a challenge more or less dissimulated, so that the logic of challenge and riposte may only be the extreme limit toward which every communication tends, especially where the exchange of gifts is concerned' (1965: 213). In offering a gift, the donor risks the recipient's refusal. In accepting the gift, the recipient risks the donor's withdrawal of the gift. Those approaches to gift exchange that focus on tangible gifts, as do most anthropological ones, fail to recognize that the acceptance of the gift is itself a counter-prestation insofar as it relieves the donors of the risk they have taken. By not withdrawing the gift, donors give, as it were, a double gift—a tangible and an intangible one—ensuring thereby their superior position. Unlike the recipients, who always remain in debt despite their 'intangible' counter-prestation, donors appear to be debt free; that is until they are obliged, by convention, to accept a gift from the recipient.

Risk is equally at play in the pardon. Those, like the Harkis, who demand an apology, are, in effect, challenging the French—the wrongdoer—but in so doing they place themselves in the inferior, vulnerable position of a petitioner, for the wrongdoer—the French—need not apologize, maintaining, thereby, the superior political position and perpetuating the petitioner's humility. But, by refusing to ask to be forgiven, by rejecting the petitioner's demand, wrongdoers tacitly admit their guilt and, more devastatingly, their defensiveness; that is when the facts are as clear as they are in the Harki case. The French find themselves in a morally compromised position, one intensified in the case in point by their ostensible (Christian) commitment to forgiveness and the change of heart it demands. Thus, they are at once in a superior and inferior position vis-à-vis the petitioners. The Harkis have a moral hold over the French. If the French were to apologize, they would surrender their political superiority and strengthen their moral superiority. But, however praiseworthy their newly acquired moral stance, it is always tarnished by the wrongdoing they have committed. The taint can be removed, if at all, by the Harkis acceptance of their apology. Were the Harkis to refuse to accept the apology, the risk the French had taken would be worthless. The Harkis would have gained the upper hand—revenge—by humiliating them. Would the Harkis have surrendered their moral superiority by refusing the pardon? By French standards, yes. But do the Harkis share this standard? Is their approach to forgiveness premised on another set of presuppositions? Forgiveness? One correlated with revenge (*tar*)?

The old Harkis are enraged but cannot direct their rage at the object of that rage in any active manner. They cannot avenge themselves. Elsewhere, I have argued that, on occasion, through political activism, personal rage—anger—is transformed into social outrage, but that outrage, that indignation, is fragile and frequently reverts back to the anger that undergirds it, particularly when the Harkis are personally affronted (Crapanzano 2008). Here, I ask if forgiveness can ever free a victim of wrongdoing of anger, hatred or resentment? Aristotle (1941) argued in the 'Nicomachean Ethics'

(1126a) that one of the ways in which anger is dissipated is through (appropriate) revenge. He considered anger, but not forgiveness (*sungnômê*), as one of the virtues. It has often been observed that rural Algerian society is vengeful (Boulhaïs 2002; Bourdieu 1965; Servier 1955). Its history is one of family feuds, some lasting for generations. The French were quick to seize on this stereotype in their attempt to understand why villages were often split between the FLN and the Harkis. Many French officers and some Algerians argued that the Harkis often joined the French to avenge themselves. I have even heard French say that Algeria is a society of vengeance and France one of forgiveness. Such stereotyping is inexcusable on many grounds, including racist and supremacist ones.

I do not want to deny Harkis the capacity to forgive or to love unconditionally any more than I want to deny the French the possibility of revenge. I am arguing that the assumptions we make about forgiveness as an occasion for a change of heart, an expression of unconditional love, the expiation of guilt and the extinction of shame are not necessarily universal. To argue that the Harkis' demand for apology without reciprocation is embedded in a culture of the vendetta, in which honour is always at stake, would be to deny the Harkis and their children a transformational response to their historical experience. They would become wooden figures. But to ignore the possible effect of the values of traditional Algerian society on their response would be to deny an important dimension of that response. Nor do I want to deny the importance of revenge in the 'Christian' understanding of forgiveness. Given the historical circumstances in which the Harkis and the French found and find themselves, it would be egregious to ignore the interpenetration of desires for forgiveness and revenge in both of them.

(I should note, parenthetically, that there may well be a marked difference of attitude towards—indeed conceptualization of—apology (*skir*), forgiveness (*smaha*) and revenge (*tar*) between the Harkis themselves and their children who were brought up in France. I cannot pursue this argument here other than to note that, in my experience, attitudes towards forgiveness vary considerably among the Harki children. I remember an impassioned discussion between two Harki sons: one, an adamant political activist, would not hear of accepting an apology; and the other, more psychologically insightful, was far more ambivalent about forgiving.)

Hannah Arendt suggests that 'Without being forgiven, released from the consequences of what we have done, our capacity to act would, as it were, be confined to one single deed from which we could never recover; we would remain victims of its consequences forever, not unlike the sorcerer's apprentice who lacked the magic formula to break the spell' (1958: 237). Arendt's metaphor is far more penetrating than she realized. Forgiveness does not necessarily 'release us from the consequences of what we have done'. It undoes neither the irreversibility of time nor the deeds done, though it may, magically, as it were, diminish the psychological consequences of those acts and facilitate their burial in forgetfulness. It gives us at least the illusion that we are rid of the past and thereby open to the future. Forgiveness relates to notions of atonement, expiation, contrition and redemption, all of which, in Arendt's terms, serve to 'release' us from the witting and unwitting harmful consequences of our acts—to undo or give the illusion of undoing history. Arendt's depiction of what would happen if forgiveness were impossible bears an uncanny resemblance to the situation in which the old Harkis find themselves. They ruminate. They are fixated on having been betrayed and abandoned. Again and again, they punctuated my conversations and interviews with them by repeating 'betrayed and abandoned'. Does this fixation spare them acknowledgement of their fatal decision? Or do they dwell on the decision itself, as was implied by several of the Harkis with whom I talked?

Italian sociologist Gabriella Turnaturi argues that betrayal presupposes a shared experience—'a We relationship', which, I would add, need not be symmetrical (2007: 8). Its artifice and fragility may be recognized or defended against by all parties to it. It may be fraught with tension and suspicion, which are controlled, if they are controlled, by custom, law or institutional (military) regulation, as it was for the Harkis and the French. Of necessity, it is intensified in combat situations where dependency on one another is a matter of life and death. But even in such circumstances, mistrust is not infrequent. Betrayal occurs, Turnaturi argues, when the relationship is attacked from within the confines of the We (2007: 9). It always involves abandonment. One does not betray a person or group but a relationship, she argues (2007: 13). It is not an aggressive act directed towards the other or others but a 'more or less intentional act aimed at destroying that relationship or withdrawing from it' (2007: 13). (Similar arguments have been made for forgiveness.) Whether or not one can separate the relationship from the person—I have my doubts about that—the betrayed personalize the act of betrayal and understand it as an aggression directed at them. (The betrayer per contra can depersonalize and justify the betrayal by focussing on the relationship, legalistically, pragmatically, rather than on the person. By deflecting the betrayal from the person to the relationship, the betrayer may well diminish the moral and psychological consequences of the act (guilt, for example) which would have resulted from the immediate recognition of the personal injury he or she had committed.) Certainly, the Harkis personalized what they took to be a betrayal. They had no doubt that it was directed at them. Though they sometimes referred to specific officers who had sent them home without arms or without explaining their choices, for the most part they depersonalized the betrayer—paradoxically, in an act of condensed personification it was the French who betrayed them; the officers were simply following orders. It is, of course, possible that the betrayer became more abstract for the Harkis as time passed and as they subsumed their own experiences in the Harki story.

As the Harkis have been continually reminded of their collaboration by people around them, most notably by Algerian immigrant workers and, at times, close family members, the 'treachery' attached to their decision or nondecision, regardless of their motives, echoes forward to their being betrayed. Betrayal is a breach of trust—of implicit if not explicit promise—and with that breach, the future loses whatever certainty it may have had. It is the promise, Arendt argues, that attenuates 'the chaotic uncertainty of the future' (1958: 217). As such, it, too, can offer no escape from what one of the Harki children referred to as the 'prison of memory'.

I should note—but cannot pursue here—that the Harkis I spoke to never expected recognition of responsibility, recompense or an apology from the Algerians. They were simply infuriated by them. When I asked them 'Why?', several said, 'What can you expect from the Algerians?' Others did not hold all the Algerians responsible. They stressed the fact that the carnage was committed or triggered by the ALN—the military wing of the FLN—and the Marsiens. But none of their answers seemed satisfactory to me. They were not, in my observation, being evasive. They had not asked themselves the question or preferred not to think about it at all. They too are—or were—Algerians.

I have heard from both the French and Algerians, as well as several American colleagues, that the Harkis cannot expect anything from the Algerians, that they cannot even blame them, because they are guilty and, accordingly, direct their rage at the French with inordinate intensity. Such answers are pat; they coordinate with our psycho-mechanics. And they may soothe us, at least the French and the Algerians, but they certainly do not conform to my experience of the Harkis and their children. I found little evidence of guilt among them. If anything, they were ashamed of having been duped by the French, and so I prefer to leave the question open. We are concerned with breaches of the most fundamental requirements of consociation and the taboos buried deep within the psyche.

Griswold (2007) and other philosophers have argued that the state and other institutions can apologize, but they cannot normally ask for forgiveness; that such apologies are by proxy, and, as public events, differ from the moral intimacy—the singular interlocution—of personal apologies and acts of forgiveness. After all, one cannot expect a change of heart from the state, a corporation or some other institution, except, perhaps, at an extravagantly metaphorical level. No doubt analytically correct, the philosophers' arguments (despite their historical examples and their psychological presuppositions) fail to acknowledge the ritual—the dramatic—force of public apologies on even the most cynical representative of the offending institution and the most sceptical of its victims. (I am not referring here to those apologies that are written, say, in a letter or legal instrument.) A political apology, at least in its public performance, is performative and to be efficacious requires among its felicity conditions the conventionally appropriate attitude of the performer. The representative of the French state would have to express in a sincerely personal manner contrition, remorse and repentance, even if he or she were in no way responsible for the offence. It is reasonable to assume that many *porte-parole* ('spokespersons') are 'carried away' by their performance whether through heartfelt sympathy, real or vicarious remorse or as a defence against their own hypocrisy or that of the performance itself. Put another way, the proxy is caught between personal performance and public representation—between a personally presumptive ritual form and a morally disquieting content the responsibility for which he or she cannot assume.

The victims of the offence are also caught: in an emotionally charged asymmetrical relationship with the proxy. The proxy speaks for the state but addresses a group of individuals who are not necessarily institutionally conjoined. In the Harki case, though there are around eighty important activist associations, none of them can claim to represent the Harki community as a whole, if indeed the Harkis can be said to form a community. I have called them, following Francesca Cappelletto (2003), a mnemonic community—one loosely united by memories of a common set of stigmatizing experiences—a story that subsumes individual experience in its frozen narrative. There is, in other words, no authorized representative of the Harkis who can accept or reject the apology and offer or refuse to offer forgiveness. Individual Harkis would have to respond to France's apology. I am quite certain that were France to apologize the Harkis would not be immune to the quality of the proxy's performance—his or her expression of sincerity, contrition, remorse and repentance—even as they recognize the artifice of the performance. Such responses to institutional apologies are not uncommon.

It could be argued, if there is any validity to my assumption, that the personalization of the proxy's apology sets the stage for either forgiveness and the possible reduction or erasure of resentment or its refusal. Both the vindictive refusal to forgive and the cynical, albeit realistic, recognition of the artifice of the apology might serve to protect the Harkis from the identity loss I mentioned earlier that might well follow an act of forgiveness. This is, of course, speculative since France has not apologized and the Harkis have not forgiven.

APPENDIX

Betrayal and abandonment, the desire for recognition, the insistent demand for an apology—for an impossible revenge—figured in the meetings I had with the Harkis and their children. By 'figured' I mean that they affected both the substance and the dynamics of our conversations. If they agreed to talk to me, the old Harkis wanted, so it seemed to me, affirmation of what they had suffered. Neither they nor their children wanted expressions of what they considered to be excessive sympathy. That would have been to appropriate their feelings. For the most part, the old Harkis remained silent, waiting for one of their children or someone whom they felt could mediate between them and whoever I was for them. Experiencing prolonged silence requires patience, the ability to remain silent and an empathy that I liken to those moments in Japanese Noh theatre in which the actors say nothing, do nothing, but yet convey something: a battle, for example. The wives of the old Harkis who were present at my interviews often expressed the emotions that their husbands seemed incapable of expressing, at least in my presence. They were like the chorus in a Greek tragedy. There was something protective about the wives' role in these interviews. Sometimes I thought that they were afraid their husbands' anger would explode or that they would fall into paralytic sadness, escape from which lay in drink.

The children's response was far more variable than their parents. After all, they had grown up in France, were younger, had other interests, family and work and were comfortable with the speech genres, including the interview, that remained foreign to most of their parents. I worked with a number of activists, who immediately co-opted my interviews, turning them into testimonies (*témoignages*, they called them) that were so legalistic that they sounded like legal briefs. Their immediate response to me was that of a *porte-parole* who would bring their plight to the attention of the English-speaking world and elicit their support. I explained that I could not be their advocate, however sympathetic to their cause I might be. I promised to tell their story as accurately as I could. With one exception, they all accepted my position, even though some of them must have thought that with time I would become their advocate. For them, at least, facts always had a rhetorical function. Whatever their truth value, they were also meant to persuade me of the justice of their cause. I often felt bullied by their intention—their insistence. They repeated their story—the Harki story—again and again, not just to me but to themselves as they spoke. They subsumed their own stories in the Harki story. With each repetition, their story lost more of its vitality. It had become frozen, but still it offered them a sense of identity, membership in the Harki community and protection through membership in that community from an unwelcoming, at times hostile, world. They often spoke to me about French racism.

I soon realized that I was not reaching the Harkis and their children through interviews and they were not reaching me. I changed my approach, entering immediately into conversation, even argumentative conversation, with them. They seemed (and I was) more comfortable with this approach. It required monitoring on my part, lest I lead them in directions they might not otherwise have gone. I knew that my monitoring could only be partial since I myself was engaged in the conversation. I was not particularly troubled by this, since even the most objective, the most neutral, of interviews requires monitoring and is subject to the same failures. I find that the open-endedness of conversation permits freer expression and is more revealing of the dynamics—the plays of identity, for example—that lie behind that expression than are revealed in the more generically constrained interview.

For the most past, the men focussed on their activism, their protests, their *manifs* (protests), the bureaucratic entanglements they found in themselves in and the organizational details of camp life and its aftermath. Like their fathers, many of them faced their situation with stoical outrage. But there were exceptions: men who could not contain their anger or who cried as they remembered the atrocities they witnessed, or were so emotionally knotted, as they described their fathers' shame, that they could not speak. It was as though they were participating in that shame. Often, it was difficult to determine when they were talking about themselves, their fathers or the Harkis more generally.

Many of the Harki daughters I talked to, particularly the activists, were exceptionally eloquent. Although they were as indignant and angered by the Harkis' history, they were not as weighed down by it as were the men, it seemed to me. Often, once they found out what I was doing, they would launch into the Harki story, their story, their protests, the humiliation and insults they suffered and, I hasten to add, their successes. Those who were educated were particularly proud of their education. Not only had they overcome the obstacles the French had created but also the objections of their fathers, who, as traditionalists, did not want them corrupted by the 'promiscuity' of school life. Though they also subsumed their own stories in the Harki story, the daughters' accounts of their experiences focussed on everyday life, the little incidents that in some of their accounts became epiphanies, resonating with the emotional tenor of, yes, the incident, but more generally of the Harki story or some part of it. They injected it with the emotions that that story was losing in its repetition and its furtherance from the original. Loss, forgetting, effacement and death made up the undersong of much of what they had to say. And yet, beside their sadness, the traumas (their word) they and their families had suffered, they were often far more open to life than the Harki sons.

I am, of course, generalizing here. Each interview, each conversation, was in its way unique. Respect, mine and theirs, played an important role in all of them. I made friends with some of the Harkis. With others I maintained a collegial relationship, which they accepted. As many of them had had little contact with Americans, I became, I imagine, also a subject of their ethnographic interest. As an American, I had an advantage, I believe, over French researchers who were too implicated in fact and symbolically in the Harkis' experience. Sometimes I glimpsed a Harki's surprise at something I said or revealed through a gesture or facial expression. The Harkis are, in my experience, keen observers. No doubt they have to be.

I am quite certain that forgiveness played a role in my encounters with the Harkis, but it would be presumptuous to assume what that role was. Certainly there were times when I wished that I could do something to undo their sadness and pain, but I, as they, knew this was impossible. And they knew, as I came to know, that that undoing, were it possible, would be a demeaning appropriation of their experience.

Notes

1. For details and bibliography see my book, *The Harkis: The Wound That Never Heals* (2011) as well as Crapanzano 2008, 2009a and 2010. Among others, see: Abrial 2001; Benamou 2003; Besnaci and Manceron 2008; Chabit 2006; Hamoumou 1993; and Roux 1991.
2. Muslims are prohibited from drinking or eating blood.

3. The breaking of an informant's silence in anthropological research should be treated with the utmost tact; it can have serious consequences. The old Harkis have chosen to remain silent for many reasons, including their culture's stress, as I note in the body of the text, on silence before hardship (*sabr*). It serves too as a defence against the recollection—the reliving—of painful events (war experiences, the shame and anger of having been duped and betrayed by the French, life in the camps, etc.). One young Harki student of psychology attempted, on her professor's advice, to have the old Harkis speak of their experiences in group-therapy–like sessions. For the most part, the Harkis refused to talk; they were visibly distressed by her insistence. Harki wives who participated in the project were very hostile. I am by no means convinced that confessional and 'talking' therapies necessarily alleviate the consequences of traumatic experiences at least in those societies in which silence—stoicism—rather than confession are valued.
4. As the French do not distinguish family origins in their census, it is impossible to know how many Harkis, their children and grandchildren are living in France today. Estimates range from seven hundred thousand to one and a half million. It is clear that the majority have disappeared into one sector or another of French society—some with extraordinary success. Others seem destined to remain in the ranks of the unemployed migrant workers.
5. Derrida would, no doubt, argue that just as forgiveness is impossible in his terms so is the giving of a gift (*don*) since the exchange of gifts is not unconditional. The receiver of the gift is in a debt relation to the donor. The two would find themselves in a chain of expectations and obligations. The present (*cadeau, présent*), like the excuse, is, of course, possible since the giving of a present assumes—or does not deny—its conditionality (Derrida 1991: 51–94; Caputo 1997: 160–1; see also Jankélévitch 2005 and per contra 1986). Its idiosyncrasy notwithstanding, Derrida's understanding of the gift challenges the Maussian assumptions generally accepted in anthropology.

References

Abrial, S. (2001), *Les enfants de Harkis, de la révolte à l'integration*, Paris: L'Harmattan.

Arendt, H. (1958), *The Human Condition*, Chicago: University of Chicago Press.

Aristotle (1941), 'Nicomachean Ethics', in R. McKeon (ed.), *The Basic Works of Aristotle*, New York: Random House, 927–1112.

Benamou, G. M. (2003), *Un mensonge français sur la guerre d'Algérie*, Paris: Robert Lafont.

Berthelier, R. (1994), *L'homme maghrébin dans la littérature psychiatrique*, Paris: L'Harmattan.

Besnaci, F. and C. Manceron (2008), *Les Harkis dans la colonisation et ses suites*, Paris: L'Atelier.

Boulhaïs, N. (2002), *Des Harkis berbères de l'Aurès au nord de la France*, Villeneuve d'Ascq: Presses Universitaires de Septentrion.

Bourdieu, P. (1965), 'The Sentiment of Honour in Kabyle Society', in J. Peristiany (ed.), *Honour and Shame: The Values of a Mediterranean Society*, London: Weidenfeld and Nicolson, 191–242.

Brillet, E. (2001), 'Les problématiques contemporaines du pardon au mirroir du massacre des Harkis', *Cultures et Conflits*, 41(2): 1–18.

Cappelletto, F. (2003), 'Long-Term Memory of Extreme Events: From Autobiography to History', *Journal of the Royal Anthropological Institute*, 9: 241–60.

Caputo, J. (1997), *The Prayers and Tears of Jacques Derrida: Religion without Religion*, Bloomington: University of Indiana Press.

Chabit, T. (2006), *Les Harkis*. Paris: La Découverte.

Crapanzano, V. (2008), 'De la colère à l'indignation: Le cas des Harkis', *Anthropologie et Sociétés*, 32: 121–38.

Crapanzano, V. (2009a), 'The Dead but Living Father, the Living but Dead Father', in L. Kalinich and S. Taylor (eds), *The Dead Father: A Psychoanalytic Inquiry*, London: Routledge, 163–73.

Crapanzano, V. (2009b), 'Half Disciplined Chaos: Thoughts on Contingency, Fate, Destiny, Story, and Trauma', Rappaport Lecture presented at the Joint Meeting of the Society for Psychological Anthropology and the Society for the Anthropology of Religion, Pacific Grove, California.

Crapanzano, V. (2010), 'The Wound That Never Heals', *Alif*, 30: 57–84.

Crapanzano, V. (2011), *The Harkis: The Wound That Never Heals*, Chicago: University of Chicago Press.

Derrida, J. (1991), *Donner le Temps: La fausse monnaie*, Paris: Galilée.

Derrida, J. (2001), *On Cosmopolitanism and Forgiveness*, London: Routledge.

Firth, R. (1967), *Tikopia Ritual and Belief*, Boston: Beacon Press.

Griswold, C. (2007), *Forgiveness: A Philosophical Exploration*, Cambridge: Cambridge University Press.

Hamoumou, M. (1993), *Et ils sont devenus Harkis*, Paris: Fayard.

Jankélévitch, V. (1986), *L'Impréscriptible*, Paris: Seuil.

Jankélévitch, V. (2005), *Forgiveness*, Chicago: University of Chicago Press.

Jordi, J.-J. (1999), *Les Harkis, une mémoire enfouie*, Paris: Autrement.

Ricoeur, P. (2000), *La mémoire, l'histoire, et l'oubli*, Paris: Seuil.

Roux, M. (1991), *Les Harkis: Les oubliés de l'histoire*, Paris: La Découverte.

Servier, J. (1955), *Dans l'Aurès sur le pas des rebelles*, Paris: France Empire.

Turnaturi, G. (2007), *Betrayal: The Unpredictability of Human Relations*, Chicago: University of Chicago Press.

Wensinck, A. (2009), 'Sabr', in *Encyclopaedia of Islam*, 2nd edn, Leiden: Brill.

–10–

Integrating Interviews into Quantitative Domains: Reaching the Parts Controlled Trial Can't Reach

Alexandra Greene

Informal interviewing has a long history of being used as a method for collecting information in social anthropology (Bernard 1995). Traditionally, this type of unstructured interviewing took place away from home and within the context of long-term participant observation. This style of interviewing can be distinguished from the development of more structured interviews in health services research (HSR), which are more inclined to consist of a questionnaire or a list of fixed-choice questions which the interviewer is trained to ask in a systematic and standardized manner (Britten 1995; Patton 2002; Ritchie and Lewis 2009; Sobo 2009). Despite this structured approach, the interview, with its emphasis on subjective perceptions and the contextual details of social interaction has, until recently, been viewed by many quantitative researchers in HSR as rather oppositional to more evidence-based methods (EBM). The history of quantitative techniques and procedures currently known as EBM (or evidence-based health care) started at McMaster University in the mid-1980s and escalated in the United Kingdom after the Bristol case (Smith 1998), where cardiac surgeons were shown to be underperforming, leading to what the General Medical Council (GMC) called unacceptable injury and death toll among children with heart disease. One time editor of the *British Medical Journal* (*BMJ*), Smith argues that the trust that patients place in their doctors 'will never be the same again, but that will be a good thing if we move to an active rather than a passive trust, where doctors share uncertainty' (1998: 1917). This change, he suggests, will bring about growing evidence that patients will become equal partners in the doctor–patient relationship and that their involvement to improve services will ensure that services are monitored and satisfactory to health care users as well as being cost-effective.

EBM is intended to herald the rise in the transparency of health services research, performance indicators and guidelines for clinical standards. This shift has meant that clinicians must no longer base their practices solely on personal experience and preferences but on a complex array of processes that can be graded strictly into hierarchies of evidence; the most robust of which is said to be the randomized controlled trial (RCT). These processes follow strict protocols which regulate the reliability and validity of the data collected and the results these produce to ultimately deliver services for the public and to monitor doctors' personal performance.

This process is evident in the development and evaluation of complex interventions in HSR, which this chapter refers to, which are health interventions that may constitute a set of individually complex interventions, such as health, education, housing and life expectancy, which may act independently or interdependently, with important health consequences (Campbell et al. 2007; Craig et al. 2008). The nature of complex interventions means that their development is inextricably bound together with the complex process of evaluating their acceptability, effect and cost in the service context. The shift towards quantitative approaches being developed to tackle 'real world' questions through complex and pragmatic designs has meant that social science, and mixed methods approaches in general, are now viewed as important parts of a more integrated approach to developing health services.

This change has been matched with more anthropologists being applied, which Rabinow (2005) sees as both a problem and strength. As qualitative methods and the subdiscipline of medical anthropology become globalized, anthropologists find themselves in what may be called morally charged domains in which the forms and values of individuals are problematized in the sense that they are subject to technological, political, EMB and medicine (see also Muller 1994). Other anthropologists, such as Franklin (2005), argue that the global production of EBM deserves careful observation of the processes that involve both individual and collective practices.

This chapter draws on an empirical study and relates to my position as both an anthropologist in a health services research unit (HSRU) who has witnessed the monopoly of EBM over other research approaches and as a member of a multidisciplinary team working on an exploratory project designed to develop a screening programme for hypertension and required to defend and promote qualitative and ethnographic approaches to research. As one of two qualitative researchers in the team (the other being a sociologist and my coworker) my aim was to interview health providers on their views of our proposed screening programme. In the event, I found myself needing to also develop a more informal type of interview closer to long-term participant observation, as a way of exploring the disparities and differing expectations that arose between the qualitative and quantitative members of our team.

Using the Interview Space to Glimpse the Field of Evidence and the Place of the Long-term Interview in the Randomized Controlled Trial

The RCT was introduced in the 1950s as the most rigorous way of capturing data and determining whether a 'cause–effect' relation exists between a course of treatment or intervention and its outcome. Its introduction is said to have had, more than any other technique, a major effect on the practice of medicine. Fundamental to the RCT is the opportunity to create economic models with which to assess the cost-effectiveness of the treatment being investigated (Sibbald and Roland 1998). Our study design, common for the development of a complex intervention RCT (Campbell et al. 2007; Craig et al. 2008), involved a first-stage exploratory (or feasibility) study to test whether the screening programme we were proposing was feasible. If it was, the team would be in a good position to apply for additional funding to develop our study into a full-blown RCT. Being involved in an RCT is considered highly prestigious in HSR, but they are costly and all the more difficult to secure in the current political and economic climate of scarce funding.

Despite the move towards mixed methods approaches, HSR maintains a strong tradition of biomedical research and a propensity towards conventional quantitative and experimental methods. Qualitative research by comparison has been criticized for lacking scientific rigour, being too anecdotal, impressionistic, ungeneralizable and subject to a researcher's bias. Moreover, qualitative methods generate large amounts of detailed information about a small number of settings compared with typical research approaches in public health where epidemiological approaches are the common currency of exploration. As Mays and Pope suggest: 'to label an approach "unscientific" is peculiarly damning in an era when scientific knowledge is generally regarded as the highest form of knowing' (1995: 109). These authors, along with many other social scientists involved in health research, believe that the pervasive assumption underlying all these criticisms is that quantitative and qualitative approaches are fundamentally different in their ability to ensure the validity and reliability of their findings.

This view has meant that strategies are now in place within qualitative research to protect against bias and enhance the reliability of its findings. Methodological checklists have also been developed to help qualitative researchers assess the quality of their own and others' research. This shift in social sciences in HSR may be understandable, particularly with the fierce competition for funding, but it has also set up the idea that qualitative research is less effective because its value and rigorousness can be measured against the highly standardized techniques and practices of quantitative research. It makes the more informal, long-term qualitative approaches I trained in as an anthropologist seem misplaced and inadequate in the HSR arena. It ignores the opportunities that entirely different approaches can bring to research and the idea that differences can be complementary rather than oppositional, and that the necessary tensions between them can provide a broader lens through which to explore the situations being studied.

Barbour (2000) argues that concerns about the value of qualitative research in medical research have now been replaced by concerns about how rigorous qualitative research can be made. Social science checklists have come about to comply with various procedures that pertain to quantitative guidelines for respondent validation and multiple coding. This, she warns, is pragmatic but has wider repercussions, because qualitative approaches cannot respond to overly prescriptive designs or be solved by the more experimental, formulaic processes of EBM: 'If we succumb to the lure of "one size fits all" solutions we risk being in a situation where the tail (the checklist) is wagging the dog (the qualitative research)' (Barbour 2000: 1115). The danger is that if the rigour of qualitative research is attempted without embedding it in a broader understanding of qualitative research design and data analysis, we risk compromising the unique contribution that systematic and in-depth qualitative research can make to HSR.

Similarly, Lambert (2006) explores the techniques of appraising and applying EBM in health research. She suggests that the application of research evidence and its evolution into evidence-based healthcare has grown out of the increasing recognition in the 1960s that many of the mistakes caused by the medical professions were due to practices being based on tradition or preference. This has given rise to sets of standards to make medicine safer through the practice of EBM. However, she describes this process as a pedagogical innovation which intends to transform the cultural, social and experiential dimensions of medical knowledge and practice into systematically reviewed and critically appraised evidence of effectiveness that is generalizable, quality assureable and affordable. What she finds is an 'indeterminate and malleable range of techniques and practices characterised not by particular kinds of methodological rigour, but by the pursuit of a new approach to medical knowledge and authority' (2006: 2633).

Other critics of EBM are those within medicine who are sceptical that medical data, devoid of clinical experience, can be translated easily into services for individual patients (Parker 2002; Schattner and Fletcher 2003; Sullivan and Macnaughton 1996). Rawlins, writing in the *Lancet*, criticizes the imagined imbalance between qualitative and quantitative approaches which he argues gives the idea of 'hierarchies [of evidence, which] place RCTs at their summit with various forms of observational studies in the foothills' (2008: 2152). He quotes Hill (1966), the designer of the RCT, who admits that 'any belief that the controlled trial is the only way would mean not that the pendulum had swung too far, but that it had come right off the hook' (2008: 2152). These critics suggest that research approaches cannot be understood outside the context of their research relations, which requires that we explore how qualitative and quantitative research has been ideologically constructed in the science of EBM (Oakley 2000). For Oakley, the energy put into maintaining the divide between qualitative and quantitative approaches should be used instead on 'how to develop the most reliable and democratic ways of knowing, both in order to bridge the gap between ourselves and others, and to ensure that those who intervene on behalf of other people's lives do so with the most benefit and the least harm' (2000: 3).

For Nutley and colleagues (2007), attaching labels of 'evidence' to particular types of 'knowing' is a political act and one that is highly complex, constantly shifting and ambiguous. In a similar vein, writing from a research ethics perspective, anthropologist Engelke (2008) questions whether anyone or any discipline has the right to judge another's way of knowing or to choose what is or is not the expert paradigm and the yardstick by which other research paradigms should be measured. His concern is that as the different research groupings jostle for power, deploying their own worldviews about what is or is not a truth, a process of judgement is set up which challenges the way others construct their ways of knowing. His unease is that notions of a research divide can set up uncomfortable positions where the tone of debate is controversial, offensive and exclusive (see also in Engelke: Hastrup 2004; Bloch 2005). To ignore this tendency, as Engelke cautions, is to miss out on discussions about what evidence means to the different groups.

Engelke's concern about the lack of debate warrants attention because mixed methods projects are becoming more common in HSR. To some extent, this is pragmatic, brought about by funding commissions and the Research Excellence Framework (REF 2010) preferences for mixed methods projects and what O'Caithain and colleagues (2008) describe as research yield, or publications and funding opportunities. McKee (2009) is equally cautious about the move towards mixed methods approaches. Funding bodies, she suggests, work in responsive mode or prioritize and commission research to address particular health issues or questions. Correspondingly, teams of health service researchers, made up of different disciplines, come together in responses to either of these modes of research funding. While this in itself is not problematic, the research team is often led by a member of staff who favours a particular qualitative or quantitative slant on how the health problems should be studied, what types of questions get asked and how the research findings should be interpreted and used. What may occur is that different researchers can be brought into a team as a bit of an afterthought to make the project seem more mixed methods.

The worry for McKee (2009) is that this opportunistic assembly of teams, in what she calls 'the scramble' to secure funding, may leave little time to consider a shared modus operandi among members, where individual members may hold fundamentally different philosophical or paradigmatic approaches to the health problem being studied. In her experience, it is usually the qualitative component in a study that suffers what she calls an 'epistemological squeeze' by being poorly attended to or exploited by members who may be less inclined to defend the qualitative perspective in the overall study.

These arguments hold up in Lewin and colleagues' (2009) systematic review, which found that qualitative studies were rarely included in RCTs and when they were, there was evidence to suggest that strategies were used to ensure that the qualitative techniques for collecting data were tightly controlled and the 'effects' of their findings minimized and poorly integrated in the final report of the RCT and were rarely published. Part of the problem, they believe, stems from the tendency in trials to use linear models for evaluating clinical interventions, which inhibits the more iterative approaches of qualitative research.

Developing an Ethnographic Interview to Reflect on My Position in the Team

A team of trialists is usually made up of multidisciplinary members who have differing expertise in organizing the running of a range of different types of trials. This could be an early-stage, exploratory trial, as ours was, or a full-blown randomized controlled trial, which our study was aiming to be. The role of each member ranges from recruiting and assigning participants (sometimes called volunteers or subjects) to a study, developing and/or undertaking the intervention or drug(s) to be studied, deciding when the study should begin and ensuring the random allocation of volunteers into the appropriate groups that will either receive treatment (there may be a number) or be part of the control group. The most important advantage of proper randomization is that it minimizes any bias in the trial results (Moher et al. 2010). The Medical Research Council (MRC) recommends that studies, particularly those relating to complex interventions (as ours was) employ a phased, mixed methods approach to allow a holistic interpretation of the effects of the intervention or drugs being tested (Craig et al. 2008).

Our exploratory study team was made up of mostly trialists and was the first stage of a potential RCT. It aimed to explore the feasibility of developing a screening programme that would be acceptable to health providers in the service context and effective, both costwise and in the detection of hypertension (high blood pressure), which is important to prevent long-term cardiac conditions (e.g. strokes, heart failure), kidney failure and shortened life expectancy. Trials, even exploratory ones like ours, are highly complex systems to run because the techniques and practices used need to be tightly monitored and audited if a case is to be made for applying for an RCT.

The other aim of our multidisciplinary team was to develop the methodology of mixed methods approaches to trials and in this way, become a flagship for a more inclusive approach to trials research. Our team was made up of statisticians, clinicians involved in treating hypertension, trial managers, systematic reviewers, health economists, psychologists, a sociologist and myself, an anthropologist. Several of us were invited to write the research proposal to be submitted to the MRC, and if successful to lead the specific phases of the project. I had been working in the HSRU for several years and was invited to lead the qualitative phase of the project. My role was to first, oversee the recruitment of health providers working in services related to hypertension in hospitals, general practice and the community, across the United Kingdom and in both the National Health Service (NHS) and the private sector (e.g. doctors, nurses, allied health professionals and policy makers) and second, develop the semi-structured interviews (see Creswell 2007; Sobo 2009). The sociologist, my coworker, was a highly experienced qualitative researcher who wanted to gain experience in HSR and in trial research in particular. The findings from this part of the study were intended to feed into the corresponding quantitative phases of the research. In trial language, the phases were a way of systematically 'harvesting' evidence which could be written up as a new proposal for an RCT.

The Nature of the Interview in the Trial

Concerns continue in social science research about the widespread and uncritical view of the interview as a method for revealing the personal narratives of the subjects spoken to. Nor, as Chamberlayne and colleagues propose, does it render the informants' voices 'fully intelligible' (2000: 8) or offer any 'biographical evidence' (2000: 22) about the power relationships among the team members. We cannot assume, as Cohen and Rapport caution, 'That what we hear is an expression of the speaker's consciousness. The sense we make of it is also, of course, an expression of our own consciousness' (1995: 12). Similarly, Atkinson and Silverman warn us against putting 'special faith' (1997: 304) in the interview as a valid instrument of data collection or viewing it as a research method that will reveal any 'underlying reality' of events (1997: 306).

The semi-structured interviews that the sociologist and I intended to design for the health providers are not the interviews that this chapter focusses on. However, they are important to it because they became the catalyst for the disparities that developed between us (the social scientists) and other members of the quantitative team and are used throughout this chapter to highlight our differing expectations. The motivation for this chapter is, instead, an informal, ethnographic interview, more commonly associated with anthropological ethnographies (Marcus 1998) that I needed to develop to deal with the differences in opinion building up between us.

My ethnographic interview had an organic nature because I had not expected to experience any long-term awkwardness with the team members, save from the occasional differences in opinion that might be a feature of every multidisciplinary team. The ethnographic interview became my way of developing a system for trying to understand and critique why it seemed so difficult to dispel the tensions that developed. It was not, as commonly referred to by the range of applied disciplines using it today, merely a tool of qualitative data collection, such as 'observation' or the 'interview' (Savage 2000; Brink and Edgecombe 2003). The unpredictable nature of my field (the team) meant that my methods of critique needed to be fluid and iterative so that I could weave back and forth between the processes of data collection, analysis and theoretical generalization. This, as Kerby (1991) states, allowed me to recount the series of temporal events and put them together in a meaningful sequence as well as taking responsibility for supplying the construction and slant I developed to fill in the gaps of meaning and their significance (Greenhalgh and Hurwitz 1998). In this sense, my long-term interview could not be treated as a neutral event (as Fischer-Rosenthal (2000) claims) because it came out of the difficulties I was experiencing. Moreover, I needed to find a way of overcoming these difficulties and not merely categorize my colleagues as unreasonable (see James 1995) so that I could remain a member of the group and be privy to the study information. As Fontes suggests, we need to find pragmatic ways to 'make it happen in situations that may be far from optional' (2008: 403). Accordingly, this style of long-term interview bears little resemblance to the well-defined steps that James Spradley (1979) lays out in his version of the ethnographic interview, and is more akin to ethnographic studies carried out by Silverman (1987), James (1993), Atkinson (1995) and Souhami (2007).

The prominent feature of my ethnographic interview was that it took place within the context of long-term participant observation: when I worked in HSR, before the study, where relationships with the team members were highly amicable and during the study, when our relationships began to deteriorate. These broader ethnographic practices appeared to enrich my interview and allowed me to triangulate my observations with a host of other data sources, for example study and policy documents, steering and advisory group meetings, emails, telephone calls and informal chats, that feed in to the overall story (Sobo 2009). It allowed the generation of organizing principles for systematic multimethods inquiry (Parker and Harper 2005). In this way, it supported the collection of data through informal as well as formal means and meant I could compare reported with actual behaviour and it underpinned my analysis of the socio-culturally situated nature of our very different ways of knowing about what constituted 'evidence' (Moses and Knutsen 2007).

Its potential was the interview's ability to relate the abstractions of trial procedures, algorithms and evidence beside the realities of the health practitioners, who would have to operationalize the screening programme (Huby et al. 1998). The iterative nature allowed a simultaneous use of immersion and structured data collection which helped to balance my positions of being a team 'insider' with an 'emic' view of the cultures and social situations, and an 'outsider' observer with an 'etic' view. This helped me to consider the different perspectives on hypertension, both from 'within' and 'without' the health problem under study. It provided a space from which, as McCaffery suggests (see chapter 12, this volume), to scrutinize my ethnographic practice and to think about, as Josephides says (see chapter 3, this volume), the interviewer's place within the scheme of relations. It became for me a way of developing the methodologies mixed methods teams and a way of reconfiguring the boundary of the problem for the health providers (Lambert and McKevitt 2002). In this way, the interview became my personal account and a bibliographical repository (Atkinson and Silverman 1997) for reflecting upon my observations of events over the eighteen-month duration of the study between 2008 and 2010.

The Interview: Being a Member of the Team or Being 'the Other'

I do not believe that the challenges that arose among the team members were ever intended to be personal. What became evident was how nervous they felt about the type of qualitative results we might produce. For example our approach appeared difficult to fit within the formulaic confines of the quantitative data and our interviews with the health providers seemed to suggest that the screening programme we were proposing would not be successful. For Sobo (2009) the qualitative and quantitative divide relates to the way the qualitative researcher needs to go to where the participants are in order to study them in their own environment, while the experimental researcher must take the 'subjects' out of their environment so that the setting can be controlled and examined. In the latter, it is necessary to control the environment of a study because the aims of the experimental methods are to test hypotheses about the relationships between several variables (measurable factors), while ensuring that other variables (not the ones being tested) do not influence (or bias) the outcome, and can be generalizable.

Another problem was related to the exploratory and generative nature of our work. While the sociologist and I worked closely together with the rest of the team to come up with the frame of questions that would keep us on track, in terms of the research questions needing to be answered, we also needed to make sure that the style of questioning was loose and provided enough leeway for the interviewees to add their own interests and concerns, which might lead to further questions that had not been expected.

Not being in a position to use a tape recorder, none of the following comments from the team and my responses to them are verbatim. They are representative of what I wrote down and remember and aim to highlight the disparities and differing expectations that appeared to exist between us in the main team meetings.

Mary (M) (the clinician and lead investigator on the project): Ok, Alex, I've had a word with Jane (the psychologist). We're a bit worried that the questions you came up with aren't specific enough, so we've come up with your interview schedule for you.

Alex (A) (the author): That's very kind of you, but I'm not sure it was really necessary. Perhaps we could design the schedule together?

M: You sound a bit put out, Alex. We thought you'd be pleased.

A (looks at the three pages of tightly typed questions): Well no...yes, a bit, I suppose. I can see where you're coming from with these questions but I'm not sure they would, in the strictest sense, qualify as qualitative questions. I probably need to develop them a bit...condense them.

[Jane (J) (the psychologist) picks up on my bewilderment]: You did say your interviews normally lasted an hour. The questions should be fine then.

A: I can see why you want to ask these questions, but from my perspective this (pages of questions) is more of a questionnaire than an interview. I don't think I could confidently say I'd done qualitative interviews if I used this list.

M: Alex, I think you're being a bit touchy. You see, this study is up against the clock and because your phase leads, we need to be able to show that we've answered the research questions rigorously and succinctly. If I'm honest, Alex, I'm not sure we can afford to beat around the bush, as your questions do. Take our help as a learning experience. It will be good for you to learn how we do it and why. Sorry, I hope that doesn't sound too harsh. It's not meant to be. I hope you can understand that I get nervous. The responsibility rests with me and I have to deliver. The rest of the team are depending on me.

The need to deliver, as I learned, didn't relate solely to getting the project and report in on time. It seemed as much to do with producing results that would suggest that our proposed screening programme was feasible for an RCT and would therefore be looked on favourably by funding bodies and journals. Concern about not letting the rest of the team down related to the members of the team benefitting from additional funding and publications. However, success is never just collective. The lead investigator would gain additional points for fronting the project, managing it and shouldering the setbacks if it failed. It seemed also that the chance to succeed was inevitably bound up with one's feelings of achievement and chances for promotion.

M: Look Alex, we're friends, so you know how important this study is to me. You know I've had a bit of a rough time. If it carries on (becomes an RCT) it will suit everyone.

As Sobo (2009) suggests, in comparison with the rest of the team, the interviewer (both the interviews with health practitioners and my personal, long-term interview) can seem too naturalistic (carried out in the natural setting) with no control over variables. In the meetings I had taken time to explain that the qualitative approach had very tried-and-tested methods for building an interpretation. The difference seemed to be that qualitative studies focus on the links between events or activities in the study, while quantitative research focusses on the links between variables (e.g. feasibility, cost and effectiveness). The link between these preplanned variables forms the unit of analysis, while in qualitative research, the whole study, or field, is the unit of analysis (Sobo 2009). I could see therefore how qualitative methods for collecting and analysing the data might seem too imprecise and our findings too random and risky.

Mark (statistician): I agree with Mary; I don't think you get it, Alex.

M: You have to understand that we're not trying to be difficult, but we need to know that you're asking the right questions... about what we need to know for the development of the screening programme.

A: Yes, I do appreciate that the questions need to attend to the research questions, but I need to be able to pick up on what's important to the interviewees. There might be things that they come up with that we haven't thought of that will help us to finely tune an RCT... the exploratory nature of the interview is important. It's about being able to give the interviewee enough leaway to talk about what's important to them, while also having the skill to pull them back again to answer the questions we need to ask, otherwise the interview just becomes a list of questions that you don't really need a qualitative researcher to do.

J: I don't think you do get it, Alex. We're only trying to help.

M: Ok, is there any way of measuring your results?

A: Well, no, but that's sort of the point...

M: You see we need to make your work systematic. We need to be able to make a large table from your results... to help us to build an evidence base that we can feed into the economic model. We just can't standardize your questions and so your results aren't compatible.

Compared with the sort of interviews I wanted to do with the health providers, the quantitative researchers interview was highly formalized, permitting little participant observation or interviewee–interviewer interaction and requiring quantifications at certain stages. What worried me most was that a moderator seemed necessary who could apply a very directive approach to the interviews and rely on highly structured questions that could be answered in a very specific order.

A: Yes, I do understand where you're coming from... we all wrote the grant proposal together... You knew that I would have a particular approach that would be very different from your own. We wrote the proposal so that the mixed methods complemented one another.

M: Don't treat me like a fool. I've done qualitative research. I know exactly what it entails and I think you're being very pedantic.

Mary had told me earlier that she had done a two-day course on qualitative research methods. Seeing herself as a mixed methods expert gave her a kudos among the rest of the team which was very difficult for the sociologist and me to contest. It made it difficult to explain that qualitative methods were not in themselves qualitative research, but required a broad understanding of qualitative research design and analysis necessary to ground the appropriateness of the methods used. Consequently, most of what we said in the meetings was either ignored or treated as if we were just being obtuse.

A: Can I just confirm that the interview is meant to find out what's important to the practitioners... to see if our ideas for a screening programme will work?

M: Yes, of course, but I've already spent a long time explaining how I want the interviews to be done.

Two weeks later:

Mark: I don't think you get it, Alex. Have you read the research proposal?

A: Yes, I think so. If you remember I was part of the team that wrote it.

Mark: Look Alex, you have to understand [he hands me a journal paper] there is evidence that qualitative research is problematic... you know what I mean... It can sabotage feasibility studies. There's evidence of that in this paper.

What the paper missed saying was that qualitative researchers were not deliberately setting out to sabotage studies. If a study failed it was usually because the qualitative findings revealed the gaps that were not evident or predictable from the quantitative aspect, or in the original hypothesis.

Three months later:

Mark: I just don't think you get it, Alex.

A: I understand where you're coming from, but I need to be rigorous in my own approach; I need to be able to show my own audit trail.

M: Don't patronize us, Alex.

A: I'm happy to help fill in your matrix, but I don't think you need a qualified anthropologist to do your questionnaire.

M: Oh don't be so touchy.

Six months later:

Mark: Alex, I don't think you get it.

A: I think you need to trust me on that one, Mark.

M: Oh you mustn't think that we don't trust you, but there's the time factor too. Your approach takes years, doesn't it?

On meeting the team members halfway, I had agreed to use some of their questions; nevertheless, some members of the team felt it was important to restrict the practitioners I spoke to.

M: You can't interview him.

A: Don't we need to interview more clinicians?

M: Yes, but I know him, he'll give you the wrong impression... bias the findings.

A: Look, Mary, I don't mean to be rude but I feel as if I'm just being allowed to interview your friends.

M: No, they're not friends, just practitioners that I know will give you a good interview. I'm trying to help.

The team's willingness to restrict my sample might have arisen because members from the first group of practitioners we spoke to felt that our proposed screening programme would not work because they believed that the incident hypertension did not warrant a screening programme.

M: Your findings are suggesting that screening can't go ahead unless the current system is changed... But then we can't go forward and do the trial.

A: I'm not trying to be difficult, Mary, but that does seem to be what the practitioners are saying.

J: Did you use the questions we gave you?

The eighteen-month study left the sociologist and me with a dilemma. Either we made life easy and complied with the rest of the team's wishes, using their questions to interview whom they wanted us to speak to, or we agreed to find a solution that would suit us all. It is difficult to explain why the sociologist and I felt so compromised. Were our reactions related to feeling that our expertise (however we might substantiate that) was not being taken seriously enough and consequently that we would be letting down our side of the qualitative divide? Was it related to the frustration we felt at not being taken seriously and feeling as if we were token contributors to secure funding for the study? Was it the disappointment at not being listened to or trusted enough? Was it because the lack of open-ended, interactive discussion between the interviewee and interviewer would result in a very thin analysis, and in turn give us little credibility with our own scholarly institutions? Looking back it was probably a bit of all of these feelings over the course of the eighteen months.

For Greenland, investigator bias (when the results are skewed towards the results that want to be found) can take several forms from 'outright fabrication to subtle and even unconscious bias in design and analysis choices' (2008: 593). The point he makes is that bias is usually a desired a priori choice by the investigators, and is related to financial input, leading to the adoption of dubious or even 'deadly treatments' (2008: 593). Our problem was how to raise this issue with the members of the team, even though the very structures put in place to ensure EBM (and to avoid bias) are meant to encourage transparency, critique and openness about uncertainty.

Conclusions

HSR focusses on public health reforms and the importance of introducing cost-efficiency, improved governance mechanisms, transparency and quality control. Part of this focus relates to ensuring that health care users and the public can inform service design and development and contribute to improving practice, outcome and quality. The mechanism for achieving this is a set of techniques and practices based on systematically reviewed and critically appraised evidence of effectiveness (Lambert 2006).

Atkinson describes the RCT as a 'collection of culturally prescribed devices' (1995: 149) whereby the work entailed is achieved in a stable and predictable way and where, on one hand, actions and opinions can be shared and challenged and on the other, colleagues can be controlled, regulated and scrutinized. The basis of any successfully funded trial research is the researchers coming up with a hypothesis, which the study then seeks to prove or disprove. Looked at logically, disproving one's hypothesis is a form of success, because it provides evidence to show that the success of an intervention or drug shouldn't be taken for granted. The failure to prove one's hypothesis, however, is rarely looked on in this way, because it usually means the termination of the research machine that leads to a full-blown RCT.

In our study, the hypothesis stated that we could design a programme that would successfully screen for hypertension in the community. Results from an exploratory (or feasibility) study that suggested otherwise would not be highly welcome. Pisani quotes Kwiatkowski, when he says: 'developing a hypothesis [in the evidence machine] is a way of fabricating a justification for an experiment, because if you say at the start that you don't know what you'll find, you'll get marked down [by funding committees]' (2010: 56), which results in quantitative scientists trying to fit their work into a model that does not necessarily reflect reality.

By comparison, the nature of qualitative interviews embraces a more bottom-up approach, where observations develop into patterns and tentative hypotheses that the researcher can explore. In HSR the qualitative interviewer may be required to take on a more top-down approach which begins with him or her adhering to specific research hypotheses (often as laid out in the research proposal) against which his or her data can be tried and tested (Lindlof and Taylor 2010).

As Hammersley and Atkinson suggest, 'the differences between participant observation and interviewing are not as great as is sometimes suggested' (2007: 109). This provides, as Goffman said (Miller 1959), an ongoing conversation in which we are not aware of the beginning and also unlikely to be aware of its end. Here, ethnography and ethnographic interviewing treat interviews as contextualized conversations which are not only used to answer research questions but provide the researcher with time to pause and reflect on the context. Ethnographic interviews are not devoid of ethical consideration, however. In my case, it allowed me to reposition my own sense of power and control and my rights as a researcher. This required a consideration of the difficult distinction between overt and covert interviews with the members of the team and how, in my endeavour to overcome the problems, I took for granted their consent and disclosure. In this way, it gave me permission to ask some critically applied questions that had their roots in my anthropological background and helped to cushion the blow I experienced when the qualitative findings were not evident in the final study report. It has provided me with an important outlet for my frustrations and the disappointment from feeling I (or the sociologist) was not being treated as a bonafide member of the team, but more like an interlocutor with the mechanisms to sabotage the trial. While it is I who writes this story, as the anthropologist in the study, I write it in mind of my coworker, the sociologist, whose experiences were so raw at the end of the study that she thought about taking her own life.

In view of this, my long-term interview allowed me to explore the members' quest for evidence and to see how this incorporated the human element and the quest for power games and ambition. While relativism may be an approach for different or difficult behaviour, the long-term interview showed me how it can seem more like an intellectual excuse for bad behaviour. Moreover, personal interests can supersede any arguments for the greater good. The interview was my mechanism for understanding how research, in any form, is provincial and culturally constructed, and that the nature of it inevitably brings with it subjectivity and intrinsic values. Once we understand the values in hand then we can cease to worry about their relationship to the evidence, and in this way, create some sort of moral environment where mixed methods researchers can work together with a better understanding of what makes better health services research.

References

Atkinson, P. (1995), *Medical Talk and Medical Work: The Liturgy of the Clinic*, London: Sage Publications.

Atkinson, P. and D. Silverman (1997), 'Kundera's Immortality: The Interview Society and the Invention of the Self', *Qualitative Inquiry*, 3(3): 304–25.

Barbour, R. (2000), 'Checklists for Improving Rigour in Qualitative Research: A Case of the Tail Wagging the Dog?', *British Medical Journal*, 322: 1115.

Bernard, H. (1995), 'Qualitative Data, Quantitative Analysis', *Cultural Anthropology Methods*, 8(1): 9–11.

Bloch, M. (2005), 'Where Did Anthropology Go? Or the Need for Human Nature', in M. Bloch (ed.), *Essays on Cultural Transmission*, Oxford: Berg, 1–20.

Brink, P. and N. Edgecombe (2003), 'What Is Becoming of Ethnography?', *Qualitative Health Research*, 13: 1028–30.

Britten, N. (1995), 'Qualitative Research: Qualitative Interviews in Medical Research', *British Medical Journal*, 331: 251–3.

Campbell, N., E. Murray, J. Darbyshire, J. Emery, A. Farmer, F. Griffiths, B. Guthrie, H. Lester, P. Wilson and A. Kinmonth (2007), 'Designing and Evaluating Complex Interventions to Improve Health Care', *British Medical Journal*, 334(7591): 455–9.

Chamberlayne, P., J. Bornat and T. Wengraf (2000), *The Turn to Biographical Methods in Social Science*, Abingdon: Routledge.

Cohen, A. and N. Rapport (eds) (1995), *Questions of Consciousness*, London: Routledge.

Craig, P., P. Dieppe, S. Macintyre, S. Mitchie, I. Nazareth and M. Pettigrew (2008), 'Developing and Evaluating Complex Interventions: The New Medical Research Council Guidance', *British Medical Journal*, 337: 979–83.

Creswell, J. (2007), *Qualitative Inquiry and Research Design: Choosing among Five Approaches*, London: Sage Publications.

Engelke, M. (2008), 'The Objects of Evidence: Anthropological Approaches to the Production of Knowledge', *Journal of the Royal Anthropological Institute*, 14(1): 1–21.

Fischer-Rosenthal, W. (2000), 'Biographical Work and Biographical Structuring in Present-Day Societies', in P. Chamberlayne, J. Bornat and T. Wengraf (eds), *The Turn of the Biographical Method in Social Science*, London: Routledge, 109–25.

Fontes, L. (2008), *Interviewing Clients across Cultures: A Practitioners' Guide*, New York: Guildford Press.

Franklin, S. (2005), 'Stem Cells R Us: Emergent Life Forms and the Global Biological', in S. Collier and A. Ong (eds), *Global Assemblages: Technology, Politics, and Ethics as Anthropological Problems*, Oxford: Blackwell, 59–78.

Greenhalgh, T. and B. Hurwitz (1998), *Narrative Based Medicine: Dialogue and Discourse in Clinical Practice*, London: BMJ Books.

Greenland, S. (2008), 'Accounting for Uncertainty about Investigator Bias: Disclosure Is Informative', *Journal of Epidemiological Community Health*, 63: 593–8.

Hammersley, M. and P. Atkinson (2007), *Ethnography: Principles in Practice*, London: Taylor and Francis.

Hastrup, K. (2004), 'Getting It Right: Knowledge and Evidence in Anthropology', *Anthropology Theory*, 4: 455–72.

Huby, G., M. Porter and J. Bury (1998), 'A Matter of Methods: Perspectives on the Role of the British General Practitioner in the Care of People with HIV/AIDS', *AIDS Care*, 10(Suppl. 1): 83–8.

James, A. (1993), *Childhood Identities, Self and Social Relationships in the Experience of the Child*, Edinburgh: Edinburgh University Press.

James, A. (1995), 'On Being a Child, the Self, the Group, the Category', in A. Cohen and N. Rapport (eds), *Questions of Consciousness*, London: Routledge, 60–76.

Kerby, A. (1991), *Narrative and the Self*, Bloomington: Indiana University Press.

Lambert, H. (2006), 'Accounting for EBM: Notions of Evidence in Medicine', *Social Science and Medicine*, 62: 2633–45.

Lambert, H. and C. McKevitt (2002), 'Anthropology in Health Research: From Qualitative Methods to Multidisciplinarity', *British Medical Journal*, 325: 210–13.

Lewin, S., C. Glenton and A. Oxman (2009), 'Use of Qualitative Methods Alongside Randomised Controlled Trials of Complex Healthcare Interventions: Methodological Study', *British Medical Journal*, 339: 729–34.

Lindlof, T. and B. Taylor (2010), *Qualitative Communication Research Methods*, London: Sage Publications.

Marcus, G. (1998), *Ethnography through Thick and Thin*, Princeton: Princeton University Press.

Mays, N. and C. Pope (1995), 'Qualitative Research: Rigour and Qualitative Research', *British Medical Journal*, 311: 109–12.

McKee, L. (2009), 'Multidisciplinary Working: Is It Working? Implementing Multidisciplinary Research in the Context of Health Care Organisations', Paper presented at Academy of Management Annual Meeting, Symposium 'Organisational Behaviour in Health Care: Diverse Perspectives and International Dimensions', Chicago, 7–11 August.

Miller, H. (1995), 'The Presentation of Self in Electronic Life: Goffman on the Internet', Paper presented at Embodied Knowledge and Virtual Space Conference, Goldsmiths' College, University of London, June.

Moher, D., S. Hopewell, K. Schulz, V. Montori, P. Gøtzsche, P. Devereaux, D. Elbourne, M. Egger and D. Altman (2010), 'CONSORT 2010 Explanation and Elaboration: Updated Guidelines for Reporting Parallel Group Randomised Trials', *British Medical Journal*, 340: c869.

Moses, J. and T. Knutsen (2007), *Ways of Knowing: Competing Methodologies in Social and Political Research*, Basingstoke: Palgrave Macmillan.

Muller, J. (1994), 'Anthropology, Bioethics, and Medicine: A Provocative Trilogy', *Medical Anthropology Quarterly*, 8(4): 448–67.

Nutley, S., I. Walter and T. Davies (2007), *Using Evidence: How Research Can Inform Public Services*, Bristol: Policy Press.

Oakley, A. (2000), *Experiments in Knowing: Gender and Methods in the Social Sciences*, Cambridge: Polity Press.

O'Caithain, A., E. Murphy and J. Nicoll (2008), 'Integration and Publications as Indicators of Yield from Mixed Methods Studies', *Journal of Mixed Methods Research*, 1(2): 147–63.

Parker, M. (2002), 'Whither Our Art? Clinical Wisdom and Evidence-Based Medicine', *Medicine, Health Care and Philosophy*, 5: 273–80.

Parker, M. and I. Harper (2005), 'The Anthropology of Public Health', *Journal of Biosocial Science*, 38: 1–5.

Patton, M. (2002), *Qualitative Research and Evaluation Methods*, London: Sage Publications.

Pisani, E. (2010), 'Has the Internet Changed Science?', *The Prospect,* 177: 54.

Rabinow, P. (2005), 'Midst Anthropology's Problems', in S. Collier and A. Ong (eds), *Global Assemblages: Technology, Politics, and Ethics as Anthropological Problems*, Oxford: Blackwell, 91–104.

Rawlins, M. (2008), 'De Testimonio: On the Evidence for Decisions about the Use of Therapeutic Interventions', *The Lancet*, 372(9656): 2152–61.

Research Excellence Framework (2010), REF2014, http://www.hefce.ac.uk/research/ref/, accessed 20 October 2010.

Ritchie, J. and J. Lewis (eds) (2009), *Qualitative Research Practice: A Guide for Social Science Students and Researchers*, London: Sage Publications.

Savage, J. (2000), 'Ethnography and Health Care', *British Medical Journal*, 321: 1400–2.

Schattner, S. and R. Fletcher (2003), 'Research Evidence and the Individual Patient', *QJM: An International Journal of Medicine*, 96(1): 1–5.

Sibbald, B. and M. Roland (1998), 'Understanding Controlled Trials: Why Are Randomised Controlled Trials Important?', *British Medical Journal*, 316: 201.

Silverman, D. (1987), *Communication and Medical Practice: Social Relations in the Clinic*, London: Sage Publications.

Smith, R. (1998), '"All Changed, Changed Utterly": British Medicine Will Be Transformed by the Bristol Case', *British Medical Journal*, 316: 1917–18.

Sobo, E. (2009), *Culture and Meaning in Health Services Research*, Walnut Creek: Left Coast Press.

Souhami, A. (2007), *A Transforming Youth Justice: Occupational Identity and Cultural Change*, Cullompton: Willan.

Spradley, J. (1979), *The Ethnographic Interview*, New York: Wadsworth Thomson Learning.

Sullivan, F. and R. MacNaughton (1996), 'Evidence in Consultations: Interpreted and Individualised', *The Lancet*, 348: 941–3.

–11–

Recalling What Was Unspeakable: Hunger in North Korea

Sandra Fahy

Anthropologists have explored the topic of silence in a variety of contexts (Basso 1970; Tamen and Saville Troike 1985; Tyler 1987). A consistent theme is that silence is powerful because of its inherent ambiguity; an ambiguity widely accepted as a 'form of withholding' (Achino-Loeb 2006b). In contrast, the 'breaking' of silence, where the trauma narrative for example finds voice, is seen as a departure from the original violence and an act against perpetrators both for those who listen and those who speak (Herman 1992; McKinney 2007). However, theories of analysis for silence are as yet unfixed (Sheriff 2000). In recent years, perhaps because scholars have lost their fear of acknowledging that informants go quiet, the topic of silence in interviews has received a lot of attention (Angrosino 2002; Bernard 2002; Cuéllar 2010; Ervin 2000; Fernandez 2006; Jaworski 1997); it has been viewed as an aspect of the cultural frame in which it emerges (Randall and Koppenhaver 2004), as something both imposed and embraced (Allison 2011). The silence of informants is not necessarily a pure silence, but can take many forms. In a similar way, the unspeakable also takes different manifestations such as the nonverbal utterance, the word left incomplete or the phrase that trails off. Some informants may testify to the inability for words to carry forth accurate communication about the experience, particularly in cases of trauma (Desjarlais et al. 1995: 175; Jenkins 1998: 187); while some trauma is so complete as to render the experience fully unspeakable (Engdahl 2002: 10), some informants speak vociferously *no matter how I tell you, you will not understand*, signifying an effective silencing on the topic.

To my imagination, such vocalized silences are like curtains behind which the experience under discussion unfolded. I use this metaphor of curtains deliberately because it evokes another key topic under consideration here: the capacity of censorship to veil communication.[1] Perhaps the informant has pulled the curtain deliberately, or she had the curtain pulled on her. Perhaps she wants to pull it back, but cannot find the opening, the start or end to the fabric. Sometimes it is not the right time, perhaps the audience is inappropriate and unresponsive. In this chapter I will explore not only what is silenced or unspeakable at the time of the interview, but also what was unspeakable at the time of the experience and how these relate to each other. Do sites of suffering which limit articulation also limit articulation after the fact?

The example under consideration here is collective social suffering in the form of protracted hunger which occurred in North Korea in the 1990s. The oral accounts I collected from survivors of the famine, resettled in Seoul and Tokyo in 2006, demonstrate a complex relationship to silence and the unspeakable.[2] The purpose of this examination is to demonstrate how contexts shape articulation during as well as after the fact. Let us bear in mind that for atrocity to come into being, whether it is famine, genocide, the Shoah or other types of rights violations, for these acts to come into being and for them to continue, there must also exist a sociopolitical discourse that generates, reproduces and reinforces the truths upon which the atrocity is justified. Thus, it is natural that articulation 'after the fact' about experience from that time and place will bear the print of that discourse within itself. This leads to the question of whether silence is a consequence of atrocity or evidence of its mechanisms of manufacture Silence and the unspeakable in interviews are useful for understanding how silence and the unspeakable functioned at the time of the experience.

* * *

Contexts of famine invariably involve violence, whether between individuals, nonstate actors or governments. One of the operational features of violence is its ability to censor, to obfuscate, to play with meaning, to make ambiguous while simultaneously destroying lives. Indeed, connections between famine and censorship have long been historically observed (Article 19 1990; Devereux 1993; Leshuk 2000; Sen and Drèze 1999). Therefore, it is not amiss to recognize several levels of silencing which occur on national, collective and individual levels long before the stage when the informant and researcher sit down together. It is clear that the language of informants can tell us a great deal about those former stages of silencing and this can reveal aspects of the social environment where the violence took place. The language used by North Korean famine survivors in their oral accounts demonstrates consistent patterns in speech that I classify as ambiguous because they require context to achieve full meaning. These expressions can be understood as 'silencing' and making 'unspeakable' their experiences in the North because that original context is so impenetrable, both physically and somewhat ideologically, for many listeners. Indeed, it could be argued that these expressions continue to make experiences unspeakable after survival, in South Korea or Japan, because truly accurate communication could endanger family members and friends still living at home.

One of the reasons ambiguous expressions appeared in the oral accounts is due to the fact that sociopolitical structures in North Korea necessitated and prescribed precisely this type of communication. Perhaps through habit, or because it struck them as the most suitable way to express themselves, these terms, metaphors and expressions emerged again and again in interviews producing an aggregate trend across a host of informants demonstrating that it was not mere coincidence. In the North, this type of speech meant that individuals could maintain fairly accurate communication about their immediate conditions while at the same time remaining safely within an ambiguous cloak of language that did not directly criticize the country, the leadership, the food shortage or even hunger itself. Consequently, once they were safely resettled in South Korea or Japan, the interview became a space where linguistic traces of acceptable speech inside the North emerged and bore evidence to how the government shaped interpretation of the food shortage through discourse. The curtain was pulled back on the famine.

* * *

In North Korea, in the 1990s, at the tail end of long-term vulnerability a famine emerged claiming upwards of nearly two million lives.[3] Poor agricultural decision making, loss of Soviet bloc trade partners and poor policy choices left the country vulnerable to natural disasters (Lee 2000: 23; Woo-Cummings 2002: 27–9). In addition to these factors, the failure to allow the population the means by which to alter its entitlement to food access (Haggard et al. 2007: 22) resulted in many years of famine and over a decade of food shortages in many parts of the country (Schloms 2004: 127). Preexisting inequalities such as nutritional discrimination according to family background and regional access to food meant that those in the northernmost regions were worst affected (Cha 2004; Haggard et al. 2007: 16). Concern over too much involvement with the international community led to strict limits on aid activities within the country, which severely hampered efforts to provide aid to the most vulnerable population groups (Scholms 2004). Inside North Korea, throughout the 1990s and well into the present day, the famine and food shortages were euphemistically phrased in the media and public discourse. The famine was not in fact a *famine*, but a 'March of Suffering'—the official term most often used. 'Famine', I was told, 'was something related to South Korea, or Africa' (Lee (F) interview 2006) and did not have any association with North Korea. Being incongruous politically, ideologically and socially, it did not make sense to use the term. In other ways, which I will explore in this chapter, whole bodies of language grew up in the space left behind in the absence of accurate expression.

When I embarked on this research I presumed many informants would be shy, reluctant and maybe even a bit embarrassed to tell me about their personal experiences of surviving the famine. Instead, it was nothing like that. Every person I asked said that they would be happy to share their experience, adding 'no one has ever asked me to talk about it'—which surprised me as much as their abundant willingness to share their stories with me. Their only insistence was that they remain anonymous, so as not to implicate family and friends back home. They let me record our discussions, asking whatever question I wished. Only once was I refused an answer, when I asked a young man what factors precipitated his departure from the North. My interviews were unstructured, open. I was intentionally vague. I always started with a request to hear about their home town before things got bad. That usually set the oral account in motion. Interviews lasted between one and two hours, and I tried to encourage a monologue narrative with as little interruption as possible. It was not perfect though. There were awkward moments and embarrassments. Sometimes I found a banquet of food waiting for me at an informant's house and over this great mass of food we discussed the famine.[4] I tried to keep an accurate population distribution among the group of informants. Some came from the capital, Pyongyang, while others came from the more northern remote regions of Musan or Chongjin. Their ages ranged from seventeen to seventy, and there were equal numbers of men and women. One-fifth of my informants resided in Tokyo, the rest in Seoul. The Tokyo group were ethnic Koreans who had family in Japan, but had gone to North Korea during the 1960s and 1970s during an ethno-nationalist campaign by North Korea.

Erasing Famine, Hunger and Starvation

The *Konan ŭi Haenggun*, or March of Suffering, originally referred to Kim Il Sung's 1938 historic march to Manchuria with his anti-Japanese guerrilla troops in 1938–9 (Choson Ensik'lip'edia 1995: 179–81). But in the 1990s, the same term was used to identify the famine. In a few instances the famine was also referred to as 'the Red Banner Spirit'[5] and for a short time in 1997 it was called 'the Forced March to Final Victory' (Oh and Hassig 2000: 32), but the March of Suffering was most common. Survivors reported that if these official terms were not used, 'economic downturn' and 'food downturn' took their place. It was unheard of to refer to the *Konan ŭi Haenggun* as a famine. Miss Lee explained, 'They did not use the expression "famine" nor did they use the expression "hunger" rather they used the term *shingnyang t'agyok*, food ration downturn. Starvation was a term we really didn't use. I had been taught that starvation was happening to the beggars in South Korea, and in that instance we used the term a lot. But for the situation we were going through with the food, we didn't use that term' (Lee (F) interview 2006).

The terminology used to express the situation needed to be inaccurate—it needed to transpose the imaginary onto the real. Accurate articulation of lived experience would dissolve this imaginary; those who articulated lived experience accurately were not heard from again. The built structure of ideology required constant maintenance under conditions which tested its declarations; without this maintenance the structure would crumble. Control of speech necessitated physical control of the population to reinforce correct ways of speaking. Informants reported disappearances during the famine and there was an awareness that this could happen to them if they did not speak carefully. There was an awareness of the link between these—the act of speaking and disappearance. Appearing as antecedent and subsequent events in the sentence, the act of speaking and disappearing are correlated and identified as relevant to each other: the one creates the probability of the other (after Ochs 2004: 271). As Mr Kim explained to me: '...I could not say that my grandfather died of hunger, because if we say that they'll take us away. The party will have my family and close acquaintances banished' (Kim interview 2006). Another North Korean, Mr Om, described the behaviour of a senior woman in his community who spoke openly, out of doors and in public, about her frustration with the food shortages. The antecedent event of speaking openly and outdoors is established as the cause of the subsequent event, her disappearance:

> There was no way that the hunger could be spoken about. There was an elderly woman who was very hungry, she was about eighty years old, she went out saying 'Oh my gosh, I'm so hungry. How are we meant to live like this?' and that very night she was taken off somewhere. (Om interview 2006)

Hunger and starvation were words which could not be spoken. Starvation deaths were said to result from food poisoning, high blood pressure and, most ambiguously, pain. Mr Yoon shared a similar observation:

> In North Korea there is no term called *famine*. At the moment there is nothing they would call a famine. *Refugee* is another word they don't have; there is no starvation-death. First of all they don't declare it that way. North Korean correspondence, intelligence, newspapers, magazines—if you look at these it'll say the North Korean economy is having difficulties. 'The people are dying of hunger, the people are escaping into foreign countries...' there aren't scholars or workers who have ever seen such things written, I know. There is no word for famine, in North Korean society tens of thousands can die of hunger, but there is no word starvation-death, in the media that truth is absent. (Yoon interview 2006)

These awkward metonyms are in keeping with cultural norms that enabled articulation without directly implicating the government. 'Hunger' was inconsistent with the metaphor established through the terminology of the *Konan ŭi Haenggun*; pain on the other hand was not. This type of conversion occurred throughout several survivor accounts. In fact, some used such deep metaphoric descriptions as to nearly lose the topic of famine altogether. Consider the following explanation from Mr Kim:

> When a person is cold, the freezing starts at the end of their fingers and then their feet freeze, later it comes to about here. Why? They are far from the heart, the heart is far away so the blood that comes out at first is hot, but it cools as it goes out. It gets colder. So the fingers freeze. In North Korea, likewise, we call Pyongyang the heart. Near to Pyongyang they are giving out the PDS.[6] Then, further away at the tips of the fingers far away in Hamgyongbukdo, Yanggangdo and so on from 1991, 1992 they weren't giving PDS. Then by February of 1996 little by little they weren't even able to give out any PDS in Pyongyang, the blood was starting to freeze...So if you think of it as a person,

> if they are frozen up to here, to the heart, then they are going to die. Then at that time the warehouses were nearly run empty and Kim Jong Il took a countermeasure against it. From that time on, Kim Jong Il was telling the population, 'Yeah, because of our natural enemy, the bastard Americans, we are unable to farm and so there is no food, so it is difficult to give the PDS.' (Kim (M) interview 2006)

The progression of the famine is narrated through the metaphor of a body (the nation) gradually overtaken by chilblains (the famine), where only the heart is saved (to save the whole, as a consequence, unnecessary extremities must be sacrificed). On one level, we have the associated articulation of the national experience of suffering. On another, significantly, we have the articulation of individual suffering. Both of these pain expressions are separate from the starvation experience. Chilblains is selected as a metaphorical carrier perhaps because it provides the convenience of drawing a relatively clear image of gradual, fatal and inevitable exposure to the 'natural' elements without directly implicating the individual body in hunger. In this metaphor, the question of the body (the nation) causing chilblains is absurd. The starving individual is extracted from the metaphor entirely, reference to the famine is only hinted at in the cessation of food ration deliveries and then this is draped in the metaphor of blood flowing from the heart. The choice of metaphor was not incidental but rather culturally contingent. The analogy of the human anatomy had long been used to educate the population about the leading ideological framework of the country, known as the *Juche* Idea (Lee 2003: 111).[7] The brain makes decisions (the Great Leader), the nervous system carries out those decisions (the Party) and the bones and muscle execute the orders (the People). The body and the nervous system are the population, while the head is the leadership (Oberdorfer 1997: 20). Within this analogy, sacrifice of less vital parts is really not too much to ask. The metaphor, and the message carried within it, is consistent with the ideas historically put forth by the government.

Through this type of metaphor, the famine is established as an inevitable experience and as such culpability fell on the natural environment, not on the government. This is consistent with the ideas put forward in North Korea's leading newspaper, the *Rodong Sinmun*, where revolutionary agricultural methods are a means of lifting the country out of the food shortage (see Gabroussenko 2009). Quasi-scientific methods used to bolster agriculture and food production—such as irrigation, electrification and mechanization of agriculture—were not amiss, but they were not sufficient to the task (Hwang 1997: 59; Scott 1998: 5). However, science offered a kind of logic where nature did not.[8] It also reinforced the idea that the government's treatment of the famine was logical and that it could be trusted.

Ambiguity operated on a wide scale in the North. It extended beyond attributing the famine to nature and its solution to science, beyond that of simply omitting questionable nouns and verbs such as 'I am hungry' and 'I'm hungry because of X.' The tendency to camouflage information is part of the country's ideological apparatus, an apparatus noted in other socialist states (Todorov 2003: 44; Watson 1994: 1). It is not at all surprising that this same tendency to speak behind veils would appear in the language of those who lived under such ideology. Whether intentionally or not, the language communicates the mentality prevalent at the time of the famine: government inaction was obfuscated and the countless lives lost were an inevitable price. The government provided the population with language that helped to prop up its perspective on the famine and this language circulated widely, but not without ordinary North Koreans putting their own twist on it. This enabled them to speak at different levels simultaneously. This type of communication has been observed in other socialist states (Humphrey 1994: 23–7), but also in nonsocialist contexts. Working with an understanding of the dynamics of power in colonial and class struggles, James Scott (1998) put forward the idea of the 'hidden transcript' as a means whereby historical memory—which was not officially sanctioned—could be transmitted in spite of forces which dictated otherwise. These hidden transcripts could be exchanged during social gatherings where certain categories of people could express themselves to one another.

* * *

During the famine, state-sanctioned discourses were enforced and the population largely adopted these though they effaced accurate description of events. What emerges in interviews then is a blend of different types of ambiguity, which were highly useful while in the North because they enabled individuals to communicate vital information—about black market selling or famine foods, for example—where direct communication would endanger individuals. The expressions of survivors (articulate or otherwise) go some way to describing the overarching sociopolitical structures which gave them shape. Scholars working with survivors of collective social suffering have encountered the silence of informants. In fact, many survivors find themselves forced to encounter their own silence too; there are no words to describe what I experienced is a common refrain. 'No matter what I say, you will not understand what it was like', Mr Yoon told me. This came at the end of the interview, after two hours of discussing his life in North Korea. Was he saying this to establish its validity? As Todorov has explained, 'understanding' can make something seem ordinary (2003: 123). Perhaps Mr Yoon was trying to impress upon me how extraordinary the experience was—how beyond normal. Perhaps if I achieve understanding, particularly as someone who has not experienced the famine, that understanding will lead to justification. Where social suffering is concerned, understanding as a goal is said to lead to justification (Primo Levi, in Scheper-Hughes 1992: 83) and to suggest that such things can be justified is like siding with those who generated the suffering in the first place. Whether or not one can *understand* is an issue beyond the scope of this chapter. Instead, here, I consider those two hours where Mr Yoon, and many other informants, used language to render life in North Korea. What do their word choices reveal about the impact of the external social environment on shaping their articulation and possibly their memory of the experience?

Not unlike other nations that experienced famine throughout history, the North Korean government offered up a picture of the famine that adhered to preexisting nationalist values.[9] Editorials from the most prominent national newspaper of the country, the *Rodong Sinmun*, throughout the 1990s, and particularly during the latter half of that decade, made repeated reference to a collective and revolutionary approach to solving the food shortage. The famine in North Korea was understood according to acceptable cultural parameters and methods for dealing with the crisis fell well within this remit. In the late 1990s, the *Rodong Sinmun* simultaneously acknowledged the food shortage while putting the responsibility for overcoming it squarely on the shoulders of the population through prescriptive calls for revolutionary and collective action (Gabroussenko 2009). Indeed in 1998, the same newspaper called for more loyal adherence to *juche* methods of farming (Gabroussenko 2009), confirming a leading North Korean defector's claim that the media increased ideological messages about solidarity and endurance during the famine (Hwang Jang Yup, in Oh and Hassig 2000: 32). As a result, both how the famine was understood and the behavioural responses by which it should be survived were kept in check. There was a very public obfuscation of the famine, a public remaking of it as something standard, something to be collectively endured. In this way, coping with the 'food shortage' could be framed as collective revolutionary efforts useful to the government. Obfuscation of the famine occurred from the terminology used to refer to it, right down to the nouns and verbs used to describe what survivors experienced on a bodily level.[10]

Humour, Ambiguous Speech and Memory

As a means of gathering deeper descriptions of the experience, I began to ask survivors questions that seemed incongruous to the topic of famine itself. I asked if they could recall any humour from that time, jokes that people shared, sarcasm or witty phrases. It has not missed my attention that asking whether there was any humour that could be recalled from the famine was a provocative and evocative question which may have triggered off memories. This proved more valuable than I could have anticipated. When I asked Mr Yoon if he could remember any humour from his days in North Korea during the famine he insisted he could not remember anything, but then he suddenly remembered the Worker's Department Store:

> But it's been many years since I've come over from North Korea, I was in China three years, and here quite a few, it's been seven years now. So a lot of the humour we used is forgotten. A lot of it is gone, and I hate to think about that side, so most of the humour the people used is no longer in my memory. Like the *paekhwachom* [Department Store]. We called the farmer's market the 'Worker's Department Store'. However, the country had made it just a shell operating as a store, and if you went inside there wasn't anything

> you could buy. Of course, there were lovely looking bottles of alcohol, cigarettes, crockery and clothes on display, but these were only for show and you certainly couldn't buy them. Labourers and farmers would never have such a fate. The things the farmers and labourers could buy were at the markets, the black markets, they were the only place. So when we talked about the farmer's market we'd call it the 'Worker's Department Store'. (Yoon interview 2006)

In Korean the word for department store has a posh connotation and this contrasts sharply with the image of a black market, highlighting the incongruity clearly. Of course, the fact that the Worker's Department Store was devoid of purchasable goods, juxtaposed with the implicit notion of bounty in the name they gave to it, shows not only the dry and black humour of North Koreans, but the 'evocative transcript' which applies criticism to the country (Humphrey 1994). However, the speaker of such humour is saved by the fact that the Worker's Department Store was in fact that, but in reality not that. Mr Yoon explained that it was a common expression; and because they used language which was totally acceptable to the government and anyone else listening, there was little chance that one would get in trouble for the true meaning embedded in what they had said. Within these 'evocative transcripts' are two messages carried in what is said: First, there is the acceptable message of the speaker referring to where he is going; and second, there is the highly unacceptable message which highlights the incongruity between what exists and what is said to exist.

There were other examples of 'evocative transcripts' occurring among North Koreans in everyday life during the famine. Mr Yoon shared his experience with famine foods.

> It was called 'substitute food products' so in place of food we had weeds, the leaves of trees, the bark of trees, lots of different things all mixed together, 'substitute food products' officially. Formally it was called 'substitute food products', but between people when we spoke of it we called it 'substitute fuel'…coal, gas, diesel…use substitute fuel. And when we spoke to each other we'd ask, 'Hey, did you use the substitute today?' Oh, it's kind of funny isn't it? Fuel. Fuelled machines, like cars, trucks, trains this kind of thing. It isn't appropriate to use the term for people. We're living creatures, sentient beings and physical entities, not machines, not equipment. Hmm…so, we used that metaphor, but there is no gas in North Korea. So, in the morning you'd go hungry, lunch you'd just skip, and for dinner you'd sleep. So, between those three meals when would you have time to eat? There wasn't time. So given that, when could you eat? At that time we'd say, 'Hey! How did you manage to get by this morning?' That's the kind of way we talked about it. (Yoon interview 2006)

Mr Yoon's narrative reveals that two objects of discontent could be simultaneously critiqued without too much risk of implication. The difficulty in finding food and fuel, both severely lacking in North Korea, are brought together here for observation.

Food and fuel are synchronized both in terms of their lack and in how they are replaced with other items. Many cars and trucks in North Korea have been converted to run on wood, just as the population was expected to convert their eating habits and adapt to famine foods.

While explaining the changing power dynamics which emerged from people having newly acquired money through the black market, a young informant explained: 'the security police eat securely...there was an expression to refer to it. The secret police eat secretly and the security police eat securely' (Lee (F) interview 2006). She did not elaborate the extent to which such expressions were used, but for a woman who was very young at the time of the famine to remember this is an indication that such expressions had a certain lasting power. These expressions indicate that some North Koreans were not only aware of their circumstances, but also knew that the articulation of that awareness required clandestine and careful means of communication. Perhaps the transcripts also point to a human need, regardless of conditions, to articulate observed incongruities and receive confirmation of what is observed. This negotiation of safety within articulation, this maintenance of preexisting relationships with real or potential perpetrators has been observed in the speech of conflict survivors elsewhere (Argenti-Pillen 2003; Brenneis 1988; Hoffmann and Oliver-Smith 2004).

The Shape of Memory

The social environment in North Korea lends itself to a sustained lack of clarity as regards accurate information on factors which lead up to famine and consequential events such as public execution, disappearance and rumour. This lack of a means by which to access sustained clarity on events—recall that the ambiguous speech of my informants was of necessity brief while in the North—helps to engender uncertainty and doubt within the population as to the validity of explanations and justifications not emerging from the government. Doubt and denial were common expressions used by informants to describe the various stages of the famine. And yet doubt and denial are the very elements which, if present in a listener or audience, are said to hinder a survivor's ability to remember and speak; the need to be believed, the necessity to not face denial and doubt are essential to the maintenance of memory and the desire to speak (Herman 1997). When the anthropologist encounters survivors from contexts like North Korea, there are multiple hurdles to overcome. The language of my informants reveals the control of both word and deed in their home country which ensured adherence to appropriated ways of living during this internal crisis, and yet they managed to develop a highly specialized form of communicating which brought humour, sarcasm and creativity to their experiences, creating enclaves of relative safety.

Within these narrowly circumscribed spaces of safety, what kinds of memory emerge later when living comfortably in Seoul or Tokyo? Do these former coded and ambiguous ways of speaking help to preserve memory? If the articulation of experience was restricted, surely this might impact the recollection of things after the fact. Caroline Humphrey further developed Scott's idea and made it applicable to socialist cases such as Mongolia where the 'evocative transcript' served to evoke meaning beyond surface meanings while remaining obscure; within state socialism subordination and domination exist in all lives simultaneously (1994: 23–7). In North Korea, Scott's hidden transcript could not safely emerge and thus a more subtle communication developed, the understanding of which occurs when the listener can appreciate the analogy and the precedent embedded within what is said. In other situations of potential volatility, it has been noted that the ambiguous expression of suffering is essential so as not to awaken the sleeping violence which exists between perpetrators and victims in small-scale settings (Argenti-Pillen 2003: 198–9). Perhaps these ambiguous expressions became so rooted in daily life as to remain even after survival and to readily awaken when the topic of famine is discussed again.

The language of North Koreans demonstrates the dynamics of power during the 1990s, and the sturdy nationalist discourse is carried through it. The interviews describe not only a mental landscape of North Korea, but also these forms of expression give a deeper sense of the structures of power that ordinary people participated with. While this may have resulted in a kind of metaphoric censorship, to use Bourdieu's term (1991: 138), the language shows the mentality through which the suffering was understood. As Althusser has explained, what ideology represents is not 'the system of the real relations which govern the existence of individuals, but the *imaginary relation* of those individuals to the real relations in which they live' (1971: 166, my emphasis); or in other words, ideology is a manifestation of their imagined reality made 'material' through the actions and practices of those who live within that imaginary relationship to 'truth' (Althusser 1971: 165, 166, 169). The articulations of North Koreans reveal the deeply embedded efforts to maintain this imaginary relationship to the real. While trauma systematically silences people through suffering (see for example Jenkins 1998: 187; Kleinmen and Desjarlais 1995: 175), the government of North Korea provided the population with a nationalist framework by which to understand and interpret its suffering. Bruner, writing on culture and narrative, explains that 'one important way of characterizing a culture is by the narrative models it makes available for describing the course of a life' (1987: 15). So while the government failed to take full action to avoid or remedy the famine in the 1990s, it went to great lengths to ensure the population understood things in ways consistent with established historical models. It was surely never intended to aid North Koreans in recalling details of the famine, yet it did just that.

I began this chapter by asking whether sites of suffering limit articulation after the experience, just as they might have during the experience. The survivors of famine who shared their personal stories with me demonstrate that the limits on communication during the famine years created pockets of site-specific communication that, if questions were posed in a way to provoke them, revealed a host of memories that not only shared features of the famine itself, but the social and political context of its emergence.

Notes

1. For a discussion of the impact of censorship on language and its veiling capacity see Sheriff (2000).
2. Over two dozen former North Koreans were interviewed in Seoul and Tokyo from January to November 2006. Interviews were conducted, recorded and transcribed in Korean by the author.
3. Reportedly between two hundred thousand and three and a half million people died in the North Korean famine. These figures are clearly very rough estimates. The low estimates represent North Korean government figures while high estimates are those of aid agencies; the former is not transparent in its information gathering, while the latter are restricted by the North Korean government in their in-country information gathering. No source offers a truly accurate picture of famine mortality impact. The North Korean government claims that two hundred twenty thousand died from famine. Good Friends (or *Chungt'o* in Korean) estimates 2.8–3.5 million, while North Korea scholars Andrew Natsios (2002) and Marcus Noland calculate two and a half million and six hundred thousand to one million respectively (Good Friends 1998, 2000, 2004; Goodkind and West 2001; Pomnyun 1998a,b,c; Woo 2004: 65). People who died from famine-related disease, those who died from accidents resulting from failed coping strategies and those who died from punishments for coping strategies considered antithetical to the North Korean government are a significant aggregate not counted among these numbers.
4. Scholars working with Holocaust survivors reported similar tendencies (see Favaro et al. 2000).
5. 'Red Banner Spirit', or 'the Red Flag', *Pulkŭnki Chaeng Chi'wi Undong*, first appeared in an editorial in the *Rodong Sinmun* on 9 January 1996. Further details are available in Korean at http://www.kcna.co.jp/calendar/2005/11/11–18/2005–1118–004.html and at https://www.dailynk.com/korean/read.php?cataId=n00700&num=7828, both accessed 6 March 2009.
6. PDS stands for Public Distribution System; this is the means by which food and other items are delivered throughout North Korea.
7. In Kim Il Sung's own words, *Juche* means 'being the master of revolution and reconstruction in one's own country. This means holding fast to an independent position, rejecting dependence on others, using one's own brains, believing in one's own strength, displaying the revolutionary spirit of self-reliance, and thus solving one's own problems for oneself on one's own responsibility under all circumstances' (quoted in Lee 2003: 105).

8. For further discussion on socialism's relationship to science see Todorov (2003: 33).
9. For other examples of this, see de Waal 1989; Sen 1981; Kelleher 1997; Yang 1997.
10. Not to be overlooked is the fact that survivors from other cases of collective social suffering—Russia during the Great Purges and China during the Great Leap Forward—have remarked in their writing on the changes that took place for them on the level of language and explicability (Shalamov 1994: 74; Zhang 1994: 61–2, 82).

References

Achino-Loeb, M. (2006a), 'Silence as the Currency of Power', in M. Achino-Loeb (ed.), *Silence: The Currency of Power*, New York: Berghahn Books, 1–19.

Achino-Loeb, M. (2006b), 'Silence and the Imperatives of Identity', in M. Achino-Loeb (ed.), *Silence: The Currency of Power*, New York: Berghahn Books, 35–51.

Allison, J. (2011), 'Conceiving Silence: Infertility as Discursive Contradiction in Ireland', *Medical Anthropology Quarterly*, 25(1): 1–21.

Althusser, L. (1971), *Lenin and Philosophy and Other Essays Part Two*, trans. B. Brewster, New York: Monthly Review Press.

Angrosino, M. (2002), *Doing Cultural Anthropology: Projects for Ethnographic Data Collection*, Prospect Heights: Waveland Press.

Argenti-Pillen, A. (2003), 'The Global Flow of Knowledge on War Trauma: The Role of the "Cinnamon Garden Culture" in Sri Lanka', in J. Pottier, A. Bicker and P. Stillitoe (eds), *Negotiating Local Knowledge: Power and Identity in Development*, London: Pluto Press, 189–214.

Article 19 (1990), 'Starving in Silence: A Report on Famine and Censorship', http://reliefweb.int/node/22631, accessed 4 April 2012.

Basso, K. (1970), 'To Give up on Words: Silence in Western Apache Culture', in P. Giglioli (ed.), *Language and Social Context*, New York: Penguin Books, 67–86.

Bernard, R. (2002), *Research Methods in Anthropology: Qualitative and Quantitative Methods*, Walnut Creek: AltaMira Press.

Bourdieu, P. (1991), *Language and Symbolic Power*, Cambridge: Polity Press.

Bourgois, P. (1990), 'Confronting Anthropological Ethics: Ethnographic Lessons from Central America', *Journal of Peace Research*, 27(1): 43–54.

Brenneis, D. (1988), 'Language and Disputing', *Annual Review of Anthropology*, 17: 221–37.

Bruner, J. (1987), 'Life as a Narrative', *Social Research*, 54(1): 11–32.

Cha, V. (2004), 'North Korea's Economic Reforms and Security Intentions', Testimony of Dr. Victor D. Cha to the United States Senate, 2 March 2004, http://

nautilus.org/publications/books/dprkbb/transition/dprk-briefing-book-north-koreas-economic-reforms-and-security-intentions/, accessed 4 April 2012.

Choson Ensik'lip'edia (1995), *Choson Ensik'lip'edia 2*, Pyongyang, DPRK: Paekhwasacho, 179–81.

Cuéllar, A. (2010), 'Unravelling Silence: Violence, Memory and the Limits of Anthropology's Craft', *Dialectical Anthropology*, 29(2): 159–80.

Desjarlais, R., L. Eisenberg, B. Good and A. Kleinman (1995), *World Mental Health: Problems and Priorities in Low-Income Countries*, New York: Oxford University Press.

Devereux, S. (1993), *Theories of Famine, From Malthus to Sen*, Hemel Hempstead, UK: Wheatsheaf.

De Waal, A. (1989), *Famine That Kills: Darfur, Sudan, 1984–1985*, Oxford: Clarendon Press.

Engdahl, H. (ed.) (2002), *Witness Literature: Proceedings of the Nobel Centennial Symposium*, Stockholm: The Swedish Academy.

Ervin, A. (2000), *Applied Anthropology: Tools and Perspectives for Contemporary Practice*, Boston: Allyn and Bacon.

Favaro, A., F. C. Rodella and P. Santonastaso (2000), 'Binge Eating and Eating Attitudes among Nazi Concentration Camp Survivors', *Psychological Medicine*, 30: 463–6.

Fernandez, J. (2006), 'Silences in the Field', in M. Achino-Loeb (ed.), *Silence: The Currency of Power*, New York: Berghahn Books, 158–73.

Gabroussenko, T. (2009), 'North Korean "Rural Fiction" from the Late 1990s to the Mid-2000s: Permanence and Change', *Korean Studies*, 33: 69–100.

Good Friends Centre for Peace, Human Rights and Refugees (2000), 'Human Rights in North Korea and the Food Crisis, A Comprehensive Report on North Korean Human Rights Issues', www.goodfriends.or.kr/eng/data/NKHR2004-final.doc, accessed 4 April 2012.

Good Friends Centre for Peace, Human Rights and Refugees (2004), 'Human Rights in North Korea and the Food Crisis, A Comprehensive Report on North Korean Human Rights Issues', www.reliefweb.int/node/416884/pdf, accessed 4 April 2012.

Good Friends *Chungt'o* (formerly Korean Buddhist Sharing Movement) (1998), 'The Food Crisis in North Korea Witnessed by 1,694 Food Refugees', www.reliefweb.int/rw/rwb.nsf/db900sid/ACOS-64C4RL?OpenDocument, accessed 4 April 2012.

Goodkind, D. and L. West (2001), 'The North Korean Famine and Its Demographic Impact', *Population and Development Review*, 27(2): 219–38.

Haggard, S. (2007), *Famine in North Korea: Markets, Aid, and Reform*, New York: Columbia University Press.

Herman, J. (1992), *Trauma and Recovery: The Aftermath of Violence from Domestic Violence to Political Terror*, New York: Basic Books.

Hoffman, S. and A. Oliver-Smith (eds) (2004), *Catastrophe and Culture: The Anthropology of Disaster*, Houston: SAR Press.

Humphrey, C. (1994), 'Remembering an "Enemy": The Boyd Khan in Twentieth-Century Mongolia', in R. Watson (ed.), *Memory, History and Opposition under State Socialism*, Santa Fe: University of Washington Press, 21–44.

Hwang, D.-E. (1997), 'Agricultural Reforms in North Korea, and Inter-Korean Co-operation', *East Asian Review*, 4(3): 57–75.

Jaworski, A. (ed.) (1997), *Silence: Interdisciplinary Perspectives*, Berlin: Walter de Gruyter.

Jenkins, J. (1998), 'The Medical Anthropology of Political Violence: A Cultural and Feminist Agenda', *New Series*, 12(1): 122–31.

Kelleher, M. (1997), *The Feminization of Famine: Expressions of the Inexpressible?* Durham: Duke University Press.

Lee, G. (2003), 'The Political Philosophy of *Juche*', *Stanford Journal of East Asian Affairs*, 108/3(1): 105–11.

Leshuk, L. (2000), *Days of Famine, Nights of Terror: Firsthand Accounts of Soviet Collectivization. 1928–1934*, 2nd edn, trans. R. Rueger, UK: Europa University Press.

McKinney, K. (2007), 'Breaking the Conspiracy of Silence: Testimony, Traumatic Memory, and Psychotherapy with Survivors of Political Violence', *Ethos*, 35(3): 265–99.

Natsios, A. (2002), *The Great North Korean Famine, Famine, Politics, and Foreign Policy*, Washington, DC: United States Institute of Peace Press.

Oberdorfer, D. (1997), *The Two Koreas*, Reading: Addison-Wesley.

Ochs, E. (2004), 'Narrative Lessons', in A. Duranti (ed.), *A Companion to Linguistic Anthropology*, Oxford: Blackwell, 269–89.

Oh, K. D. and R. Hassig (2000), *Through the Looking Glass*, Washington, DC: Brookings Institution.

Pomnyun (1998a), 'May 21st "The Food Crisis of North Korea 770 Witnessed by Food Refugees"', www.goodfriends.or.kr/eng/report/report.htm, accessed 16 November 2010.

Pomnyun (1998b), 'The Food Crisis of North Korea 1,019 Witnessed by Food Refugees', www.reliefweb.int/rw/rwb.nsf/db900SID/ACOS-64BRCQ?OpenDocument, accessed 16 November 2010.

Pomnyun (1998c), 'The Food Crisis of North Korea 1,694 Witnessed by Food Refugees', www.reliefweb.int/rw/rwb.nsf/db900sid/ACOS-64C4RL?OpenDocument, accessed 16 November 2010.

Randall, S. and T. Koppenhaver (2004), 'Qualitative Data in Demography: The Sound of Silence and Other Problems', *Demographic Research*, 11(3): 57–94.

Scheper-Hughes, N. (1992), *Death without Weeping: Violence of Everyday Life in Brazil*, Berkeley: University of California Press.

Schloms, M. (2004), *North Korea and the Timeless Dilemma of Aid: A Study of Humanitarian Action in Famines*, Berlin: Lit Verlag.

Scott, J. (1998), *Seeing Like a State: How Certain Schemes to Improve the Human Condition Have Failed*, New Haven: Yale University Press.

Sen, A. (1981), *Poverty and Famines: An Essay on Entitlements and Deprivation*, Oxford: Clarendon Press.

Sen, A. and J. Drèze (1999), *The Amartya Sen and Jean Drèze Omnibus, Poverty and Famines, Hunger and Public Action, India, Economic Development and Social Opportunity*, Oxford: Oxford University Press.

Shalamov, V. (1994), *The Kolyma Tales*, trans. J. Glad, London: Penguin.

Sheriff, R. (2000), 'Exposing Silence as Cultural Censorship: A Brazilian Case', *American Anthropologist*, 102(1): 3–28.

Tamen, D. and M. Saville Troike (eds) (1985), *Perspectives on Silence*, Norwood: Ablex.

Todorov, T. (2003), *Hope and Memory: Reflections on the Twentieth Century*, trans. D. Bellos, London: Atlantic Books.

Tyler, S. A. (1987), *The Unspeakable: Discourse, Dialogue, and Rhetoric in the Postmodern World. Language Arts and Disciplines*, Madison: University of Wisconsin Press.

Watson, R. (ed.) (1994), *Memory, History and Opposition under State Socialism*, Santa Fe: School of American Research Press.

Woo, S. (2004), 'North Korea's Food Crisis', *Korea Focus* (May–June): 63–80.

Woo-Cummings, M. (2002), 'The Political Ecology of Famine: The North Korean Catastrophe and Its Lessons', in Asian Development Bank Institute Research Paper, 31 January, http://www.adbi.org/research%20paper/2002/01/01/115.political.ecology/, accessed 4 April 2012.

Yang, R. (1997), *Spider Eaters: A Memoir*, Berkeley: University of California Press.

Zhang, X. (1994), *Grass Soup*, trans. M. Avery, London: Secker & Warburg.

–12–

Re-presenting Hopis: Indigenous Responses to the Ethnographic Interview

Nick McCaffery

Introduction

This chapter engages with recent ideas around the concept of an 'interview society' and explores the idea that the interview has become one of the contexts through which an authentic cultural identity can be articulated. Reflecting upon ethnographic data collected from my research amongst the Hopi Indians of northeastern Arizona in the United States, I explore whether the interview should be seen as not simply another research method, but instead as a 'constitutive feature of our everyday lives' (Gubrium and Holstein 2002: 11). The ethnographic interview has certainly become viewed by some of the Hopi research participants with whom I worked, on both an institutional level and amongst 'ordinary' Hopis, as a medium through which inauthentic or invalid representations can be challenged. As such, the potential benefits of the ethnographic interview were often articulated by Hopis, particularly as the interview was such a familiar concept amongst this research population. However, as many Hopis are well aware of the behaviour and responses expected of them from the ethnographic interviewer, the utility of relying solely on interview data is questioned—particularly data that seemed to dispute responses gathered from noninterview research.

I argue that the widespread familiarity with the ethnographic interview has led some Hopi people to use these occasions for their own interests; in particular to construct a very rigid and formal definition of an authentic Hopi identity that could be somehow authenticated by academic researchers. But while this essentialist rhetoric concerning an 'authentic' Hopi identity was often present in interview contexts, many observations made in noninterview contexts suggested a more malleable, flexible—even possibly less academic—approach to Hopi identity. Clearly, both approaches seemed to be valid reactions to the ethnographer's presence, and both reflected the local understandings of the ways in which this indigenous population could make use of academic research for its own purposes. This suggests that there has been a shift in the balance of power between interviewee and interviewer at Hopi; but rather than see this as one side now taking advantage of the other, I argue that this reflects a move towards more positive collaborative research methods with Native American communities. As such, this chapter explores local reactions to anthropological research in general and the ways that Hopis managed being interviewed by me or evaded my interview attempts. Further, it examines some of the reasons *why* Hopis have had to develop ways to manage their representations in a nonlocal context.

A First Attempt at the Ethnographic Interview

To an outsider, Hopi land can often feel like a strange place to be. There are very few amenities for the visitor to avail of and very few signs to guide one's visit or advise of the preferred behaviour expected by locals. There are twelve Hopi villages, all historically and politically independent, spread over the three mesas that rise up from the northern Arizona desert. Aside from the publicly performed aspects of the Hopi ceremonial calendar known as *Katsina* dances, there often seems to be no real reason for visiting the area. Each village is nothing more than a cluster of homes and outbuildings that are increasingly more functional than aesthetic, and are all located somewhat off the beaten track. Most Hopi villages are not 'on the way' to anywhere else such as the Grand Canyon or other more popular tourist attractions in the state. In short, one would have to have a very good reason for being there. Hopi land is not the sort of place that has intentionally attracted visitors, but a variety of visitors do come, and locals have learned to deal with them in various ways.

As a doctoral research student I often asked myself precisely how I had got there and what I was proposing to do whilst I was there. In my head it had been simple—go and do some anthropology. In reality it was more difficult. This was largely because the relationship between Hopis and non-Hopis is more complex than I had at first assumed. And my mere presence at Hopi was always framed in complex and politically sensitive contexts that made ethnographic research quite complicated. My first real interview with a real live Hopi went a little like this.

I had arranged to meet with artist Mike Kabotie at his work studio on the grounds of the Museum of Northern Arizona. We had met a couple of days before, although this first meeting had not gone well. I had been rather abruptly 'introduced' to Mike by an overzealous colleague keen to get my research started for me as soon as possible. She had led me through a throng of visitors in a very busy museum gallery where Mike had been talking to a small group of representatives from the nearby Indian community at Zuni about his murals on display. My 'colleague' pushed me through this small group of religious and political leaders and presented me to Mike as the 'anthropologist who needed to speak to him right away'. I was very fortunate in that Mike was a patient and humorous man who clearly saw the panic in my own eyes at being introduced to him in such an abrupt way, and we arranged a time to meet when both of us were a little less occupied.

And so I found myself outside Mike's studio two days later, armed with notebook and pen, a back-up pen, a back-up notebook, a spare pen, a pencil and a list of questions. I had been advised by a well-meaning colleague not to use any recording equipment with my Hopi interviewees—although I now question whether this was an entirely rational decision.[1] I knocked on the door and waited, and after a few minutes and a couple of half-hearted coughs and hellos I made my way to the back door, where I found Mike sitting outside his studio, drinking coffee and relaxing in the morning sun.

Mike smiled warmly and pointed me to the chair sitting opposite him, which I took gratefully. 'I wasn't sure if you were in,' I said, 'or whether you had remembered our meeting.'

'Oh, I'm here,' said Mike, as he picked up his newspaper from under his chair, opened it fully, brought it up between us as if he were some spoof private detective concealing his presence from an unwanted observer, and proceeded to ignore me completely for a full three-quarters of an hour. We sat in total silence. After this tediously slow and uncomfortable forty-five minutes, Mike peered over the top of his *Arizona Daily Sun* and said, with a wink, 'Same time tomorrow then?' I was more than a little confused. Was this a success, or had I not tried hard enough to gain Mike's trust? Was he teasing me or just testing me; seeing if I would relax in his company, or if he could relax in mine? Had he fallen asleep? I was certainly aware that Mike had appeared uncomfortable at the pushiness of my colleague two days earlier, and I was determined not to place myself in the same category as her, but forty-five minutes of silence? For the life of me I cannot recall how or why I went along with this void of noise. At least the transcription was easy.

Despite this initial teasing, or perhaps because of it, Mike became a very good friend through my time at Hopi, and we subsequently spent many hours in conversation with each other. Whether this shift was due to a sense of familiarity with each other or a genuine interest in my research topic is unclear, but regardless of the reasons Mike introduced me to a wide range of other people who helped in my research and he was always very open. I even managed to interview him eventually. In due course, I realized that Mike was using a very successful method of avoiding misrepresentation in our first meeting. This long silence, aka 'the avoidance technique', is one of the many ways that Hopis have developed to deter the would-be ethnographer.

Another very successful method was the way that potential interviewees who had been specifically recommended to me due to their expertise in a particular matter would calmly deny any knowledge of a specific subject; but would happily recommend another person that I should get in touch with. I often went from one 'perfect interviewee' to another without interviewing anyone. It took a long time to stop feeling like a parcel being passed from one hand to another without really getting anywhere. But these techniques did not appear from nowhere, and some context is needed as to *why* Hopis feel the need to manage their relationships with academics and other visitors.

New Age Appropriation and Other Inauthenticity

My research was based on the idea that Hopis are aware of and opposed to the continued commercialization of Hopi culture by non-Hopis—in particular the appropriation of Hopi-ness within New Age spiritual networks that exist on a global scale. This New Age appropriation of Native America in general and of Hopi-ness in particular is relatively easy to locate and present, and there is an increasing negative reaction to this appropriation from within Native America (Welch 2002; Aldred 2000). There is little doubt that the noble Indian has a certain cachet within a global alternative spirituality context (Rose 1992; Dilworth 1996), and the use of Hopi symbols, people and, in particular, Hopi prophecies are commonplace. These New Age versions of Hopi-ness are generally based upon essentialist depictions of 'the other' that many of my Hopi informants would consider inauthentic representations of their culture. These are often framed using the Hopi term *qahopi*, which loosely translates as un-Hopi. It is mainly employed in relation to Hopi ritual clowns whose *qahopi* behaviour reflects how not to behave (Hieb 1972).

Examples of New Age Hopi-ness range from those considered pure fakery, such as Hopi ear candles (the invention of a German company), to the more complex realm of New Age travelogues that claim to reveal the esoteric nature of the tourist's spiritual reawakening encountered whilst visiting these 'peaceful people' of the desert. Prior to my fieldwork at Hopi I tried to prepare myself by collating a great deal of data from books, archives and the Internet that depicted the Hopi in an overtly romanticized, stereotypical and essentialist manner (Kimmey 1999). However, these depictions were not stereotypes that necessarily stressed the primitive or the savage, but instead reflected the apparently optimistic opportunities that traditional indigenous knowledge holds for the well-being of all people. As such, these romantic New Age glorifications of Hopi culture did not seem immediately insulting, but I knew from prior experience of research at Hopi that they were not representations that many Hopis were happy about. This prior research experience deserves some explanation for it is the key to understanding the ways in which Hopis are actively engaging with global networks of representation, from the esoteric to the academic. This is, in part, because there are many people at Hopi who do not differentiate between New Age representations of Hopi culture and anthropological representations of Hopi culture.

A Poor First Attempt at Research at Hopi

My doctoral fieldwork of 2001–3 was not the first time that I had visited Hopi. The first time that I had visited Hopi was as an undergraduate five years earlier attempting to conduct anthropology for the very first time, and with the naïve expectation that Hopis would welcome me into their villages and homes and reveal to me the answers to every question that I could muster. All that I had to say were those magic words that would open every door to me: 'Hi, my name is Nick and I am an anthropologist…'

It's not fair to say that Hopis don't like anthropologists; I was often made to feel very welcome, and my endless questions were even tolerated, like the constant background chatter of an inquisitive child. But what is fair to say is that Hopis claim to *understand* anthropologists, and they are very aware of the role that we play in the representations of the people we choose to work with. When I first arrived at Hopi as an undergraduate student in the mid 1990s I was not prepared for this active engagement with the discipline that Hopis have held for over a century. I was certainly not prepared for the negative reaction to my proposed presence as a researcher. I am unsure whether my surprise at this negative reaction was a result of unfamiliarity with Native American politics in general (understandable considering that no member of staff at my home university in the United Kingdom had any Native American experience), or that I had simply not done enough individual research before deciding to immerse myself in the field.

Nevertheless, my presence as a researcher, or as an anthropologist, or even as an unqualified, underprepared, undergraduate anthropology student who wished to explore comparative data concerning religious elements of ritual clowning was frowned upon. I remember very well a phone call with the Hopi Tribal employee who told me that I was not welcome to visit Hopi land and that if I was found attempting to conduct research without tribal permission I would be arrested by the Hopi police and escorted off Hopi tribal land. 'Your white men's clowns are nothing like our Hopi clowns,' I was told, rather abruptly.

This reaction was not a personal rejection of my work per se, but an institutional response to the idea of treating Hopi religious and cultural information as purely academic data. I was proposing to conduct a small research project that would not benefit the Hopi people in any way. For this reason I was told not to bother. There would be no option for any dialogical approach to fieldwork, there would simply be no fieldwork allowed. I was not prepared and not committed enough to conduct effective anthropological research despite my good intentions. This type of research proposal was classified by the Hopi tribe as a good example of bad research.

The Transformation from 'Bad' Researcher to 'Good' Researcher

> 'Hopis do not oppose research per se, but Hopis will continue to support "good" research' (author interview, April 2004).

The Hopi Tribal Council has a department called the Hopi Cultural Preservation Office (HCPO). This office acts as a buffer zone between local Hopi interests and potential non-Hopi investigations. The office is concerned with four key areas: language preservation; cultural resources management; archives; and dealing with museums and repatriations. The HCPO assesses prospective research proposals and decides whether or not to grant research permits. It was this office that had denied my research plans as an undergraduate, and it was through this office that I eventually developed a more collaborative approach to research when I decided to return to Hopi as a doctoral researcher a few years later. Through this office I learned that research clearly does exist at Hopi, and Hopis are often very welcoming towards researchers; but with a long history of unwanted academic intrusion into their lives, most 'ordinary' Hopis are content to allow the Tribal Council to assess the impact of any proposed cultural research (both negative and positive) and to decide whether or not any research should be permitted.

Looking back on my undergraduate research I now understand what was so offensive about my proposed work. First, I was an undergraduate and so my research was not considered to have the same weight as professional or doctoral research. This was going to result in a brief unpublished paper, not a widely read piece of work that would be of any utility to the local population. My approach was representative of the continuing attitude amongst many undergraduate students, both nationally and internationally, that indigenous communities were to be viewed as 'research labs' for developing one's skills. The reality is, of course, that these are not 'research labs' but communities of real people. These are people's homes and places of work and any intrusion into Hopi lives would be better served by a more thorough commitment of both time and energy than many undergraduate programmes can allow.

The other reason that my undergraduate research was flagged as potentially harmful was that I was an anthropologist and looking to investigate the role of ritual clowning in Hopi society. Dealing with any kind of religious phenomena at Hopi is almost always a topic that will be rejected outright. And that is quite a difficult decision to make for the HCPO, considering the ubiquitous nature of religious observance at Hopi. However, the flag that goes up whenever anthropology is mentioned is perhaps better explained through the prevalence of informal attitudes towards the discipline shown by ordinary Hopis, rather than the more formal HCPO attitudes towards us 'anthros'.

'Every Hopi Family Has a Pet *Pahaana*'

Pahaana is a Hopi word of some significance. On an everyday level, it just means 'non-Hopi' people, or more specifically 'white people'. However, the root of the word comes from a part of the Hopi emergence myth describing the lost white brother destined to return to Hopi at a time of great transformation. Throughout the summer Hopi land is awash with *Pahaanas* of varying hues. Some are simply visiting for a cultural experience, some are seeking something more spiritual—I even met one or two who claimed to be the *Pahaana* of Hopi myth, ready to bring peace and unity to the Hopi people. But the quote 'every family has a pet *Pahaana*' refers to the fact that many Hopi families have a non-Hopi friend or two that keeps coming back. These *Pahaanas* stay in touch, they bring gifts when they return to Hopi land, they even get invited into the homes of friends and relatives and will often get ushered into prominent positions in village plazas on days when the Hopi *Katsinam*[2] are dancing. These family pets are teased and tolerated, and I was fortunate to become one myself through the good patience of the family that I stayed with in the village of Hotevilla.

In this context of pet *Pahaanas*, I was also often teased for being the HCPO's pet 'anthro'. This was largely because my doctoral research had been accepted as an example of potentially 'good research' by the HCPO, and I had developed a collaborative working relationship with the director, Leigh Kuwanwiswma. This acceptance existed because I was proposing to investigate the allure and extent of Hopi-ness in a New Age context. I was not at Hopi to uncover any religious data or to extract sensitive information from village elders. I was there to investigate the sphere of interaction between Hopis and New Agers. My research zone, if you like, was the contact area where Hopis and non-Hopis met, and was therefore an already public sphere. I was not attempting to delve too deeply into the more sensitive and private areas of Hopi religious and ceremonial life. I was asking what it was about the Hopi that New Agers found so appealing and why was it so important for Hopis to stress the inauthentic nature of these New Age representations of their culture. In short, I was in a very fortunate position to investigate a phenomenon that the Hopi people were interested in as well and, as such, I was in a position to conduct interviews with a wide range of people at Hopi; at least, in theory.

Explaining this institutional acceptance to people at Hopi was often more difficult because most Hopis have a valid expectation of what it means to be an anthropologist and because most anthropologists at Hopi have not gone unnoticed. Most anthropologists at Hopi are placed into the same compartment as grave robbers and culture thieves. The contemporary folklore about us 'anthros' is that we are there to take and rarely there to give anything back. A lot of people at Hopi still think that 'anthros' have ignored the concept of reciprocity whilst conducting their research—a concept central to most Hopi social and religious dealings. The impact of this local perspective is that many Hopis have an opinion as to the utility and value of ethnographic research. It is not uncommon for some Hopis to assume that the 'anthros' are there like spies, recording everything, feeding data back to the ivory towers of academia. And, in truth, it is not an entirely unfounded accusation.[3]

'My Friend the Reverend Voth' and the Difference between Interviews and Ethnographic Conversations at Hopi

The notoriety surrounding us 'anthros' at Hopi is easy to explain. We have a long history of poor behaviour, and a bad reputation is always going to stay around longer than a good one. Stories abound of prior researchers who would trick people into revealing sensitive information or recruit individuals with alcohol-related problems into selling sacred objects and valuable artefacts. There are even many Hopis who still define the discipline of anthropology in relation to an incident at the end of the nineteenth century when a researcher apparently drew a gun on a Hopi priest in order to demand access to a private ceremony (James (1974) 1994: 110). These folktales have left contemporary anthropologists with an uphill struggle. We may be aware of the need to shift attitudes and to develop more collaborative research projects, but we also have to make sure that the Hopi individuals that we work with recognize this shift in our attitude! Today's scholars of Hopi recognize the need to call a halt to the kind of research that is developed, conducted and published with little regard for the wishes or needs of Hopi communities. But there are still so many Hopis that I worked with who, when hearing of my identity as an anthropologist, would refer to my 'friend' the Reverend Voth, a Mennonite missionary of the nineteenth century renowned for his lack of humility and his eagerness to delve into areas that Hopis were not happy for him to explore. Reverend Voth was still a haunting presence that reflected the way that many Hopis viewed contemporary academic activity; we were all just one step away from pulling that gun and demanding access to restricted areas so that we could publish our tales and make our fortunes.

The idea of anthropological investigation does not sit well at Hopi and one reason for this is the difference between wanting to know something and being *entitled* to know something. At Hopi, so much knowledge is compartmentalized and restricted along lines of clan, age and stages of initiation that the concept of academic freedom for the sake of understanding more about Hopi culture is quite alien. Hopis have defended their decision to restrict access to non-Hopi investigators for some time, and have even maintained that many Hopis should not necessarily have access to some published anthropological material. A key example of this is the *Hopi Journal* of nineteenth-century ethnologist Alexander M. Stephen that contains detailed accounts of several Hopi rites and ceremonial information that many contemporary Hopis consider simply unsuitable material for all but a few Hopi individuals (Parsons 2005). This compartmentalized approach to knowledge is reminiscent of many recent debates stemming from Aboriginal Australia (see Weiner 1999). For Hopis to reveal information to a non-Hopi individual there must be a sense that the data revealed are not sensitive at all and are therefore permitted for all Hopis to hear or read. It is this kind of research that is generally permitted by the HCPO, and it is only then that potential researchers are permitted to begin conducting research amongst the local population.

And so we come back to Mike Kabotie's method of avoiding answering any questions in an interview technique that reflects the explicit understanding of the nature of ethnographic interviewing and deals with it precisely; how can one mistake what is being said and present data in an inaccurate or inappropriate manner when nothing has been said at all? With a research population that was all too aware of the rules of engagement, my ethnographic research, and in particular the ethnographic interview, had encountered a shift in power relations between the interviewee and the interviewer. The Hopis were clearly in control.

However, I quickly discovered that my presence at Hopi, sanctioned as it was by the HCPO, resulted in a remarkably creative environment. There were very few occasions where the line between anthropologist and guest was transgressed. With the local understanding of the nature of ethnographic research being so ubiquitous, I was able to talk with a range of individuals about my area of investigation with a clear understanding that I was always 'on duty' as a researcher and that anything discussed would be included in some kind of research output. This local familiarity with the discipline mixed with a reliable and active Hopi grapevine meant that most people knew who I was before I knew who they were. When people saw me coming, they assumed that I was there to 'do anthropology' with them. The majority of people, after a good deal of teasing, reacted positively to my area of research and were very willing to offer their opinion. Several people even offered to go beyond the realm of informal conversations and asked to be officially interviewed by me.

From a relatively early stage, the distinction between interview and noninterview behaviour was established. But the local understanding of anthropological research methods meant that this distinction is not the same as being on or off the record,[4] as every meeting began with some reference to my research—why else would I be talking with them? Every conversation I had was considered to be contributing to my research, but whilst many of my research participants preferred not to be interviewed per se, others sought to establish a more formal context in which to articulate their ideas to me. Indeed, there were several occasions when I was refused access to an interview as this would feel too formal, but I was ushered into homes so that I could sit and listen to people's opinions about my research in conversations that often lasted for two or three hours! And so, to me, the interview at Hopi felt like something that needed to be worked up to: I had to get to know someone, or have them get to know me, before they felt comfortable enough to formalize their conversations. In this context it was my research participants who distinguished between interviews (marked by a series of open-ended questions where the responses were recorded on paper) and ethnographic conversations (where information was divulged through dialogues and tended not to be accompanied by notebooks).

The only problem with this difference between interview and noninterview behaviour was when I simply didn't believe what was being offered to me as data. I felt uncomfortable when the reciprocal relationship that I had entered into became unbalanced through the introduction of clichés and stereotypes. Although I never felt as though I was being lied to maliciously in any interview, I often felt that some of the responses that I was getting seemed to be too formal, too prescribed, too 'Hopi'! Was I becoming a pawn in the game of representing Hopi-ness to outsiders? Had I actually become the HCPO's pet 'anthro', and been given the task of authenticating an official version of Hopi identity (cf. Theodossopoulos 2007)?

Hopi Rhetoric and the Constructivist Essentialist Debate

In the face of so many local claims to the inauthentic nature of New Age representations, it became one of my aims to explore local ideas of an authentic Hopi identity. If so many Hopis were opposed to the inaccurate ways in which Hopi-ness was presented globally, what did it actually mean to be Hopi locally? Where were the New Agers going wrong in their depictions of Hopi-ness? These proved to be very difficult questions to answer, but were nevertheless recurring topics in interviews. The inauthentic nature of New Age stereotypes was, in a way, holding a mirror up to the Hopis themselves. The existence of these overtly positive, but falsely romanticized depictions of Hopi-ness required a dialectic response from the Hopis. If these New Age versions of Hopi-ness are wrong, what is the right version? It was here that I began to feel uncertain as to the validity of my interviewee's responses.

Nick McCaffery: How would you define Hopi? Who is and who is not a Hopi?

Leigh Kuwanwiswma: I guess there is a tangible answer and a philosophical answer. The tangible way is: one—you have to be a member of a clan, and that clan has to be gained through a Hopi matriarch, through the mother, you have to have a Hopi mother. Second, Hopis define their mother village, where your clan is rooted into…Third, the thing defining yourself as Hopi is your language…I have been taught that you never call yourself a Hopi person because you must let others judge you. You define yourself through your clan, where you're from—your village, and the ability to speak and understand your language, and the extent that you can uphold the Hopi way of life. But you let others decide, you never state 'I am a Hopi'.

These building block elements of Hopi identity kept recurring in both interview and noninterview conversations. First you had to have a Hopi clan, and the only way that this is technically possible is through matrilineal descent. Second, you have to show your affiliation to a particular Hopi village—rather than have a generic tribal identity. Third, the issue of speaking and understanding the Hopi language was stressed. Finally there was a category of being Hopi through doing Hopi things—this may include undertaking some farming or gardening activity or being involved in village religious affairs.

But the ways in which these essential elements of Hopi identity were presented in either interview or noninterview behaviour were often distinct from each other. In casual conversations and in less formal observations the malleable, constructivist nature of Hopi identity came to a fore whereas in formalized interview contexts, the essential elements of blood quantum and cultural affiliation were more prominent. In short, the flexibility of Hopi-ness was present in less formal conversation but less so in interview responses. Compare the previously cited extract of an interview with the director of the HCPO (a Greasewood Clan man from the village of Bacavi) with the observations made with Hopis engaged in casual conversation with me.

Driving from Flagstaff to Hopi, Mike Kabotie and I, talked casually about the differences between life in the city and life on the reservation and the issues of blood quantum levels. 'It's different out here [at Hopi], out here some of these half-bloods know more about being Hopi than most of those full-blooded Hopis who live in the city.' I heard similar sentiments chatting with another friend prior to their village preparing to host a big *Katsina* dance that would attract a lot of Hopis returning to the village for the weekend: 'Those city Indians don't know shit.' There seemed to be a spectrum of valid Hopi-ness encountered in everyday conversation that did not necessarily rely upon the simple building block approach presented by my interviewees. The flexible nature of Hopi-ness within the Hopi community was evident in various places. I came across several examples of individuals of mixed Navajo/Hopi parentage who chose to enrol with the Hopi tribe rather than with the Navajo Nation or vice versa for such practical reasons as access to educational grants. I also became aware of individuals with non-Hopi mothers being adopted into Hopi clans and therefore being given access to a variety of roles within other social and religious institutions. For the most part, Hopi social and religious organizations such as clans or societies should be seen as inclusive institutions that serve to cement relationships between individuals and connect them to a local idea of Hopi-ness rather than exclusive clubs that seek to separate themselves from their neighbours based on ideas of purity. Through a variety of observations and conversations I could readily conclude that Hopi-ness was a flexible concept. But this was not the kind of malleable identity that could be used to easily challenge apparently inauthentic accounts of Hopi-ness.

There is a saying that if you find two Hopi men agreeing with each other for more than five minutes, then one of them is lying. I must admit that there were times in both interview and noninterview contexts that this little snippet of wisdom kept coming to mind. I found myself in a complex situation wherein I felt compelled to distinguish between various versions of authentic Hopi identities. Let us take two imagined versions of Hopi individuals: Hopi A has a clan identity ascribed at birth through his Hopi mother. He is actively involved in the political affairs of his natal village, is initiated into several religious societies, speaks Hopi fluently and is a productive farmer. Hopi B has a Hopi grandfather, lives in California, visits Hopi occasionally, is not initiated, does not farm and does not speak Hopi. The question is not 'Which one is Hopi and which is not?' The question is 'What are the ways in which these individuals connect to something called a Hopi identity?' And also, what are the *contexts* in which different Hopis stress the essentialist or constructivist versions (truths?) of Hopi-ness? Where are Hopis defining the boundaries of Hopi-ness and how are individuals negotiating these boundaries (cf. Barth 1969; Cohen 1993, 2000)?

Creating Authentic Identities through the Ethnographic Interview

There were clearly at least two truths circulating about authentic Hopi identity. One was that Hopi-ness was something that you were born with; the other that it was something you had to earn. Both of these ideal types were authenticated by different Hopi people. For the sake of clarity, it may help to return to the inauthentic claims to identity that have pushed certain individuals to stress a more essentialist approach to identity. Let us take a third 'imagined' version of a claimed Hopi identity. Hopi C is white. She has no ethnic connection to any Native American community. From her existing interest in New Age spirituality, she becomes interested in the alternative politics of a group of Hopis opposed to the idea of a unified Hopi tribe that works with the federal government, and instead stress the importance of following traditional forms of village-based governance. This message of defiance is almost always presented in prophetic rhetoric. Hopi C visits with one or two of these 'Hopi traditionalist' families and helps to spread their message through activist networks on an international scale. After her host dies, she publicly refers to herself using an adopted Hopi name and continues to conduct workshop and activist events throughout the country acting as a Hopi messenger for peace. According to most Hopi people, Hopi C is not a Hopi. But the people that Hopi C is trying to convince are not Hopis either. They are the people running workshops and seminars in cities around the world who are looking for a taste of authentic indigenous culture that they can incorporate into their own lives. If Hopi C was only claiming that she knew a few Hopis, or if she used a non-Hopi name, she would not appear to be as 'authentically native' as she does with these attributes.

There is a global Hopi identity that is at odds with a local reality at Hopi. This is largely through the actions of a small number of these traditionalist Hopis who were highly effective at utilizing networks of alternative political activists and New Age spiritual seekers to spread a prophetic message of impending global change. These messages even found their way to the United Nations (see Clemmer 1978, 1995; Geertz 1994; Nagata 1979). Their message was rooted in Hopi myth and prophecy and was very quickly made welcome in New Age contexts alongside Mayan prophecies, Buddhism, the I Ching and a range of alternative belief systems (Geertz 1994). This global Hopi identity is rooted in a local identity and clearly contains recognizably Hopi characteristics; but it is not the kind of identity that most Hopis, and in particular the institution of the Hopi tribe, feel comfortable with. I was given the distinct impression that the romantic infatuation that New Agers have with Hopis did not seem to contribute to a better standard of living for today's Hopi population. I also felt that part of my role as an anthropologist in this context of representing Hopis was to challenge the claims that these non-Hopis were making.

Although it is an effective technique for assessing researchers, or even avoiding unwanted questions, silence in an ethnographic interview only gets one so far at Hopi. There needs to be a more effective channel of communication open in order to challenge the apparently inaccurate or inauthentic representations of Hopi-ness that are currently circulating. Silence from Hopis on this matter may be seen as a passive form of complicity, and as such a firm retort against them was necessary. Moreover, these challenges need to contain an alternative, locally articulated depiction of Hopi culture to replace the unwanted romantic adoration. The message from the Hopi tribe was clear in my interviews—only Hopis are allowed to be Hopis, and it is our responsibility now to promote the kind of 'good research' that follows this agenda of cultural preservation. If concepts of Hopi identity seemed too rigid, too structured, too essentialist in my interviews, this was because so many of the Hopis that agreed to be interviewed wanted an authentic alternative to the inauthentic Hopi-ness currently circulating within global New Age networks.

Conclusion

Hopi life has changed a good deal over time, but there are still a variety of cultural features that seemed to be recognizably 'Hopi' about the people that I worked with.[5] The late Hopi scholar Hartman Lomawaima referred to this as '*Hopification*' (1989), the concept that Hopis keep moving forwards, adapting to or adopting new experiences whilst retaining a living connection to their past. It is this *Hopification* that provides a meeting point for the apparently dichotomous versions of essentialist or constructivist Hopi-ness that I encountered whilst interviewing or conversing with Hopi people. This *Hopification* reflects recent work on authenticity in the anthropology of tourism that distinguishes between static (essentialist) and dynamic (constructivist) versions of authenticity (Xie and Lane 2006). In this context of defining a Hopi identity, a static authenticity was favoured in interviews, whereas a dynamic authenticity was favoured in more casual conversation. I argue that Hopi behaviour in a formal interview context departed from their 'ordinary' behaviour because they saw the interview as a context through which they could establish a firm alternative to inauthentic (*qahopi*) representations of Hopi-ness.

In 'ordinary' conversations the rigidity of Hopi identity was challenged, and the boundaries of ethnicity became seen as more flexible (cf. Barth 1969; Cohen 1993, 2000). There were many people with whom I spent much time discussing the complexities of both tangible and philosophical approaches to Hopi identity, such as those individuals who were in a position to favour one tribal identity over another for such practical reasons as access to tribal funds for education. These discussions were often framed in reference to the 'ideal' Hopi individual: born into a clan, linguistically fluent, immersed in political and religious spheres of village life, a farmer, someone who was both humble and had a 'good heart'. They were the kind of ideal Hopi constructed from essentialist anthropological building blocks.

These two approaches only merge when ethnographic interviews are analysed with reference to data collected from other research methodologies. The way that I witnessed the fusion of dynamic constructivism and static essentialism was a moment of epiphany and, once again, down to the wisdom of my friend Mike Kabotie. It was the way he explained, in casual conversation, the New Age appropriation of Hopi-ness in a very Hopi way. He told me once that he thought that New Agers behaved like the Hopi clowns who appear alongside the dancing *Katsinam* in the plazas of Hopi-land. When the clowns first arrive in the plaza, they see the *Katsinam* dancing and they are overjoyed, taken aback by their beauty, their presence. The clowns watch them dancing and singing and are elated. But then they become greedy and want to keep the *Katsinam* for themselves. They want to take what doesn't belong to them and stop anybody else from getting what they see as theirs. The clowns start to round up the *Katsinam*, herding them into groups and boasting to each other about how many beautiful singers and dancers they now own. It is here that the clowns have gone wrong. They have overstepped the line. The clowns are like the New Agers. They are in awe of the beauty they see, but they want to take it for themselves. It was a beautiful example of drawing upon historic Hopi themes and concepts to explain a contemporary phenomenon. It was a classic example of relating to a new problem using existing cultural symbols. It was a dynamic approach that drew upon static ideas.

I argue that Hopis feel it is necessary to resort to essentialized rhetoric in formal ethnographic interviews because they feel the need to state publicly that there are boundaries around what can and cannot be taken from Hopi people. What Mike failed to mention in his analogy is that once the clowns start behaving greedily, acting in a way that is *qahopi*, they are then beaten quite vigorously by a group of warrior *Katsinam.* The essentialized rhetoric that appeared in my ethnographic interviews is a way of redressing the balance for Hopis without resorting to violence. If the message that emanated from Hopi was that Hopi identity was malleable, flexible and inclusive then Hopi-land would be awash with prospective adoptees (McCaffery 2005), for if Hopis can stretch the boundaries of ethnicity then anyone can become Hopi. Hopis are therefore managing their representations by stressing the exclusive nature of Hopi-ness over the flexible nature of identity.

As such, the ethnographic interview at Hopi is a 'constitutive feature' of everyday Hopi life. Because the *Hopification* strategy is one that looks inwards as well as outwards. This strategy is not solely concerned with addressing the romantic versions of Hopi-ness held by New Agers or other visitors, but it also relies upon stressing the benefits of Hopi culture to a young generation of Hopis who are becoming increasingly aware of a wide range of non-Hopi cultural influences. By highlighting the advantages of clan identity, of linguistic ability, of village affairs, the Hopi are managing to retain a particularly Hopi identity in an increasingly heterogeneous environment. If Hopi-ness can be seen to be vibrant, alive and exclusive then there will be more young Hopis willing to carry their identity forwards with a sense of pride. This pride may not be expressed in the same way that their parents or grandparents necessarily did, but I personally witnessed some evidence for its existence.

I am sitting in the living area of a double-wide mobile home. The living room contains a handful of non-Hopi students from the local university, two or three adult Hopi men and women, and half a dozen teenagers from one of the villages. We are all tired after a day of clearing weeds from fields and planting corn, and I am drooling over the smell of cooking coming from the kitchen. One of the students is interested in clan identities and asks the teenagers which clan they are. The responding grunts and awkward stares speak volumes about the international nature of teenage communication. One of the more outspoken teenage boys finally speaks up. He is dressed in black jeans, a black T-shirt with various skull motifs and is draped in a leather jacket: 'I'm Black Widow Clan'.

The student is confused. There is no Black Widow Clan at Hopi.

'You mean you're Spider Clan?', she inquires.

'I know what I mean', says the teenage boy, and sinks further into his seat with a peculiar sense of cultural pride. For this young man, at least, there is something to be said for being Hopi in the twenty-first century.

Notes

1. The logic behind this advice reflected a local distrust of recording interviews connected to complex themes of intellectual property rights, storage of and access to Hopi cultural knowledge, and even elements of espionage.
2. The *Katsinam* are the spirits/ancestors/deities of the Hopi; they are personated by initiated men throughout certain parts of the year and sing and dance in the villages.
3. This is clearly not an issue unique to the Hopi considering recent debates concerning the role of ethnographers in Iraq (see Gusterson 2010).
4. There were occasions where I was asked to put down my notebook and pen and informed of some detail that should not be included in any output but needed to be raised in order for me to help understand subsequent information. These occasions were not common.
5. Without wanting to appear overtly simplistic and list these features as the ingredients of Hopi identity, there were people who would identify and be identified as Hopi rather than Navajo, or Irish or Bulgarian.

References

Aldred, L. (2000), 'Plastic Shamans and Astroturf Sundances: New Age Commercialization of Native American Spirituality', *American Indian Quarterly*, 24(3): 329–52.

Barth, F. (1969), 'Introduction', in F. Barth (ed.), *Ethnic Groups and Boundaries: The Social Organization of Culture Difference*, London: Allen & Unwin, 9–38.

Clemmer, R. O. (1978), *Continuities of Hopi Culture Change*, Ramona: Acoma Books.

Clemmer, R. O. (1995), *Roads in the Sky: Hopi Indians in a Century of Change*, Boulder: Westview Press.

Cohen, A. P. (1993), *The Symbolic Construction of Community*, London: Routledge.

Cohen, A. P. (ed.) (2000), *Signifying Identities: Anthropological Perspectives on Boundaries and Contested Values*, London: Routledge.

Dilworth, L. (1996), *Imagining Indians in the Southwest: Persistent Visions of a Primitive Past*, Washington: Smithsonian Institution Press.

Geertz, A. W. (1994), *The Invention of Prophecy: Continuity and Meaning in Hopi Indian Religion*, Moscow: University of Idaho Press.

Gubrium, J. F. and J. A. Holstein (eds) (2002), *Handbook of Interview Research*, Thousand Oaks: Sage Publications.

Gusterson, H. (2010), 'Do Professional Ethics Matter in War?', *Bulletin of the Atomic Scientists*, http://thebulletin.org/web-edition/columnists/hugh-gusterson/do-professional-ethics-matter-war, accessed 6 June 2011.

Hieb, L. (1972), 'The Hopi Ritual Clown: Life as It Should Not Be', PhD dissertation (unpublished), Princeton University.

James, H. C. ((1974) 1994), *Pages from Hopi History*, Tucson: University of Arizona Press.

Kimmey, J. (1999), *Light on the Return Path*, Eugene: Sacred Media.

Lomawaima, H. (1989), 'Hopification, Strategy for Cultural Preservation', in D. Thomas (ed.), *Columbian Consequences*, Washington: Smithsonian Institution Press, 93–9.

McCaffery, N. (2005), 'Global Hopi—Local Hippie: An Anthropological Study of Hopi Identity in Relation to the New Age', PhD dissertation (unpublished), Queen's University Belfast.

Nagata, S. (1979), 'Political Socialization of the Hopi Traditional Faction: A Contribution to the Theory of Culture Change', *Journal of the Steward Anthropological Society*, 11(1): 111–37.

Parsons, E. C. (ed.) (2005), *Hopi Journal of Alexander M. Stephen* Eastford: Martino.

Rose, W. (1992), 'The Great Pretenders: Further Reflections on White Shamanism', in M. A. Jaimes (ed.), *The State of Native America: Genocide, Colonization, and Resistance*, Boston: South End Press, 403–21.

Theodossopoulos, D. (2007), 'Encounters with Authentic Embera Culture in Panama', *Journeys*, 8(1–2): 93–115.

Weiner, J. F. (1999), 'Culture in a Sealed Envelope: The Concealment of Australian Aboriginal Heritage and Tradition in the Hindmarsh Island Bridge Affair', *Journal of the Royal Anthropological Institute*, 5(2): 193–210.

Welch, C. (2002), 'Appropriating the Didjeridu and the Sweat Lodge: New Age Baddies and Indigenous Victims', *Journal of Contemporary Religion*, 17(1): 21–38.

Xie, P. F. and B. Lane (2006), 'A Life Cycle Model for Aboriginal Arts Performance in Tourism: Perspectives on Authenticity', *Journal of Sustainable Tourism*, 14(6): 545–61.

Epilogue: Expectations, Auto-narrative and Beyond

Marilyn Strathern

Towards the end of these encounters with the interview, we are given a glimpse of a history lying behind attempts to improve standards for qualitative data collection. Such attempts have been introduced, for example, into the devising of mixed methods approaches in health services research, where the well-meaning expectation is that different methods should be aligned with one another. When it comes to 'qualitative' research, what is at issue is the scrutability of the questions posed and the rigour of the data they are meant to elicit. Qualitative research, in this view, needs to be protected against bias and needs to enhance the reliability of its findings. There is puzzlement when its practitioners resist: it should, after all, always be possible to construct hierarchies of evidence and provide indicators for assessment. Now what comes out of Greene's account (chapter 10) is not resistance to the search for rigour but an understanding of some of the consequences of trying to effect such an alignment, of zeal misplaced. The division between quantitative and qualitative research works in certain contexts, and often works well as a blunt reminder of diversity in social science approaches. But when the 'qualitative' in qualitative research is regarded as though it were signalling just another variant of quantitative research, truly the search for rigour by measurement has 'not got it'. So what other expectations might there be?

I mean expectations on the anthropologist's part. In turning to this book for an answer, I have been conscious of an order of detail or attention, to example and conceptualization alike, to be found in the various contributions that can be no more than shadowed here. At the same time, I do not step outside the book. One of the editor's visions was that the collection was to be an interrogation of the interview, an extended interview of it, if you like. So, as a postinterview of a kind, these closing words confine themselves to what has already been said. I thus note where different points have come from, mainly by chapter number, sometimes by contributor's name, and diversely from the arguments being expounded and other works being cited. The result may look clumsy, but perhaps the reader will take the brackets as a set of postinterview annotations.

Expectations

The chapters collected here are all conscious of the way in which the concept of 'the interview' raises an expectation about form. As in Rapport's opening account (chapter 1), the interview may be presented as formalized version of what may happen informally in the course of encounter and conversation, or rather, as he goes on to suggest, interview and conversation merge and bifurcate depending on context (and see chapters 9 and 12). In other chapters, the interview appears as an exchange of words removed from naturally occurring conversations (as Montgomery mentions in chapter 6), which also means that it can be deployed by itself in situations where more wide-ranging encounters are not possible, or not looked for (chapter 1 again, and chapters 4 and 7). Local conventions about formality may come into play (chapter 12). However, all contributors seem agreed that in broad terms the form of the interview they wish to take up for discussion is one suited to qualitative research. In chapter 2 Hockey and Forsey explicitly address a further question that anthropologists in particular might raise, that is about the relationship of interviewing to ethnography at large. I return to this.

These chapters prompt the reader to ask what specific elements constitute 'qualitative' data in an interview setting. One such element is surely the discursive character of the narration, which implies that the information being imparted is not of a kind that can be handled by a survey or by an online consultation procedure. It does not matter how fragmentary or disjointed the questions and answers are—and in chapter 10 'the interview' is spread over a long period—or how partial the story, the form of the interview at once requires and enables the parties to sustain an interlocutionary flow. The narrative is expected to unfold over a duration of time. Usually the duration is of a piece, so that suspended in the short-term memory of interviewer and interviewee is what has just been said. An obvious point, but this means that there is always the possibility of internal reference between later and earlier parts of the interchange. To anyone who has filled in electronic questionnaires that refuse to move to the next window until preformulated boxes have been ticked, there is a freedom here we never knew (until, that is, online surveys became ubiquitous) that we had.

The interview thus allows for, if it does not always effect, an evolution of subject matter, interpretation and cross-reference so that the interchange builds up its own context. And, depending on how it is recorded, the interview can be picked over in retrospect. I am thinking of Rapport's 'incremental zigzag' (chapter 1) or the potential for 'escalating creativity' that Wulff reports in her encounters with dancers (chapter 7). I am also thinking of the place that afterthought has, as in the ethnographer's realization of the moment at which ethnographic experience is made into ethnographic evidence (chapter 8, for example).

Of course the ethnographer is not the only actor present. Absent entities of all kinds figure in what is sayable, such as the state for many of those to whom Fahy talked (chapter 11), or all those people to whom the actions of the professionals in

Gore, Rix-Lièvre, Wathelet and Cazemajou's account (chapter 5) are oriented. Interviewees bring other actors in their train, and are invariably—of course—themselves actors in a strong sense. Particularly interesting is the situation in which reflection on the part of those being interviewed has to be cultivated during the interview process precisely to the extent that it is absent elsewhere, as chapter 5 further demonstrates. Josephides (chapter 3) adds a pertinent commentary when she describes the way the interview prompts reflection in a context where assertions are constantly the subject of remarks by others. Lives become entangled together. It is a common expectation (on the part of interviewer and interviewee alike) that reflection, including reflection on people's self-narratives, is not going to be a solitary act.

What routinely differentiates most of the kinds of interviews presented in this collection from diverse other interactions, then, is the formalism or framing that at once separates interviewer from interviewee and conjoins them, a boundary case perhaps begging the question where those being interviewed do not recognize the format (chapter 6). And although the interview could be about anything that fell within the interviewee's competence to talk about, almost all the contributors make evident the extent to which the subject of the interview simultaneously enrolls the interviewee who thereby becomes the subject too. What expectations are there here?

Auto-narrative

Svašek and Domecka (chapter 4) introduce a specific technique, the autobiographical narrative interview, which comes with protocols for biographical storytelling as stand-alone sources of information. Whatever else is brought to the interchange, here the interviewee becomes the subject through the idea of having a 'life' to tell. Conversely, it is clear that any of the interviewees in this volume will also be talking about themselves in talking about other things, as several chapters (for example chapters 2, 8) make clear.

Elsewhere the interviewee's self may be more elusive in the face of events brought to recall, and indeed the 'self' may be a less useful category than (say) 'representative'. I am thinking of Crapanzano's evocation of the silences of a generation betrayed (chapter 9)—individual stories subsumed by a collective history, as he puts it. Silence can link the experiences being brought to recall and the present moment of recall more poignantly than talking. This is similarly true of the unspeakable in North Korea, though people may also insist that being voluble need not be illuminating: words can silence a topic, Fahy observes (chapter 11). Then again, there are situations in which the crucial issue is who has the right to speak, as both Josephides (chapter 3) and McCaffery (chapter 12) emphasize.

The working asymmetry between talking partners is brought up by Skinner early on. This is the asymmetry between the one who, in seeking out the interviewee, has the questions to ask and the one who, knowing he or she has been sought out for what he or she has to say, expects to be the target of the questioning and—whether we are in chapters 1 or 4—may seize the social opportunity for his or her own ends. Another asymmetry, then, one found again in those moments when people appear to be talking to themselves. So there are several senses in which, however partially or inadequately or misleadingly, the interviewee is the subject of the interchange. In a different register one encounters, too, a sense in which the interviewer reveals himself or herself, in one case (chapter 6) the interview in effect turning out to be the interviewer's own biographical repository. In other words (after chapter 3), meaning is given to the individual life.

The interviewee can be the subject of the interview from a further point of view. Leaving aside selves and representatives, the interview constructs the interviewee as a 'person', that is a social entity of a specific kind, whose enactment of relationships—whether aligned with the questioner's agenda or not—is through prompted description. (Reflection is not a solitary act.) So there is a necessary tension between the person being recreated through the interview itself and the person whose experiences or life or opinions, that is, whatever is formed outside and beyond the interview context, is the subject of discussion. The tension may be a productive one, as in the example of the elicitation of embodied knowledge; the comment made by Gore, Rix-Lièvre, Wathelet and Cazemajou (chapter 5) that while first-person accounts are crucial, so too is the negotiation and objectification of the tacit during the process of recall applies more widely. But the tension may also be left ambiguous or unresolved or simply confusing (chapters 6, 9 and 11 offer instances). And one is in special terrain, Svašek and Domecka (chapter 4) indicate, when people are unfamiliar with the performative demands of self-disclosure.

While there are numerous interview types, as chapter 7 reminds us, the expectation on the actors' part that there will be an element of formality about the interview, if only in the asymmetry of the questioning, leads to one interesting contrast with informal situations. Formality may license the interviewee to talk about things that an informal conversation inhibits. Montgomery (chapter 6) invites the reader to consider one such situation, where the interviewee hazarded a view about the difficulty of speaking about certain things with fellow sufferers. This is given a political twist in chapter 12, where the formal interview is seen as a platform for expressing views in a particular way, or in chapter 9 as a blatant opportunity to deliver a testimony. Sometimes the exposé is a manifestation of the world to which Skinner alludes: the extent to which one is dealing with an 'interview society'. McCaffery implies as much (chapter 12) in reference to the Hopi expectation of the role the interview plays in everyday life. Sometimes the interview may work as a kind of shadow confidence-telling, a sort of reverse question-and-answer where the person wishing to confide co-opts, to use Crapanzano's verb (chapter 9), the other party into being a recipient. Although much of the work of the interview is the work of elicitation, the interviewer is also being positioned by the interviewee, with greater or lesser consciousness, into being a particular kind of recipient. Rapport (chapter 1) records coming away from an interview with a sense of privilege.

Beyond Expectations?

There is an open-endedness to the relationships that emerge from the interview. I do not mean between the interviewer/interviewee as such, interesting as that is, I mean between elements of what is being constructed in the course of the interview. Speaking from the questioner's viewpoint, what relationship will there be between any one particular interview and others; between the recording and narrative; between the narrative and the text; between the text and everything else that is known about the interviewee; between the interviewee and the conditions of his or her talking at all, and so forth? The interview comes over as an intensely person-centred technique, but one advantage in reflecting on it is to remind ourselves of just how many nonhuman actants crowd round the table as well. They at once keep the interlocutors going and nudge them in various directions. Then, when the conversation has become the record, the holder of the record (rather than the one answering the questions) is faced with innumerable choices of direction to take with respect to what, postinterview, has materialized as an artefact.

The material traces of the interview is the subject of chapter 8. Florescu develops the analogy of collecting, and its attention to the particular circumstances of acquisition that are simply not amenable to generalization and to its quite proper alienation of knowledge from experience. ('No matter what I say, you will not understand'; chapter 11.) The interview, she suggests, can be seen as a way of learning about the 'collections' of memories that inhabit others.

The range of possible practices appearing in this volume that go under the name of 'the interview', and made evident in the introduction, is not just a matter of luxuriant growth, of the variety and diversity one might find in any compartment of social activity. Without going so far as to say there is no such thing as 'the interview' (and in chapter 12 it does almost disappear in the ploys of a prospective interviewee), the variety of its modes of elicitation or of the shifting positioning of players, and the diversity of artefacts created or of aftereffects registered, speak to some—though surprisingly few—disagreements as to where emphasis should be laid. Important, and there would be no disagreement on this, they also speak to the place of unpredictability in 'qualitative' inquiry. This renders any prescriptive characterization of what is to be expected from an interview—whether we think of method or of research—an absurdity. The unpredictability of outcome encouraged by the interview practised for the ends of qualitative research is bound up with the practice itself. Two brief comments are in order.

First, as a matter of method, one point of the interview is to take advantage of a counterpart unpredictability, namely that of human interaction. However closely a schedule is kept to or however incidental the answers appear to the questions, you can never tell how people are going to spark each other off; or, as Florescu (chapter 8) reminds us, just how many opportunities there are for misunderstandings. Chapters 9 and 10 make both of these evident. The data capture at issue is precisely what cannot be anticipated, cannot be preconceived (chapter 1). Failures of communication feed into this (chapter 7).

Second, with respect to research, is it not the case for social anthropology at large, to return to Greene's situation (chapter 10), that measurement and standardization come after the fact (of data collection)? 'Purification', and the analytical work that implies, begins when the record is at hand. It is not, in any rigorous way, feasible in advance. I emphasize the rigour: one can imagine all manner of outcomes, but it is an illusion that one can jump from question to answer to anything that would stand up as a finding. Other things are, or need to be, happening. Josephides (chapter 3) emphasizes the ethics: what are the implications of postfieldwork activity that mines or harvests the talk? How does one provide the means for a posteriori verification (chapter 5)? And how would one evaluate what is yet to happen, where for example what is covered or uncovered in the interview renders it a rehearsal of processes of covering and uncovering that, painfully so for the Harkis in chapter 9, lie not just in the past but lie ahead? As these chapters attest, at the end of the interview the work of the interviewer has only just begun, and that may go for the interviewee as well. Anyone who thinks that the qualitative interview should strive, as an aim held in front of it, for outcomes whose measure is already taken really has not got it.

End

This brings the discussion back to ethnography. Of course 'the interview' exists, but only ever as part of something else. Thus it does so as one among numerous other devices or methods for finding things out, or as an element in an overall research orientation towards enquiry into varieties of knowing and talking. A degree of equivocation is shown across the contributions to this volume as to where, then, one should put the anthropologist's concept of 'ethnography'. Is an ethnographic impetus already contained within the notion of the qualitative interview? Hockey and Forsey (chapter 2) put their finger on it when they argue, in relation to the kinds of interviews that are the subject of this book, that the interview should be considered a form of participatory research. As such, and for all that the term *ethnography* covers, it can yield ethnographic knowledge. And specific skill is needed, as Wulff reminds us (chapter 7). So with ethnography as a reference point, we might want to look again at interviews that—whether conducted by anthropologists or others—do not meet the expectations that ethnographers would place on the concept of participatory research.

At the end of this interview I come away with a sense of privilege: the interrogation on which this volume embarked has proved its worth. In retrospect, I would say now, the brackets are more than citations to a broad and generously conceived set of essays. They are meant, too, to indicate everything that could not be said in these closing words. And they can be read, all over again, as the places where the reader can find the contributors' already recorded response to the comments here, perhaps agreeing with them or perhaps answering back.

Index